For Feathered Pets.

SPRATT'S

MIXED

BIRD SEEDS.

Sold in Packets or Tins.

Sold in Packets or Tins.

SPRATT'S PATENT, LTD.,

Head Office and Appliance Show Rooms,

24 & 25, FENCHURCH STREET, E.C.

THE CANARY BOOK.

LANCASHIRE PLAINHEAD CANARY.

THE CANARY BOOK:

CONTAINING

FULL DIRECTIONS FOR THE BREEDING, REARING, AND
MANAGEMENT OF CANARIES AND CANARY MULES;
CAGE MAKING, &c.;

FORMATION OF CANARY SOCIETIES;

EXHIBITION CANARIES, THEIR POINTS, AND HOW TO BREED
AND EXHIBIT THEM;

AND ALL OTHER MATTERS CONNECTED WITH THIS FANCY

Illustrated.

By ROBERT L. WALLACE.

THIRD EDITION.

*Enlarged and Revised, with many New Illustrations of Prize
Birds, Cages, &c.*

LONDON:
L. UPCOTT GILL, Bazaar Buildings, DRURY LANE, W.C.

NEW YORK:
CHARLES SCRIBNER'S SONS, 153-157, FIFTH AVENUE.
1904.

LONDON :
L. UPCOTT GILL, LONDON AND COUNTY PRINTING WORKS,
BAZAAR BUILDINGS, W.C.

PREFACE

TO THE THIRD EDITION.

IN consequence of the great and rapid progress that has been made during the past ten years in the art of Canary-breeding, I have found it necessary to issue a Third Edition of the "CANARY BOOK." In doing so I have endeavoured to treat fully and accurately upon every subject of interest to lovers and breeders of these delightful pets.

I have now given a full and complete account of ' those direful maladies, Typhus and Scarlet Fever, the result of over twenty years' experience and study since my first discovery of these diseases attacking birds. Their cause, prevention, and general treatment are fully discussed. Further, I have included information on some maladies not hitherto mentioned, and have extended my remarks on other complaints from which birds are known to suffer. Other subjects not previously dealt with in this or any other work on Canaries are also treated, and I have endeavoured to set right several matters that have hitherto given rise to contention and heart-burning among fanciers generally.

On several varieties of Canaries, including Yorkshire Fancies, Norwich Plainheads, Lancashire Coppies, Lizards,

London Fancies, and Germans, I have considerably extended my remarks, and have given the fullest information possible about the Modern Crested Norwich, Cinnamons, Cinnamon Crests, Evenly-Marked Cinnamons, and the Modern Scotch Fancy birds of the most approved types; with instructions how to breed, rear, and prepare them for exhibition. Particulars of the variety now known as the "Border Fancy" are also included. In fact, I may fairly claim that the book is brought completely up to date.

Several new plates of birds of the most modern type have been added, while those which I consider out of date have been removed. The latest and most reliable recipes for obtaining the best specimens of Red- and Yellow-fed birds will be found, as well as formulæ for the preparation of other foods to be used during the breeding- and moulting-seasons.

All the information given in my previous editions which will enable amateurs and others to trace the progress that has been made in this science during the past eighteen years, has been retained, and the present edition may, I confidently think, be fairly considered as complete and searching as the most fastidious fancier could desire it to be.

THE AUTHOR.

CONTENTS.

THE CANARY BOOK.

CHAPTER I.

CAGES AND CAGE-MAKING.

THE ingenuity and skill of man are so vast and varied, and the success which has been attained in the art of cage-making is so prodigious and wonderful, that it would be a task of no inconsiderable difficulty to any person to attempt to give anything approximating to a full and lucid description of all the different patterns of cages that are to be met with in this country; nor do I propose to do so, but simply to give a description of those which I consider best adapted to the wants and requirements of the times; for cages can be met with of every conceivable form and size, from an overgrown mouse-trap to a moderately comfortable apartment—that is, so far as length and height are to be considered—and in form they may be procured from that of a common fig-box to a miniature representation of the Crystal Palace at Sydenham. I have seen cages of almost every imaginable pattern, representing cottages, abbeys, castles, cathedrals, and palaces, with fine fluted columns, porticoes with pediments, stained glass windows, &c., rich and varied in design, and in every known style of architecture, including Gothic, Doric, and Ionic, and displaying great taste and marvellous mechanical skill. Cages of this description are generally the production

B

of some ingenious and industrious fancier, and whilst I admire them as works of art and masterpieces of workmanship, I regret I cannot recommend them as fitting habitations for birds; for, with very few exceptions, all such cages lack that most essential requirement—utility. Every consideration of comfort and convenience is sacrificed to carry out the design in its entirety, and hence many of those cages are, despite their external grandeur, mere dungeons for canaries and other birds. Nevertheless, I am a great advocate for handsome cages; but what I admire most is artistic skill, combined with elegance of design, practical utility, and sound, substantial workmanship; for I consider a good bird worthy of a good cage, upon the same principle as I contend that a good picture is deserving of a good frame.

It is the highest ambition of some fanciers to possess high-class birds, and, so long as they succeed in accomplishing this object, they care little as to what kind of tumble-down, broken, twisted, rickety, rusty, patched-up cages they keep them in. They appear to go upon the principle of the bucolic Scotchman, who, so long as he received good victuals, did not care in what fashion they were served; whereas an epicure—which in this instance I will compare with a genuine lover of birds—is generally as particular about the manner in which his viands are served as he is about the viands themselves. I have heard it said that half the enjoyment of a good dinner is in the way it is placed on the table, and in order to enjoy a good bird I consider it ought to be seen in a suitable cage; in this I feel confident that all true lovers of those pretty little choristers will agree with me. I consider it a gross insult to good taste to place birds of undoubted excellence and merit in cages which are not worth as many pence as their occupants are worth pounds. Besides, a good, well-made cage will outlast a dozen flimsy common ones, to say nothing of the difference in appearance.

CAGE-MAKING.—If you have a latent tendency to the mechanical in your composition, and are possessed of a little ingenuity as well, you only require patience, perseverance,

and practice to enable you to become your own cage manufacturer. It is a tedious occupation, to be sure, and more
particularly so to those, I should imagine, who are not
fanciers themselves; but with a genuine love for birds, and
your enthusiasm wound up to fever-heat, it is astonishing
what feats of enterprise and skill you can accomplish.

If you resolve to make a trial of your talents in this
direction, I would advise you, in order that you may have a
fair chance of success, to rig up a temporary bench to work

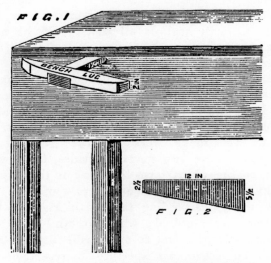

FIGS. 1 AND 2. TEMPORARY CARPENTRY BENCH.

at. A strong old table or, better still, a good old kitchen
dresser, which may usually be had for a trifle at a sale by
auction, will answer the purpose admirably. Fit on to this
what is called in joiner's vernacular "a bench lug"—that is,
a piece of wood projecting from the left-hand corner of the
bench, in front, say from 6in. to 12in. in length, and
fastened to a piece of stout wood forming an arm from the
under-part of the top of the bench; it must be set at an
acute angle, and appear as in Fig. 1. This is to hold the

B 2

wood you desire to plane in an upright position. You will likewise require an angular piece of wood, called a plug, to fix it firmly between the bench and the "lug" (see Fig 2). The board to be operated upon with this contrivance must be placed on edge next the bench, and the plug put in between it and the lug, and wedged tight with a wooden mallet. When you wish to plane the flat surface of the board, you will need a small iron hook driven well into the bench with the point projecting towards you; fix the end of the board with the hook in order to keep it steady during the operation. There are proper contrivances for this purpose, but a small hook is all that would be needed in cage-making.

In addition to a bench you will require a set of tools as follows: Three saws—a handsaw, a dove-tail saw, and a key-hole saw, and if you intend to make ornamental cornices to your cages, a small frame-saw as well; two planes at least, a smoothing-plane and a trying-plane, and, if you like, a "jack" plane for rough work besides; I would likewise recommend you to get two grooving-planes, to "groove and tongue" the boards which form the back of the cage. These planes are known in the trade as a "pair of ploughs," and are of different sizes according to the thickness of the wood for which they are required; when for $\frac{1}{2}$in. deals they are called half-inch ploughs, and so on. Glue in the "tongue," and this will not leave any aperture or receptacle for bird vermin to enter and conceal themselves. You will require a square, a gauge, a pair of compasses, a 24in. rule, a spoke-shave, a few chisels, a stone to sharpen them upon, a brace and four bits, $\frac{1}{4}$in., $\frac{1}{2}$in., $\frac{3}{4}$in., and 1in., a couple of hammers of different sizes, a few bradawls (commonly called prickers), a few gimlets of various sizes, a wooden mallet, two pairs of pliers (one pair of which must be wire cutters), a pair of pincers, a hand-vice, a stout pocket-knife, a glue-pot, and, if you take my advice, an instrument called a "sash-fillister," used for what is technically termed "rabbeting"—that is, to let the back of the cage flush with the ends the same as will be observed in the back of a chest of drawers, &c., as this plan likewise assists to keep out the parasites, for I find they avoid cages where good lodgings are not procurable. Get a supply of glass and emery-paper, wood and wire, nails, flaws, and screws of various sizes, a piece of chalk, and a stout lead pencil, and you ought to be thoroughly equipped for the business of cage-making.

Do not let the formidable list of tools which I have enumerated frighten you from an attempt at making cages, for there is no necessity to purchase all the articles mentioned at an ironmonger's shop, unless you can afford to do so and feel so disposed, as you can generally meet with most of the tools at a furniture dealer's store at a moderate price, especially if you live in a large town; and, besides, you can frequently pick up a few of them at least at some sales by auction for a mere song.

The best wood for the tops, bottoms, backs, and ends of breeding-cages is American pine, from half-an-inch to five. eighths inch thick in the rough, and well seasoned (purchase it from a well-established timber merchant, if possible), so that when it is dressed it will be reduced to about three-eighths-of-an-inch in thickness. For the fronts use hard wood, either oak, teak, rosewood, mahogany, or walnut; the two last-named kinds are what I prefer myself, and when well dressed off and nicely polished they look really superb. The ends, tops, and bottoms of the cages ought to be stained and varnished; but I will treat upon this part of the subject more fully hereafter. Make the body of the cage first; measure off the timber and cut it to the sizes required, then proceed to dress it, fit it, and lastly put it securely together. Having satisfactorily accomplished this, cut out the wood for the front of the cage, and act as before directed; if you decide upon using wood rails for bars, as shown in Fig. 7, it will be advisable to make them ready for wiring before you fix them permanently. This is a most important feature in cage-making, for if you do not have the holes exactly in a line with each other, in the top, bottom, and bars, the wires will be thrown out of a perpendicular line, and will in consequence be offensive to the eye. Compasses are mostly used for measuring off the holes, but they are apt to get compressed or extended if not handled with consummate care, in which case they would be sure to mislead you; therefore you will find it better to use a good stout two-pronged table-fork, with the prongs about half-an-inch apart, as a gauge for setting off the correct distances between the wires. If you prefer wire bars to wood ones, as shown in Fig. 3, you will find the task of boring less difficult; still you cannot be

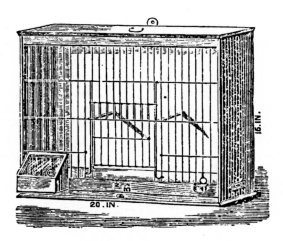

FIG. 3. BREEDING-CAGE, SINGLE COMPARTMENT.

too particular in the performance of this part of the work, and the difference in appearance betwixt a well-wired cage and one carelessly and slovenly executed is immense.

If you use wire cross-bars and you can handle a soldering-iron, solder the wires instead of binding; it makes a far stronger job and looks much neater and better, but it is a somewhat difficult operation for a beginner. Before commencing to wire a cage it is a good plan to prepare a bradawl or pricker for boring the holes; it should be exactly half-an-inch long in the prong. You can cut down an ordinary one to the size required, and then file it until it is of an equal thickness throughout; the point should be made perfectly round and sharp, and it should be as nearly as possible of the same thickness as the wire you use, but if anything the least shade thinner, so as to let. the wood grip the wire. The wire can be forced up or down, whichever you require, with the small pliers; this makes the wiring firmer. By using a

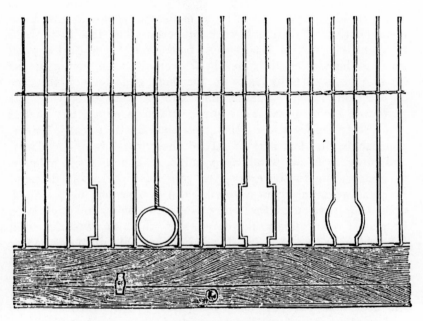

FIG. 4. SPECIMENS OF WIRE OPENINGS FOR BIRDS TO GET AT THEIR FOOD AND WATER.

pricker of the above description you will not, with ordinary care, be likely to split the wood, and the principal advantage to be gained by it is that all the holes will be of the same depth, for it is intended to force it home to the handle each time, so that after you fit one wire you can cut the remainder the same length, which it is best to do ere you begin the process of wiring.

As I said before, if you can use a soldering-iron, it will be better to solder the wires than to bind them with wire binding; but it is not an easy task to those who have never attempted it before. Get a medium-sized soldering-iron and a "stick" of solder from a plumber—it is simply a mixture of pewter, lead, and block tin; but, as only a small quantity will be needed, it is cheaper to buy it ready made than to make it. Heat your iron to a moderate heat—do not make it too hot, or it will not work properly. The test is to hold it about six inches from your face, and if you feel a good glow of heat arise to your cheek from it, then you may use it; if you happen to make it too hot, and destroy the face of the iron, file it a little, and rub it well among a little powdered resin spread on a piece of brown paper, but heat it moderately before you do this. As soon as it is ready for use you can begin; but first of all fix the wires into their places, and place them as plumb as possible, and, before you attempt to solder them to the cross-bars, you must put a few drops of muriatic acid, to which a small piece of zinc has been added, upon that portion of the wires where the union or joint is to be made; resin, finely powdered, and which is generally used for soldering tins, &c., is of no use for this purpose. After you have joined a wire in this manner, you ought to have a little diluted liquor of ammonia in a vessel of any kind, dip a piece of cotton waste or rag of any sort into this liquid, and rub over that part of the wires that you touched with the acid, so that its effect thereon may be neutralised at once.

You can form the holes for the birds to feed or drink through by turning the wire across a round piece of hard wood, about three-quarters-of-an-inch in circumference. Grip it firmly with the pliers before you proceed to wrap or coil it, for you must do this to the extent of half-an-inch or more to make it hold firm, or you can make the hole with a double instead of a single wire, if you prefer it. It is simply done, and you will only require to examine one already made to see how easy it is of accomplishment. There is, however, a simpler method even than this, and that is to bend a wire thus: leaving half-an-inch at the bottom to go into the wood to hold it firm; but if you make the round holes you will have to fasten the wire to the bottom stay of the cage with a small wire staple, or by making a small groove in it to let the wire into. This you can do with a sharp knife, but you must not make it any deeper than is necessary to hold it firm (see Fig. 4).

If you can manage to "dove-tail" the tops, bottoms, and ends of the cages together, by all means do so; if you are unable to accomplish this feat, try to "rabbet" them together; failing in this likewise, use glue, in addition to flaws or screws, to fasten them together, as it will make closer joints, and thereby prevent crevices being left, which must by all means be avoided, as they only serve as harbours of refuge for bird vermin. If the wood you use is not well seasoned, the tops or backs may possibly "spring" a little, especially if the cages are exposed to a strong heat, either from a fire or the direct rays of the sun in summer time. If such an event should happen, be sure to take them off the first time you clean the cages out and re-fit them. It is a commendable plan to make the fronts of breeding- and show-cages with framed wire fronts, to screw on and take off, so that they can be easily removed for the purpose of painting, white-washing, or thoroughly cleaning the cages; or the framed fronts may be secured by a pair of small brass hinges on one side, and a brass hook or button on the other, or by fitting in two pieces of wire instead of hinges, to lift in and out.

It is better to make the compartments of the breeding-cages a little too large than too small; the birds get more room for exercise, and the air is not so liable to become vitiated as it is in a too circumscribed space.

CAGE DOORS.—Fig. 5 shows three descriptions of cage doors, all of which are simple in construction. The first and second (*a* and *b*) are a combination of wood and wire, and are secured to the cage by passing one of the wires, forming a portion of the front of the cage, entirely through the two projecting pieces at one end, and fixing it in the bottom stay. These ends should be neatly rounded off. The door can be placed either to the right or left side; the projecting pieces forming the opposite end being thinned away and notched out to allow the wire to fit in to the notches and make the door quite level.

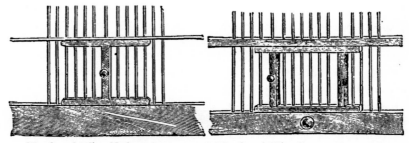

a Wood and Wire H-shaped Door.   *b* Wood and Wire Square Framed Door.

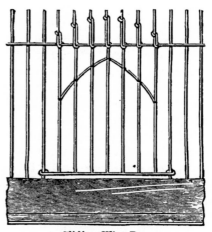

c Sliding Wire Door.

FIG. 5. CAGE DOORS OF WOOD AND WIRE.

The other (*c*) shows a sliding wire door. Many more descriptions of doors could be given of an ornamental kind, but they are generally beyond the capacity of an amateur to manufacture.

WIRE-STRAIGHTENER.—Fig. 6 is a contrivance for straightening wire, and it not only saves a great amount of time, but, if properly made and used, a pound of wire can be made quite straight in a marvellously short space of time, which would take anyone a long while to do with the old-fashioned method of straightening on a block of hard wood, with a wooden mallet, and by using pliers. This instrument is made of hard wood, mahogany or oak, and wire. The one from which I have made a sketch is constructed of a piece of well-seasoned mahogany, 14in. by 3½in., and ¾in. in thickness. At one end is a wire hook, fastened to the under-side first, by the wire being bent and sharpened at both ends and then driven into the wood, and afterwards secured by two small wire hooks in the form of staples, one placed over

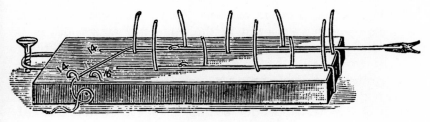

FIG. 6. WIRE-STRAIGHTENER.

each wire separately and driven home. This wire hook is to secure the machine during the operation of drawing the wire, and it is placed over a nail or hook driven into the workbench or otherwise. The wire loops are for the purpose of guiding the wire and keeping it in its place during the operation of straightening. The wire is passed through one of the front loops first, and then between the uprights and beneath the inner loop which prevents it from jerking out of its place. In making an instrument of this description, you must use a piece, or pieces, of wire the same gauge as those you wish to straighten; bend them over at one end of the wood, the one opposite to the one containing the hook, and bend them thus :

C⸺, and drive them into the end; the other ends of the wires being left free. Next drive firmly into the wood some stout pieces of wire in an upright position on each side of the gauge-wires, as close to them as is possible. These upright wires should be left projecting about an-inch-and-a-quarter, and should be slightly bent over in a slanting posture, the one made to lean one way and the other the other alternately. Much of your success will depend on the inclination of these wires, and you must bend them backward or forward, as is necessary, until you find that the wire drawn through them comes out straight, or nearly so. A little practice, combined with patience and perseverance, will enable you to do it satisfactorily.

If you fail to get the wire quite as straight as you could wish, you can cut off the lengths required and place them on a block of hard wood, and beat them with a wooden mallet, turning them in your hand in the same way as a smith does a piece of heated iron to get it hammered round; but there will be no necessity for this if you succeed in getting your wire-straightener made properly.

Any good-natured wire-worker would supply you with an article of this description for a shilling; but, if he were inclined to be ill-natured, he could easily make it of no use to you.

COLOURING AND PAINTING CAGES.—After you have finished making a breeding-cage, or, better still, before you begin to wire it, it ought to be coloured inside. I generally give mine a coating of thin glue-size first, and after that is quite dry I proceed to colour it with the following composition: Paris whitening and pipeclay, equal proportions. I mix them well together, and then add a small quantity of ultramarine blue (lapis lazuli), which may be obtained from any colourman, and at most chemists' and druggists', just sufficient to make it what is termed a "French white," that is, white with a sort of invisible blue tint. It prevents it from turning yellow, and looks much better. Add to these ingredients a little skimmed milk, sufficient to make it into a thin paste, and afterwards dilute it with soft water to the required consistency for use; the milk makes it adhere more firmly. It is considered an objectionable practice to paint the inside of a cage of this sort. The same composition may be used for colouring-out show-cages, only more blue should be added in this case, and also a small, very small, quantity of rose pink, or vermilion, to give it warmth; but, for my own part, I prefer to paint show-cages inside, as the colouring matter is liable to be rubbed off, for birds very frequently wash themselves in their drinking-tins whenever they are supplied with fresh water, and afterwards rub themselves against the backs of their cages, and thereby get besmeared with the colouring matter, which is detrimental to their chance of obtaining a prize. They are never many days together in a show-cage; hence the paint, after becoming thoroughly dried and hardened, can do them no harm. I give mine a coat of oil paint first (white), and afterwards two coats of "flattening," which is paint without oil. I mix white lead, lime blue, and turpentine together for this purpose; you can regulate the shade of colour according to your taste. I fancy that a bird of any variety looks best in a cage coloured-out with pale blue (cerulean or azure blue); it looks far cleaner and nicer than dark or even a medium blue. Some people colour their cages black inside to show clear jonque and mealy birds in, thinking that the greater the contrast the more advantageous it is to the birds. I have tried nearly all colours and shades of colours experimentally, and the colour just recommended I consider best. The outsides of show-cages may be either painted, stained and varnished, or coated over with the ordinary black varnish. If the latter is used, they should have either a coat of black paint or glue-size, in which some lamp-black or ivory-black, finely powdered, has been previously mixed. This adds much to the appearance both in colour and lustre. If you prefer to paint them, I would recommend dark blue (Oxford blue); but the black varnishing looks exceedingly well, and is very serviceable. Breeding-cages ought to be cleansed out and re-coloured inside twice a year, just prior to the breeding-season and again at the close. Show-cages, too, are none the worse for being frequently re-painted, re-coloured, and re-varnished ; they not only look better, but I always think that they enhance the appearance of the birds.

Some fanciers prefer to lime-wash their breeding-cages with quicklime whiting, made by dissolving a piece of quicklime, known as a "clot," and weighing from 1lb. to 2lb., in a gallon or two of boiling water, with the addition of a small handful of salt, and applied whilst warm ; others enamel their cages with Aspinall's Enamel, which looks well, and assists materially in keeping down the little mischievous parasites which are so detrimental to bird-breeding. Before using enamel the crevices in the cages should be puttied up or filled with a preparation made of two parts slacked lime finely powdered and one part silver sand, with sufficient linseed oil to make it of the consistency of putty; this if properly prepared sets as hard as iron. When quite dry enamel should be applied in accordance with the manufacturer's instructions. The cages are afterwards easily cleaned, and the appearance is very good.

STAINING, VARNISHING, AND POLISHING CAGES. — The tops, bottoms, and ends of breeding-cages look best when stained and varnished, and are more easily kept clean. Mahogany and oak are the prevailing woods imitated. You can purchase a sixpenny bottle of mahogany stain from any oil and colourman, and in country towns from most chemists; this will suffice for a good number of cages, as it needs to be well diluted with water before being used. There are several different makers of this stain. I generally use Mackie's, though Stevens's is very good. Mahogany stain can be made by mixing Venetian red and a little brown umber together, and then using it with thin glue-size; when it is quite dry it should be sand-papered down and varnished. Carriage varnish is the best kind to use. To imitate oak, use a little sienna or burnt umber, mixed with sour beer or thin gum and water, with a little moist sugar added to it. To make it light or dark depends entirely upon the quantity of pigment

used. After you have given a cage a coat of the staining-
liquid, if you think it is too light in colour, make it darker
by giving it a second coat. After the stain has dried
thoroughly, you may proceed to varnish. The following is an
excellent recipe for spirit varnish: Gum shellac (orange), 6oz.;
gum sandrac, ½oz.; amber resin, ½oz.; methylated spirit, or
"methylated finish," 1 pint. Bruise the gums together or
separately in a mortar, put into a stone bottle (earthenware),
and add the spirit; shake it up well frequently for a day or
two; strain it through a piece of muslin, and it will be
ready for use. Varnish must not be laid on too thick; after
the first coat is quite dry give it a second, and a third if
necessary.

Do not varnish the fronts of the cages when made of hard
wood, such as walnut, &c., as they will look far better French
polished. If you desire to make your own polish, I can
strongly recommend the following formula, as it is one of the
very best for making really good French polish: Orange
shellac, 3oz.; gum benzoin (Benjamin), 1¼ drachms; methylated spirit, or finish, 1 pint. It must be made in precisely
the same manner as the varnish. Before you commence to
polish any wood you must give it a coat of raw linseed oil—
some polishers use a little finely-powdered Paris whitening as
well—to fill up the pores of the wood. If you are going to
polish mahogany, and desire to improve the colour of the
wood, add some alkanet-root or dragon's blood to the oil, and
place it near a fire for an hour or two before using. Dip a
piece of wool or cotton in the oil, and rub it well into the
wood. When you commence to polish, take a piece of wool
or cotton wadding, and roll it into a small ball; saturate
this with the polish, and cover it with a cotton rag or two;
moisten the rag with a little of the linseed oil before you
begin to polish, and be sure to go over the whole surface of
the wood under operation at a tolerably rapid rate. Begin at
one end, and work your hand round and round until you
cover the entire surface; then work backward and forward,
never allowing the polish to dry in until you obtain the

bright surface you require. You may be obliged to replenish your polishing-pad or rubber from time to time—this you must do with the utmost dexterity; but do not forget the oil or the polish will not work—it will dry and peel off. You will find that with care and practice you will soon become an adept in this line of business. If the varnish or polish gets too thick at times, add a little more spirit or finish.

BREEDING-CAGES.—The single-compartment breeding-cage, shown in Fig. 3, is well adapted for Yorkshire Fancy canaries, Manchester Coppies, &c., and may, if desired, be used for the smaller varieties, such as Lizards, Norwich Fancy, &c. The dimensions are as follow : Outside measurement — length, 20in.; height, 16in.; width, 10in.; the main front stay (bottom) is 3½in. deep; three-quarters-of-an-inch of which represents the front of the "false bottom" or "draw-board"; the top stay is 2in. in depth; the wires forming the front of the cage are fixed into those stays; the seed-hopper is 4in. long and 2¼in. wide, and 2in. deep in that portion which forms the trough, the sides extending 3in. higher, and tapering away to a-quarter-of-an-inch, forming an acute angle. A narrow groove must be made on each side of the outer edge of these, which admits of a piece of glass being put in; this forms a cover to keep out the dirt from the seed; it likewise prevents the birds from throwing the seed over the hopper, and enables you to see without removing it when a fresh supply is required. An egg-drawer, 2in. wide and 3in. long, made of tin, with a tin, wood, or brass front, or a porcelain drawer, must be placed in the end of the cage, about 4in. from the front. A drinking-trough, made of tin, zinc, or sheet iron, can be hung on the front of the mainstay, or a glass trough used if preferred, but by all means do not use those tall glass fountains; the water soon becomes turbid and foul in them; they are perfect abominations. At the opposite side to the water-trough hook on the seed-hopper. A perch must be placed inside the cage the whole length of the front, about two inches behind the mainstay, and about one-and-a-half-inches below its level; this is for the birds to feed from, and to enable them to reach their food and water easily. Two other perches must be placed about the centre of the cage, on each side of the door, as shown in Fig. 3. Fix a half-inch screw in the centre of the cage, and another in the centre of the end opposite to the one containing the egg-drawer, to hang the nests on, about 4in. above the perches, or one at each side of the perch. Sometimes tin troughs are used instead of drawers for eggs, &c.; but you are apt to frighten the birds, and especially the young ones, when about to fledge, by having to put your hand inside the cage to place them in and take them out. It is a clumsy contrivance, therefore avoid it. Put a neat half-round beading about three-eighths-of-an-inch in thickness round the extreme edge of the draw-board. This prevents the sand from slipping off it, and makes a more substantial job; but be sure to put it well and firmly on, so as not to leave a crevice; or you can simply use the front lath only as a dummy draw-board, fixed to the cage with a wire pin put through it from the bottom; this is a more simple contrivance, and answers quite well. Wire the front with tinned wire No. 17. For the cross-bars use No. 13, and bind them with tin, brass, or copper binding-wire — that is, wire as fine as thread; copper binding is more durable, and does not cost more than the brass; it is about 2s. per pound. For No. 13 wire I pay 7d. per pound, and for No. 17 1d. more.

In making a sliding wire door you will require two upright wires for the door to run upon. I have left the door in the drawing of cage Fig. 3 partly open, and have shown the form of it so plainly that it would be superfluous for me to do more than call attention to it; a close examination of the engraving will enable anyone to see how it is constructed and the principle upon which it works. I prefer doors of this kind to all others, for if they are properly made and oiled occasionally they ought to close themselves; another advantage is that they cannot by any possibility be opened by the birds, so there is no danger of their getting out and being lost (see also Fig. 5).

C

Cage Fig. 7 is adapted expressly for breeding Belgian canaries in. The dimensions of this cage are as follow: Extreme length, 4ft.; height, 19in.; depth, 11in.; the main-stay, including draw-boards or false bottoms, should be 3½in. high. The cornice can be made according to taste. The cross-bars in this cage are made of mahogany, the same as the front, and are three-eighths-of-an-inch in thickness. The sliding doors at the ends of the cage are useful for running the birds out into show-cages. The doors in front are framed, and are made of mahogany, the same substance as the bars; the feet are made of brass, and are globular

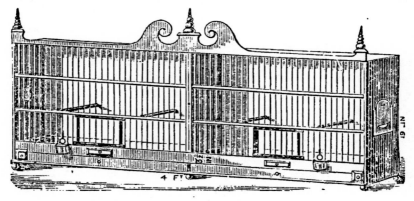

FIG. 7. BREEDING-CAGE FOR BELGIAN CANARIES, TWO COMPARTMENTS.

in form, with a steel screw in the centre, and are procur-able at any ironmonger's; the spires upon the cornice are made of mahogany. These you can get turned for a small sum by any professional wood turner, or you can use a plain or base moulding in preference to the cornice if you desire to do so; but I think a cornice looks infinitely better, and is almost as easily made. In the centre of this cage is an upright draw-board, running between two mahogany bars, a-quarter-of-an-inch in thickness, and rounded at the edges. It is used during the breeding-season for shutting off the cock or young birds, as described in the chapter on "Breeding":

after the breeding-season you can, by withdrawing this board altogether, form an excellent fly- or flight-cage for the young birds. Some fanciers prefer to make a three-compartment cage of this description; others, one with four, six, eight, nine, or twelve, and so on; but I have always found one with two compartments only most handy.

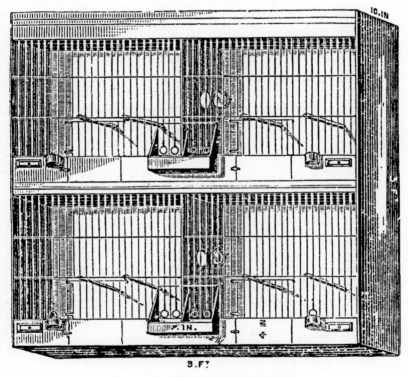

FIG. 8. BREEDING-CAGE, FOUR COMPARTMENTS.

Cage Fig. 8, four compartments, will be found very convenient for mule-breeding, and it may be used for breeding any of the small varieties of canaries, such as Lizards, Norwich Fancy, &c. It is 3ft. square, and 10in. in breadth. with small communicating doors between each compartment.

c 2

I generally give a pair of birds the benefit of both compartments. If the male bird is mischievous, or troublesome to the hen during incubation, I shut him off by himself; if not, I allow him to remain until the hen has commenced to sit again. I then shut off the cock and fledgelings from the hen until the young brood can cater properly for themselves. After the hen has again hatched, and when her brood are eight or ten days old, I remove the fledgelings to another cage, opening the door of communication as before. But, before doing so, I have found it a good plan to give the male some water in which to bathe; if he bathes, open it at once; if he does not, take a mouthful of water and spurt it well over him, for if you do not take this precaution his ardour may be productive of mischief. The doors in this cage are made partly of wood and partly of wire, and are cut through the stay to the bottom, so as to be cleaned out more easily on account of it being destitute of draw-boards. The bars in this cage are made of wire No. 12. As all the other belongings are clearly shown in the engraving, it is unnecessary to describe them further.

Some fanciers are fond of breeding with two female canaries and one male. I am no advocate for this method myself; but when it is considered desirable to adopt this plan, I would recommend a cage with six compartments in place of the one represented, that is, one with three compartments to each flat, with communicating doors between each compartment, so that the male bird can be run either to the right or left as circumstances may require.

There are a great many different kinds and descriptions of breeding-cages; but, from my own experience, I have great confidence in recommending the adoption of cages such as I have endeavoured to describe and illustrate, and I am quite sure they will be found to be thoroughly adapted to the requirements of all who desire to breed either canaries or canary mules. I do not recommend cornices to these cages, so that other cages may, when required, be placed on the top of them to economise space.

Fig. 9 represents a London-made breeding-cage. It is divided into three separate compartments — viz., a cage, breeding-loft, and a nursery, the breeding-loft being subdivided into two compartments by a wired partition. I cannot say that I am greatly in favour of the construction and arrangement of these cages. They appear to me cumbersome, and are somewhat difficult to clean out and whitewash, and I think the dimensions generally used will admit of improvement; nevertheless they have their admirers. The space set apart for the birds to breed in is, as already mentioned, divided into two compartments by means of a wired partition; two small doors are placed at the end of the

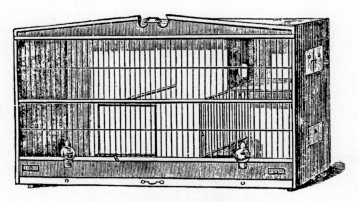

FIG. 9. LONDON-MADE BREEDING-CAGE.

cage to give easy access to clean them out, and to remove the eggs, as is usually done, until the third egg has been laid, when they are replaced, or to examine the young brood, or to search for parasites as the case may be. The nursery is placed below the breeding-loft, and has a two-fold object— first, to keep the young birds from interfering with the mother bird during incubation; and, secondly, to prevent the parent birds, when so disposed, from plucking their progeny; and as these cages are used principally for breeding the London Fancy and Lizard canaries, this arrangement is very necessary.

The nursery is divided from the breeding-cage by a sliding partition, wired, with an opening between the wires greater than the front of the cage, so that the young birds can get their heads through, and so enable their parents to provide

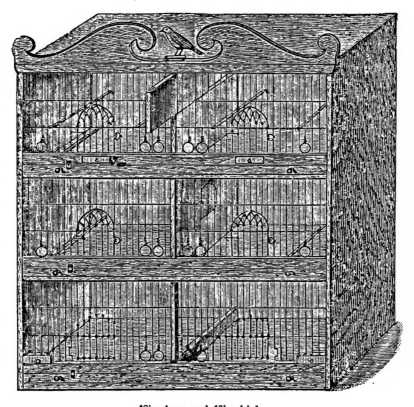

42in. long and 48in. high.

FIG. 10. FOUR-COMPARTMENT BREEDING-CAGE, WITH BOTTOM FLIGHT-CAGE.

them with food. The only thing to be guarded against is not to make them too wide, so that the birds can get through bodily; about three-quarters-of-an-inch will suffice between each wire. An egg-drawer and a water-trough are all that is needed in this division of the cage, for as soon as the young birds are able to feed themselves they should be removed to an ordinary breeding- or similar cage, and when they are capable of breaking the seed, they may, if found desirable, be placed in a flight-cage. A door at the end is necessary in this compartment also. These cages are obtainable, ready made, at most wire-workers' and ironmongers'. Their dimensions are, as a rule, about 25in. in length, 15in. in height, and 12in. in depth, from back to front. The breeding-loft is divided into two compartments, 6in. square. The nursery 10in. by 12in., or thereabouts.

Fig. 10 is a drawing of a four-compartment breeding-cage, with a fly- or flight-cage beneath. The latter can be made with a sliding partition in the centre, the full height of the open space in front. It can then be used either as a fly- or as an additional breeding-cage. Two pieces of wood, one top and one bottom, the depth of the top and bottom front stays of the cage, should be grooved and fitted for the slide to work in, these pieces, of course, being the full width of the cage, and they must be fixed before the front is wired; two thin pieces of wood are also fixed in front to form an opening for the slide and to hold it firmly. The slide should be toothed away at the top and bottom edges—wedge-shaped —to make it glide in and out easily, and also to make it look neater and more compact and workmanlike. A cage of this description is well adapted for a recess in a sitting-room, and should be well made of good materials, and French polished.

The doors in the first four compartments of the cage are fitted with a spiral wire spring for self-closing; this is fixed to an adjoining wire. It is on the same principle as the wire springs used for the lids of mouse-traps, and will be found an excellent contrivance, as they are self-closing, and cannot by any possibility be left open; hence they prevent accidents which not unfrequently happen through a door being left open unthinkingly.

The other doors in the lower portion are the ordinary sliding wire doors. Other descriptions of doors can be used

if preferred, but we advocate those shown in our drawing
in preference to all others.

Fig. 11 is a four-compartment breeding-cage with nurseries. The nurseries are in the centre, and are separated
from the breeding-compartments by wired frames made to
slide in and out, the wires being left sufficiently far apart
to enable the old birds to feed their .young. It is advisable

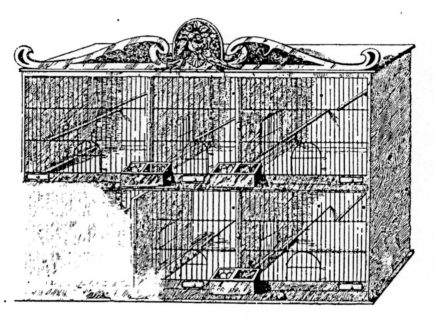

Length, 52in.; depth, 11in.; height, 32in.

FIG. 11. FOUR-COMPARTMENT BREEDING-CAGE, WITH NURSERIES
IN CENTRE.

to have solid wood divisions also; the latter to be used during
the period of incubation, and the former when it is necessary
to remove the young birds from their parents. Wooden partitions may be used instead of the wired divisions, with a
space wired for the purpose mentioned at one end, but this

is not nearly so satisfactory as the first-named method. For a cage of the above dimensions the breeding-compartments should be 19in. and the nurseries 14in. in length.

I consider the Lancashire breeding-cage (Fig. 12) one of the best single-compartment cages adapted for canaries. It can be used for every known variety; is simple in construction, ample

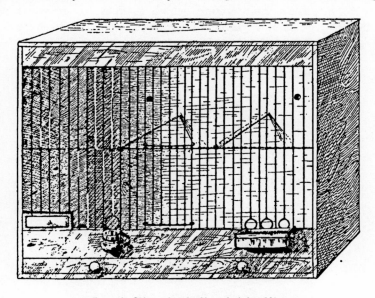

Length, 21in.; depth, 9in.; height, 18in.

FIG. 12. LANCASHIRE BREEDING-CAGE.

in dimensions, and is easily cleaned out. A cage of this description is best made of mahogany or cedar-wood and French polished. The nests are hung inside on screws.

SHOW-CAGES.—The description of show-cage generally used for exhibiting Norwich Fancy, Cinnamons, London Fancy, and Lizard canaries, and canary mules in, is represented in Fig. 13. It should be made of American pine wood, three-quarters-of-an-inch in thickness, in the rough, as it is necessary to make these cages extra strong to enable

them to withstand the ordeal of rough usage to which they
are liable in the course of transit to and from shows; the
length of the cage should be 13½in., height in front the same,
depth 6in. The top should be placed at an acute angle,
as shown in the engraving; the original idea for making the
top in this style was to throw a reflected light over the
birds to intensify their colour, which it does to some extent
when the cage is not placed in a direct light. It used to be
the practice to place the sides of the cage at an angle as

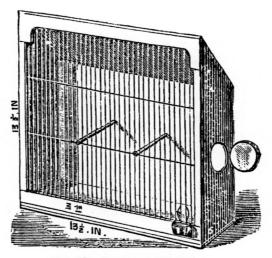

FIG. 13. ORDINARY SHOW-CAGE.

well, with the same view, but certainly not with the same
result, but that idea is now exploded. The chief advantage
in making the tops angular is this: Most fanciers place the
cages face to face, with a piece of cardboard or strong
brown paper between them, to prevent the birds getting
their heads through the wires during transit to and from
exhibitions, and thereby preventing them running the risk
of being injured or killed; the cages are then tied together
firmly with twine and secured in a canvas wrapper. The

tops being made in the manner described, they form, when packed, an angular roof; and this in a great measure prevents the servants of the railway companies from placing heavy packages upon the tops of them, which they would be very likely to do if they were made flat, and thereby incurring the chance of breakage or damage. The main stay at the bottom, in front of the cage, is 1½in. in depth, and the top stay 1in. except at the extreme corners, which are shaped so as to give it the appearance of the top of the capital letter T. At the end of the cage, towards the right hand, is a circular door, 4in. in diameter, and bevelled in such a manner as to prevent it going inside the cage (see Fig. 13). The bottom of the cage should project about a-quarter-of-an-inch beyond the front. Two stout wire bars, at equal distances from the top and bottom of the cage, and from each other, should be placed across the front of the cage. No. 11 wire should be used for cages of this kind, and No. 13 for the uprights, as they need to be very strong; they should be placed three-quarters-of-an-inch apart, and firmly secured either by wire binding or solder. I generally bend two wires a little at the bottom at one end of the cage (it is immaterial which end) for the convenience of the bird to drink through, the drinking-tin being hung opposite this aperture; be careful not to make it too large, or the bird might get out. Place two perches in such a manner as to rest upon the lowest cross-bar, insert a piece of stout wire into the end of each perch, about 1½in., allowing it to project about three-eighths-of-an-inch, and fix it into the back of the cage in a straight line; cut away a portion of the under-part of the other end of the perches to the extent of a quarter or three-eighths-of-an-inch back, to one-half their thickness, round or bevel off the top edge, and make a notch in it so that you can slip it across the upright wire to make it firm, for it is a great misfortune when a perch falls down, especially when there is only one, for it prevents the bird being seen to advantage when it has to be examined by the judges on the floor of the cage. Some fanciers use only one perch, but this is a

most objectionable practice, and very reprehensible, as a
timid bird is sure to dart into the bottom of the cage, or
against the wires, at that critical moment when it is under-
going the ordeal of the scrutinising gaze of the judges, and
a judge is very apt at such a moment to lose his temper
over it, which is by no means to be desired; but when there
are two perches it will in most cases content itself by
hopping to and fro from one to the other, and by this
means show itself to much greater advantage. The perches
should be placed about four-and-a-half inches from each
end of the cage, or upon the sixth wire.

If you choose to do so, you can make the front of the cage
solid, by making it in the form of a frame; in this case it
should be made to fit inside a little way, and should be
fastened with small screws at the sides. The advantage to
be derived by this contrivance is the ready means it affords
you for re-painting or colouring-out your cages. It is not
customary to make seed-drawers for cages of this sort, the
seed being thrown inside the cage. I generally sprinkle a little
sand over the cage bottom first; some people use oat-, barley-
or wheat-chaff instead, and others nothing but the seed. These
cages ought to be coloured inside or painted before you commence to wire them, as you can do it so much more readily at
that time. The outside can be either painted or stained and
varnished, it is all a matter of taste, but it is advisable to
coat the wires with black varnish, as it forms an excellent
contrast with the colour of the birds; and more particularly
is this visible when the occupants are Clear Yellow or Buff
Norwich birds. It is the practice of some fanciers to cover
the perches of their show-cages with scarlet flannel or crim-
son velvet, and with others to tint the front ends of them
with rose pink or carmine, or to have them gilded
with gold leaf. Whether their object is to show the great
value or the affection they entertain for their pets, or what
their motives are, I am unable to say; but it is certainly
an objectionable practice, and, I think, ought to be put a
stop to by show committees, as all such conspicuous and

distinguishing marks act as a key to judges, and lead to remarks the reverse of complimentary to those who adopt these peculiarities.

Fig. 14 represents a Scotch fancy show-cage. Some of these cages are got up in splendid style, and look really exquisite; in fact, to give Scotchmen their due, as cage-makers they stand unsurpassed. It is quite impossible to give anything like an adequate conception of these cages in a drawing; the workmanship is of the very best in all parts,

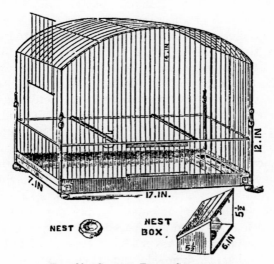

FIG. 14. SCOTCH FANCY SHOW-CAGE.

the wires are neatly soldered, and, in fact, nearly all the cages that I have seen at Scotch shows are put together and finished in such a manner as almost to defy competition. The wood-work is generally made of the finest descriptions of wood procurable, and most frequently of walnut, rosewood, or Spanish mahogany, and finished in the highest style of workmanship and beautifully French polished. In front is a seed-drawer, and a "dummy" or imitation drawer front to correspond at the opposite corner, and these are generally inlaid

with ebony and satin-wood in various devices; the front stay
or margin is likewise inlaid with a beading or cross-banding
of mahogany or other wood, and a draw-board is placed at
one end of the cage. The length of a cage of this sort may
be from 17in. to 18in., height 13in. to 14in. in the centre, and
from 7in. to 8in. wide. There is a door in the front fitted
with wooden bars top and bottom. There are four pillars,
one at each corner, extending about midway up the cage,
about three-eighths-of-an-inch square, and ornamented by
being cut with a sort of diamond pattern down the outer
edges; a wooden bar of the same thickness extends round the
cage about an-inch-and-a-half below the top of these pillars,
as shown in the engraving. On the tops of the pillars are
bone ornaments, having a hole through them, and they slide
up and down the corner wires. There is a running wire door
at the end opposite the seed-drawer, in addition to the
ordinary door, so that the birds can be run in and out the
more readily. It is also used for hanging a nest upon, such
as is shown in the illustration: for Scotchmen are naturally
very economical, and when these cages become shabby or get
damaged they use them for breeding. They place them upon
shelves, and either put a wood partition between each cage or
cover the ends with paper or calico, to prevent the birds from
seeing each other as much as possible during the breeding.
season. The nests proper are made of leather and lined with
flannel; the leather is damped, and then fastened on to a
wooden block made for that purpose, of the exact size and
shape of the nests. The holes in the nest-boxes are bored
with a large ungainly-looking brace and bit, made specially for
the purpose, the latter being in form not much unlike a monster
claw; it has a point in the centre, and is hollowed away in an
eccentric fashion, leaving another sharp point or edge which
cuts the piece out solid, like a wheel for a toy cart. The
feet of the cage are made of hard wood, stained black and
varnished. The nest-box is made of very thin deal, the top is
wired and may be either solid or made to open like the door
of the cage in front; size of nest-box 6in. long, 5½in. wide.

and 5in. in depth, with wire hooks fixed in the top cross-bar of the nest-box to hook on to the cage; the hole for the nest is 3¼in. to 3½in. in diameter, the water-trough (glass) is hung on the side beside one of the perches, the wire that supports it is made to shut up as if on hinges, and a small wire handle is fastened on the top of the cage.

Fig. 15 exhibits a Belgian show-cage. The lower portion is made of wood with a draw-board and seed- and egg-drawers; the remainder of the cage is made entirely of wire,

FIG. 15. BELGIAN FANCY SHOW-CAGE.

except the ornament at the top, the base of which serves . as a receptacle to let the wires .into. The cross-bars are made of No. 13 wire, the upright wires being No. 17. The wires ought to be soldered together; at the end is a sliding wire door. The dimensions are: length 14in., height 13in., and width 7in. Some fanciers make them rather smaller, and with semi-circular tops. The show-cages used by the fanciers in Belgium are heavy and ungainly looking, framed with bars, having uprights at the corners and cross-pieces;

the body is square and the tops dome-shaped; the uprights
at the corners, which are made of half-inch laths, square,
extend about four inches below the bottom to form legs,
and give a cage the appearance of being on stilts.

Fig. 16 represents a Yorkshire show-cage, the lower portion
of which has a 2¼in. wooden frame all round, the remainder
of the cage being made of wire. Thin mahogany or other
hard wood may be used for the frame. If made of fir, the

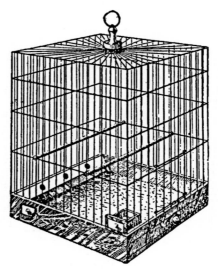

Length, 9½in.; depth, 7in.; height, 15in.

FIG. 16. YORKSHIRE SHOW-CAGE.

whole cage ought to be black varnished; if of hard wood,
polished or varnished, and bright tinned wires should be used.

The improved show-cage (see Fig. 17) is eminently adapted
for showing Lizards and Crested birds. The upper portions
of the wires are circular, and fit into a piece of wood 2in.
wide, secured to the ends and back of the cage. These should
be made of mahogany and French polished, a brass handle

being placed on the top for the convenience of moving it about. One or two perches may be used, one for a Crested bird, and two for a Lizard.

Fig. 18 is a composite cage. It answers three purposes: first it can be used as a moulting-cage, and is well adapted for crested birds, which should, if intended for show, be kept apart from others, to prevent damage to their crests

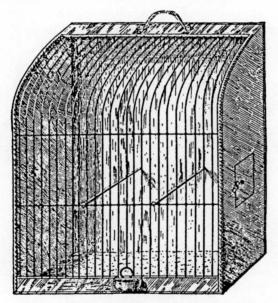

Length, 12in. ; depth, 6in. ; height at front, 12in.

FIG. 17. IMPROVED SHOW-CAGE.

and plumage; secondly, they are most useful for keeping show-birds in of any variety of the Norwich, Cinnamon, Lizard, or smaller specimens of the canary family, as it is not prudent to put show-birds together or with other birds during the exhibition season for fear of injury through quarrelling and fighting, which frequently occur when male birds especially are grouped together in the same cage;

D

thirdly, by removing the seed-hopper these cages can be used as show-cages, but when so intended I recommend a width of 6in. only, as birds do not look nearly so well in a broad cage as they do in a narrow one. These cages can be made entirely of deal and painted, or stained and varnished, or with hard wood fronts, polished or varnished; mahogany and walnut look best, to our taste.

TRAVELLING-CAGES.—The travelling-cage shown in Fig. 19 is suitable for despatching birds a long distance. The door is

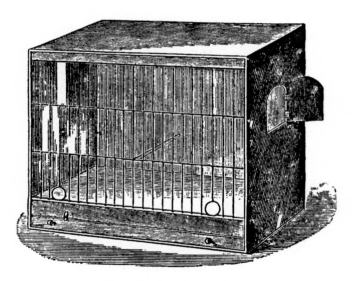

FIG. 18. COMPOSITE CAGE.

at the back of the cage, hung on small brass hinges, and secured by a hook or button. A perch should be fixed the full length of the cage, 2in. from the bottom and an equal distance from the front and back. Wires must be bent or two round holes made to allow the birds to get at the water-tins, which should be hung in front of these apertures. A piece of flannel or thin canvas ought to be tacked on to the front and over the door, pieces being cut out opposite the water holes.

Any railway servant would give them a drink of water during a long journey. Seed should be thrown on the floor of the cage together with a piece of breadcrust, soaked in cold water and broken into small pieces; a bit of sweet apple may also be put in the cage. It is a good plan to let in a piece of glass at one end, and fasten over this a piece of perforated zinc to prevent it from getting broken, as by this means the birds can see to feed during a long journey.

To accommodate four birds the dimensions would be correspondingly less, say 11in. by 7in. and 8in., and for two birds only 9in. by 7in. and 7in., or for one 7in. by 7in. and 6in. wide. It is necessary in sending valuable birds a long

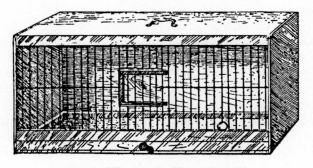

Length, 15in.; depth, 7in.; height, 9in.

FIG. 19. TRAVELLING-CAGE TO ACCOMMODATE SIX BIRDS, to be sent any distance.

distance to allow plenty of space to prevent them from getting cramped or damaged in plumage. For short distances an ordinary wooden box, with ½in. holes bored at each side and a perch placed in the centre, would suffice.

CAGES FOR SINGING - BIRDS. — Those best suited for canaries and mules are neat wire cages, with wood bottoms, oblong in form, with arched roofs, waggon shaped; they should have a draw - board, a seed-hopper, and a glass drinking-trough—those made of brass wire are very objectionable, for, when they get wet, as they are sure to do every time the bird washes itself, verdigris is produced, and it is

D 2

a deadly poison. I do not like those fancy painted cages. either: the paint is baked on, and the birds can peck it off quite easily, which they invariably do, and disaster follows.

FLIGHT-CAGES.—Where a fancier breeds young canaries by the hundred he is obliged to have recourse to temporary places of abode for them, to save him not only the expense of a large outlay for cages, but a great deal of labour in feeding and watering the birds. If you have a good deep recess at the side of a chimney in your bird-room, you can easily put a few shelves across it, about four feet apart, a few wood uprights and cross-bars, and wire it; but the better plan is to make a solid framed front to each compartment; this can be hung with hinges or fastened on with small screws or metal "buttons," the same as are used for closet doors, but smaller; if you desire to be very economical, or are wishful to save yourself much labour, you can cover the front with half-inch diamond-shaped wire-work, which you can buy in the piece at any professional wire-worker's—use the galvanised, which will last for a number of years. I have a fly made in one corner of one of my bird-rooms; it is placed 4ft. from the floor, and extends in height to the ceiling, which forms the top, the wall forms the back and one end, the other end extends from the ceiling to the floor, and is part wood and part glass; the wood-work is about five-and-a-half feet from the floor of the room. I have a hole cut in it 8in. deep, framed round and wired like a cage front: upon this I hang two troughs made of zinc with glass fronts; they hold about three half-pints of water each. The front is formed of glass frames, being part of a glass case such as chemists use; the centre frame is hung with hinges and forms a door, and is fastened with a brass button; this framework rests upon a stout lath 2½in. wide and 1½in. in thickness; below this are two deals 6in. in depth, hinged at the top, and each extends half of the whole length of the fly—they lift up to enable me to clean it out, which I can do with a small iron rake. I give them water

to bathe in through one or other of these apertures. At
the other end I have a large drawer which holds 7lb.
of seed; this is covered with a fixed wood frame inside with
a sloping top and a wired front; it is 12in. deep at the
back and 9in. in front. This is to allow the light to
penetrate inside, and to enable the birds to see their food;
the perches, with the exception of the one to feed from
and the other to reach their drinking-water readily, are all
placed at different distances and various heights, care being
taken not to have one above the other, or in such a way
that the birds would be likely to foul each other. It is
lime-washed out, and the perches are made to "ship" and
"unship" at pleasure. It accommodates forty birds, and I
generally place those in it that I intend to dispose of. If
they fight, as they often do about Christmas, I darken the
apartment, which has the effect of restoring order.

BEADS FOR CAGE-DOORS.—In Norwich I observed that most
fanciers, including the Mackleys, have their cage-doors some
distance from the cross-pieces, both top and bottom, and this
they manage to do by putting in two large glass beads, placed
on the wire that the door works on, in opening and closing it.
This is to prevent parasites from congregating there.

AVIARIES.—The illustrations, Figs. 20 and 22 are represen-
tations of outdoor aviaries. That shown in Fig. 22 may be
placed on a lawn or in some convenient situation in a
garden or pleasure-ground. It can be made to any dimensions required.

The aviary shown in Fig. 20 should be erected against a
wall in a sheltered situation, and with a south or south-
westerly aspect, and should be constructed with an inner and
an outer compartment, as shown.

A friend of mine has one which answers the purpose admirably. It is about fifteen feet in length, and about seven feet
in width. It is constructed of wood and wire, in the form of a
"lean-to." A wall some seven or eight feet in height forms
the back. At one end is a sort of small room, forming the

FIG. 20.—OUTDOOR "LEAN-TO" AVIARY.

inner dwelling, which is made of deal, tongued and grooved.
It should be formed with double boarding, about three inches
apart, and the space between the boards should be filled with
sawdust, to make it warm. The front part of this compartment extends about six feet; in it is placed a small window,
about twelve or fourteen inches square, and about five feet
from the ground. This not only admits light to the compartment, but enables anyone outside to see its occupants
without unnecessarily disturbing them. It ought, however, to
be covered over with a piece of wire-work, for fear of an
accident. The remaining portion is all wired similar to an
ordinary breeding-cage. The door, which is about five feet
six inches in height and two feet six inches in width, is wired
in the same way, and placed in the centre; but I should
prefer it at the end, with an outer entrance in the form of a
portico, with a second door to prevent the escape of a bird
when anyone enters the interior of the aviary for the purpose
of cleaning it out or otherwise. It is fitted with perches in
various positions, and has a few trees and some fancy cork-
work placed against the back wall, the latter being fixed in
a variety of ways to give a pleasing appearance, and for the
birds to rest on. There are nest-boxes of various kinds hung
about here and there, including cocoa-nut husks, cocoa-nut shells
in halves, wooden nest-boxes and baskets suspended by wire
and strings from the ceiling, and other contrivances of a
similar kind, which give it a picturesque and imposing appearance. Self-supplying seed-hoppers are placed about in different positions against the wall and in other convenient
places, and water-fountains, also self-supplying, are placed
about the floor. There are also tins for German paste and
other special compounds to suit the different kinds of birds
which occupy it. The top is made of deal, covered with
roofing-felt, and tarred to make it impervious to wet weather;
these boards should be tongued and grooved, but where
expense is not a consideration I would recommend slates in
preference to wood. In this aviary is kept a great variety of
both British and foreign birds and canaries, and they appear

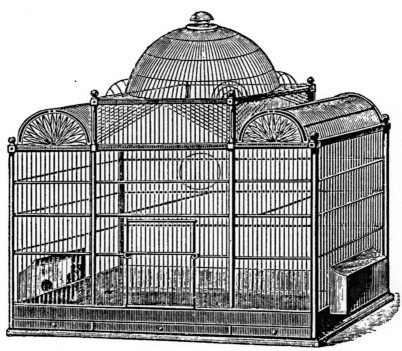

FIG. 21. THE CRYSTAL PALACE INDOOR AVIARY.

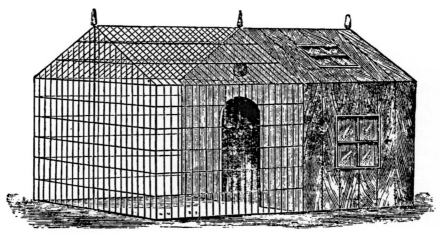

FIG. 22. OUTDOOR AVIARY, WITH ROOM FOR MOULTING SHOW-BIRDS.

to agree wonderfully well. I also noticed pigeons and doves among them. The British birds comprised thrushes, blackbirds, starlings, bullfinches, greenfinches, brown linnets, reed buntings, skylarks, hedge sparrows, winchats, blue tits, robins, and many other kinds. Among the foreign varieties I noticed cardinals, spice birds, Java sparrows, budgerigars, &c., and all seemed to thrive well and agree in a wonderful manner— almost a happy family. I must not omit to say that the ground forming the bottom of the aviary was got out to the extent of twelve inches or more, and this was filled in with sand and fine gravel, and a garden rake passed over it once or twice a week made it always look clean and nice.

To anyone who has a taste for this sort of thing, I can recommend it as a most interesting and instructive hobby; but birds do not breed so freely where such a quantity and so many different varieties are grouped together. I should think there were about eighty birds of one sort and another in this ornithological domicile.

DRINKING-TROUGHS.—Fig. 23 is made of tin or zinc, and furnished with wire hooks to hang on in front of the cage. A piece of wire is run round the top rim of the trough, and two pieces are left projecting in front, so that they can be bent over to fit the cages they are intended for. Either wire that has been tempered by heating in a fire, or copper wire, should be used, as ordinary tinned wire breaks readily, and iron wire rusts and decays soon. Fig. 24 represents a glass trough which is secured to the front of the cage by passing a piece of wire round it, boring two holes at the required place through the front stay of the cage, and securing the two ends by bending them downwards inside; care being taken that no sharp points are left to injure the birds. The top of the glass should be fixed level with the top of the stay and arranged to be central with the aperture made for the bird to drink through. Fig. 25 is a drawing of a cover to be placed over it. This can be made of tin or zinc, and a wire passed round the bottom projects, as in the tin trough, to form two hooks to hang it on to the front stay of the cage : this contrivance prevents mice from entering the cage through the water-hole.

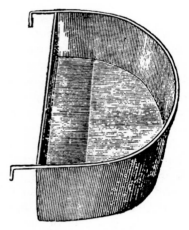

FIG. 23. DRINKING-TIN.

The drinking-glass (Fig. 26) and wire (Fig. 27) for holding the same are intended for the Composite cage (*vide* Fig. 18).

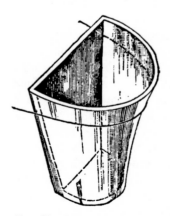

FIG. 24. DRINKING-GLASS.

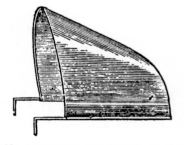

FIG. 25. TIN COVER FOR DRINKING-GLASS.

Another contrivance, and a good one, is to have some small tins made, as per pattern (see Fig. 28). The front portion is put through the drinking-aperture, and a small phial, with a longish thin neck, and filled with water, is placed in the other portion outside the cage, and upside down; this is secured to the cage by a piece of wire being passed round the middle of the bottle thus ⌒⌒, and secured to the wire. It forms a self-supplying drinking-trough, and the supply will last for

FIG. 26. DRINKING-GLASS FOR COMPOSITE CAGE (Fig. 18).

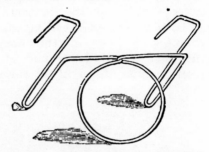

FIG. 27. HOOK-ON WIRE, FOR HOLDING DRINKING-GLASS.

two or three days or more. It is easily cleaned out with a small bottle-brush, or a few shots, or a little sand. This arrangement entirely supersedes the conical water-fountains frequently used, and which I consider most objectionable, as they get very foul, and the water in them becomes turbid in

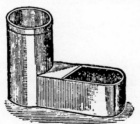

FIG. 28. WATER-TROUGH.

a few days, as they are difficult to cleanse out properly, owing to their construction.

I need hardly point out that pure and wholesome water for birds is of the greatest possible importance, being essential to the comfort and well-being of all caged birds.

SEED-HOPPERS.—The self-supplying seed-hopper, as shown in Fig. 29, will be found very useful for aviaries, and also for group- and large-sized fly- or flight-cages, where a goodly number of birds are kept all together. It may be made of deal or hard wood, whichever is preferred. The one represented is 8in. long, 6½in. high (at the back), and 5in. wide (extreme width at the bottom). It has a solid wood back and bottom; the ends can be made solid likewise; that portion forming the body of the hopper or seed-box being 2¾in. wide; but at the lower end of each a piece should project in an angular form, 2¼in. farther, making 5in. altogether;

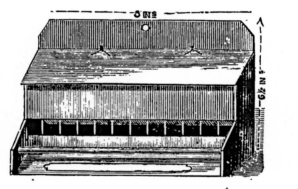

FIG. 29.   SELF-SUPPLYING SEED-HOPPER, WITH SIDE SECTION—showing Interior Arrangement.

these projections are 2¼in. in depth next the body of the hopper, and taper away to 1in. at the extreme outside. These pieces of wood or projections support a perch for the birds to rest upon whilst feeding. The bottom of the hopper has a hole cut through it (as shown in the engraving) which extends about three-fourths of its entire length, and about three-quarters-of-an-inch wide, and is midway between the feeding-box and the perch, to allow the husks of the seed, &c., to fall through. From the bottom of the hopper, and forming part of the front of feeding-box, is a stay or lath 1¼in. deep; and 1¼in. above this is placed a wood cross-bar.

The space between the stay and bar is wired with stout wires, set 1in. apart; this is where the birds feed through. Above this is a piece of glass extending from the cross-bar to the lid of the hopper, and this forms the front of it, and enables you to see when a further supply of seed is required. Inside of the hopper is fixed a piece of thin wood the entire length of the front; it extends from the cross-bar, which supports the glass, to within ⅜in. of the back, and is placed at an acute angle, and 1¼in. from the bottom of the hopper or feeding-box. This forms the aperture for the seed to fall through; and so long as there is a supply of seed

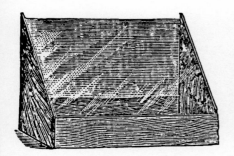 

FIG. 30. SEED-HOPPER FOR BREEDING-CAGE, to supply Two Compartments.

FIG. 31. SEED-HOPPER FOR COM-POSITE CAGE (Fig. 18), to supply One Compartment only.

in the upper portion or box the lower portion or feeding-trough is kept constantly supplied by this contrivance. A small hole should be made in that portion of the back which projects above the lid, to hang it up by. The lid is made of wood and secured with two pieces of wire, which act like hinges. The illustration fully explains anything further that is required to be known. The hopper should be made of wood from ¼in. to ⅜in. in thickness when dressed ready for use.

Figs. 30 and 31 are made of wood with glass cover or front, arranged to slide in and out of grooves made at each side with a stout hand-saw. They are so constructed as to fit close to the cage front, with the object of preventing mice getting at the seed. By using hoppers of this description, together with a glass water-trough and cover, as already described, and having the cages wired closely, with the wires about two-thirds-of-an-inch apart, it is impossible for mice to intrude in the cages; and only breeders know the difficulty experienced in preventing these nocturnal depredators from interfering with their stock, and the incalculable mischief they do when they gain access *ad libitum* to the sanctuary of a valuable lot of choice birds. The cages should be hung against a wall or partition, for if left on a stand, or table, the probability is that these pests to fanciers will gnaw a hole through the back or end of a cage. Ornamental hoppers can be made by

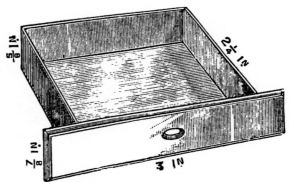

FIG. 32.   EGG-DRAWER FOR BREEDING-CAGE.

the skilful use of a fret-saw. The pattern should be first drawn on paper, and then cut out and pasted on the wood to be operated on, for a guide. Hoppers of this description add much to the appearance of a well-made cage; but unless cages are made of mahogany, walnut, or some similar wood, and French polished, the labour would be wasted.

EGG-TROUGHS.—Fig. 32 is a sketch of a tin or zinc trough —tin preferable—with a brass or wooden front, for a breeding-cage, and Fig. 33 represents another tin or zinc trough to be used for any cage in which provision has not been already made for one, or for a show-cage when required. Being made long and narrow it can easily be inserted in any cage, bending two of the wires backward a little way with a pair of small pliers, just sufficient to admit the trough. The length makes up for the deficiency in width. These tins will be found very useful to breeders and exhibitors of canaries.

Pearl-white egg-drawers made of enamelled earthenware are desirable, as they are easily kept clean, and keep the food cool and fresh. They may be obtained, with nest-pans of the same material, from Mr. Green, of 96, Gray's Inn Buildings, London, or of Mr. Tams, Drury Works, Longton, Staffordshire.

FIG. 33. EGG-DRAWER FOR BREEDING- AND SHOW-CAGES.

PACKING-CASES.—Figures numbered 34 and 35 represent travelling-cases for packing cages in to send to shows. Fig. 29 is a box made of thin deal, and stained and varnished. It is made to hold two Scotch Fancy show-cages; the length of it is 18in., outside measurement; the width and height are equal, each being 16in. It has a metal handle at each end, two brass hooks and eyes in front to secure the lid, and likewise a stout leather strap, or rather two leather straps forming one. When fastened, the ends of the straps are secured on the back and front sides of the box with small screws, and one portion of the strap is made with a handle to carry it by. There is a hole at each end of the box, 1in. in diameter, to let in a supply of fresh air. These holes are covered inside with a small plate made of perforated zinc to prevent a draught. Any further information

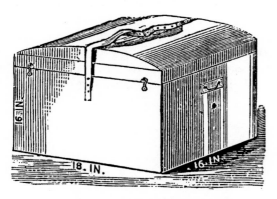

FIG. 34. CASE FOR DON SHOW-CAGES.

that is needed can be gathered from inspecting the engraving. Fig. 35 represents a travelling-case made to hold half-a-dozen ordinary show-cages, such as are used for

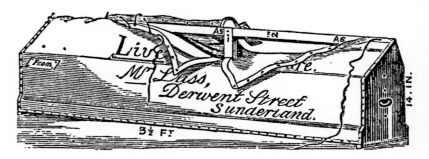

FIG. 35. CASE FOR ORDINARY SHOW-CAGES.

showing Norwich Fancy and the smaller varieties of canaries and canary mules in—three on each side. It is 3½ft. long, 14in. high, and 14in. wide, inside. The bottom and ends are made of wood, stout deal, ⅞in. in thickness in the rough. Between the ends, across the top, is a stout rail or bar, 2½in. deep and 1½in. thick, let into the ends, mortised to make it firmer and look better. At the bottom of the case, and in a parallel line with the top rail, is fixed another lath, 1½in. in depth and breadth; and in the centre of the case between these rails is fastened an upright stay or support, which is mortised at both ends, placed across and secured to the cross-bars with screws to give it strength. The cages rest against the bars, top and bottom, and this creates a space for air. Opposite this space at either end are three air-holes, each ½in. in diameter. A metal handle is placed at each end of the case to facilitate its carriage up and downstairs or at shows, and a brass handle is fastened in the centre of the top rail for the convenience of moving it about or carrying it if necessary. A thin lath, 2in. deep, is nailed on each side, in front, next the bottom, to keep the cages firm. It is covered with canvas, first tacked on with very small tacks, and afterwards bound round with "list" or binding to make it firmer and more durable; the latter is likewise tacked on. Along the top on each side small round holes are made, and worked like button-holes; these are laced up with two pieces of stout twine, secured firmly at each end of the case, and meeting in the centre, where they are tied securely. It will be found necessary to cut the canvas cover a little way down on each side in the middle, to let the cages go in more easily. The portion so cut should be bound with stout linen binding, and made to fasten up with buttons and button-holes; 6in. or 8in. will be sufficient for these openings. At one side (outside) you can have a square piece of canvas bound round with the same kind of binding, and secured at the top edge with a needle and thread to the cover of the case; this should be made to turn over, like the lapel of a coat, to form a reverse label, with the word "From" on one side, and the word "To" on the other. Make it with two button-holes at the lower corner, and place two buttons above

E

and two below to secure it by, as shown in the illustration. Opposite this you can print with ink and a piece of wood, sharpened like a wooden skewer, your name and address in large characters, so that they may be readily seen; and above the address print the words, "Live birds, with care." By using these precautions, your birds are sure to be returned to you in due course, and you avoid the risk of any error being made inadvertently by committee men, or other persons connected with shows, in the bustle and excitement of packing for the return journey. A great many fanciers send their birds to exhibitions in canvas wrappers, whilst others merely fold the cages containing the birds in paper covers. Both these plans are objectionable, and entail an unnecessary amount of labour upon both secretaries and other persons who assist at shows, besides running a great risk of having the cages damaged, and their occupants maimed or killed, through their being improperly packed by some inexperienced person. The cost of these cases is very trifling, and they are so exceedingly light that the extra carriage, if any, is very small, and, when compared with the comfort and security which they afford, sinks into utter insignificance.

In addition to these, wicker-work baskets can be obtained, but the wooden frames covered with canvas are doubtless the best. The canvas covers can be coated with two coatings of boiled linseed oil, and afterwards with two coats of paint, which will make them more durable, and render them to a great extent impervious to rain and snow. Baskets or hampers I consider too draughty, and not sufficiently warm in cold weather.

CHAPTER II.

BREEDING AND MANAGEMENT.

CANARIES, THEIR TEMPERS AND DISPOSITIONS. — Birds, like human beings, are very differently constituted—each bird has its own temper and disposition, its likes and its dislikes, its own peculiar fancies and ideas, quite as much so in its limited sphere as beings more highly favoured and gifted than they. I need not, therefore, point out to the observant and thoughtful mind the necessity there exists for each fancier, as far as possible, to endeavour to familiarise himself with the tempers and dispositions of his feathered captives, as much really depends upon his knowledge in this respect for his ultimate success in producing high-class young birds. True, there are some birds that it is impossible to lead into the way in which you fain would have them go; but I hope to show, however, that even vicious birds, by judicious management, can in some instances be reformed from ways which are neither pleasing nor profitable to their owners.

FLIGHTING STOCK-BIRDS.—Having selected the birds required for breeding, which is generally done between November and February, run the hens into a roomy flight-cage or aviary, or what is better, a small room; the amount of exercise which they get in this way is conducive to their health and well-being afterwards. The cocks, too, would be all the better for being put into large cages or aviaries in batches of from two to twenty, but not more, as they are generally more

E 2

mischievous and quarrelsome in their disposition than the hens. Of course, it would not do to put show-birds together in this way, for fear they might injure their plumage, and it will be found necessary to separate them about Christmas, or before, if they are observed to disagree.

SEPARATE ROOMS.—If possible, keep the cocks and hens in separate rooms; if not, endeavour to keep them in such positions that the opposite sexes cannot see each other, for it not unfrequently happens, as the spring approaches, that an intimacy arises between them, and when a cock or hen has selected a partner in this way—and they generally select the one which is not intended for them—they prove sulky and malevolent if compelled to mate with birds not of their own choice and selection, and the result is that the hen not unfrequently frets and will not feed her young, and the cock, on the other hand, breaks the eggs or destroys the progeny. These results do not always proceed from this cause, but generally so, and I have noticed repeatedly that in cases where the parent birds appear attached and affectionately disposed to each other, they very rarely fail to rear their young.

PREPARING BREEDING-CAGES.—Having selected the birds intended for breeding, and having decided which to pair, in the early part of January commence to prepare the breeding-cages. First scrape them thoroughly, next scald them well out with boiling water; after they are quite dry coat them well inside and out with the following mixture: Spirit of turpentine, ½ pint; camphor, ½oz.; spirit of tar, 4oz.; dissolve the camphor in the turpentine, and then add the spirit of tar, or carbolic acid diluted with water, one part of acid to three of water may be used in preference, or a strong solution made of soft soap and washing-soda, used scalding hot, is very destructive to the bird parasite. Some fanciers use kerosene and some fir oil. I have used the first two preparations for some years, and have found them efficacious, especially if the cages are first thoroughly washed with hot water to which soft soap and soda have been added. Either preparation must be laid on with a small new paint-brush; rub well into all the crevices of the cage, where the parasites or bird vermin usually harbour, so that they may all be dislodged and destroyed, as there is great difficulty in rearing birds where those troublesome pests exist in large quantities. After this is done, allow the cages to be exposed to the weather for not less than forty-eight hours, but a few days would be still better; next wash them out with warm water in which a small quantity of washing-soda has been previously dissolved. Rinse off with pure water; and, lastly, whitewash them out.

Another remedy is to slightly coat the crevices and corners or joinings of the cage with turpentine or wood naphtha with

FIG. 36. SMALL IRON RAKE—for Cleaning Dirt out of Cages.

a painter's brush, and then fire with lighted paper; but this is rather a rash experiment, and needs care and caution in its use. It is undoubtedly an effectual remedy. Quicklime, when procurable, is best for whitewashing; when not, use common whitening and pipe-clay in equal proportions, and add a small piece of alum. After the cages are quite dry, they are ready for use.

Be sure always to sprinkle the bottom of the cages liberally with coarse sand—the coarser the better—or very fine gravel. I prefer sea-sand myself, but any kind will do. Sand or gravel is essential to assist birds in the process of digestion. Powdered cuttle-fish, the shells of the eggs of fowls crushed fine in a mortar, but not made into a

powder, or old lime hammered into very small pieces should
be mixed with or strewn among the sand at the bottom of
the cage, as these not only promote health and digestion, but
they form the shell of the eggs to be laid by the birds.
These are essential during breeding-operations, and are beneficial to the young birds. Clean out the birds as often as
possible without unnecessarily interfering with the hens
whilst sitting, using a small iron rake (see Fig. 36) for this
purpose. A little charcoal added and mixed with the sand
will be found useful, not only in keeping the birds in health,
but it prevents an accumulation of parasites.

PAIRING.—Having prepared your breeding-cages properly,
the hens can be put into them at once. If two hens are to
be run with one cock, keep the hens together in the same
compartment for some time first, until they are observed to
be on friendly terms, after which they very rarely exhibit any
symptoms of jealousy towards each other. Before the cocks
and hens are put together, which is usually done in February
or March, according to the climate, state of the weather, and
locality, it is advisable to place them in such a position in
separate cages as they may be able to see each other; in fact, to
be as close to each other as possible, in order that an intimacy
and familiarity may spring up between them, for if a male be
placed beside a female without this precaution it frequently
happens that a severe quarrel and a serious conflict is the
result, especially if the male be of an amorous and ardent
disposition. The hen is almost certain to resent his advances,
and hence an ill-feeling is engendered which is very detrimental to their future well-doing, and frequently leads to
results not at all to be desired. The best plan is to put
them into a cage with two compartments, commonly known
as a "double-coupled cage," with a wired division or slide
between them, or into two single wired cages placed close to
each other. As soon as a mutual understanding exists between
them, they may be placed in the breeding-cage. A great deal
more depends upon the careful coupling of the birds for future
results than is generally supposed or acknowledged.

After the birds are properly paired—that is, when they are thoroughly reconciled to each other, and on a friendly footing— it will be advisable to separate them for, say, two or three days, which generally tends to strengthen the attachment already formed. This can be done by closing the communication between the compartments of the breeding-cage, but when "single-coupled" breeding-cages are used, the cock should be put into another cage, and placed as closely as convenient to the one containing his partner or partners. Care should be taken, however, to prevent either, if possible, from seeing other birds of the opposite sex: this can be accomplished in a variety of ways, which, doubtless, will suggest themselves naturally; such, for instance, as forming lines with common twine and covering with a thin material of any kind, or old newspapers, so as not to exclude too much light. When a cock is placed beside two hens, he will sometimes show a preference for one, and proceed to persecute the other; in such a case, remove the hen he appears to despise into another cage, and after the one he first selects has laid three eggs and commenced to sit, remove him from beside her, and proceed, as at first, with the other hen. Some male birds become so much attached to a particular hen as to resent all others, and *vice versâ*, but such cases are of rare occurrence.

BREEDING-SEASON.—The best time to put birds together is from the 10th to the 21st of March, although some fanciers put them together much sooner; but unless they are constantly kept in a room with a fire in—which must be avoided when possible—it is not prudent to do so; in fact, I prefer the latter to the former date, and rarely put my birds together before that time. The result of a too early commencement is, that the hens are frequently seized with the cold, and become so weak and prostrate that they have not strength to deposit their eggs, and unless promptly attended to succumb in the effort; at other times they lay them irregularly, get out of condition, and will not sit upon them; or presuming that these difficulties have been overcome, the easterly winds, which are usually prevalent at this season of the year, carry off the early nestlings, despite the attentions of a good mother; or, supposing that they are reared, they are often weak and puny, and not unfrequently die when they commence to moult. It is better, therefore, not to be in too great a hurry to begin to breed. Of course, much depends on the weather and the part of the country in which the fancier resides. In Devonshire, Cornwall, Kent, Sussex, Hampshire, and all counties situated in the south, south-west, and west of England, operations in bird-breeding may be begun from three weeks to a month earlier than in the extreme north of England and most parts of Scotland, and in the Midland counties a time midway between February 14th and March 23rd should be chosen.

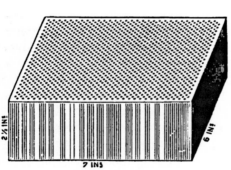

FIG. 37. BREAD- AND EGG-SIEVE.   FIG. 38. SPATULA.

FOOD FOR NEWLY-PAIRED BIRDS. — When the birds are put together finally, feed them liberally; give them hard-boiled egg, chopped fine or grated through a piece of perforated zinc. For this purpose get a small fig- or cigar-box, knock the bottom out, and nail the zinc on in its place, or make a small box, 6in. square by 2½in. deep (Fig. 37), and obtain a wooden or an iron spatula (Fig. 38). Take as much egg as is required, free it from the shell, and press through the zinc with the spatula or a knife having a stout blade, or a chisel will do as well; next rub through the same machine, or in your hands, an equal portion of bread, not too new, mix them together, either with a knife, or rub them together in an old newspaper; give about two teaspoonfuls of this to each pair of birds daily; every alternate day give them a little maw or hemp - seed (the former preferred), and occasionally a little linseed and millet-seed. After the birds have been together two or three days give them a nest.

CRUSHING-SEED.—A large number of Norwich fanciers use a small coffee- or pepper-mill for crushing hemp and other seeds, which I noticed some of them gave their birds whilst breeding. After crushing, the husks must be removed: this may be accomplished either by blowing them away or by sifting.

PREPARED FOOD.—A good mixture of dry food can be prepared as follows: Breadcrusts, rusks, or biscuits, 8oz.; ground linseed, pure, 2oz.; finely-ground oatmeal, 3oz.; ground rice, 3oz.; crushed hemp-seed, freed from husks, 2oz.; powdered loaf sugar, 4oz.; salt, ½oz.; maw-seed, 2oz. This food should all be reduced to a fine powder, except the maw-seed, which may be added whole, and the mixture should be rubbed well together in a mortar, or other suitable vessel, and kept in a tin canister in a dry place. It is invaluable as a food for birds, and may be given to them *ad libitum* if desired; they are very fond of it. It should be mixed with hot water to a moderate consistency, and given to the birds when cold, or nearly so. A teaspoonful of this mixture is sufficient for any bird for one day when not breeding. It keeps them in health and condition, and you need use no other food for rearing young birds unless you choose, but be careful not to let it get sour, and keep the feeding - tins scrupulously clean. It increases the bone and muscle.

The crusts, rusks, biscuits, and sugar can be powdered as finely as you please by using one of Hancock's Patent Bread-crumbing and Sugar-Mills, sold complete for a few shillings. These machines are most useful to breeders who keep a lot of birds, and can be procured from F. and C. Hancock's

Dudley. The preparation mentioned above is of my own invention; it far surpasses any of the compounds I have been able to purchase, and can be made for about one-eighth of the price.

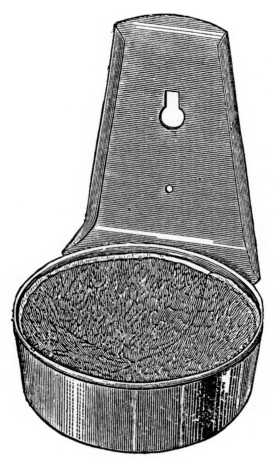

FIG. 39. TIN NEST WITH FELT LINING.

NESTS.—The nests that I prefer to all others are round tin nests, the bottoms of which are slightly globular in form,

and made of perforated zinc, having an upright tin back
(Fig. 39), with a hole in it by which to hang it up.   Fix a ½in.
screw-nail in each breeding-compartment in such a position
as will allow the top of the nest to be about one inch above
the perch, and 1in. from it, to enable the birds to feed their
young from the perches; the zinc bottoms let air into the
nest, which is necessary.   I line these tins with felt; any
kind of felt will do, so long as it is soft and pliable—an old
felt hat, for instance, but I prefer the thick felt used for lining
saddles, which can be procured from any saddler.   This I split

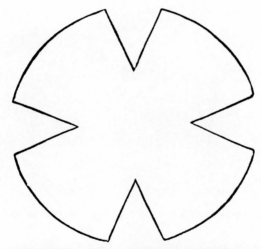

FIG. 40.   PATTERN OF A FELT LINING FOR AN ARTIFICIAL NEST.

in two; I place the outside of the felt at the bottom of the
nest, as the inner surface is much softer for the hens to sit
upon.   I generally have three sizes of these nests.   The first
is 3in. in diameter and 1½in. deep; these I use for the hens
to sit in during incubation.   The second size is 3½in. in diameter and 2in. deep, and the third 4in. in diameter and 2in.
deep; these I use for transferring the young birds into when
eight or nine days old.   I use them according to the number
of young birds.   Second size for three or four, and the larger

for any number exceeding that just given. In Fig. 40 I give a pattern, on a reduced scale, showing the shape of the felt or lining. I first cut it round, and then I cut out the angular pieces, and, drawing the parts together where the vacancies exist, I sew the edges firmly and neatly together. If carefully cut and sewn, they form nests precisely the shape of the tins. I then sew them through the perforated zinc bottoms, which keeps them quite firm. Fig. 41 represents a wooden block used for fitting the felt linings into the tin nests. It is made of hard wood. The block is for pressing them into shape after this has been done. I always tease out a piece

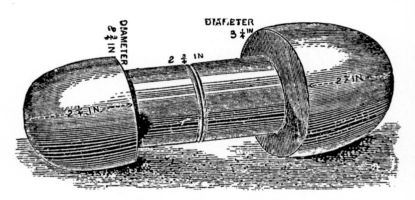

FIG. 41. WOODEN BLOCK FOR FITTING FELT LININGS IN TIN NESTS.

of felt and place it over the seams, and by screwing the block backwards and forwards, or round and round, it causes the teased-out felt to adhere firmly to the lining and makes the nest look smooth and neat. The block will likewise be found very useful when an old felt hat is used for a lining. In this case the felt is cut round, but is not notched. It must be steeped in hot water for an hour or so, wrung out tightly, and while hot stretched well over the block and tied securely. When it is dry it will be found the proper shape, and ready for use. It may be done overnight, or dried at a slow fire. Before putting in the felt, if a little sweet-oil be rubbed round the tin, or a little snuff, or Keating's Insect Powder be sprinkled inside, not many parasites, or "bird lice," will be found to exist. These linings can be taken out and washed after each brood, and they will last for years.

Fig. 39 is the tin nest with the lining, ready for use. Where tin nests cannot be readily procured, get a cocoa-nut and cut the shell into pieces as nearly the size to those given as can be obtained; put on a wooden back and line them the

FIG. 42. COCOA-NUT NEST, on mahogany frame, fastened with screw through bottom.

FIG. 43. COCOA-NUT NEST, fitted with piece of wood and wire.

same way, only I find a coating of thin glue-size round the top edge answers best for this description of nests to fasten in the felt. My birds all prefer nests of this sort, and I imagine that I can make a nest with the best architectural canary in existence. Canaries generally are bad architects. I likewise give them a piece of well-dried short moss and a little cow-hair; these dispose them to breed with more

freedom, though I seldom find them make good use of the
materials, and ultimately, as a rule, they throw them all out
ere they lay, evidently satisfied that they cannot improve
upon the "original," although occasionally I find a hen
construct a very neat nest from this material. These
materials likewise prevent them from plucking their progeny.
Instinctively they all have a notion of making a nest; but
only instinctively, I consider. As a general rule I am. no
advocate for the "square box" and "dried grass and wool
nests," although I know they are much used. Next to what
I have described, I prefer those used by Scotchmen generally—made of leather lined with flannel and let into a piece
of wood with a round hole cut in it, with wooden sides
fastened to it, wired top and back, and hung with wire hooks
on to a square hole made in the end of the cage. Tease out
a piece of the felt or saddle-cloth or a piece of wool carpet as
fine as possible, and place it in the wires of the breeding-
cages; this will induce the hens to take to the nest all the
more readily. Figs. 42 and 43 show method of fixing cocoa-nut
nests.

Glazed earthenware nest-pans are used by some fanciers, but
I prefer those I have already described, as I think earthenware too cold for general use. Such pans may be beneficial
in very hot weather, or in cases where hens are known to
sweat their young brood. These pans can be had from both
Mr. Green and Mr. Tams, whose addresses I have already
furnished (see page 47). Wooden nest-boxes and wicker nest-
baskets are preferred by some fanciers. The former are
made from three to three-and-a-half inches square or in
diameter, and one-and-three-quarter inches deep, inside measurements, with a projecting angular back, the latter being about
four-and-a-half inches in length, with a hole near the top by
which to hang it up, and a few small holes made in the
bottom, front, and sides for air to get to the nest. Where
these are used dried grass or hay, moss, and cow-hair must
be supplied for the birds to build their own nests. I should
prefer a zinc bottom perforated.

GREEN FOOD, &c.—When a hen carries material to the nest
and works freely with it, she will probably lay soon; therefore a
little moist sugar must be added to the egg and bread, and a
little green food, such as winter lettuce, watercress, groundsel
—if ripe, not otherwise—or the leaves and stalks of broccoli—
should be given.

A little beef-suet and a piece of raw apple should be placed
between the wires of the cage for the birds to peck, and if
a hen has a difficulty in laying her eggs, or seems thick, dull,
and husky, put a few drops of castor oil on a piece of sponge
cake, soaked in sherry and squeezed partly dry first,
and either place it between the wires or put it in the egg-
drawer; this will generally give relief.

In the middle of February, when ordinary green food is
difficult to procure, a good substitute may be obtained by
putting into a pan or vessel of any kind, long and not too
deep, a quantity of rape-seed—sowing-rape, which ought to
be procured of a seedsman, and not runch-seed, or spoiled
turnip-seed, which is very frequently sold by grocers in
country towns for that article, and which is injurious to the
birds—spread it equally over the vessel, then pour in a
quantity of water, sufficient to float the seed well, and place
it where it will get the most light and heat; a greenhouse is
the best place, but a kitchen window, especially with a south
aspect, will do quite well. This, of course, is merely a make-
shift for the beginning of the season, as plenty of green food.
is procurable in the month of May. When it is tolerably
well grown it can be cut out in pieces, roots and all, and
placed in the breeding-cages; it is best to put it in a small
cup or salt-server in water. The birds eat it readily, and
appear to like it. With this treatment the hen will rarely,
if ever, be egg-bound. I have known fanciers, in the spring
of the year, when green food is very scarce, feed their young
birds with dandelion-leaves. Where such food is resorted to
it is essential that it should be immersed in lukewarm water
over night, especially if the weather is frosty, otherwise its
use will be attended with fatal consequences.

Some fanciers prefer not to give green food to their birds during breeding operations, only egg food and seed. I have tried both plans, and prefer giving wholesome green food in moderation, preferring ripe chick-weed, groundsel, dandelion, and young lettuce to all other kinds; in excess green food is decidedly objectionable.

I have seen it asserted that the giving of green food causes the hens to sweat their young; this is in my opinion a mistaken notion, and not tenable by any rule of logic or common-sense, and in my experience it certainly proved fallacious. Birds are sweated by the hens sitting too close, and the oftener you can tempt them to leave the nest, the less likely are they to become too hot, and thereby overheat their progeny. Nothing will tempt them to come off the nest sooner than a fresh supply of green food, which should be well washed and given to them damp, inside the cage in a suitable vessel; they will be sure to have a refresher by settling on the top of it, and trying to turn it into a substitute for a bath. It has also been advocated to feed birds solely on seed soaked in water, and given fresh frequently. Such advice I consider can only be given by persons of limited experience, and I regard it as an absurd and impractical suggestion, and one contrary to the natural instincts of the birds themselves, as can be easily proved by placing the two foods—soaked seed and the prepared egg food—side by side, and allowing them their choice. I knew a working-man, a bird fancier, who, owing to ill-health and misfortune, could not afford to purchase eggs and luxuries for his birds, one season reared several young ones on boiled potatoes mixed with bread previously soaked in water, and on this diet they thrived, and appeared strong and healthy. This is a much more sensible method than the sole use of seeds for such delicately-constituted things as newly-hatched canaries.

EGG-BOUND.—When the hens are about to lay they should be closely watched, and if a hen is expected to lay, and she does not do so before nine o'clock in the morning, but appears dull and drooping, and sitting with her feathers ruffled up,

take her out of the cage and examine her. If she be found
to be egg-bound, drop a few drops of salad, olive, or almond
oil on the vent; and, if she does not get better, or lay within
an hour after this treatment, roll her up in flannel and place
her beside a brisk fire, taking care to leave her head out; if
she gets worse, give her two drops of castor oil—open her
bill as wide as possible and get some one to drop it over
her tongue with a warmed knitting-needle. After she has laid
replace her in her cage, and give her a little sponge cake
soakèd in sherry wine, and add more sugar to the egg and
bread. If she has a difficulty in laying her eggs afterwards
keep her in a warm room until she lays her complement.
Be careful not to break the egg before it is laid, or the bird
will die.

Another commendable plan is to take the hen about to lay
in your hand (having first well warmed it), about three-
parts fill a cup with hot water, cover it with a
thick piece of flannel, or two folds of a thinner material, and
rest the lower portion of the bird's body and vent on this
for a space of fifteen or twenty minutes, taking care not to
scald the patient during the operation. The best plan is to
retain the bird in your hand, spreading your fingers wide
apart to let the steam have as much play on the body as
possible, as it is from this that the benefit is chiefly derived;
by adopting this method there is no danger of having
the water too hot. The vent of the bird should likewise be
oiled. A little scalded rape-seed and green food given for
a few days prior to the bird's laying will generally prevent
egg-binding. · In bad cases I have found that half a teaspoonful of whisky or brandy mixed with the drinking-
water is of great service; it acts as a gentle stimulant and
revives the patient wonderfully.

REMOVAL OF EGGS WHILST LAYING.—When the hens
commence to lay, remove their eggs, one by one, until each
hen has laid three, giving them instead a nest-egg, unless,
as sometimes happens, though but very rarely, that a hen
only lays two, in which case they must be given to her;

F

this is easily known if she fails to lay on the third morning.
It sometimes happens, too, that a hen only lays one egg;
under these circumstances I never permit her to sit, as it
is a sign that the hen is not in really good condition, and
hence the probability is that the egg will be fruitless,
and it will be a waste of time to set her; in instances of this
kind feed the birds liberally and give them plenty of
fresh air—which is an essential element at all times in
bird-breeding. When a hen has laid three eggs she ought
to be set.

Before the brood of young are fit to be removed from
the parental care, the hen begins to lay another batch of
eggs, and the young birds frequently leave their own nest
and go beside their mother. If the eggs are not removed
as soon as laid, they are not infrequently fouled; in all such
cases the eggs should be carefully removed and immersed
in lukewarm water, the shells cleaned of the excrement
and gently dried with a soft silk handkerchief or piece of
fine linen rag. It is a somewhat delicate operation, requiring
much care, or the eggs will get broken or damaged. Bird-
fanciers should keep their finger-nails cut short during the
breeding-season.

NEST-EGGS.—The best kind of nest-eggs to use are those
made of bone, wood, or ivory; but when these are not
procurable take a few fruitless eggs, make a hole at each
end of them, and blow out the contents. These answer
very well. The wooden eggs are easily made with a penknife, a file, and a piece of sand-paper.

INCUBATION.—The period of incubation is usually fourteen
days, although in hot weather hens have been known to
hatch at the end of thirteen days, and others will sit fifteen
days. At the end of four or five days blood vessels begin
to form if the eggs are fruitful, and at the end of eight
days they are quite opaque. This can be discovered by
holding the eggs in a strong sunlight between the forefinger and thumb.

PARENTAGE OF YOUNG BIRDS.—Where a large number of birds are kept it is necessary to adopt a regular system, and make such arrangements as will prevent the possibility of a doubt as to the parentage of the young broods. In

FIG. 44. BOX FOR STORING EGGS DURING THE BREEDING-SEASON.

all cases it is necessary to keep a diary, and a "Stud Book" will be found very useful, especially to breeders of exhibition birds.

In the first place, number those cages which contain each pair of birds, consecutively—small paper labels gummed on to the front of them will do—after the birds have been

F 2

placed in the cages; it will be found advantageous to name them, or simply to call them number one, two, and so on, for distinction and future reference; keep a separate register of their pedigrees, &c., at least of those deserving of mention elsewhere. Having done this, make a box, say one-and-a-half to two inches deep, with as many divisions as there are pairs of birds; make each division from two to two-and-a-half inches square, and label them so as to correspond with the numbers upon the cages; in these compartments may be placed a quantity of bran or sawdust, and the eggs should be placed in them, small end downwards. See Fig. 44.

SINGLE PAIRS: HOW TO MANAGE.—If it is decided to breed the birds in single pairs, that is, a cock to each hen, then I would recommend the use of a "two-coupled" cage for each pair: remove the slide, and let the birds have the entire space to breed in. After the hen begins to sit, the cock may be left in, but it will then be necessary to observe him pretty closely; if he is very troublesome to the hen, or breaks an egg, close the slide at once, separating the cock from the hen. If, however, he conducts himself with becoming propriety during the process of incubation, he will, in all probability, do so afterwards, although I have known instances of cocks when too fresh destroying the progeny even after having fed them for several days; when this happens remove the male bird at once, and do not allow him to be placed beside the hen again until the young birds are at least three weeks old. Whenever a cock eats the eggs, the best cure for this very unnatural practice is to give him one or two eggs that have been sat upon for a fortnight, and have proved unfruitful; they are then rotten, and very rarely fail to effect a cure, although, if too many are given they are apt to make a bird ill.

The hen will, in all probability, have commenced to lay again at the end of three weeks; this, however much it might be regretted could not, under the circumstances, possibly be avoided, for if the cock is what may be termed a cannibal, there is no alternative—for if he be placed beside the hen sooner he will assuredly kill the young birds; and even at the age of three weeks I have seen cocks of this nature attack them in a most savage manner. When I observe it I remove the cock at once, and merely run him beside the hen periodically —say twice a day for one or two hours together—usually in the morning and evening, which is the best time, until she has laid three eggs, when it is not necessary to do so longer. If the hen should lay before the cock is replaced, the eggs will, of course, be fruitless; but should the hen lay an egg when the young brood is, say, twenty-one days old, and the cock is put in at once, the third, fourth, and fifth eggs will be, as a rule, fruitful. In this case either the eggs must be given to another hen, or she must have two or three artificial eggs for a few days to keep her sitting until it is certain that the young nestlings are able to feed themselves; but unless a hen is a good sitter there is a danger in the latter plan of her forsaking her eggs ere she hatches, as by its adoption it causes her to sit much beyond the usual period of incubation, which is from thirteen to fourteen days, or in some rare instances even fifteen. If, however, the hen has laid, say, two eggs before it is discovered that she has done so, let her have her own way—that is, let her lay her batch and sit as she pleases; she will, if a good mother, come off the nest and feed her young regularly until they can take care of themselves, but should she be observed sitting too closely, and neglecting her nestlings or fledgelings, remove the eggs and nest altogether. When the young birds are one month old there is no danger of losing them, and they may be confidently removed to a cage by themselves, taking care to place the food, &c. (egg and bread, fresh greens and water), so that they may be found readily.

. In Lancashire, bird-breeders take a piece of thin wood, about two inches broad, and fasten a narrow lath in front of it, and two pieces of wire to the back; with these wires they fasten it to the front of the cage opposite the door, inside, and place upon it a quantity of moist food, such as egg and biscuit moistened with water or milk. This is generally done when the young birds are about three weeks old. It is considered a good plan to get them to feed themselves early. In an ordinary way, that is when a cock has been removed from a hen either for being troublesome to her or for the purpose of pairing him to another hen, it is best to return him to her again (if she hatches) when the young birds are from seven to ten days old. He is sure to take to them at once (if not a cannibal) and assist the hen to rear them. As soon as the hen lays three eggs she may be set, and the nestlings can be left in the care of the cock, who will bring them up himself. If, on the other hand, the cock be not returned until the progeny are fourteen days old or upwards, it not unfrequently happens that he will not take to them at all, and I have known instances (though rare) where young birds have perished from this cause. In all cases where a cock is first returned to a hen with young ones, he ought to be watched, unless he is a tried and faithful servant; but that must be so arranged as to enable them to be seen without their being able to see the watcher, or even to be aware of his presence, as that alone would deter them from acting in the way they would do in the absence of any one; and if a cock really will not feed them, then the plan hereinbefore mentioned must be adopted.

HATCHING.—When a hen is about to hatch, a supply of egg and bread and green food must be given her, and also a little linseed and maw-seed, or even hemp-seed, but very sparingly, a change of diet being beneficial to both the young and adult birds; this treatment ought to be continued until the young fledgelings are at least six weeks old, when they will be able to feed themselves with seed, which is much better for them. A few groats may be given to them at this time, which will be of great service, and care must be taken to clean the cages frequently and supply the birds liberally with sand and fine gravel.

DIFFICULTIES EXPERIENCED IN BREEDING.—Having given the course to be pursued in canary-breeding, I will proceed

to enunciate the chief obstacles which are usually met
with, more or less, by all breeders, and will endeavour to
point out, so far as my own experience enables me, the best
means of obviating and overcoming them.

In the first place, it is necessary to take care that the
birds are in robust and vigorous health, for, if they are not,
disappointments often occur after they are paired. This is
readily discovered by their movements. If a bird bounds
briskly from perch to perch in a rapid and lively manner,
and moves its wings quickly and almost incessantly with a
sort of semi-flapping motion, it is a sure indication of good
health and a sound and vigorous constitution: but if, on the
other hand, it sits dull and mopish, or moves about in a
listless and phlegmatic manner, it is a certain sign of ailment
or delicacy of health, and I would strongly advise all breeders
to discard such a bird, however good in quality, for stock
purposes; as, although birds may be reared from parents
slightly affected with asthma, consumption, and similar diseases, the progeny are never really healthy nor satisfactory,
and great difficulties are experienced in endeavouring to rear
them; besides, they very frequently die during the process
of moulting, even if they are reared thus far.

UNHEALTHY BIRDS.—Never put a sound bird with an unhealthy one, or it will be found, in most cases, that in a
short time the sound bird becomes affected in like manner.

BIRDS OUT OF CONDITION.—I must likewise impress upon
breeders the necessity of thoroughly satisfying themselves
that both birds are in fine form before they are placed
together in the breeding-cage, for if the male be fresher
than the female he will most assuredly proceed to ill-treat
her, and *vice versâ.* This is an essential point that is too
frequently neglected by beginners.

BREEDING-BIRDS FOR EXHIBITION.—I would sincerely
recommend all fanciers to breed from the best strains that
can be procured if they desire to breed birds for the purpose
of exhibition, as it is merely a matter of outlay in the first

instance. High-bred birds do not cost any more to keep than common birds, and with careful and judicious management they are nearly as easy to rear; and the pleasure to be derived from breeding prize birds is immeasurably greater than breeding what may be termed mere cage- or aviary-birds, although, be it remembered, prize birds are, as a matter of course, rare and exceptional, even from the best blood procurable. It is, nevertheless, a well-authenticated fact that they cannot be produced without the proper material. It is an old saying, and a true one, that "like produces like," and this observation holds good with birds as well as with horses, dogs, &c.

There is no doubt that a great deal depends upon the birds being properly matched for future results, in addition to being well bred. See chapters on the different varieties.

YOUNG HENS TO BREED FROM.—It is best to breed from young hens (first year) and cocks from two to three years old, providing they are strong, healthy birds, as young hens are generally more vigorous than old ones, and hence produce hardier and better young ones. I never care to breed with a hen more than three seasons, and a cock, four. The principal objection to young cocks—that is to say, one-year-old birds—is that they are generally too ardent, and consequently prove mischievous and troublesome; besides, a cock that has bred a season or two, if a good parent, teaches the young mother her duties towards her newly-hatched nestlings. I have seen an old-experienced cock, the moment he observed a hen hatch an egg, go direct to the feeding-trough, and, having procured a supply of food, hasten back to the hen and commence to disgorge the contents of his crop into her upturned beak. Having given her a portion of the food he brought, his next anxiety was to get access to the newly-hatched brood; and it was both amusing and interesting to observe the various devices and manœuvres he used to induce the fond and vigilant mother to permit him to give the remaining portion to her newly-hatched little "birdies."

Of course, there are some mothers which rise instinctively as soon as their partners have supplied them with provender,

and commence without ceremony to administer it to the small
objects that have just been ushered into being; but many
hens act with a watchful jealousy towards their first charge,
and prefer taking the opportunity of feeding their young
when the cocks, after having vainly endeavoured to coax them
to gratify their humour, have returned to the egg-trough for
a further supply of food. Cocks of this sort are always
good parents, and valuable on this account; but there are
others who pay very little attention to the domestic pursuit of
assisting to rear their young, and permit the hens to use their
own pleasure in the matter entirely. I always look upon this
conduct as a bad omen so far as a cock bird is concerned,
and, unless a hen is naturally a good mother, there is considerable danger of losing the progeny, especially if she be of
a jealous and sulky nature. Whenever I notice this disposition I remove the male bird at once—as all such hens feed
much better without them—for a week or ten days, by which
time the hen loses this feeling of jealousy to a considerable
extent, and there is a very slender probability, if they have
been hitherto well cared for, of losing the young after this
period, and therefore I then return the cock with confidence.

LEAVING COCKS BESIDE HENS DURING INCUBATION.—
When a cock and hen are found to agree, the best plan is
to leave them together during the process of incubation and
afterwards, providing the cock does not interfere with the
newly-hatched birds. Some cocks destroy them as soon as they
are hatched; such birds ought to be removed as soon as the
hen is set, and not returned until the young birds are at least
fourteen days old—from that to three weeks; if he interferes
with them at that age, that is, if he commences to pluck
and otherwise ill-treat them, do not leave him with the hen
for any length of time; he may be run beside her for about
an hour, and then removed until it is convenient to repeat
the operation. After he has paired with the hen two or three
times, it is not necessary to renew the connection. A bath
may be given to a hen during incubation twice or thrice a
week during hot weather.

HENS SWEATING THE YOUNG BIRDS.—A bath given daily at this time will be found of great service. Some hens, although good and attentive mothers, sit too closely upon their nestlings, especially in hot weather, and overheat them to such a degree as to prevent their thriving, or, to use a common aphorism among fanciers, "sweat them to death." In cases of this kind take one or two pieces of stick, cut very thin and round—common lucifer matches with the brimstone ends broken off will answer the purpose—and place them firmly across the nest, pretty closely together, and as near the young birds as possible without touching them ; this will keep the hen from getting too closely upon them, and consequently prevent her "sweating" them. But as the birds grow, fresh pieces of wood will be needed, and they must be removed accordingly, say, every two days, until the nestlings are about eight or ten days old, when it will not be necessary to continue it any longer.

Canary hens sweat their young from various causes, but, I think, mostly from over-affection. In some cases, no doubt, hens that are not over strong naturally become weakened during the process of incubation, they get exhausted, and become inert. In such cases provide a basket-nest to let in air freely, and give plenty of moss to build their nest with, as it absorbs moisture, and not too much hair to line it with, as it creates heat. These are the best preventives against this unfortunate practice, which greatly weakens the progeny and prevents the growth of the feathers, and often causes the young birds to be weakly. It is one of the most difficult problems that a fancier has to deal with. Sweating-hens should be placed in a cool part of the room where the direct rays of the sun cannot reach them, a small glass vessel should be placed inside the cage, to be used as a bath, and water in which a small piece of alum or borax or a teaspoonful of salt has been dissolved may be put in this vessel for the purpose named, and given fresh every morning; if a hen can be induced to use it it will be found very beneficial.

A sweating - hen should always be supplied with a large nest; if a wooden box be used the bottom should be covered with perforated zinc. I have often thought that a nest made entirely of open wire work—a sort of skeleton frame covered with some thin material inside—would be very advantageous in such cases; but whatever might be used for a lining it would have to be light and porous, such as muslin or calico, and would to a great extent obviate this serious difficulty, for young birds which are exceedingly sweated are much weakened and rarely feather properly.

When the young birds are from twelve to fourteen days old, the hen will be desirous of going to nest again; she must, therefore, have another nest given to her for this purpose, and likewise a little moss, or material of this kind, to build with; for although a hen may have a well-made artificial nest, she has the instinctive desire to build one herself; and during the period of pairing she will work assiduously in carrying the material to and from the nest. Nevertheless, she often throws it all out just before she lays; but if she has not something to build with she not unfrequently proceeds to pluck her progeny, and when hens once commence this vicious practice they seldom forget it. At such times I have seen hens pluck their young brood to such an extent (when the above rules have been neglected) as scarcely to leave a feather upon them, and I have seen the poor nude, miserable, semi-devoured wretches so horrified at their brutal and unnatural parents that hunger alone could induce them to approach the parent birds.

PLUCKING OF YOUNG.—Prevention is better than cure, and the means above recommended will be found to answer in nineteen cases out of twenty. When they do not, place the young birds in an open wire cage, and tie it on the front of the breeding-cage where the parents are; bend the wires back a little, here and there, in both cages, taking care that the corresponding wires are bent and placed opposite each other before the cage containing the young birds is secured, so as to allow them to get their heads through. The parents will feed them in this way.

SELECTION OF BREEDING-PLACE.—It very often happens that a hen wishes to build in the same part of the breeding-cage as she reared her first brood, and will commence to peck at her half-fledged nestlings long before they are ready to leave the nest, in order that she may force them to give up possession of it to her for her further convenience. When this is observed, remove the nest containing the young to another part of the cage, and put the new nest in the place thus vacated.

SCREW-NAILS FOR TIN NESTS.—Before I commence to use a cage for breeding I always put three screw-nails into each —one in the centre and one on each side of the two perches (outside), or at each end—so that it is an easy matter to re-move the nest from one nail to another. This little device is generally successful.

HENS REFUSING TO FEED THEIR PROGENY.—It will be found in some rare instances that under no circumstances can a hen be induced to feed her young. This arises mostly from bad health, a sulky disposition, or a very nervous temperament. If from ill-health there is no remedy; if from the other causes named they can, to a certain extent, be overcome and sometimes entirely cured. Speak kindly to such hens whenever you have occasion to go near them, and always address them by the names you have given them; they will soon get accustomed to, and know them. Treat them gently, and try to gain their confidence. If they are very wild or intractable remove their food and water for four or six hours, beginning in the morning. When these are replaced remain close by—as close to the cage as you can get: if they still appear timid and nervous, and refuse to come near, remove the food, &c., for two hours longer, then replace them again, acting as before, and continue this treat-ment at short intervals until the birds are tamed. In time they will learn to know their master, and will not exhibit

any signs of fear; by such treatment I have known hens
. that refused to feed their first brood ultimately become good
mothers.

FIRST BROOD.—Do not part with a hen simply because she
fails to rear her first brood—always give her another chance;
for it sometimes happens that the fault is not hers; the young
birds may be weak and puny, and consequently too delicate
to rear. I have known hens prove bad mothers one year and
good ones the next.

DELICATE HEALTH.—Other hens, again, I have known to
rear their first nest, and let the next die. This, as a rule,
will be found to proceed from a delicate constitution; the hen
becomes weakly and enfeebled by breeding, and, falling into
a bad state of health, becomes listless, and hence lets her
progeny die for want of strength and energy to feed them
sufficiently. Give such hens a rest, feed them liberally, and
try to induce them to bathe.

HAND-FEEDING.—Some hens refuse to feed their progeny,
and others feed so sparsely as to need assistance. In such
cases hand-feeding is necessary if you have no foster-mother
at hand, but unless the birds are valuable, or you desire to
show forth as a philanthropist, it is scarcely worth the
amount of trouble and sacrifice of time that is needed to
rear them. The instrument to be used for this purpose should
be a quill, abstracted from the wing of a goose, duck, or
fowl, and cut in the shape of a pen nib; or you may use a
piece of stick or wood similarly cut. The birds should be fed
at first about every forty minutes, after four days old every
hour to the sixth or seventh day, after that a further interval
of half-an-hour more may ensue up to ten days; after they
reach this age feed every two hours, from 6 a.m. to 7 p.m.
Prepare the food in the following manner: Grind some arrowroot biscuits to fine powder in a mortar, mix well with
the yolk of a hard-boiled egg, and moisten with warm water
to the consistency of Devonshire cream or cream cheese. When
the birds reach the age of six or seven days, a little finely-

ground German rape-seed may be added; this should be ground in a fine-set coffee-mill, and passed through a hair sieve before using. In all cases the food should be given warm. At the age of ten days you may give a little seed in addition to the food recommended. When the birds reach the age of twenty-three or twenty-four days they should be able to feed themselves, and you may then substitute the ordinary egg food, giving in addition a few lettuce-leaves, or a piece of ripe chickweed or groundsel. When five weeks old they will be able to crack seed, a supply of which should be provided for their use.

FOSTER-MOTHERS.—Fanciers who keep a large number of high-class birds will find it necessary to keep a few common canary hens as nurses. Endeavour to get them to begin to breed at or near the same time as the hens whose eggs or young ones it may be desirable for them to have; so that, in the event of a high-class hen failing to feed her own progeny sufficiently, they can be transferred to one of these nurses. Where there are only one or two young ones they can sometimes be given to other known good mothers who happen to have offspring about the same time.

In cases of emergency, and when highly bred, I have given newly-hatched young to other hens which have only been set from two to five days—well tried feeders—and they have in all cases reared them. In one instance, where a hen had only sat two days, I removed her eggs and gave her a nest of birds a few days old to rear; at first she was greatly puzzled and mystified, and appeared in great doubt how to act; she remained off the nest for several minutes, going occasionally to inspect the contents, and evidently trying to account for the sudden and unexpected transformation, but after the lapse of nearly a-quarter-of-an-hour she settled down upon them quietly and reared them satisfactorily.

DIFFERENCE IN AGES.—There ought never to be more than two or three days' difference in their ages, or the stronger and older birds will get all the nourishment from the mother, and ultimately may trample the younger and weaker birds to death.

DISTINGUISHING MARKS.—If the young ones transferred should be of the same variety as those they are placed beside, and so young as not to be distinguishable, then it will be necessary to put a mark upon them whereby they can be recognised—such, for instance, as tying a piece of coloured silk loosely, but in such a manner as to prevent its coming off, round one of their legs, so that it can be readily removed when the birds are feathered.

A SOLITARY NESTLING.—One young bird is more difficult for a hen to rear than a nestful; at the same time, I prefer giving her an opportunity of doing so, otherwise she might be spoilt for the rest of the season. If, however, it is seen that there is but a meagre chance of its being brought up, and there are other reliable hens with broods about the same age, it will be better to transfer it to one of those than allow it to die.

WEANING YOUNG BIRDS.—After the young birds are removed from their parents, and they are able to feed themselves, continue to give them egg and bread and green food until they are at least six or seven weeks old, or even longer as too sudden a change of food is very frequently attended with bad results, and engenders ailments which sometimes prove fatal; but I do not mean that the full allowances should be given after they attain the age of six weeks, as they can crack seed pretty well before this time. Gradually leave off giving so much egg. After they attain this age, I generally give them the leavings of the other birds, provided they are fresh and wholesome; and this, especially if it has stood over-night and gets rather dry, weans them from it better than anything, and is not attended with bad results.

LIME AND SAND.—Fresh water and perfect cleanliness, as well as fresh air and a liberal supply of sand, or fine

gravel, are essentials in bird-breeding. A little old lime
may be given occasionally; but if a plentiful supply of sand
is given it is not really necessary. I never give my birds
old lime—nothing but sand gathered from the sea-shore—and
yet I never have a shelless egg, commonly known as a "wind
egg." Where sea-sand cannot be procured, freestone bruised
small will answer the same purpose, and a little strong
salt water, made artificially, and thrown over it, will be found
to make a good substitute.

DIRTY FEET AND LONG CLAWS AND BEAKS.—It is highly
desirable to clean the feet of birds and cut their claws before
they are placed in the breeding-cage. If this be not done,
hens with dirt adhering in little hard knots to their feet, or
with long overgrown claws, are very apt to indent their eggs
whilst turning them—a necessary process during incubation—
and if the abrasion admits the air, the egg is spoilt in consequence. I remember a case, however, where an egg was
accidentally damaged and a piece of transparent plaster was
put over the bruised part very neatly; the egg was
hatched, but this was a case where the egg had not been
previously sat upon. I do not think it would have succeeded
under other circumstances; at least, I have never found it so
during my experience. Get a pair of sharp scissors and have
some tolerably warm water in a suitable vessel at hand—a
teacup or even a saucer would answer the purpose; take hold
of the bird gently, but with sufficient firmness to prevent it
escaping, hold it on its back, and place the leg you intend to
perform upon between your fingers as to avoid any involuntary
action at the moment you are about to operate upon its
claws. If you can, cut them clean through with one cut,
about the centre of the curve of each claw; be careful not
to take too much off them or you will cut them into the quick
and run the risk of laming the bird. After this operation is
completed, immerse the feet in warm water, wash them properly,
and dry with a soft cloth. Sometimes the bill, too, gets overgrown and has to be cut; this is a somewhat delicate operation, and requires considerable skill and care in its performance.

The scissors used for this purpose must be very sharp. Placing a little may-shell, or even a knob of loaf sugar occasionally in the wires of the cage for the birds to peck at will prevent any overgrowth in this direction.

UNFRUITFUL EGGS.—This untoward event sometimes proceeds from totally different causes. It may happen through a male bird having lost a hind claw, or even through his having sore and tender feet, but not frequently so. It is usually caused through one or other of the birds not being in robust and vigorous health, frequently from ailments contracted during the process of moulting. Thus it will occasionally be found that a bird is prolific one year and have no produce the next; this almost invariably results from a bad or very late moult. But as I purpose to treat more fully on this subject under the head of "Moulting," I will not notice it further at present.

BARREN HENS.—I have known instances of young hens failing to breed the first year, but amply rewarding their owners the following season. This, however, is a very rare occurrence. There are other hens which are permanently barren. This results chiefly from old age, although an unsatisfactory moult will sometimes produce it. These hens go to nest with all the regularity of a prolific hen, and generally make excellent foster-mothers, sitting eggs and rearing young birds with great care, attention, and regularity, and they are sometimes found valuable to an extensive breeder.

SINGING-HENS.—I have known hens, though not many, commence to sing like cocks, and with such gusto and vehemence that no one but a thoroughly practical and experienced fancier could possibly discover the sexes by their song. These hens, when put up to breed, almost invariably proceed to destroy their eggs or progeny, and are known among fanciers as "unnatural mothers." My advice to breeders is never to try them. I remember a friend who once had a hen of this description for a great number of years, but I never could persuade him that it was a hen until one day it laid an egg

G

at the bottom of its cage, and immediately gave up the ghost. He always contended that it was one of the best singing-canaries he ever heard, and as a cock it was regarded by all his acquaintances and friends who were not adepts in the "fancy."

IRREGULARLY LAYING-HENS.—Some hens lay an egg and then miss two or three or more days ere they lay another. This is very often attributable to putting a hen up to breed too early in the spring; the cold seizes her as the eggs are "coming upon her"—to use bird phraseology—but, to speak more correctly, maturing within her, and completely disorganises her system. It may likewise proceed from age or a delicate constitution, but from the first-named cause much more frequently. When a hen once goes wrong during the breeding-season she cannot be relied upon afterwards—for that season, at all events.

SECOND AND OTHER BROODS.—After a hen rears her first brood she sometimes gets her feet completely clogged with dirt. When this is the case, take care to clean them properly before she is re-set; remove the young birds to another cage properly prepared for them, as previously pointed out, clean out the cage in which she is breeding, strew it liberally with sand, and take care to give her a clean nest. If the cock is with the young birds, and feeding them, they may be removed as soon as the hen has laid her third egg; otherwise, not until they are twenty-eight days old, as they cannot feed themselves properly before they attain that age.

YOUNG BIRDS CAST OUT OF THE NEST. — It sometimes happens that a hen throws one of her newly-hatched birds out of the nest. If a cock is with her, and it is not discovered immediately, he will most assuredly mutilate it. When the hen is by herself it is rarely molested, and mostly found where it had the misfortune to fall. It is astonishing how long they will live in this way, especially in warm weather. When a young bird is found in this predicament, and to all outward appearance dead, lift it as gently as you can, place it in the palm of your hand, partially close it, and commence to breathe upon it as vigorously as possible, and as long as you conveniently can do so without ceasing. Persevere for some time, and you will succeed in ninety-five cases in every hundred in restoring animation. As soon as you observe such symptoms of life as convince you that there is a reasonable chance of its recovery, return it to the nest; the warmth of its mother will soon restore it to its wonted appearance. Never put a bird found in this way beside a hot fire, or in most cases it will succumb. I presume the excessive heat affects the brain, and likewise prevents the lungs—which must have nearly collapsed—from exercising their proper functions freely.

BREEDING BELGIANS.—Of all the varieties of the *Fringilla canaria* family, probably the most tender, and consequently the most difficult to rear, are those known among fanciers as pure Belgians. It is not at all an uncommon occurrence to find newly-hatched young birds of this variety so weak and delicate that they have not sufficient strength to hold up their heads, so as to enable the parent birds to administer to their pressing necessities. I have been greatly interested, and sometimes astonished, whilst watching (through an aperture in the door of my bird-breeding room) a thoroughly reliable good-feeding hen endeavouring to give food to diminutive objects of this species. I have seen her exert her utmost ingenuity and skill in her anxious endeavours to assist them to obtain the succour which she instinctively knew they required. I have watched her single the young birds out and place them separately in turns under her in such a position as to yield them support by her legs; and, failing in this manœuvre, she has tried to feed them by resting on her side, half buried in the nest, as their little heads and slender necks were bobbing from side to side, but without avail.

When there are young birds of this description, it will be advisable to render them some assistance until they are sufficiently strong to receive nutriment from the hen in a proper manner. The method I have found to answer best is to give them the yolk of a moderately hard-boiled egg—boiled, say, for five minutes and allowed to cool—mixed with a small quantity of finely-grated biscuit (pic-nics answer very well, but any kind of biscuits containing sugar will do equally well) moistened with a little water to soften it, and stirred well together with the point of a knife to a thin consistency. Get a quill and cut it in form similar to a pen, only not quite so sharp at the point; hold the young bird in the left hand in such a manner as to render the most support to its head and neck, and proceed to feed it with the above food. Give a small portion at first, which may be gradually increased daily. This operation should be repeated every fifteen or twenty minutes, from daylight to dusk in the evening. When the birds are three days old they ought to be able to receive food from their parents without further assistance; if not, there is but a slender chance of their being reared. The great objection to this mode of treatment is the danger there is of making a hen jealous, which would prevent her from feeding them when they are ready for her attentions. Nevertheless, it is the only chance they have, and they are sure to perish without artificial aid. If any one should be induced to continue this process until the birds are sufficiently matured to feed themselves, I can only say that his perseverance will merit any reward that the birds are likely to bestow, however good they may ultimately turn out to be. Of course, in such an event a little seed would be required with the egg and biscuit after the birds are six days old; and it would be necessary to have it thoroughly well crushed and the husks removed—a pestle and mortar, which has been previously well washed and dried, or even a paste pin, in an emergency, would do for this purpose. Canary-seed answers best, and occasionally a few groats and a little maw-seed may be added, or hemp-seed sparingly. As the birds advance in size they will not need to be fed so often, but regularly, and at intervals of, say, fifteen, twenty, five-and-twenty, and thirty minutes.

AVIARY BREEDING.—Breeding birds in aviaries and in rooms without cages is a pastime enjoyed by some people, and answers very well for dealers who breed for profit, or for

amateurs who merely breed birds to sing; this latter
accomplishment being considered by everyone who is not
initiated in the knowledge and mysteries of the " fancy" as
the great *sine quâ non* of bird-breeding; whereas to a real
fancier the song of a bird is quite an after consideration—
size, shape, contour, colour, feather markings, crest, &c., are
the grand points in his estimation, according to the different
varieties of the birds. He wants birds to show, not to sing;
and, therefore, unless they come up to the standard of "show
birds" they are of little value to him except as breeding
stock, if the strain be reliable and well known.

In aviary breeding a dozen hens with three cocks will,
with moderately good luck, produce a great number of young
birds ; as in cases of this kind they pair promiscuously.
Sometimes the cocks assist in feeding the young birds, but
not always. Branches of trees or shrubs may be placed in
the room or aviary, or artificial nests may be hung here
and there. If branches of trees be used, they should be cut
from large evergreens, such as holly or laurel, or pine boughs
(*Pinus pinea*, Linn.), which should be cut in January or
February, as they will not then shed their leaves, and placed
in large flower-pots or small tubs, filled with earth and made
firm. If real trees or shrubs be used the birds will pluck
and destroy them. They prefer the orange tree to all others
to build their nests in. One great drawback to this plan of
breeding is that two or more hens are apt to select the
same spot in which to make their nests, and a brisk conflict
is the result. As soon as one hen commences to build, the
other will pull out the material, and then a warfare is begun
which is not easily quelled. First one hen is master of the
situation, and then the other, and it is astonishing to witness
the pertinacity which they display on such occasions. I have
known a hen make a nest, and as soon as she has finished
it another hen has gone and taken forcible possession of it
In all such cases war, and "war to the knife," is certain,
and very often a hen's full complement of eggs is broken in
the affray

To attempt to breed different varieties, such as Lizards, Cinnamons, London Fancy, Norwich Fancy, &c., mixed up in an aviary, is simply a waste of time; and even suppose one variety only was bred, and there were a few pairs together, you could not rely upon the parentage of the birds. The only satisfactory method of breeding birds for exhibition is to breed them in separate cages.

BIRD ROOM: ASPECT, HEATING, &c.—Where space is not an object, it will be found advantageous to keep a room entirely for the purpose of bird-breeding. One with a southerly or south-western aspect is the best; but this is not an essential consideration, as any situation will do. The more retired it is the better the birds will like it, as they prefer quietude at that season. If it can be warmed during the winter by artificial means, such as hot-water pipes, or by passing a sheet-iron stove-pipe through it, heated from outside, it will be very desirable to do so. A coke stove, with hot-air pipes attached and suitably arranged, is a good method of heating a bird room, or an open fire-grate may be used during the day and allowed to go out during the night time without causing any ill effect to the birds. Some people use oil stoves, and others gas stoves, but none of these are satisfactory, and are at all times attended with great risk and danger, and are besides extremely unhealthy. There are a great many contrivances, but the coke stove and hot-air or water pipes are the simplest and best, and next to these I prefer an open grate, or a covered-in stove with an 8in. stove pipe carried into a chimney, the stove being placed as nearly as convenient to the centre of the room. Under no circumstances would I advise the use of gas, as it is very pernicious in its effects on the constitutions of birds, and will set them into the moult in an incredibly short space of time. If the room is quite dry, and situated in an inhabited house, no fire is absolutely necessary, but during frosty nights the cages should be closely covered with quilts, shawls, or rugs. If the water freezes it will cause no harm, but should be thawed in the morning, and again during the day if necessary.

END ELEVATION.

FRONT ELEVATION.

THE AUTHOR'S BIRD HOUSE

END ELEVATION.

FRONT ELEVATION.

THE AUTHOR'S BIRD HOUSE

We have known birds under such circumstances nibble the ice, and thereby allay their thirst. Most canaries, except Belgians, can endure an immense amount of cold.

DETACHED BIRD HOUSE.—I have had a bird-house built at the rear of my dwelling-house (see Plate). It is a semi-detached building; I had it constructed specially for birds and plants. It faces west and south; on the north it adjoins another building which acts as a shelter for it. It is 10ft. high at the back, 12ft. long, 7ft. wide, and 7ft. 4in. high at the front. It faces due west, and the end the south. At this end and in front is a wall 3ft. 3in. in height, and above this to the roof is framed woodwork, glazed in long narrow stripes like an ordinary greenhouse. The whole of the front is made in sashes and hung on hinges, which can be opened for ventilation when required. The south end is also framed, with a framed and panelled door in the centre, the upper half of which is glass. The front and south end are shelved for plants, and the back and a recess at the north end are also shelved with 11in. boards for the breeding-cages. The shelves at the back are supported by wooden trestles fixed to the wall in five rows, the first being only 10in. from the ground. It is built like a room, and has a step, 7in. in height from the ground, leading into it; the floor is formed of 6in. buff-and-red tiles laid obtusely or anglewise, to resemble oilcloth in the pattern, on a 4in. bed of concrete. The walls are all plastered and coloured dove colour, with fixed colours. The roof is lathed and plastered to form a ceiling, and in the centre is a framed sky-light, 24in. by 18in., which opens when needed for ventilation. In addition to this I have a small iron ventilator inserted in the brickwork, which closes with a slide. At the north end is a properly-constructed chimney with a registered fire grate, and a mantle-piece; and the whole room is skirted round with a 7in. moulded skirting. This being a separate building, it is necessary, in cold, damp, and frosty weather, to have a little fire in it, and in order to prevent it getting overheated I have a contrivance to cover the whole of the open space above the bars, and so constructed

as to fit round the moulding of the grate to prevent smoke
coming out during adverse winds. It has a large steel knob
in the centre to lift it by. At the top, on the inside, is a
piece of iron like a square hook which goes inside the grate
to prevent it being blown forward, and it is fixed on the
bars by another hook at the bottom; it is made of sheet-
iron; this instrument acts as a "blower," and makes the
fire burn well, but it also consumes the coals rapidly, and
requires frequent attention. I can regulate the heat in cold
weather to about 45deg., and in moderate weather to 50deg.
or 55deg.; however, 6in. hot-water pipes with a No. 2 com-
bustion stove would be more satisfactory, but in a circumscribed
place this is out of the question. I only breed birds for my
own gratification, amusement, experiment, and study, not for
profit, hence I never put up more than about twelve pairs
of birds. Besides this house, I have an aviary in which I
can turn my young birds that are to be used for breeding
purposes only. The house is very light in appearance, and
the birds thrive in it splendidly. It is painted white outside
and French-white inside, excepting the shelving, which is dark
stone colour.

The roof is slated and spouted, in all respects like an
ordinary dwelling. I have the town water laid on, which I
find very convenient. Anyone who has sufficient ground space,
and as much as £25 to spare, I would recommend to have
a house of this sort. I must not omit to mention that I
have a wood-and-wire frame for the centre window and the
sky-light, which is all that is necessary to be opened, and
in hot weather I shade the front with calico coverings.

Birds create a great deal of dirt, and fanciers who happen
to be blest with wives of cleanly habits, fastidious tastes, and
pungent tempers, are not generally without a knowledge of this
sublime fact. Besides, most fanciers have friends who are
also fanciers, and consequently frequent visitors, especially in
wet weather, when they cannot very well spend their time in
out-of-door pursuits elsewhere, and they as well as the birds
make dirt. A house such as I have described obviates this.

Another consideration is that bird-rooms, wherever situated, are harbours for moths, who patronise them very extensively, and enjoy their precincts exceedingly.

LATE BREEDING.—Cease breeding as soon after the middle of August as possible, or even earlier; for when that advanced period of the year has arrived it is quite time the old birds were commencing to moult; late moulting is exceedingly objectionable, and very detrimental to the health of birds, and ought, therefore, by all means to be avoided. When any of my hens lay after the 10th of August I never permit them to sit. I throw their eggs out, and as soon as their last broods can cater for themselves I remove the mothers into a large flight cage or aviary; but before doing so I pull their tails out, which appears to encourage or promote the process of moulting. If the hens commence to breed in the early part of April—as they ought to do, if in blooming health and condition—or even, sometimes, at the latter end of March, there is ample time to obtain four nests of eggs from each hen, which is quite as many as it is prudent to take in one season. For a hen to lay too much is weakening and injurious to her constitution, thereby paving the way for disorder, which is almost the inevitable result. Ailments thus engendered, and not discovered until too late, are frequently attributed to the moult, whereas the weakness caused by excessive laying is so enfeebling that the constitution is completely undermined, and the moult—which is at all times an eventful period in the life of a bird—establishes the activity of disease.

INCUBATION.—There are probably few subjects less understood—that is, from a scientific point of view—than incubation. The reason of this arises from a variety of causes, one of which, doubtless, is that few fanciers care to destroy a fertile egg, as there is a feeling that it might develop into a prodigy. Much that is valuable and interesting might be learnt from a few careful experiments.

I have experimentalised a little in this direction, and have discovered that eggs can be removed the day prior to that

on which they are due to be hatched, and left totally un-
protected for a period of six hours in warm weather, and
even a much longer time, and if again replaced under the
hen, they will be hatched, and the chicks survive. I have
likewise found that eggs which have been sat upon for a
period of two days may be removed for a corresponding
period, and afterwards returned to the nest without injury
to them; but, as a matter of course, they must be sat upon
the full time—*i.e.*, thirteen days—before they will hatch.
These facts are worth knowing, and it would be well if fanciers
would make sacrifices by way of experiment occasionally, and
give the results of their labours for the edification and en-
lightenment of their brother fanciers. Eggs have been known
to be hatched that have been kept for a period of eight days
before being set, and it is quite possible that eggs kept even
for a period of twelve days might prove fruitful.

CHAPTER III.

MULE BREEDING.

AMONG the many pleasures to be derived by bird-fanciers from breeding birds, there is none which affords such an amount of pleasure, instruction, and amusement, as mule breeding; that is, provided good specimens of the hybrids are obtained. Herein lies the difficulty, but when once it has been surmounted, a full reward for all past labours, perseverance, and patience is reaped.

UNCERTAINTIES OF MULE BREEDING.—It is a well-known fact that many men have bred mules for a great number of years, between the goldfinch and the canary, and likewise between the linnet (*Fringilla Linota*, Linn.)—commonly known as the grey or brown linnet—and canary, and have never once succeeded in producing a single specimen worth 5s.; whilst others, who have only been recognised as "fanciers" but a short time, comparatively speaking, have managed to obtain birds worth as many pounds sterling each, and no doubt a great deal of this success depends upon intelligence and observation.

GOOD MULES.—Up to within a very recent period, any fancier who happened to produce a good specimen of a lightly-marked mule was looked upon as either an exceedingly fortunate individual, or a man that really knew something—a sort of seer in "birdology." No doubt, solitary instances are on record of persons having bred a good specimen, as it were by mere accident, that is, at a first attempt; whilst others, as I have before stated,

have bred mules for many years or, as I have frequently heard it
expressed, "all their lives," and never were fortunate enough
to "get anything worth looking at."

INFLUENCE OF PARENTS ON THE PROGENY.—There are a
great many theories in vogue as to how good mules are produced,
especially goldfinch mules; and I have heard fanciers express a
very decided opinion to the effect that it was attributable to
breeding with a particular kind of goldfinch, whilst others as
implicitly believe that the description of the finch has nothing
whatever to do with the result. One thing, however, is pretty
certain, and that is, that when a hen has been found to breed
pied mules with regularity, her offspring may be relied upon, as
a rule, to do the same thing. This being an established fact,
any man who is in possession of a well-known hen of this
description is almost certain to be besieged with applications for
young hens bred from her; and fabulous prices have occasionally
been paid for them. Fanciers who are in possession of the
genuine type of birds for producing prize mules can seldom be
induced to part with them, and I have known what I should
consider most tempting offers to purchase blankly refused.

All those who are genuine admirers of our feathered favourites,
and have been in any way associated with the "fancy" during
the last twenty-five or thirty years, must have a vivid recollection
of the names of some of our most famous mule breeders. I refer
to breeders of birds which have obtained great celebrity, such
as Lenny Moore, Tempest, Robson, Brent, and many others, and
not the mere exhibitors; as it is now notorious that a number of
our largest and most successful exhibitors very rarely breed
a single specimen of the birds they show, they being simply
the purchasers, and, consequently the possessors of the birds.
Of course, there are some exceptions, but this rule applies
pretty generally.

GOLDFINCH AND CANARY MULES.—When commencing to
breed mules, my advice is, confine yourself to those obtained
between the goldfinch and canary, linnet and canary, or goldfinch
and bullfinch, as they are best calculated to reward you

pecuniarily for the trials and disappointments which are almost
certain to beset you at the beginning; but you must persevere,
and if my instructions are strictly followed, I have every
confidence that your labours will terminate satisfactorily.
Other kinds of mules can be obtained, such as siskin and
canary, bullfinch and greenfinch, &c., but of these I will treat
more particularly under their respective headings.

The goldfinch and canary undoubtedly produce by far the
most beautiful of all the canary hybrids, as such variety and
diversity of colour and markings are obtained as cannot be
had by any other cross. The first thing to be aimed at is to
get a strain of canary hens that can be relied upon to breed
marked mules, as it is beyond dispute that the majority of
hens chosen at random, or even selected, as they sometimes
are, by breeders who imagine that they know "a thing or
two," very seldom produce the merest semblance of a pied
bird, although they have tried season after season with hens
of totally different strains. When first I commenced to
breed mules, which is a good many years ago, I began, like
a great many more fanciers, with no more idea of anything
further being required than simply to place a male goldfinch
and female canary together in a breeding-cage, give them a
nest, and await the result. Experience has taught me very
different. After breeding mules for several years, with no
better success than, as a mortified old fancier illnaturedly
observed, "getting a houseful of sparrows"—for such are
dark mules sometimes designated—I began to turn my attention
to the subject more closely.

SIB-BRED BIRDS.—Having determined to enquire into this
subject, I paid a visit to a person who had obtained considerable notoriety in his neighbourhood among the "fancy,"
from the fact of his having bred, during the previous five or
six years, two or three very good goldfinch and canary
mules. He was a carpenter by trade, and I found him
shrewd and intelligent, and inclined to be communicative.
As a matter of course, I asked him the usual "thousand and
one" questions, but all the information of a practical

character that I was enabled to obtain from him was that all his canary hens used for this purpose were of So-and-so's "celebrated" strain. I visited another and another, with a like result, and not being satisfied I determined to visit Mr. So-and-so himself. This gentleman was none other than a knight of the shovel and pick; or, to speak more plainly, a pitman, or hewer of "black diamonds." This individual I found to be exceedingly reserved, cautious, suspicious, and cunning in his manner. When I began to question him as to how he managed to obtain the hens that had bred him such excellent mules, he was very mysterious in his demeanour, and his answers were given after considerable deliberation on his part. He evidently regarded my visit and catechising him with much disfavour. Finding that my tactics in asking straightforward questions were not at all appreciated, I resorted to a different plan altogether, and with apparently much better success. I bought a marked mule from him at a good price, and also a young canary hen "of the mother of the mule" I had bought—so he informed me. She ought to have been, for the price I paid for her; but whether she was a daughter of this particular hen or not, I can only say that she failed to emulate the deeds of her parent. After repeated visits and much manœuvring, I fancied I had learned something. He told me he had possessed the strain for upwards of twenty years; and in answer to further questions, I discovered that they were all very nearly allied in blood relationship. This gave me an idea, and I resolved to follow it up.

Whenever I heard that any breeder had produced a "pied" mule, I made it a rule to go and try my utmost to trace the parentage of the hen that bred it. Sometimes I succeeded to a certain extent, but not generally; and I found it a slow process and terribly up-hill work. It often happened that the hen had been bought from a dealer, or the person had forgotten where he purchased her, and had merely run a goldfinch to her as an "off chance," in hopes of getting "something good." Still the little information I was enabled to accumulate in this way strengthened my first impression, that the chief secret lay in the in-and-in breeding (consanguinity).

In or about the year 1872, I visited an old man in a small country town in Northumberland, who had been a bird breeder for a great number of years; he bred mules principally, and had obtained some very handsome specimens—chiefly evenly-marked birds. I could not glean much from this individual himself, as he was by no means of a communicative disposition; but I learnt from a neighbour of his, who had the same strain of hens, but had been a little less fortunate in obtaining good mules, that the origin of them had been the produce of a common hen canary and a "London Fancy" cock. I failed to learn anything of the antecedents of the hen as to parentage; but the cock, I ascertained, was bred by a gentleman who had bred London Fancies for several years, and during the whole of that time he had not introduced a change of blood.

When I got north of the River Tweed, I visited one day a very old fancier, who had had the good fortune to breed and rear some excellent mules. I found him to be a respectable and trustworthy man, and consequently I courted his acquaintance. I was too familiar with the peculiarities of the Scotch people to begin to exhibit any inquisitiveness at first, but as time rolled on our friendship waxed greater, and I ventured to ask him how he procured the hens which bred him his good mules. He replied, "They are sib bred." "Sib bred!" I repeated; "what is that?" He said, very gravely, "Weel, sib bred is sib bred, an I thocht that onybody kenned what that was." However, I found that the meaning of the words was consanguinity; and thus the idea which I had naturally formed was practically confirmed. He further informed me that all the hens he had bred mules from were as "sib bred" as they could be, and that all the principal Scotch breeders attributed their success to this cause. My theory is that the blood becomes so thoroughly pure in one direction by the process of breeding in-and-in that the admixture with a foreign or opposite species produces little change in it; and I have no doubt that this is the veritable solution of the "secret" which has been so closely kept for so many years. No doubt, there are other adjuncts needed for the production of mules of a superior class, having in view the improvements, size, colour, and feather, which I will point out in the course of my remarks; but, before I do so, I will give the result of my own experiments, which, being practical, will be valued accordingly.

Being now thoroughly convinced that I had discovered the true method of producing marked mules, I procured a clear buff Norwich cock canary, bred from clear birds, by a friend who had bred with a few pairs for four or five years, merely for his own amusement, and, therefore, had not deemed it worth his while to introduce a fresh strain. I put this cock to a clear yellow hen, bred from two evenly-marked Norwich birds by myself, which were pretty closely related. I kept two hens and a cock from this pair, and having paired these again, I got three young canaries from one hen and two from the other. I then placed a male goldfinch with each of the hens, and during the season I bred some nicely-marked mules—scarcely good enough to show in this age of marvels, but notwithstanding, good birds. Fired by my success to more vigorous exertions, I determined to extend my chances, and hearing of a person who had some hens very "sib bred," I purchased one, and two more goldfinches.

The following year I put up two young hens, one yellow and one buff (the remainder being all cocks), bred as before stated, and also the "sib bred" hen which I had purchased. She was a clear buff hen, of the variety known as "Norwich Fancy," and was the produce of clear buff parents. I first took a nest of canaries from each of these hens, and afterwards introduced them to the "goldies." One of the young hens started at once, and laid a nest of eggs which proved fruitful, and were hatched; but the young birds were weak and delicate, and only lived two days. They had all the appearance of being light mules, as their skins were like newly-hatched canaries'; I was much pleased with my success so far, although doomed to disappointment by the loss I sustained when they succumbed. Scarcely, however, had I become reconciled to my first misfortune, when a second and worse befel me; for, a few days afterwards, the mother of them died also. I was now left with nothing but the two hens, as I had previously parted with the others; and in one of these I must confess my expectations were very limited. They each laid about a week after the first-named hen, but both their eggs were barren; so I exchanged the goldfinches, and the following nests proved fruitful. I set them both together, as they laid on the same day; but before the period of incubation had expired, I thought it prudent to exchange their nests, as the young hen I bred myself was not a good feeder, and it was with difficulty that she had managed to rear one bird from her first brood; whereas the other hen had proved herself to be thoroughly reliable in this respect.

As their time for hatching drew near, my anxiety and anticipations increased, and culminated one morning when I entered my bird-room and heard a low chirping sound—familiar to the ears of old experienced fanciers—proceeding from the corner in which the cage containing the two hens in question was hanging. I made straight to the spot without a moment's delay, and listening with an eager and attentive ear, I soon discovered that both of them had hatched. I proceeded at once to give them the usual viands as quickly as I could, and made my exit rather abruptly, as I was afraid to disturb the hens any more than I could help on this occasion. My desire to have a peep at the little strangers, the produce of the hen I had bred, became more intense as each day passed by; but when the fifth day arrived I could not restrain my curiosity any longer, so I ventured to poke the hen off her nest, which I took out of the cage and conveyed to that part of the room where I got the most light. A minute inspection followed, and although I found them fairly good mules, I must confess they were not so good as I had expected; so I returned them to their foster-mother more disappointed than pleased. On the following day I was feeding my birds, as usual, when I casually noticed the other hen which had charge of the other mules off her nest; and, singularly enough, about these I had felt no matter of anxiety, and very little

H

curiosity, but I thought I might as well have a look at them when an opportunity was afforded me. Guess my astonishment and gratification, then, when I discerned two light mules there! I removed the nest in the twinkling of an eye, and found, to my dismay, that the poor little hungry-looking wretches' had been half-starved for want of better attention from the mother, and must, unless some succour was immediately forthcoming, perish.

My first impulse, on finding the two light-coloured mules among the half-starved youngsters, was to transfer the brood to the other hen; but, seeing the great disparity that existed between the size of the one lot and that of the other, I resolved not to adopt this plan, as I well knew that the larger and stronger birds would be pretty certain to smother their small and weakly companions. My next notion was to throw out the darkest, and consequently least valuable birds, to save the others; had I done this I should have acted wisely, at least in a pecuniary point of view; but, like thousands of other people in this world, I adopted a "penny-wise and pound-foolish" policy.

I felt reluctant to lose any of the birds so long as there appeared the least possibility of saving them; and beside, I had some qualms of conscience, I am bound to admit, when the idea of killing those poor unoffending little birdies crossed my mind. I was in a dilemma, that is quite certain, and how was I to get out of it puzzled me not a little. At last I made up my mind to take the mule which I considered of the least value from under the hen which was feeding her young to my satisfaction, and give it to the one which was not behaving properly to those under her care. I then removed the clear mule—for such it really was—and put it in the place of the one I had taken away, thereby effecting a transfer, so that each hen in reality got one of her own progeny by the change.

There was still a grand mule left underneath the neglectful foster mother which I was most anxious to save, and having a canary hen with a brood of young birds some three or four

days old, I effected a second transfer between these hens, on
the same plan as the first. This appeared to me to be the
most satisfactory arrangement I could make, as the only risk
I had was that of losing a moderately-marked mule and
a Norwich canary; but I was quite willing to make this
sacrifice if I could only succeed in rearing the two mules of
such excellence and promise. As I said before, one of them
was quite clear, and the other had beautiful evenly-marked
wings, seven dark feathers in each in the upper part of the
wing, and corresponding exactly, with all the appearance of
being clear elsewhere, with the exception of eye marks, which
would still further have enhanced its value. At the age of
thirteen days, however, this bird died, and the clear mule
expired a few days before; so I gave each of the hens their
first charges back to them, by no means benefited in appearance or condition by the change.

The loss of these birds was exceedingly mortifying to me, and
I do not need to tell those who know anything about mule
breeding what a serious one it was; but perhaps I ought to
warn those who intend to pursue this pastime that they must
be prepared to meet with similar disappointments.

When the hen which bred me the good mules had reared
those under her care, I took a nest of canaries of her, and
afterwards another nest of mules, four in number, which
consisted of one dark and three marked birds. I twice showed
the best of the marked ones, and obtained a "high commendation" on one occasion, and a "very high commendation"
on the other. From the other hen I got two more nests of
mules, and among them were two very good specimens, being
nicely marked, although small; both were hens, and consequently of little value. In the autumn of the same year
some kind of distemper, which proved very fatal, got among
my birds, and I lost a great number of them; the only birds
I had left to begin the following season with of the mule
breeding strain were the two hens, and two young cocks from
the hen that produced the best mules. I commenced, as
usual, with placing a canary cock with each hen for a first

H 2

nest, but I only succeeded in rearing one young canary,
which died at the age of fourteen days. I next put the
goldfinches with them, but on this occasion I reversed the
cocks, for this reason: One of them was what is known
among bird breeders as a "pea-throat," and he was the
father of the clear and lightly marked mules; and being
aware that a difference of opinion exists among breeders with
respect to these birds, some attributing the cause of the
mules being pied or marked to the fact of breeding with
"pea-throat" and "cheverell" goldfinches, I resolved upon
making an experiment, in order to ascertain, if possible,
whether there really was any foundation for such a belief.
In the course of twelve or fourteen days both hens laid and
were set, and their eggs were fruitful. The hen with the
"pea-throat" hatched four eggs and brought up the mules
herself—there were three of them marked and one entirely
dark, but the marked birds were not so good as those she
had produced the previous year with an ordinary goldfinch.
The other hen hatched and reared three birds, two being
dark and the other tolerably well marked. I had purposed
reversing the finches again, but before I had an opportunity
of doing so the "pea-throat" died. I thereupon ran the other
goldfinch—the only one I had left—to the hen which had
reared a brood by the "pea-throat"; the result was a nest
of three mules, all marked birds, and very similar in their
markings to her first produce. I had replaced the finch with
the other hen, and on this occasion she hatched four mules,
which consisted of two dark buff mules, one clear mule, and
the other had one lightly-marked wing and an eye mark on
the same side as the marked wing. The clear mule died at
the age of three weeks, from some cause which I never was
able to discover, as it appeared in perfect health only a few
hours before I found it dead; the other I managed to rear,
but, unfortunately, I lost the lightly-marked bird when it was
almost through the moult. One of the dark mules from this
nest I showed at the Crystal Palace, where it took first
prize.

During the moulting season the yellow hen which had bred me some very fair mules died, and also the young canary cock of this strain; the other I had sold previously, so that I had nothing but one hen and the goldfinch left, and I was so exasperated at my bad fortune that I exchanged them for a pair of good Lizard canaries with a friend, and gave up this branch of bird‑breeding; but it is my intention to try it again, and, I hope, with fewer misfortunes than I have hitherto experienced.

A gentleman who purchased from me a young cock bred from the "sib-bred" hen, mother of the best mules I had bred, put him to a clear Norwich hen canary, and a young hen bred from this pair produced two very excellent mules. I mention this fact to prove that where the blood is right it will be perpetuated in future generations. I could name several other cases within my own knowledge, if it were necessary, to verify the fact. Nevertheless, it must be distinctly understood that while this peculiar feature is traceable through an entire race of birds allied in blood, it varies much and in different degrees, even in the same family or generation. For instance, I have known three hens, own sisters, each produce mules, and although the progeny from the whole of them were more or less pied, there was a marked characteristic distinction among them, those of one particular hen being infinitely superior in quality and markings to those of the others. This, I presume, depends greatly upon the well-known fact which is familiarly termed "throwing back," that is, breeding back for several generations in favour or resemblance to certain progenitors. This is no new theory, but an acknowledged fact, and it is traceable not only in birds and animals, but in the human species also.

CHEVERELL AND PEA-THROAT GOLDFINCHES.—It is not my intention to attempt to refute *in toto* the theory held by some breeders, who consider it essentially necessary to have a " Cheverell " or a " Pea-throat " goldfinch in order to obtain marked mules. My experience has taught me to place implicit reliance upon the canary hens, and I am fully persuaded that

unless the hens are of the right sort you will never succeed
in producing lightly-marked mules simply by breeding from
goldfinches of the description I have named. And I am quite
sure that more than two-thirds of the most successful breeders
of these birds will bear me out in my assertion; at the same
time, I know that both "Cheverell" and "Pea-throat" goldfinches are much sought after and highly esteemed by some
of the oldest and most experienced mule breeders in this
country, and a much better price can be obtained for them
than for ordinary birds. Indeed, I have known as much as a
sovereign to have been paid for a good specimen of the first-
named kind. Many noted breeders assert that hens are more
likely to "throw" a good mule with a finch of this sort than
with one of the ordinary type, and this fact I am not at all
disposed to dispute. I have great regard for the opinions of
thoroughly practical men, and for this reason I am not
desirous of endeavouring to ignore what appears to be a
settled conviction in favour of these particular kinds of goldfinches; at the same time, I consider it right to say that I
have seen several grand mules bred from goldfinches of the
common description, and this fact goes far to prove that the
theory I hold is well founded; and beside this, I can certify
that several breeders who are personally known to me have
tried the experiment with both varieties of the goldfinch above
mentioned, and hens chosen promiscuously, and have never
succeeded in breeding a pied mule of any value. This being
so, it must be evident to all that the first and principal
requirement, in order to insure success in this particular
branch of bird-breeding, is to procure a race of canary hens
upon which some reliance can be placed. I will, therefore
endeavour to instruct those who are desirous of pursuing this
interesting study in the most approved method of producing
a thoroughly reliable strain for this purpose.

CANARIES FOR MULE-BREEDING. — In the first place, I,
recommend the purchase of a pair of London Fancy canaries,
as I believe that all birds of this particular variety are very
closely allied in blood relationship, much more so than is

generally supposed. This class of birds has been in the hands of a very limited number of fanciers for the last forty years or more, and have dwindled year by year to a mere fraction of what they were at that period. They have become very delicate with in-and-in breeding, and their constitutions have been greatly impaired thereby, so that the strongest of them are now regarded as tender birds. Having procured these, get a large bird bred between a Belgian canary and a cinnamon variegated Yorkshire Fancy; let it be perfectly clear in colour, and if it "blows clear" all over, so much the better — that is, clear in the under flue, or small feathers next the skin. Many birds which appear clear are found when examined to have small black feathers beneath their outer covering. Birds of this kind should be avoided when they are intended to be matched with a London Fancy bird, as plenty of green will be had from the last-named variety. Having obtained a bird of this description of the opposite sex and colour to the "black wing" (London Fancy), they can be paired. In choosing a cross-bred bird of this sort, endeavour to get one with red or brown eyes, commonly called "pink-eyed"; it is not difficult to do so, as most birds with a cross of cinnamon blood in their veins have red eyes.

In the next place, procure a clear hen of the evenly-marked Norwich Fancy strain. The larger she is and the richer in colour the better. This hen must blow clear likewise—that is, when you blow back the feathers on the under part of the body the inner feathers or under-flue should be clear as well as the upper or top covering of feathers. When purchasing London Fancies be sure to have them both out of the same nest, if obtainable; if not, they ought certainly to be of the same parents; and I should strongly advise you to get two male birds if possible; but, if not, couple the cock bird with the Norwich Fancy hen, and the hen "black wing" with a male bird bred in the way I have already pointed out. Keep two or three of the cleanest birds obtained from these crosses; but if any of them have "pink eyes," select these in preference to all the others; mate these, and breed from them the following season. If preferred, some of the hens bred from the last cross may be run with goldfinches, when, no doubt, a few tolerably good males will be obtained from them; but the canaries must be bred in-and-in for some years longer before mules of the highest standard of excellence can be expected. They must be so crossed as to insure an intimate blood relationship; but while a pair should be collaterally related, they must not be of common parentage or of the same direct line, as the produce of these crosses are generally puny and difficult to rear.

DOUBLE-YELLOWS.—Occasionally two yellow birds must be put together. The produce of these will sometimes be found scant in feather, and when crossed the same way a second time will be still more so. Indeed, I have seen hens so semi-nude by this process of breeding that the sight of them was offensive. But these hens invariably breed the handsomest hybrids. I once saw a very beautiful evenly-marked goldfinch mule, which was bred from a hen that was so destitute of feather, so pinched and hungry-looking in her appearance, that I positively would not have had her as a gift if I had not been cognisant of the above fact.

My reason for advising you to breed from double jonques is that you are sure to get more yellow-marked mules by this method than by any other, and the yellow-marked birds are the most valuable, as they are much more difficult to obtain, and, consequently, more rare than buff-marked birds; beside, this cross greatly enriches the colour of the birds, which in itself is a weighty consideration.

DOUBLE-BUFFS.—In like manner pair two buff birds together, say, once in two or three years, as by the adoption of this plan the birds will be greatly improved in feather, both in quantity and closeness. It likewise increases their size, and materially strengthens their constitutions. A trifle in colour may be sacrificed by it, but this is readily regained by matching a bird bred from two buffs with one of the opposite sex bred from two yellows, and the blending of these crosses will be found to produce the most beneficial results in every respect.

ADJUNCTS FOR MULE-BREEDING.—When commencing to breed from the London Fancies, &c., it is a good plan to put a pair of pure Norwich Fancies together at the same time. both clears and nearly allied in kindred; also put a Belgian, Glasgow Don, or Manchester Coppy canary, with a large cinnamon variegated hen, or a clear hen bred from two birds of the latter description; cross the produce of these two pairs of birds in the same way as I have pointed out in the first instance. These birds can in the interval be utilised as nurses, but at the end of three years they will be found most valuable adjuncts to pair with what I may term the regular muling strain, and the admixture of this new blood will strengthen and invigorate them wonderfully, and without detracting from their specific qualities to any appreciable extent as mule breeders, seeing that they inherit the speciality required through the in-and-in breeding.

CONSANGUINITY.—If you breed too long on the principle of consanguinity, without an occasional admixture of new blood, there is a danger in the course of time of losing the strain altogether, although it might require a considerable period to effect so undesirable an object. Still, there can be no manner of doubt that the process of "sib" breeding tends greatly to impair the health of birds, and ultimately makes them exceedingly tender and bad to rear, and therefore an occasional cross is in reality an imperative necessity, and I may add that it is a common practice with many old mule-breeders to exchange with each other a male canary about once in every three or five years from their "noted" strains, as they find it mutually advantageous to do so.

When birds are sufficiently "sib-bred" for muling purposes they will be found to be very sparse of feathers, and wanting in the full complement of tail and wing feathers (eighteen feathers in each wing, and twelve in the tail of a bird is the full number of an ordinary specimen), and those covering the body will be found to be scant and thin; in many cases barely sufficient to cover the body in some parts. The appearance of the feathers also will be meagre, and not fully developed, but will have the appearance of being pinched and shrivelled up. " Sib-bred " birds are not unfrequently deformed in their claws and nails; some of them which have been in-bred for several generations look ghastly, weak, and puny. The best mules that have been bred and exhibited for many years have, as a rule, been produced in the northern counties of England—Durham, Northumberland, and North Yorkshire, and in Devonshire, principally in and around Plymouth. Since the " Canary Book " was first published, giving the method of producing exhibition mules, we have noticed a great number of people advertising " sib-bred " hens, and we feel it our duty to warn new beginners and inexperienced breeders to be careful from whom they purchase such birds, as very few fanciers have succeeded in establishing a breed of birds that can be relied on for producing such mules as are worthy of a place on the show bench. There are so many people now-a-days who breed and deal in birds for the sake of profit, that little reliance can be placed upon their statements,

Further experience has taught me that by breeding double-buffs and double-yellows together for a lengthened period, such birds will, apart from being " sib-bred," produce pied mules. To be more explicit, I mean to breed buffs continually with buffs, and yellows with yellows, without ever crossing them with opposite colours. This I consider a valuable discovery.

The following will be found a good method for obtaining a reliable strain for breeding light, variegated, and clear mules. Procure two evenly-marked cinnamon hens of the Yorkshire type. All evenly-marked birds from a good strain are sure to be bred nearly akin. To these hens match two clear cocks, bred from an evenly-marked strain, either Yorkshires or Norwich birds—whichever kind is preferred. The Yorkshires are best when size and symmetry are required, and the Norwich if you prefer colour to size and shape. One pair should be yellow in the ground colour, and the other pair buff. From these birds select all the evenly-marked and clear birds, and breed them together, brothers and sisters, for three generations; by this time they should throw marked mules. You may now cross the young bred from the two original pairs of birds, and then proceed as before, crossing the buffs together and the yellows together, and at the end of the sixth generation you ought to be rewarded with a breed of birds as reliable as any procurable—always, of course, breeding brothers and sisters together. This plan has been tried with success. I must, however, say that I still have great faith in the London Fancy birds for a cross, and should prefer these birds to Norwich, as they have been sib-bred for at least fifty years. I must also say that I have most faith in an old goldfinch, one from three years old upwards, if sound and in good health and plumage. Hens with pink eyes bred from a cinnamon cross, which indicates Albino blood, are preferable to any other variety for breeding variegated mules. In selecting an un·tried hen for this purpose choose one that is very pale in colour: if of the kind known as "buff," select one as nearly white as possible; if "yellow" obtain one of a pale straw colour, or as near to those colours as you can procure them, as such hens mostly breed pied mules.

DARK GOLDFINCH MULES.—Having fully given all the instructions necessary for obtaining a reliable strain of canaries for the production of variegated mules, it will probably be found advantageous to some if I give a few hints as to the breeding of dark goldfinch mules, which, although of considerably less value than their more esteemed *confrères*, the pied birds, are nevertheless, when good, much esteemed by some people. The great desideratum in these birds is size and richness of colour, and when these qualities are obtained, combined with good shape, carriage, and closeness and quality of feather, you are pretty near the top of the tree, I can assure you.

In order to establish a tribe of canary hens likely to produce dark goldfinch mules fit for the "keenest competition," it will be necessary to procure first a very rich-plumaged Norwich bird of either sex, with a clea⁻ orange-coloured breast and dark back, flights, and tail, with a clear or very lightly-marked head. Couple this bird with a green canary having a light breast, bred from the cinnamon-marked strain, or a pretty heavily cinnamon-marked bird full of Norwich Fancy blood will do quite as well. Next procure the largest-marked bird possible —one full of Lancashire Fancy properties, and marked as nearly like the Norwich bird already described as can be procured. Couple this bird with a Lizard canary, or, what would be still better, a bird bred between a London Fancy and a Lizard. Having succeeded in rearing young birds from these crosses, put the produce together the following season, and from the birds so bred select the largest and handsomest of the hens, green, or nearly all green, in colour. If there are any with clear breasts and lightly marked about the head, be sure to retain them; if not, choose those which bear the nearest resemblances to what I have described. These hens can be placed with goldfinches, and their progeny ought to be up to the mark. I like to breed dark mules from young hens, romping and full of life and vigour, with large broad heads, good in colour, and plenty of feathers.

If it be desired still further to improve the colour of the mules, and there be no objection to sacrificing size and shape to colour, cross the hens for two or three generations further with the Norwich Fancy variety. If, however, shape be preferred to colour, select large birds, such as Glasgow Dons, three-quarter bred, or pure Lancashire Fancy canaries, or some similar variety of large birds for the purpose; but take care to select the birds for these further crosses in accordance with the instructions already given, or the result might not prove satisfactory. In my opinion, size and shape are great acquisitions to a mule; and if with these elements in hand, rich colour, close feather, and, what is most admired of all, a brilliant orange band round the beak and well up over the face of the bird can be obtained, together with a rich, deep, and vividly-coloured breast, there are only required style, contour, and a graceful carriage to complete a thorough show bird and an undoubted prize winner.

CHOICE OF GOLDFINCHES FOR DARK MULE BREEDING.—As soon as the hens have been obtained from the different crosses I have recommended, look out for a few choice goldfinches. The birds I prefer for breeding purposes are what are known among the initiated as " grey-pates "—that is, young goldfinches, the produce of the last breeding season. The best time to purchase them is in the months of September and October, before they have moulted their grey faces and donned the plumage of matured birds, as you cannot then be deceived as to their actual ages; but it will be necessary to exercise great care in their selection, or you will, in all probability, get more females than males. Perhaps the best plan would be to purchase a dozen from a flight of newly-caught birds, select the male birds, and give the females their liberty; for, although instances have been known of female goldfinches breeding with male canaries, they are rare and exceptional, and I cannot in any way feel myself justified in advising anyone to try the experiment. Goldfinch hens have a natural aversion to artificial nests, and very few of them can be reconciled to these substitutes. By adopting the plan I have mentioned, you ought to be able to buy them at a low figure, say, from ten to twelve shillings per dozen, or even less; much depends upon the season, as some years they are more plentiful than others. It is not an easy matter to distinguish the males from the females, although the former, as a rule, are larger, more masculine in appearance, and bolder; they usually have longer beaks and larger heads, and the red stripe which encircles the root of the beak is broader and brighter, as is also the black on the top of the head, down the neck, and on the shoulders; the white cheeks are cleaner, and the breast and back are likewise purer and more vivid in colour. The covering feather of the wing butts are blacker and brighter in the male birds than in the females.

The " Cheverell " goldfinches are known by a clear white mark which passes clean through the centre of the red stripe which surrounds the roots of the under mandible, and the "Pea-throat" by having a round white spot, about the size and shape of a white pea, in precisely the same place (in the middle of the red band). In other respects they differ very slightly from the ordinary or common stock in general appearance, but always bring a better price. " Cheverells " (warranted breeders) are usually sold at from ten to twenty shillings each, and " Pea-throats " from seven shillings upwards, according to age, quality, condition, and other properties. Always select a light-coloured goldfinch with a clear white hind-face and collar, and with a bright, deep full blaze of rich scarlet, in preference to a dark, dull, dingy-coloured specimen to breed with.

Instances sometimes occur in which a young goldfinch fails to breed with a canary hen the first season, but does so the second; such birds, however, are usually of a timid or phlegmatic temperament, and are more suitable for singing than for breeding purposes. There are others, again, too ardent—so much so, that if they are permitted to remain with their spouses they will destroy the eggs as soon as they are laid. As a great many goldfinches are guilty of this malpractice, I think it is best to remove them from beside the hens a day or two before they commence to lay; they can, however, be returned to their domicile during the day and taken away again at night, if considered necessary. Or, if it be thought preferable to leave a goldfinch with a hen during the time she is occupied in laying her complement of eggs, then a duplicate nest should be given her—that is, if I may so describe it, a nest within a nest. For instance, suppose you are in the habit of using the artificial nests recommended by me in the first chapter, you must get a piece of felt, and make and fit it in precisely the same manner as the piece used for the original nest, only it must not be quite so large, so that when it is placed inside the other it will leave a space. Cut a small hole in the duplicate or outer artificial nest, sufficiently large for the egg to drop through, and place it inside the nest proper, or cut the end of a cocoa-nut, make a large hole through it, line it with felt and use it. As soon as the hen has laid an egg it will fall through the aperture, and Master Goldie will be thereby frustrated from carrying out his malicious vagaries. The eggs ought to be removed daily until three have been laid, when the goldfinch should be taken from beside her. It must not be presumed that all the tribe of goldfinches are gifted with those vicious proclivities, and those who are desirous of leaving the twain together can do so; but be it remembered that it will be very necessary to exercise considerable vigilance, especially at the commencement of the breeding season, or a whole nest of eggs may be sacrificed ere the mischief is discovered, or worse, as has frequently happened, not until the second or even third nest of eggs has been destroyed by the finch.

INCUBATION.—There is no advantage to be gained by leaving a goldfinch and canary together during incubation, as it is an exceedingly rare occurrence to find a "goldie" assisting to rear the progeny; in fact, I have only known of two well-authenticated instances of this kind during the whole of my experience. Plenty of goldfinches will feed the canary hens whilst they are nesting and sitting; but they apparently deem it no part of their duty to succour the young birds after they are brought forth; indeed, many of them proceed to destroy the newly-hatched broods, and the majority of those which do not, ill-treat them without compunction after they have left the nest. In addition to these drawbacks there is another important consideration, and that is, that the presence of the male bird would be sure to induce the hen to commence a second brood earlier than she otherwise would do; and if she began to lay, as she doubtless would, ere the young mules could cater for themselves, there would be great danger in losing them, as they would in all likelihood perish.

NATURAL ALLIANCE, &c.—There are a great number of difficulties to contend with in mule breeding, as both goldfinches and canaries naturally prefer an alliance with birds of their own species, although rare instances have been recorded where a mutual attachment has been known to exist between birds of a totally different species. Nevertheless, in other cases it has been found literally impossible to effect an alliance of this kind, even despite repeated and protracted efforts to bring about a union; and although the birds have been kept in close communion with each other, and apart from all other birds, not the slightest traces of regard for each other could be discerned.

Presuming that you have been successful in obtaining a race of "sib-bred" canary hens and a few select goldfinches, turn them into flight cages together about the month of November; but, before doing so, satisfy yourself that the goldfinches will eat canary seed, or rape and canary mixed.

NEWLY-CAUGHT GOLDFINCHES.—It not unfrequently happens that newly-caught birds of this species refuse to eat seeds of the description named, and many of them sulk and repine—especially old birds that have bred in the open air with hens of their own tribe; these birds are not only deprived of their liberty and their domestic partners in life, but the sudden changes of scene and food are so great that a complete revolution in their systems is begun, and so powerful is the change that in many cases their lives are seriously jeopardised thereby. It is therefore advisable for a time to give them a mixture of hemp, millet, maw, and linseed, and if thistles are procurable, a few of the tops should be given them, together with a little dock seed, which is plentiful in most places not under rigid cultivation; a cabbage or lettuce leaf, or a little groundsel, may also be given with advantage, and a little white bread soaked in milk.

MATING.—After they become accustomed to their new mode of life, it will be necessary gradually to discontinue giving them those luxuries, and the ordinary food supplied to the canaries will be found sufficient, although some birds will almost starve ere they submit to this fare; there are others who take to it quite readily, and these are the birds which generally prove most valuable as mule breeders. As soon as you are convinced that the finches will subsist on the ordinary canary diet, place them in large cages with the canary hens in batches of, say, from four to six hens and from two to three goldfinches in each cage, two hens, in my opinion, being amply sufficient for one "goldie" for breeding purposes; by adopting this plan the hens, which are sometimes afraid of the finches, get accustomed to them, whilst, on the other hand, the "spinks" overcome the natural aversion which they entertain to forming an alliance with an opposite or distinctly different species of bird. As the spring of the year approaches the male birds usually commence to quarrel, and it will be found necessary to separate them; but, should an attachment appear to exist between any particular finch and canary, be sure to mate these birds. When you remove them from the flight-cages, put one goldfinch and two hen canaries together in a breeding-cage, until one of the hens exhibit signs of wanting to go to nest. Then supply that requisite, and when she is busily employed about it introduce a male canary to the hens. In the first place, he must be put into a separate cage, and hung in such a position that he can be seen by both the female canaries and the finch. If the hens have not formed an attachment with the goldfinch, they will be, in all probability, very much delighted with this introduction; whilst Master "Goldie," especially if he be attached to the hens and of an amatory temperament, will exhibit unmistakable symptoms of jealousy, and by this means his affections will be considerably strengthened, unless he be of a sulky disposition, when it is quite possible he might fret and repine, and ultimately die of a broken heart; but I have only known one case of this extreme character. After the lapse of two or three days, remove the other hen and the goldfinch into another cage, and put the canary cock with the first-mentioned hen. As soon as the latter hen has laid her complement of eggs, remove the cock canary to the cage containing the other hen; but, before doing so, take out the finch and place him in a small cage by himself, and hang it in such a position as he will be able to see both hens and the canary cock. As soon as the second hen has laid her third egg the

I

male canary should be removed, and she should be set. My
reason for recommending this method is, first, that the female
canary, having naturally a stronger desire for a mate of her
own species than for a foreigner, is thereby induced to begin
to breed sooner than she would otherwise do; for although
a hen canary will build, and sit about the nest in the presence of a goldfinch, it will be found that she rarely, if ever,
begins to breed before the end of April or beginning of
May; and I have known instances of hens postponing their
breeding operations as late as June under such circumstances;
whereas, if they had had a partner of their own tribe, they
would most probably have had eggs in March or the beginning of April. My next reason is, that goldfinches rarely
begin to breed until the middle of April, but more frequently
in May; and another reason is, that it gives an opportunity
of testing the capabilities of the hens in the capacity of
nurses; for, if a hen fail in this respect, it is useless to breed
mules from her unless you provide yourself with a few spare
hens to act as foster mothers to the newly-hatched birds. I
need scarcely say that this is not at all desirable if it can by
any means be dispensed with. A further reason is that, supposing the hen produces a nest of good mules, there is the
satisfaction of having some of her offspring for future operations. It is a generally recognised maxim among old experienced mule breeders not to place a goldfinch with a hen
canary so long as he retains any portion of the "black" on
his bill, as it is believed that until the beak is quite clear
they are unproductive. It is perhaps necessary for me to
explain here that all goldfinches, during the winter and early
spring, have a dark mark resembling an ink or pencil line,
which runs straight down the middle of the upper mandible,
and as soon as they are ready to pair this mark entirely dis-
appears; not all at once—it is a gradual process, and extends
over several weeks; but until it does so the bird is not considered in a fit condition to produce fruitful eggs. Another
peculiar feature about a goldfinch is that when moulted in
the open air it has black legs, but as soon as it becomes

domesticated, and is moulted in the house, its legs becomes clear
or flesh-coloured, although termed by the "fancy" "white-
legged;" hence you are able to tell whether a bird has been
"house-moulted" or not. It is further stated, on good authority, that if ever a goldfinch becomes clear in the bill before
the month of February it is certain to die shortly after it has
been placed with a hen canary for the first time. I have
myself known two instances of this happening. I think it is
caused through keeping the birds in too hot a room and
giving them stimulating food, which ripens them out of season,
and the unwary are sometimes imposed upon by unprincipled
people selling them birds of this description as "grand
breeding birds."

Should anyone desire to experiment with a female goldfinch
and a male canary, in preference to the usual and generally
recognised method of breeding
mules, I would advise him to
use a small room or very large
aviary for the purpose—if an
out-of-door one, all the better;
a small apple or pear tree
planted in a tub should be supplied them; and care should
be taken to keep it well
watered and manured; in addition to this, the birds will
require a quantity of moss,
lichens, fine root fibres, and a
little wool, hair (cowhair), and

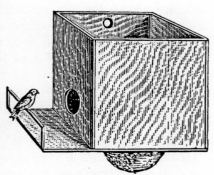

FIG 45. BOX NEST.

dandelion or thistle-down for nest-building. They ought likewise to be kept together during the winter months, or at any
rate for several weeks prior to the commencement of the breeding season. In all other respects mules must be bred and
treated in the same manner as canaries. If bred in cages use
the nest represented in Fig. 45. The bottom and sides are made
of wood, and likewise the ends; but it is an improvement to
have one end glazed with ground glass, to give more light,

or it can be fitted to slide in and out of grooves. At the other end is an aperture for ingress and egress; the bottom is extended forward to admit of a perch being fixed to it for the convenience of the birds when going to or from the nest. A large round hole is made in the bottom to admit a tin nest; the top is left uncovered for ventilation. At one side, near the top, a hole is made to hang it up to the back of a cage, or the wall of an outdoor aviary.

The nest should be placed at one end of the cage, within 2in. of the roof or ceiling; the tin nest should be lined with felt before being put in its place. It would be an improvement to have the nest fitted inside to a stout wire frame, and open wire-work surrounding it, so that the refuse from the young birds would fall to the bottom of the cage instead of accumulating in the nest box. If made with a wood bottom, the nest should project from ½in. to ¾in. above the floor, to allow sufficient space for the collection of excrement, and a nest box so constructed will require to be removed after the young birds have left it, in order that it may be entirely freed from dirt. This description of nest is preferable to all others for the purpose for which it is intended, and it will be found by experience that, where several different kinds of nests are placed in an aviary along with it, the birds will almost invariably choose the one here represented. It can be contrived to hang on the outside of the end of a breeding cage if preferred.

CAGES FOR MULE BREEDING.—The best kind of cages to use for the purpose of mule breeding are those made with three separate compartments, but constructed in such a manner that they can readily be made into two, or even one, if deemed desirable. This can be done by using sliding partitions; the best kind are those in the form of a light frame, and wired similar to the front of a cage, small screw rings or knobs being used to pull them out. They should be made to run in grooves. By having the cages upon this principle the birds can see each other, and, when they choose, have a *tête-à-tête;* the centre compartment can be used for the male bird until the young nestlings are old enough to be removed

from the maternal care, when they can be conveniently transferred to it, and a necessary change readily effected. The
wires, however, should be sufficiently wide to allow the youngsters to get their heads through, lest they should require for
a few days longer the parental assistance in feeding. The
dimensions of the cage should be as follows : Entire length,
42in.; depth, from top to bottom, 14in.; width, from back to
front, 10in.; each of the end compartments ought to be 15in.
in length, outside measurement, and the centre one 12in., or
if it be preferred, the whole of the three compartments can
be made the same size ; each one should be furnished with a
seed hopper and an egg drawer, in addition to a water trough ;

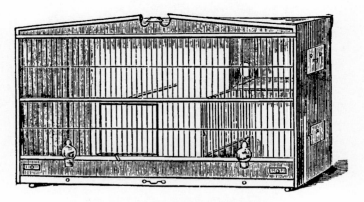

FIG. 46. CAGE FOR MULE BREEDING.

the cages should be made entirely of wood, with the exception
of the front and sliding communicators ; a false bottom, made
to draw out, so that the cage can be readily cleaned out during
the breeding season without disturbing the hens, would be
found exceedingly serviceable, or the breeding cage represented
in Fig. 46 may be used where breeding on a small scale is
considered desirable.

CAGES FOR YOUNG MULES.—Mules are very mischievous
birds ; they are much addicted to plucking each other, and

ought on this account to be kept in separate cages after they begin to moult. A large fir cage, lightly built, and divided into eight, ten, or twelve compartments, can be made to answer the purpose required at a small outlay. It may be black varnished outside if desired; the dimensions of a cage of this sort need not exceed 11in. square for each of the several compartments, and 8in. from back to front. Tin hoppers and drinking troughs, japanned, could be made to hang on the front of each compartment. For a singing bird, the drawing-room cage shown ·in Fig. 47 will be found appropriate.

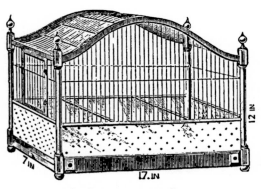

FIG. 47. DRAWING-ROOM CAGE.

LINNET AND OTHER MULES.—Brown or grey linnet and canary mules can be obtained in the same way as goldfinch and canary mules. Care should be taken, however, to procure young linnets, if obtainable; they are easily distinguished, when newly caught, by the absence of red colour on their heads, and also by the fact that the head in young birds is more profusely covered with black spots than in older birds. The russet colour of their backs, too, is spotted with dark brown and reddish white; these birds are known as grey linnets. The older or more matured birds, when first caught, are very red on the forehead; the remainder of the head being reddish ashen grey, spotted on the poll with black, and on the cheeks, the sides of the neck, and round the eyes with reddish white, besides, the feathers on the sides of the breast are nearly blood-red; and birds of this description are known among professional bird-catchers by the cognomen of "stubble" birds. Linnets alter very much in their appearance, according to age and circumstances, and if old birds are moulted in the house their rich plumage is changed into ashen grey and russet brown, and they strongly resemble the ordinary grey linnet in their outward covering.

The same rules as are laid down for breeding goldfinch and canary mules must be observed in breeding with linnets and canaries, and the same remarks apply to siskins, green-finches, redpoles, &c. By far the handsomest mules, however, are those bred between the goldfinch and canary. It is stated by some breeders that mules have been obtained by crossing a bullfinch and a canary together. I am perfectly aware that a bullfinch will occasionally pair with a hen canary, but I have never been able to find a verified instance in which the eggs proved fruitful. I have seen a bird exhibited which was said to be a hybrid of this kind; but, beyond the fact that its bill bore a striking likeness to that of the bullfinch, I could not discover another trace of resemblance to it.*

It is also affirmed by some authorities that mules will pro-pagate their own species in confinement, but I have never known a single instance in which this fact has been clearly established.

The goldfinch and bullfinch will breed together. I have seen some fine specimens of the hybrids from a male gold-finch and a female "bully;" and in the case to which I refer she took very readily to an artificial nest.

There are other varieties of the finch tribes that will breed together quite readily; but their produce are valued more as curiosities and *raræ aves* than objects of beauty.

---

* I have now seen a hybrid, the property of Mr. Williams, of Liverpool, which I believe to be bred between the canary and bullfinch. It is the only genuine specimen I have seen. A likeness of it is given in this issue of "The Canary Book."

Female hybrids, unless well marked or clear in colour, are of no value intrinsically.

In addition to the hybrids already mentioned, it has been asserted that the yellow-hammer and canary have bred together, and I have seen a mule exhibited, said to be a cross between the species named, and a prize was awarded to it. I examined it most minutely, but failed to find a trace of canary in its composition, nor could I discover anything about the bird· to lead me to believe that it was other than an ordinary yellow-hammer.

In my own experience, I have never observed any signs of affinity to exist between the yellow-hammer and canary. Besides, yellow-hammers are insectivorous as well as grain-eating, which canaries are not ; and I doubt very much whether hybrids so bred (?) could be reared on canary diet.

Mules can be bred between the goldfinch and greenfinch, the goldfinch and linnet, siskin and goldfinch, bullfinch and goldfinch, goldfinch and redpole, bullfinch and greenfinch, and bullfinch and linnet. In fact, any two varieties of the finch family may, with care and patience, and if in good health and under favourable circumstances, be induced to breed, and any of these will breed with the canary. In the latter case we prefer the hen to be the canary, and in using goldfinches we prefer the male to be of that variety. Mules bred between the greenfinch and linnet, or greenfinch and bullfinch, or green-finch and siskin—in fact, any mules bred between the green-finch and any other variety of the finch tribe, are never handsome, and are looked upon more as a *rara avis* than otherwise; by far the handsomest mules are those bred between the goldfinch and canary, and next to these are preferred the specimens obtained between the bullfinch and goldfinch, many of these crosses producing very handsome birds.

CHAPTER IV.

DISEASES.

GENERAL REMARKS.—There is a quaint old saying that "Prevention is better than cure," and there is more philosophy in that maxim than at first sight appears, except to those who may be intimately acquainted with the "Ills that flesh is heir to."

It is well known to pathologists that the most prolific causes, both in the origination and dissemination of diseases, are, first, the eating of food which is too rich and nourishing, and, secondly, the overloading of the stomach. These, as a natural sequence, are the promoters of indigestion or dyspepsia, which is the forerunner of a great variety of complaints, more particularly in those who are of a thriving constitution, with a natural tendency to obesity. Such people, if they partake too freely of the good things of this life, are prone to gout and rheumatism and other kindred ailments, and more particularly if they lead an inactive and sedentary life. Perhaps the next great evil is the want of sufficient fresh air and out-of-door exercise. Close confinement is a great enemy to health, without which life becomes a weary burden. Calisthenics, or even athletic exercise, if used in moderation, invigorate the human frame and give strength and vitality to those who without them would be weak and delicate. If, then, the science of physiology teaches us that these things are to be duly regarded, in order that we may enjoy good and uninterrupted health, how much more necessary is it that they should be fully considered and carefully weighed in administering to the wants and necessities of our feathered captives who are constant prisoners ?

CAUSES OF DISEASE.—As I have already stated, many illnesses are brought on by over-feeding, others are engendered through neglect. Some fanciers give their birds egg and bread, chickweed, cabbage, lettuce, dandelion, groundsel, &c., in unmeasured quantities, and the birds amuse themselves, after having satiated their appetites, by throwing the former into the bottom of their cages, and by pulling the green food inside as well. This is the result of giving birds more food than they can possibly consume in one day. In the course of a few days it becomes sour; and if they partake of it, as they will do at times, the consequences which usually ensue are cases of diarrhœa, or, still worse, inflammation of the bowels or intestines, which, if not promptly attended to, result in death. Others, again, give them sour greens, or bad water, or allow the water to remain in the troughs until it gets loathsome and unfit for use. These, and similar causes of neglect, produce more than half the illnesses from which birds die. Therefore, remember the adage referred to at the beginning of this chapter. Indeed, I think it would not be a bad plan if fanciers would adopt it for a motto, and have it painted in large characters upon their bird-room doors.

FOOD.—Always supply your birds with plain, wholesome diet, but never pamper them with dainties, except in such cases as I have pointed out. Be particular always to procure the best canary seed, and genuine German summer rape seed, and give in the proportion of three parts of canary to one of rape; occasionally you may give a little linseed and a few groats, and from April to September a little fresh green food, either watercress, groundsel, or lettuce. Dandelion leaves may be given sometimes, but they ought to be well washed and immersed in water for a few hours previously. In winter time a little sweet apple, with the rind taken off, may be given them once a week. When in health, and not breeding, they require no other food, except to prepare them for exhibition. Let them have as much fresh air as possible, and be sure to give them fresh water every day, or every alternate day. If there be any reason to doubt the purity of the water you give the birds to drink, it is a good plan to filter rain water for their use. Let the cages be roomy, and clean them out frequently. Use sea sand when procurable, as the salt which it contains is beneficial to them; if you cannot succeed in getting it, prepare your sand in the manner pointed out in the chapter on "Canary Breeding." By observing these recommendations you will seldom be troubled with diseased or ailing birds.

It is a mistaken kindness on the part of many well-meaning, warm-hearted fanciers, to pamper their birds with every conceivable luxury, and they little dream of the consequences which are sure to follow such a line of treatment. It will readily be seen that I am strongly opposed to feeding canaries on delicacies; so I am, and ere I proceed further I will illustrate my meaning by quoting the following facts: It is well known to a great many fanciers that people who keep canaries merely as singing birds, and who are totally unacquainted with many of the dainties that are frequently given to them, and who believe that all they require is canary and rape seed mixed, fresh water, and clean sand once a week after their cages are cleaned out, manage to keep their birds until they attain great ages. I have known one bird live to the age of twenty-three years, another to twenty-one years, and a third to eighteen years; but the most remarkable part of the story is that these birds were all living at the same time, and kept by three different families in the same village, and within a hundred yards of each other. This fact I will vouch for; and I found on enquiry that they were fed upon canary and rape seed, principally, commonly called black and white bird seed, occasionally a little apple, and during the summer months a little green food given sparingly, which latter consisted of either watercress, groundsel, or lettuce; each bird had a knob of loaf sugar constantly placed between the wires of his cage, had fresh water given twice or thrice a week, regularly cleaned out once a week, and received a fresh supply of river sand at the same time. I bred a nest of birds early in the spring of 1859, between a Belgian Canary and a Lizard, and I presented one of their offspring to an intimate friend for a singing-bird: it was living in 1875, and in excellent health. It was fed on simple food; in fact, very similar to that given to the three birds previously mentioned.

A.

APOPLEXY.—There are several kinds of this fearful disease. There is the atrabilious, cataleptic, hydrocephalic, &c. They are, nevertheless, all of them of such a tendency as to lead to a fatal termination in the lives of birds, as it would be physically impossible to subject these minute objects to a process of treatment similar to that resorted to in human beings. Prevention is the best substitute for cure. The most fruitful source of this complaint in birds is luxurious living, and intemperance in diet. Male canaries which are permitted to revel in Mormonism to any extent are likewise prone to it. If you are present at any time when a canary drops from its perch in a fit, and lies struggling at the bottom of the cage in apparent agony, lift it gently out and carry it to an open window, bathe its head with cold water, and if there should happen to be any spirit of ammonia (harts-horn) at hand, or to be procured readily, dilute a little of this with cold water, and let the bird inhale the vapour. Should it revive, keep it cool and quiet for some time, and afterwards give it some laxative medicine. You might give it two drops of castor-oil to begin with, and about ½dr. of Epsom salts might be put in its drinking water. The diet of the patient should be of the simplest and plainest description, more especially if the bird is of a full habit of body. There is likewise a species of apoplexy which is produced by the effect of the sun's rays—this is called *coup de soleil.* I have known birds hung in a window where the sun has poured upon them during the hottest days in summer, but, fortunately, in most cases, with the upper sash of the window lowered to let in the fresh air. Many birds die from this cause alone, and I wonder that there are not far more.

ASTHMA.—This is a complaint from which a great number of canaries suffer. It not unfrequently proceeds from a hereditary disposition, the result of breeding with birds affected with this disease; and I notice, with regret, that it is much more prevalent at the present time than it was twenty years ago. This, I am disposed to think, results in a great measure from keeping show birds constantly covered, as some fanciers do, during certain months in the year, with the idea that it preserves their colour and keeps them clean. To some extent, no doubt, this is so; but I do not approve of the practice being carried to such an extent as to impair health. Birds subjected to this treatment are frequently sent long journeys, and often during the most severe and inclement weather, and are therefore so much more liable to be affected by atmospheric changes, which is another frequent cause of this very troublesome and tedious disorder. Derangement of the stomach and bowels, or profuse evacuations, may likewise produce it.

This malady can be distinguished from consumption by the periodical character of its attacks, and the wheezing sound which always accompanies it is a characteristic symptom that can scarcely be mistaken. Asthma, like consumption, varies in its symptoms; in fact, there are three distinct kinds of this disease; but I do not think it necessary for me to revert to them separately in this instance, as no one, other than a medical practitioner, could possibly distinguish between one form of the malady and another, and even they in such cases, had they bird patients, would at times be sorely puzzled. When it first occurs, if it is not complicated with other diseases and is dealt with vigorously, it can be cured; but if it once becomes chronic no hope need be entertained of a perfect recovery. When any organic disease exists, according to the organ affected, asthma may terminate in inflammation and dilatation of the bronchi, emphysema and œdema, consumption, dropsy of the chest, apoplexy, &c.

Birds suffering from asthma should be fed on a light, nutritive diet. A cake made of the following ingredients and well baked will be found very suitable to their requirements: Take sound wheat flour, ½lb.; the best arrowroot, ¼lb.; four fresh-laid eggs, and 4oz. of powdered loaf sugar; mix well together, and add half-a-pint of new milk; make into a cake in the ordinary way; a little of this should be placed between the wires of the cage, or crumbed and placed in the egg drawer for the use of the patient. It should be given fresh daily. A piece of dandelion-root, previously dried and roasted, should be scalded, and, when cool, the liquid should be drained off and given to the bird instead of ordinary water to drink; this will be found very beneficial. Warmth is indispensable in the treatment of this complaint, and it is not advisable to place the invalid in a damp room; particular attention should be paid to birds suffering from this vexatious disease during foggy or rainy weather.

In all diseases, but more especially in this, much depends upon the time when the treatment is commenced; when once constant dyspnœa (difficult breathing) is induced, depending upon organic disease, little more can be done than to palliate symptoms. Whenever a bird is seized with a sudden paroxysm, with much wheezing and oppression of breathing, give the following mixture with as little delay as possible: Ethereal tincture of lobelia, ten drops; compound tincture of camphor, one drachm; syrup of ginger, three drachms; cinnamon water, one ounce; put two teaspoonfuls of this mixture to two ounces of water, give it to the birds to drink in place of their ordinary drinking water, and continue its use until the most distressing symptoms have subsided; the dose may then be reduced to one-half, and increased whenever the breathing appears difficult until the symptoms have entirely disappeared. Should the mixture recommended fail to give permanent relief, give the patient a few drops of vin. antimon. tart. (antimonial wine) and tr. hyosciami (tincture of henbane), say, ten drops of each to one fluid ounce of water, to be given according to the directions laid down in reference to the preceding mixture; this I have found most serviceable, even in obstinate cases. I have likewise found the following preparation very efficacious in prolonged and difficult cases: Tinct. of aconite 1dr., tinct. of belladonna 1dr., sp. of ether nit. 2dr. Mix and give ten drops to each fluid ounce of drinking water, in place of the ordinary drinking water, to be renewed every alternate day. It is necessary to pay particular attention to the bowels of the sufferer, and a gentle purgative should be given when required; a little of the carbonate of magnesia, or, in some cases a few drops of molasses (treacle) put into the drinking-water, will have the desired effect. By following up the treatment recommended here, all cases of recent date should be cured, and even cases of long standing, and which are so thoroughly confirmed as to defy all remedies, can be greatly relieved, and the life of a bird suffering from this tiresome complaint may be prolonged for a considerable period, for this disease is not nearly so fatal in its effects as consumption; but unless a bird is a prize-taker, and valuable on this account, it is probably not worth while to persevere with chronic cases of asthma, as it is certainly incurable.

B.

BEAKS AND CLAWS, OVERGROWN.—See under "Claws," and also p. 79.

BOWELS, INFLAMMATION OF.—See under "Enteritis."

BROKEN LIMBS.—It happens occasionally that a canary has the misfortune to break one of its legs. When an untoward event of this kind takes place, remove the perches from the cage in which the bird is placed; supply their places with a nice clean bed, made with soft hay or straw (the former preferred), cut it into short lengths and tease it well out, and remove anything of a hard or prickly nature that may by accident have been placed amongst it; make it as smooth as possible in the centre for the bird to rest upon, and in a few weeks the limb will become perfectly sound. Nothing further need be done, as the fracture will heal by the process known

in surgery by the name of adhesion. It will be necessary,
however, for you to supply the invalid with food and water,
and these should be put into suitable vessels, and placed in
such a position that the bird can supply its wants without
being necessitated to move about for them. Place the cage
containing the patient where there is a good and clear light.

BRONCHITIS.—In an attack of this complaint the bird looks
feverish, is very restless, and frequently drinks; among other
symptoms are a dry husky cough and much difficulty in
breathing, accompanied by a rattling noise in the throat.
Bronchitis usually arises from a neglected cold.

Keep the patient warm. Three-parts fill a large basin with
hot water, place across it two pieces of wood, then stand the
cage containing the invalid on these, and cover all with a
piece of flannel, the object being to give a steam bath. If
the attack is a bad one add to the water ten drops of carbolic
acid and twenty-five drops of turpentine, but in this case thin
calico or muslin should be used as a cover instead of the
flannel. The operation should last from twenty to thirty
minutes, and be repeated twice daily for three or four days.
Prepare and give the following: Boil 2 table-spoonfuls of
linseed in a teacupful of water, strain the juice through a
piece of muslin, and add to this 2dr. of the best Spanish
juice, 1dr. of gum arabic crushed to powder and dissolved
in a little warm water, 2dr. of glycerine, and a dessert-spoonful
of the best moor honey*; put a teaspoonful of this mixture
to 3 table-spoonfuls of water, and give it fresh to the birds
every morning. If the birds operated upon have been accustomed to a room without a fire, it will be necessary to keep
them in a warm room until they are quite convalescent, and
before they are again returned to it great precaution is
necessary. The patients should be gradually removed to a
part of the room farthest from the fire, and if the weather

---

* At a certain period of the year many beekeepers send their hives of bees
on to waste or moor lands, when wild flowers and the heather, &c., are in
blossom. The honey obtained in this way is considered the best, and is known
in the North of England by the name of "Moor honey."

will permit of it, the window of the room should be opened for an hour or so for two or three days prior to their removal.

C.

CATARACT AND OPHTHALMIA.—See under " Ophthalmia and Cataract."

CATARRH, OR COLD. — This complaint is most frequently brought on by birds having to travel long journeys during cold and inclement weather, and more particularly is this the case if a bird has been kept in a warm room, either at home or during the time it has been at a show. At most shows the rooms are allowed to get over-heated, especially at night when a large number of gaslights are usually employed and visitors are most numerous. The symptoms are: First, sneezing, then a dullness in the eyes, ruffled feathers, and a general "knocked-about" sort of a look. Sometimes there is a swelling about the eyes and a watery discharge.

This complaint requires prompt action, or it will probably develop into something more serious. Remove the patient to a warm room, and exclude all draughts. Prepare some linseed tea by simmering 2 table-spoonfuls of linseed in a teacupful of boiling water for twenty minutes, when cold it is fit for use. Give fifteen drops of the following mixture to each ounce of linseed tea, in place of the ordinary drinking water: Tinct. of lobelia 1dr., vin. ipecac. 1dr., tinct. aconite ½dr., glycerine 3dr. The patient should be dieted on hard-boiled eggs and bread, with a slight sprinkling of cayenne pepper, and from twenty to thirty drops of almond oil. If this treatment is not successful in the course of a few days, give the following in place of the first-named formula: Tinct. aconite 1dr., tinct. belladonna 1dr., oxymel scillie 2dr., sp. ether nit. 2dr. Mix well and give the same quantity and in the same manner as directed above.

CHOREA.—Chorea is a disease with which birds are some-times afflicted, but very rarely. I have only seen two cases of it, both in very " sib-bred " birds. The birds affected keep

K

continually turning their heads round in a very peculiar manner. It is the result of some nervous affection, or of a diseased organism. I know of no remedy for it, and birds so afflicted had better be destroyed. If such birds could be induced to breed, this might possibly remove the malady, but in the case referred to, neither of them showed any disposition to mate with other birds.

CLAWS AND BEAKS, OVERGROWN.—I must not omit to state that all birds confined in cages require their claws cutting occasionally, some more frequently than others; and their bills too sometimes, but this only in exceptional cases. These operations should be performed with a pair of small, but sharp scissors. Great care is required not to cut too much off their claws to make them bleed, or you might lame the birds; neither must you cut any more off the bill of a bird than is absolutely necessary. This is a delicate operation, and should only be performed by an experienced person. These little attentions conduce greatly both to the health and comfort of birds. (See also p. 79).

CONSTIPATION.—This can be relieved by putting a few drops of molasses in the bird's drinking water, or by giving it a plentiful supply of green food if during the summer months; if in the winter, a little white bread sopped in milk and well sweetened with moist sugar, or a little prepared egg food, with a few drops of castor or almond oil added, may be placed in the egg-pan for the use of the birds, and a little green food, if seasonable at the time when required; if not, supply a little scalded German (summer) rape seed.

CONSUMPTION (PULMONARY) OR PHTHISIS.—Perhaps one of the most difficult diseases to contend with, and one with which birds are frequently affected, is phthisis, or pulmonary consumption, and those most prone to this malady are the Belgian, Dutch, and Lancashire Canaries. It is generally contracted during the time the birds are moulting, although, no doubt, in many instances it results from breeding from parents affected with this complaint. It may originate through allowing

the birds to bathe too frequently whilst they are casting their
feathers, as at this time they are, to a greater or lesser extent,
more delicate in health, and consequently much more liable
to take cold than under ordinary circumstances; or it may
be produced through negligence or forgetfulness by leaving
the window of the bird-room open all night, particularly in
foggy or damp weather, or through the birds being placed in
a current of air (a draught). It generally begins with catarrh or
a common cold, and the first symptom usually observed is a
sort of wheezing noise, or what may be designated, and probably
is, a bird cough. As soon as you observe a bird making this
noise, you may safely conclude that it has a bad cold, and
you ought to remove it to a warm room, and cover the cage
partly to keep it cosy. Nourishing food should be given to
it at once; a little hard-boiled egg, chopped very small, and
a little arrowroot biscuit should be grated and mixed with it,
and a piece of gum acacia about the size of a pea should be
dissolved in its drinking water, and likewise a small piece of
Spanish liquorice, or a weak infusion of linseed, given in place
of the drinking water. If these precautions are neglected, the
bird will most probably get worse, become languid, and look
dull and heavy about the eyes, and will gradually become
weak and lose its flesh, and ultimately be seized with diarrhœa,
which, if neglected, soon terminates in death. Great prompt-
ness is necessary in the first stage of this disease, which
does not always appear in the same form, although catarrh is
generally the forerunner of it. Its action upon birds varies
the same as in human beings, and some linger under its
influence much longer than others; however, if it once becomes
fairly established in any form, and latent phthisis or tubercular
phthisis sets in, there is no remedy for it.

It may, however, even when very bad, be considerably allayed
by proper attention and treatment; nourishing diet and warmth
are essentials which cannot be dispensed with. A little white
bread sopped in warm new milk may be given with advantage
in this stage of the disease, but care must be taken not to
allow it to get sour. A little tincture of digitalis (foxglove)

should be given fresh every day in the bird's drinking-water, say, from fifteen to twenty drops to a wineglassful of water; this diminishes the force of the heart's action, although, if given too frequently, and particularly in overdoses, it is apt to produce unpleasant and dangerous symptoms, and ought therefore to be given with extreme caution. The bowels, too, should be kept gently open; this can be accomplished by mixing a very small quantity of the carbonate of magnesia in the drinking water (a very small piece upon the point of a knife will be sufficient); or two, three, or four senna leaves in the water will have the desired effect. In chronic cases, a few grains of the hydriodate of potass may be given with advantage ; but I prefer a little tr. opii camph. (paregoric) and a few drops of the oxymel of squills, say, fifteen to twenty drops of each to a wineglassful of water, given instead of the ordinary drinking water : sometimes a little cod-liver oil is beneficial, but I have always found the other treatment to answer best. The last-mentioned remedies are only to be given in confirmed cases of this disease. If diarrhœa sets in, a few drops of elixir of vitriol and a little infusion of gentian must be given in the drinking water—twenty drops of the former and two teaspoonfuls of the latter, which you must prepare fresh every three or four days. Get a pennyworth of gentian-root, take a piece the size of a bean and cut small, put it in a mug or jug with about an equal bulk of orange rind, and pour about one-fourth of a pint of boiling water on it; when cool, strain off and use. The addition of a teaspoonful of brandy would preserve it a little longer, and. would add to its medicinal virtues. If the purging is severe, a little prepared chalk and loaf sugar added to the egg and biscuit diet would prove useful, but, as I have stated before, unless you can check this disease in its first stage, there is little hope of a perfect cure, so that it becomes a question as to whether it is worth while to prolong the life of a bird under these circumstances. Bleeding and blistering, which are frequently resorted to with excellent results in the case of men, cannot of course be applied to little, delicate birds.

COUGH.—See under " Consumption."

CRAMP.—All birds are more or less liable to this troublesome complaint; sometimes it attacks the limbs, at other times the stomach. It may arise from a vitiated state of the bile, or from having eaten something indigestible. The most effectual remedy I know of is, when in the limbs, to immerse them in warm water and administer some gentle aperient. When in the stomach, give twenty drops of antimonial wine and ten drops of laudanum to one-and-a-half ounces of water, in place of the regular drinking water.

D.

DECLINE. — " Going light," or " wasting away," as many fanciers are pleased to term this disease, is hereditary in most cases, and caused by breeding from diseased parents. It is only the final stage of consumption (see p. 130), or gradual decay engendered by that disorder.

DEFORMED HIND CLAW.—This deformity is attributable to a contraction of the flexor tendon of the hind claw, which may result from a variety of causes. It is much more prevalent than it was a few years ago, a fact for which I am quite unable to account. Treatment: Bind back the affected claw firmly to the shank of the leg with a piece of silk thread, worsted, or cotton, but not so tight as to interfere with the circulation. In the course of a fortnight or so the binding may be cut, and the contracted claw liberated. A cure should be effected in this time. If the remedy is not applied for some time after the deformity is observed, a longer time, say three weeks, will be necessary to effect a cure. If the contraction is allowed to go on for months without the application of a remedy, it may be necessary to amputate the toe, but if attended to at once a cure is certain.

DIARRHŒA.—This term is used to express laxness of the bowels and purging. It is a symptom more than a disease, for it depends upon irritation of the stomach or bowels, which may arise from a variety of causes, the principal being cold.

or indigestible articles of food, or bad water, or anything producing acidity of the stomach or an over-secretion of bile. Too much green food will produce it, especially if it is unripe or decayed, sour egg and bread, &c. It may also, and no doubt does frequently, arise from inflammation of the mucous membrane of the intestines. This disorder consists in watery motions from the bowels, of frequent occurrence, and which are usually fœtid, and are mixed with portions of undigested food, &c.

The treatment depends greatly upon the cause of the disorder. If it depends on checked perspiration or cold, a small quantity of Dover's Powder—say, from two to three grains to an ounce of gum water, very weak—may be substituted for the regular drinking water; and two drops of castor-oil should be given internally on the point of a knitting needle; warm the needle before you put it in the oil. If the bowels appear inflamed, alternate the former with water containing twenty drops of antimonial wine to each fluid ounce. If it depends on indigestible food, put a teaspoonful of carbonate of soda into three ounces of cinnamon water, and give in place of the ordinary drinking water and the dose of castor-oil as previously recommended. If the purging still continues, mix a dessert-spoonful of chalk mixture with a wineglassful of water, add twenty drops of laudanum, and give it in the manner already pointed out. For the chalk mixture take of prepared chalk, half-an-ounce (procurable at any chemist's); refined sugar (loaf sugar), three drachms; gum arabic, powdered, one ounce; water, one pint; mix them by trituration. If this fails to check the looseness, a few drops, say, thirty or forty, of tincture of catechu may be added to the last-named mixture, which will generally be found to have the desired effect. The diet should consist principally of arrowroot biscuits sopped with new milk. After the purging has ceased the bowels should be carefully regulated by giving a little magnesia, or a senna leaf or two, in the drinking water; and as the looseness, if of any duration, is sure to weaken the patient, a little tonic medicine will be necessary for a few weeks after recovery from the attack. The best and simplest is the infusion of gentian, which can be given in the drinking water in the proportions of a teaspoonful of the former to a tablespoonful of the latter. Diarrhœa also occurs in the last stage of consumption, &c.; but in such cases little can be done to alleviate it, as checking it is sure to aggravate the other symptoms of the disease.

DIPHTHERIA.—This complaint, which is not very prevalent in canaries, affects the head and throat. The mucous membrane becomes thickly coated with secreted matter, and the throat and tongue ulcerated. It is, however, very contagious, hence a bird discovered to be suffering from this disease should at once be isolated, and, if not valuable, it will be well to destroy it in order to stamp out the malady. In valuable specimens the following treatment should be adopted. Use a lotion to the throat made as follows: 2 drachms of cupri. sulph. dissolved in 4oz. of rain water, and apply to the throat with a feather, turning it carefully round a few times before being withdrawn. Give for internal use as follows: Loaf sugar, burnt brown, 2oz., sulphate of iron 2 scruples, sulphate of magnesia 2 scruples, sulphate of soda 2 drachms, chloride of sodium ½ drachm, water 6oz. Mix in a mortar, add twenty drops of this to each ounce of water, to be given in place of the usual drinking water; or the following, 20 drops of Calvert's pure carbolic acid, 1 drachm of spirit of wine, and 6oz. of water; dose, twenty drops to each ounce of water, as before directed.

DYSENTERY.—The symptoms first observed in this disorder are a dullness and want of energy in the bird attacked, and it is usually much relaxed in its bowels for a day or two; then the evacuations become scant and thin, and consist principally of a little thick mucus tinged with blood, and there is much straining, and evidently severe griping pains as the poor patients cling close to the perches, and move from side to side in a manner that suggests great agony. Warmth, quiet, and light nourishing diet are essential—a little white bread

or arrowroot biscuit soaked in warm milk, with a few drops
of sherry wine added, may be given fresh twice a day as the
sole diet until the symptoms begin to disappear, and the bird
to recover ; then a tablespoonful of a mixture of oatmeal,
ground linseed, and white bread in equal parts, and a sixth part
of the yolk of an egg boiled for ten minutes, made into a
moderately-thick paste with warm water, may be substituted,
and renewed daily until recovery is complete. For further
treatment: Give from fifteen to twenty drops of the following
mixture to each ounce of water in place of the ordinary drinking
water : Vin. ipecac. 2dr., vin. antimon. 2 dr., tinct. belladonna
1dr., tinct. opii. 1dr., sp. æther nit. 2dr.

This disease is generally brought about by the birds partaking of sour egg or green food during hot weather, or it
may result from an attack of typhus fever. I do not think
it is contagious, but at the same time it is commendable to
remove any affected bird from among others. A great many
birds die from this complaint during intensely hot weather.

E.

EGG-BOUND. — See Chap. II., on " Breeding and Management."

ENTERITIS, OR INFLAMMATION OF THE BOWELS. — It is
sometimes a matter of great difficulty to discover the true
cause of ailment in canaries affected with sudden illness ; but
in acute or even chronic inflammation of the bowels, the symptoms are readily distinguishable. Birds suffering from this
disorder suddenly become listless and dull, and, according to
the prognosis of this complaint, they suffer acute twitching
pains in the abdomen, which cause them frequently to lie
with their bodies upon the perches in their cages in their
endeavour to procure ease. If you catch the bird, and blow
back the feathers from the under part of the body, you will
find that there is tension of the belly, and the external appearance of the skin is red, at first somewhat pale, but gradually
deepening into a much darker colour, and, as the disease

progresses, becoming intensely red, with a blackish hue beneath. It is generally accompanied with obstinate constipation, though sometimes there is diarrhœa. If the inflammation be in the upper part of the intestines, the bird frequently throws out of its mouth, with a " chit, chit ! " some dark, bilious-looking matter; but if in the lower intestines, there is straining, and a frequent desire to go to stool. Sometimes it happens that the tongue of the patient is completely covered with sores, and a disinclination to partake of food is the result. A small piece of borax, finely powdered and put upon the tongue, will mostly give relief when a bird is found to be suffering in this respect.

Thirst becomes urgent as the inflammation increases; but cold drinks only increase the pain. Inflammation of the bowels—or, as it is sometimes called by writers on birds, "rupture "—is a complaint from which many young birds die, and occasionally old ones. It is produced, I assume, in most instances, by partaking of unwholesome food, such as sour egg and bread or decayed vegetables, and in some cases by bad or impure water, or by over-gorging with egg, &c. When egg and bread have been thrown about the cage by adult birds, or a lettuce-leaf, a piece of groundsel, chickweed, or other vegetable of a like nature, and allowed to remain until sour or decayed, the birds partaking of them are pretty certain to suffer from disorder in the bowels and intestines, and ultimately from inflammation.

The treatment of enteritis requires to be active and immediate. Bleeding, blistering, and leeching cannot be resorted to with such delicate little patients as canaries; but a little turpentine, made tolerably hot, and applied with a camel or hogs'-hair brush to the inflamed part of the abdomen, will be found to give considerable relief to the sufferer. The bowels must likewise be acted upon by administering internally two or three drops of castor-oil. After they have been freely evacuated you may give the bird to drink, in place of its ordinary water, a little thin gum-water (gum arabic), to which has been added ten drops of tr. opii (laudanum) and twenty drops of

vin. ipecac. (ipecacuanha wine) to each ounce of the former. Any
sudden change from heat to cold, or from a cold room to a
hot one, or placing before a fire, is to be avoided, as it would
only tend to increase the symptoms and feed the complaint;
a moderate and uniform temperature is the best. A light diet
must always be given in cases of internal inflammation; a
little arrowroot biscuit, steeped in warm new milk, and given
fresh twice a day, or a little oatmeal, which has been lightly
browned in the oven and made into a paste with a little honey
and gum-water, may be alternated with the former.

If you succeed in restoring the bird to health, it will require
a little tonic medicine for a few weeks after its restoration,
such as iron and gentian; a rusty nail should be placed in
the water-trough, with a few drops of either the infusion or
tincture of gentian added. If, however, the disease will not
yield to these remedies, as occasionally happens, and suppuration intervenes, with frequent involuntary shivering, and
the bird discharges fœtid stools of a reddish, watery appearance, and the poor little patient seeks to bury its head deeper
and deeper beneath its wing, and persistently hustles itself
into a solitary corner of its cage, there is but small hope of
its recovery, for gangrene most probably has set in, and will
soon terminate the life of the little sufferer.

EPILEPSY. — There are three different species of this disease—the cerebral, the sympathetic, and the occasional. The
one from which birds most frequently suffer is the last-named.
The predisposing cause seems to be a nervous tendency, allied
with a delicate constitution, and is probably the result of
continual confinement. The fits are generally brought on
whenever a bird, subject to this ailment, is surprised or
frightened; anything likely to create terror must be carefully
guarded against. I have known birds subject to these fits go
off in one every time they were brought into the open air,
or every time a hand was put in the cage to take hold of
them. Whenever a bird is seized with one of these occasional
fits, sprinkle it freely all over with cold water, but more particularly about the head; dip your fingers into a basin of

water and dash it vigorously over the affected bird. It is not considered a dangerous complaint, although, if it occurs frequently, it is very apt to impair the health of birds, and predispose them to disease. A mild aperient given occasionally, with a little tonic medicine besides, such as the carbonate of iron, quinine, infusion of quassia, or gentian, are the best remedies. Some birds are very subject to this disorder during the moulting period.

F.

FAINTING OR SYNCOPE.—See under "Syncope or Fainting."

FAINTING FITS.—Some birds are subject to fits, a species of hysteric or epileptic fits, and they go into them whenever they are caught, or in some instances on being exposed to the open air, or simply by removing the cage. It is undoubtedly a complaint affecting the nerves. When a bird takes a fit of this sort, dash a little cold water over it by dipping your fingers in a basin of cold water; this will generally restore it in a few minutes.—See also under "Epilepsy."

FEATHER-EATING.—This pernicious habit is acquired when several birds are placed together in a large cage or aviary to moult. No doubt heat of the body and an itching of the skin is engendered during this process, and creates a desire to pluck out the feathers which produce the derangement. It is believed by some fanciers to originate through a liking for the taste of blood, but I think it is often done through mischief and wantonness on the part of some birds. A bath given frequently and a plentiful supply of grit and crushed egg-shells (the shells taken from the boiled eggs of fowls), liberally sprinkled at the bottom of the cage or aviary, with a moderate supply of fresh green food, and pieces of apple and loaf sugar placed between the wires of the cages, are the best preventives of this vicious and objectionable habit.

FEET, SORE.—See under "Sore Feet," and also on p. 79.

FEVER, TYPHUS.—See under "Typhus Fever."

G.

" GOING LIGHT."—See " Decline."

H.

HENS, RUPTURED.—See under "Ruptured Hens."

HEPATITIS, OR INFLAMMATION OF THE LIVER.—Birds, and
more especially young birds, are subject to this dreadful malady.
It is produced by their partaking too freely of stimulating
food, particularly hemp seed, which acts as a very powerful
excitant when given to birds, and is with them a very feeding article of diet. I have had a great number of canaries
and canary mules, and other birds, die from this disease; but
at the time I was unable to determine its nature. I thought
it was some form of fever, but whether typhus or what I
could not be certain. I tried a variety of medicines and
different modes of treatment, but without any apparent
success; and, after losing twenty or thirty birds one season,
and forty or fifty the next, and as many more the next, I
decided to have the opinion of some eminent and practical
physician on the subject, so I sent one of the unfortunate
little victims to Dr. B. for dissection and report as to the
cause of death. I subjoin his reply, which is as follows:

Dear Sir,—With the exception of an enormously enlarged liver, I
can find nothing the matter with the canary. The exception is a very
important one, as I believe it is the cause of death. Of course, not
being learned in birds, you must accept what I say as that of one
who does not pretend to speak with authority. Yet, from the utter
disproportion of the liver with the other organs, I believe it to be,
as I have said above, the cause of death. No inflammation exists
in the intestines or stomach.

Perhaps you can call to mind how the ortolans* are caused to have
such large livers, for gastronomic purposes. They are supplied with
abundance of stimulating food, and kept in a warm place. Has this
not something to do with the mortality amongst your birds?—I am,
dear Sir, faithfully yours,   C. B., M.D.

---

* Ortolans are birds about the size of larks, and somewhat of the appearance
of yellow-hammers. They are allied to the *Fringillidæ*, and are natives of
southern Europe.

I had been in the habit, for some time previous to this, of
giving my birds hemp seed *ad libitum*, but as soon as I
received the letter already quoted I set to work to make
experiments, in order to test the accuracy of the opinion I
had received, and the idea I had formed, the result of which
leaves no doubt whatever in my mind that the hemp seed
was chiefly, if not solely the cause of all the mischief. Two
of the birds I experimented upon recovered, after a severe
attack of this complaint, the disease having yielded to the
remedies used, whilst three others succumbed, and, upon
being opened and carefully examined, their condition was
precisely as described by Dr. B. From that time I ceased
to give my birds hemp seed, and have not had a single case
of hepatitis since.

Inflammation of the liver is of two kinds—the acute and
the chronic; when of the former type it makes rapid progress,
unless it is immediately dealt with. Depletion (blood-letting)
is one of the first things resorted to in cases of hepatitis
in regular practice, but this operation is out of the question
entirely with such diminutive patients as canaries. Nevertheless, I am such a thorough believer in phlebotomy in all
cases where internal inflammation exists, that I generally pull
a couple of the largest flight feathers from each wing of the
bird, as well as a few of the tail feathers, and, although
you seldom draw much blood with performing this operation,
I am disposed to think that it does good. At the commencement of this disease the bird droops, and looks lumpy and
fretful and restless, and when suffering from the acute form
there is generally a considerable amount of feverishness. The
bird appears to perspire very much, is very hot in the body,
particularly restless, and appears in search of something it
fails to find. When, however, this disease makes its appearance in the chronic form, the symptoms are developed more
gradually and with less violence, but for all that it is quite
as difficult of cure. The treatment pursued by me, and with
tolerable success, is as follows: Give, first, hydrarg. (hydrar-
gyrum) cum creta (mercury with chalk) and James' Powder

in equal parts in infinitesimal doses; open the bird's beak as wide as possible, keep the tongue down and the head well back, and, having the powder in a piece of writing-paper, made funnel-shape, slip it well down into the throat, and drop a few drops of water upon it to help the patient to swallow before you allow it to move from the position in which it has been placed in order to administer the medicine, or the powder may be placed in a piece of quill, cut open at both ends, carefully put in the bird's mouth, and gently blown into the throat of the patient. In the next place, roast a piece of dandelion-root, which has been previously washed and scraped, and put it in the drinking water. About an hour after you give the powder follow it up by giving two or three drops of castor-oil, and if it does not operate freely in a short time—say, from half-an-hour to an hour—repeat the dose. You may likewise add a few senna leaves to the drinking-water, as well as the dandelion-root. In all cases of inflammation of the liver it is necessary to act promptly upon the bowels and intestines, as in this disease, in either form, the biliary secretion is much impeded, and even when restored the fluid is far from healthy at the beginning. On this account, and to prevent chronic indurations, or the chance of present suppuration, it is necessary to reinstate the biliary secretions as soon as possible. This can only be effected by such medicines as act on the biliary organs, such as the hydrarg. chlor. (calomel), James' Powder, &c.

The diet should consist chiefly of stale bread soaked in new milk, or a little arrowroot biscuit and ground rice made into a paste with the same vehicle. In some cases, however, these means may—and will—prove unavailing, and more particularly if the bird affected is not of a robust constitution.

If the hepatic tumour continue to grow, despite these remedies, the bird will become weaker and weaker; it will pine away to a mere skeleton, the shiverings become more frequent, and it will have a sour, sweaty smell. This is a sign that suppuration has begun, and the treatment must be changed. Remove the dandelion-root and senna-leaves, and add to the drinking-water instead twenty or thirty drops of antimonial wine. Should this fail to relieve it there is no hope of its recovery. Mortification sets in, the body assumes a dark, livid appearance, and death speedily follows.

I.

INFLAMMATION OF THE BOWELS.—See under " Enteritis."

INFLAMMATION OF THE LIVER.—See under " Hepatitis."

INFLAMMATION OF THE LUNGS.—See under "Pneumonia."

INTERNAL PARASITES.—These parasites are generated in the locality of the heart and liver, and I have no doubt thousands of birds perish from this cause alone, but as to its origin, that at present is problematical, and there is a wide field open for medical and scientific men to search after truth in that direction. I am of opinion that the cause arises from the use of an improper diet, and too much stimulating heat produced in feeding for colour. Another cause may be the want of a constant supply of grit, or from giving decayed seed or other unwholesome food. I know that many fanciers think it is produced by using some kinds of green food, and more particularly watercress. I do not care for the latter, as it is frequently grown in stagnant and filthy water, and is literally swarming with animal life, and requires strong treatment before being available for use. Birds affected with these pests often die quite suddenly, and to an unobservant fancier without showing any premonitary symptoms of disease. These insects, which are exceedingly minute, will be found on the liver and viscera of birds which fall victims to this disorder. The best remedies are probably a liberal and nutritious diet and abundance of fresh air, a large flight cage for exercise, and pure water. I think these parasites are generally only present in birds that are emaciated, or of weak and delicate constitutions, brought on by a bad moult or improper feeding.

J.

JOINTS, SWOLLEN.—See under " Swollen Joints."

L.

LIMBS, BROKEN.—See under " Broken Limbs."

. LIVER, INFLAMMATION OF THE.—See under " Hepatitis."

LOSS OF VOICE.—Canaries lose their voices sometimes, and this event takes place more frequently during the process of the moult than at any other season. I do not mean their ceasing to sing, for all birds stop singing at that time of year, but they are unable to say "pretty dick!" or "peat!" and when the season of song returns the voice of the bird is mute. It probably arises through cold, which may produce inflammation of the respiratory organs or larynx, or it may originate from cramp, weakness, or paralysis. I have invariably found that a little gum arabic and a few drops of paregoric (twenty to thirty drops), put into the drinking-water twice or thrice a week, and a liberal supply of lettuce and linseed, mixed, given to a bird so affected, removes the complaint. When a bird is suffering from this affection he will distend his throat to the utmost of his power, and if otherwise in apparent good health he will throw his head back, open his bill to its widest extent, and, in fact, go systematically through all the movements usually made when singing, and with all the energy he can muster; but not a sound can be heard. A piece of rusty bacon fixed between the wires of the cage will be found of great benefit for this complaint ; another remedy, much prized by some fanciers, is to put half-a-tea-spoonful of honey in the drinking-vessel with the water, and to add a few drops of lemon-juice freshly squeezed out of a lemon.

LUNGS, INFLAMMATION OF THE.—See under " Pneumonia."

O.

OPHTHALMIA AND CATARACT.—Within the past few years a great number of crested and crested-bred birds have suffered from this complaint. It has no doubt originated through the enlargement of the crest, encouraged by careful breeding, which in high-class birds frequently covers the eyes, and thereby irritates them, causing inflammation, and it is among such birds that the disease is observed. To me it appears to have become to some extent hereditary in its tendency, affecting plain-heads bred from heavily-crested parents. This complaint is greatly on the increase, owing to the vast improvement—so far as crest is concerned—which has been made within the past ten years in this variety. I am afraid there is no appreciable remedy; for to remove the cause would be to circumscribe the crests by introducing the blood of non-crest-bred birds, which would, I fear, be distasteful to the breeders of crested birds generally.

When the first symptoms of this complaint are observed the eyes should be washed or bathed with a lotion, made as follows: Sugar of lead 2 scruples, rain water (*aqua mollis*) half-a-pint, to which should be added ½ drachm of the tincture of belladonna. This lotion should be applied once or twice a day for a month; a soft feather or a small camel-hair brush are the best mediums for applying it.

The eyes should be well opened, and the liquid placed on the pupils. In some cases cataracts are formed which could only be removed by a surgical operation by a skilled practitioner.

The first symptoms of cataract noticeable is that the bird, before venturing to leap to the perch from the bottom of the cage, looks up with its head turned on one side, and appears to have some hesitancy, hopping along a lower perch, looking up several times before attempting to reach the upper one. Birds so affected appear tamer than usual, and fly about less when you attempt to catch them in your hand, and on closely examining the eye or eyes—as frequently both are affected—a milky white film will be noticed on the pupil.

P.

PARASITES.—See under Chap. II., p. 52 ("Preparing Breeding Cages"). Parasites are produced and propagated by the

ʟ

birds themselves. It will be found that as soon as a bird falls into ill-health it becomes possessed of these objectionable pests, and propagates them rapidly; hence an ailing bird should be removed to a cage, and placed by itself away from other birds, for when once the vermin get a footing they increase rapidly, and more particularly during warm and genial weather, or where the temperature is above 50deg. If they can get no shelter in the cages they cling to the birds, hence it will be found a good plan to use hollow perches, so constructed and arranged that the parasites can easily get access to them. They should be fixed by suspenders made of wire or tin to the back and front of the cages, and a little cotton wool should be placed in each of the hollow ends, to provide a shelter, and it will form an attractive place of refuge. The perches should be removed daily, the wool extracted, and the parasites dislodged and destroyed. The birds, as well as their cages and nests, should be freely dusted at short intervals with pyrethrum powder, which is an excellent safeguard against the encroachment of these unwelcome intruders. Another remedy I have found of great service in destroying these pernicious pests is sulphate of copper, commonly called blue-stone, but it should only be used cautiously and in bad cases, as it is a strong poison. Carbolic acid and Fir-tree oil are likewise useful remedies. Birds badly attacked by these little blood-suckers should be washed in a bath strongly impregnated with alum, which will add much to their comfort by ridding them of their enemies. As a further preventive to the accumulation of these insects it will be found advisable to add a little alum dissolved in water to the whitewash with which the breeding-cages are coated out; a weak solution of alum may likewise be given with great advantage to the birds to bathe in, once or twice a week, in dry weather, as this mineral destroys the pests. Another precaution should be taken, and that is to rub the nest tins or boxes inside with a little sweet oil or butter. I have likewise found camphor, placed in small bags and hung at the ends of my cages, very useful. Some fanciers, after first scraping and washing their cages out, give them a good coating of paraffin oil; let them stand twenty-four hours, and then wash again with hot water, strongly impregnated with washing soda; and, lastly, rinse out with pure water, and then whitewash them in the ordinary way.

PHTHISIS.—See under " Consumption."

PIP.—This is so called from a small pimple on the rump —in fact, it is the bird's lubricator, so to speak, it being an oil gland, and contains oil used for trimming the plumage; it occasionally gets deranged, and swelling ensues. If it appears to contain a mattery substance, it should, when ripe, be let out with a fine sewing-needle, and a little oil or moist sugar applied to the part. When it is ready to be operated upon, the bird appears heavy and sleepy. Whenever a bird is ill it should be removed to a cage kept expressly for invalids—a sort of hospital—and when the disease is of a contagious character, it should be removed as far away from the locality of the bird-room as circumstances will permit.

PNEUMONIA, OR INFLAMMATION OF THE LUNGS.—This disease is very common among canaries, and is generally ushered in by what is known as a common cold, usually caught during inclement weather, or by travelling long journeys to shows, or otherwise when the atmosphere is humid or foggy, or in tempestuous or severely cold weather. The first symptoms observable are shivering and dullness, the bird affected appearing very quiet for a day or two, eating little, but throwing the seeds about wantonly, and evidently in search of something it cannot obtain. On the second or third day its feathers become rough, and the patient looks cramped up and almost as round as a ball; difficulty in breathing will be observed, and a sort of dry, husky cough will be noticeable. In some cases there is likewise soreness of the throat, and if these symptoms are not relieved death will supervene in about forty-eight hours, more or less, according to the constitution of the patient. First remove the subject to a warm room, if it is not already in one, and in any case it must be isolated from other birds. Give a little gentle laxative—such as a small quantity of the sulphate of magnesia, a few senna leaves, and a piece of liquorice in the drinking water. When the bowels are relieved, substitute for the above the following: Vin. ant. tart. 1dr., sp. ether nit. 1½dr., tinct. opii camph. 1dr., tinct. belladonna ½dr. Add 15 drops of this mixture to every ounce of the water in place of the drinking water, and draw a few feathers out of the tail and wings, as a little blood-letting will assist in reducing the inflammatory symptoms. Feed on arrowroot biscuits and milk, with a teaspoonful of sherry wine added, and when the bird begins to recover give egg-food and tonics; a grain or two of quinine, dissolved in a few drops of diluted suphuric acid (elixir of vitriol), and 1oz. of pure water added; a teaspoonful of this should be put to each ounce of the ordinary drinking water, and renewed each alternate day until recovery is complete. This disorder requires prompt attention to effect a cure.

A caution to purchasers of birds. When you buy birds from anyone keep them apart from your regular stock for a week or so, and if they appear in good health at the end of that time you may place them in your bird room. It is not an uncommon practice with some fanciers when they find they have got a bad disease among their birds to sell them off speedily, but the advertisement will frequently lead you to the true cause. If it be stated that the owner is going abroad or for some other specified reason, that the entire stock must be sold at once, then my advice is be careful. This precaution is hardly necessary when you purchase birds from a well-known fancier, but at the same time it can do no harm.

R.

RUPTURED HENS.—If a hen gets ruptured through laying her eggs, catch her and immerse her bowels in tolerably hot water for a few minutes, then apply a little oil to the

distended womb with a feather, and try to press it back gently
with a piece of cotton wadding fastened to the end of a
finely-pointed pen-holder; if you fail to replace it the hen
will die.

S.

SCARLET FEVER.—Next to typhus fever, there is probably
no complaint from which birds suffer that is so fatal in its
consequences as scarlatina. Several years ago I had the misfortune to have a visitation of this direful malady of the
malignant type in my family, and I lost two of my children
in consequence. During this visitation in my household several
of my birds became suddenly ill, and after lingering a few
days they died. At first I did not take much notice of this
as I was in great trouble, and the whole of my children,
with one exception (an infant), being badly affected by this
fever, and most of them dangerously ill. As time advanced
I found that the greater part of my birds were being attacked
by some disease, and at this time I had a very large collection, among them several valuable prize birds. After a careful
examination of the dead birds, and a close observation of
the symptoms of those that were ill, I came to the conclusion that they had taken the fever from my children, who
were located in bedrooms on the same landing, but a few
yards away, there being seven rooms in all, and the birds
were in the one farthest away. I mentioned my suspicion
to the medical attendant who visited my family, and he
appeared amused and surprised and said he could not think
such a thing possible. But I was so convinced of the accuracy of my diagnosis that next day I dissected two birds
which had succumbed to the disorder, and from the appearance of the tongue, throat, and viscera, I was quite satisfied
that my theory was correct, and I fully convinced the doctor
that I had made no mistake.

I at once began to treat my patients for this complaint,
and out of about thirty-five birds thus affected, I saved
twenty-one. The symptoms of scarlatina differ somewhat from
those of typhus, but before I proceed further, I must mention

that there are three species of this disorder—*i.e.*, scarlatina simplex, or simple scarlet fever; scarlatina anginosa, scarlet fever attended with inflammatory sore throat; and lastly, scarlatina maligna, that is scarlet fever with malignant typhoid symptoms and sloughing sore throat. It was the latter and most dangerous type from which my children and birds suffered. Symptoms : This complaint begins with cold shiverings and lassitude, followed by restlessness and a loss of appetite. If you catch a bird affected with this complaint and examine its tongue, you will find it rough and coated with a sort of slimy mucus or yellow fur, at first slightly red, with raised papillæ, and after a day or two the tip and outer edges become intensely so, and you will find after a few more days, if of the virulent type, that the throat becomes swollen and inflamed. In other respects the symptoms very greatly resemble those of typhus, with the addition of a sort of dry cough, and after the third day the body assumes a red appearance on the feathers being blown back. If the bird is likely to recover the eruption will begin to disappear about the sixth day; but the danger is not then over, as the fever leaves the birds languid and debilitated, and nourishing food and tonics require to be administered.

In the malignant form the eyes of the bird affected become very dull, and there is generally a slight discharge from the nostrils of acrid matter. Treatment : Firstly, attend to the bowels. Put an ounce of Epsom salts, and a piece of Spanish juice the size of a Spanish nut, into a pint bottle, and fill it with warm water; when cold, and the ingredients are dissolved, give to the birds in place of the ordinary drinking water for twelve hours. Then give half the quantity filled up with water, and add to this twenty drops of sweet spirit of nitre and twenty drops of antimonial wine to each ounce of the former, to allay the symptoms. Give this fresh every morning until the fever has entirely abated. If the throat of the patient is swollen, make a gargle with twenty drops of muriatic acid to one and a half ounces of water, and to this add thirty drops of the tincture of myrrh ; open the mouth of the bird gently and hold it firmly, dip a small feather in the gargle and pass it a few times carefully into the throat, and quietly turn it round.

The diet should consist of white bread soaked in warm milk, given fresh two or three times a day, and as an occasional change sponge biscuit soaked in sherry wine and squeezed partly dry. After the sixth day, if the patient appears to be recovering, add to the drinking water, in place of the antimonial wine and nitre, thirty drops of the tincture of gentian, fifteen drops of diluted sulphuric acid, and a small quantity of the best gum arabic.

Ventilation is a great factor in restoring health to sufferers from this malady, therefore, if the weather is at all genial the window of the room should be opened, but all draughts must be rigorously guarded against. In cases of the malignant type the birds should be removed to pastures new, and the bird room and cages disinfected in the manner pointed out under the head of Typhus Fever. I have no doubt whatever that birds are more or less prone to all or most of the ills and epidemics that human flesh is heir to, but as the poor little mites cannot tell us of their troubles or describe their feelings otherwise than by their appearance and actions, it is often very difficult, and more particularly so to an inexperienced person, to diagnose correctly the ailments from which they suffer.

SORE FEET.—These are almost invariably produced through dirt and neglect. Birds get their feet clogged up with filth, which forms into little balls, hardens, and produces sores. This state of things ought not to exist. I have known fanciers supply their birds with horse-hair or cow-hair for the purpose of building their nests, and the birds have worked on with it until it has got so twisted and wrapped round their claws and feet that the disentanglement became a work of considerable difficulty and patience to overcome; and if birds are permitted to go about with the hairs fastened round their claws in this manner for any length of time together, they will most probably lose some of them.

Whenever you discover a bird in this plight, catch it, immerse the feet in warm water to free them from dirt, dry, and proceed to cut away the hairs with a sharp penknife or a pair of scissors, and, lastly, anoint any place which appears sore with a little sweet oil.

SURFEIT.—This complaint is usually produced either by a bird eating to excess, or by its being fed too long upon one particular kind of food without having a change. During this disease the insensible perspiration is impeded, and the skin is generally covered with a small, almost invisible, eruption, and the feathers gradually disappear from the head of the bird. A change of diet, something cooling, should be given, and a few drops of lime-juice added to the bird's drinking-water. Give it, once or twice a week, a drop or two of castor-oil internally, and anoint its head with a little pure olive-oil (free from scent), lard without salt, or spermaceti ointment, and the ailment will speedily disappear.

SWEATING.—See Chap. II., on " Breeding and Management," page 74.

SWOLLEN JOINTS.—I have known instances of birds having had their feet or legs caught in a loose wire, or in the thin wire used for securing the upright wires to the cross-bars of a cage front, and with struggling in their endeavours to free themselves they have injured their knee- or ankle-joints, or other portions of their limbs, which have become swollen and inflamed in consequence, or pulled a nail off one of their claws. When an event of this kind happens, catch the maimed bird and place the injured leg in hot water, as hot as you can bear your hand in without flinching; allow it to remain immersed for five minutes, afterwards dry the limb, and apply a little compound tincture of myrrh to the affected part with a feather.

SYNCOPE OR FAINTING.—This is caused by a diminution or complete interruption of the motion of the heart and of the function of respiration, accompanied by a suspension of the action of the brain, and a temporary loss of sensation, volition, and the other faculties, of which the brain is the organ. It is sometimes caused in the case of nervous birds by the sudden appearance of a cat or dog, or anything which may produce fear or fright; or it may proceed from a mechanical obstruction to the circulation, arising from organic affection of the heart or of the vessels in its vicinity. When a bird is observed to have a fit of this kind, remove it from the cage and dash cold water upon it, and if you have any spirit of ammonia in the house sprinkle a few drops on a pocket-handkerchief and put it lightly over the head of the bird; sometimes the attack proves fatal. I remember a gentleman once coming into my bird-room with a white hat on; he came suddenly forward to admire a Scotch fancy bird, a gem, which had won me several prizes in the best of company. The bird made an involuntary dash forward, and dropped to the bottom of the cage, and, despite my efforts to revive him, he died. He was a very nervous, timid bird.

T.

TUMOURS.—Tumours, or wens, are divided into two classes, *i.e.*, solid and encysted; simple or benign, or malignant. Birds are sometimes, but not frequently, affected with these extraneous growths about their heads, and they are mostly of that kind known as encysted tumours, and commence their growth at the base of the bill, and occasionally, but rarely, at the back or side of the head. These latter are in most cases what are known as solid tumours, and are always longer in maturing.

The solid tumour is generally enveloped in a dense cellular sheath. This covering separates the diseased from the healthy parts, whilst the cyst or encysted tumours, on the contrary, must be considered as an integral part of the tumour, for should any part of the cyst be left the disease is sure to be reproduced.

The principal forms of simple solid tumour are those termed adipose or fatty, the fibrous, exostosis, or bony tumour. The malignant are those known among the medical profession as encephaloid or brain-like tumour, melanoid, fungus, hæmatodes or bleeding cancer, &c. This disease is better known among fanciers as "cancer of the bill," "yellow gall," and "warts on the head." Discutients, such as iodine and mercury, are occasionally applied for the removal of these unsightly growths, but the "knife" or scissors is the only effectual remedy. Cut away the substance carefully but effectually, and if it bleeds rather freely apply a little burnt alum or a few drops of the muriated tincture of iron. Should these remedies prove unavailing, cautery must be resorted to, viz., burn the part with an iron previously heated to whiteness—a knitting-needle would be sufficient in a case of this kind; but I do not anticipate that it will ever be required, as I have never found it necessary, although I have cut off a good many and effected a permanent cure in every case. As soon as the bleeding has ceased, the part should be anointed with a little fatty matter of any sort, provided it does not contain salt; a little spermaceti ointment is as good as anything you could apply, and will, in the generality of cases, heal the wound in a short space of time. The old-fashioned and well-known cure for warts has in some cases been resorted to with success—*i.e.*, to tie a hair from the human head tightly round the extraneous growth, or a fine hair taken from the back of a horse or cow will do, and in a week or ten days the remedy will be complete, and the excrescence disappear, but success can only be expected in cases of adipose tumours.

TYPHUS FEVER.—Some twenty-five years ago, when I propounded the theory that birds suffered from fevers, such as typhus, and kindred diseases, many fanciers, I believe, thought that I had discovered a "mare's nest," but since then careful study and observation on my part, and that of several fanciers belonging to the medical profession, have proved beyond all reasonable doubt that birds as well as human beings are subject to these disorders. Typhus fever has been known to many fanciers for a long period under the common appellation of the "bird plague" or "bird cholera," but beyond the fact

that birds suffering from this malady died in a rapid and
unaccountable manner, they could form no conception as to
the real cause or nature of the disease. A careful study of
the symptoms, together with a close watchfulness of the progress of the complaint, and a post-mortem examination of
birds which died from this cause, led me to the conclusion
that it was neither more nor less than typhus fever, and my
diagnosis proved to be correct. Since then several of my
friends and acquaintances have had a visitation of this direful
malady, and among others that enthusiastic and successful
exhibitor, Mr. Thos. Thompson, of Lancaster, then living at
Preston, in Lancashire. Mr. Thompson had a most unfortunate and disheartening experience. At the time he had in
his possession probably the grandest lot of prize birds ever
owned by any fancier or combination of fanciers, and after
a most successful season, beating the Messrs. Mackley, G. E.
Russell, and all the best known and most successful exhibitors of crests, he had the misfortune to purchase some
evenly-marked Yorkshire birds, which introduced the disease
into his bird-room, and in a few weeks he lost some hundreds
of pounds' worth of the grandest crests, mules, &c., that have
ever been produced or seen in the hands of any single man,
including most of his champion crests, that had never been
beaten. He sent for me, and I did all I could to save the
remainder of his stock, but the disease had got such a hold
upon them that it was with the greatest difficulty that a few
of the best could be saved. This was in or about the year
1884. This misfortune caused him to suddenly relinquish the
fancy, and in losing him we lost one of the kindest, noblest,
and best of men that ever entered the arena as a canary
exhibitor. About 1888 or 1889, Mr. G. E. Russell, then living
at Brierley Hill, had a visitation of this scourge in his bird-
room, and that stayed his career as a successful exhibitor of
crested canaries. Many other fanciers of my acquaintance
have suffered similarly.

Birds are most liable to this disorder when about to moult,
and more particularly young birds when changing their nest

feathers for the adult plumage. At this period of a bird's life there is a great demand on the serum of the blood, and if there is not sufficient health and vigour to replenish this loss freely, stagnation or blood-ferment follows, which is supposed to create a bacillus, considered by medical men to be the origin of these disorders. There is a difficulty of getting rid of the excretory matter, and it lodges in the region of the vent, which is readily discernable on examination. This being the first symptom, the application of a purgative is at once necessary to get the bowels fully relieved: a small quantity of the carbonate and sulphate of magnesia, and two or three senna leaves, should be put in the drinking water, allowed to remain for two days, and renewed if necessary, until the excrement is natural in appearance and quantity. Some tonic medicine in the shape of gentian or camomile should also be added to the drinking water.

As soon as the malady is discovered, all birds not apparently affected with this complaint should be removed without delay from among the affected birds, and placed in fresh cages, which have been previously disinfected by the application of a solution of carbolic acid (1oz. of carbolic acid to each pint of hot water) freely used over the whole of the outside, and well saturated with Condy's Fluid on the inside. The birds should be removed, not only from the premises where the disease exists, but out of the town or village a few miles distant, and the room in which they are placed should be well sprinkled with Condy's Fluid, or have a vessel placed in the centre of it containing chlorate of lime. The birds should be kept moderately warm, and be fed with light but nutritious diet. They should have given them some mild aperient such as magnesia (20gr. to each ounce of water), and an infusion of senna leaves (1oz. to a pint of boiling water; infuse for two hours and give cold) added to their drinking water, renewed daily for three or four days, and the room should be freely ventilated during the day, but should be free from draughts.

If the slightest symptoms of typhus become observable among the removed birds, give at once two or three grains of James' Powder, six or eight drops of laudanum (in place of the magnesia and senna), and add twenty-five drops of sweet spirit of nitre as well, to every fluid ounce of water to be used in place of the ordinary drinking water. If the weather is mild, open the windows as wide as possible, and if practicable, get a current of air to pass through the room; but the night air and damp atmosphere must be entirely excluded.

The birds affected may be fed on rice cake soaked in sherry, and partly squeezed dry; and to this should be added a few drops of almond or salad oil. During the disease the following receipt will be found of much service: Tinct. of belladonna, 1dr.; Vin. ipecac., 2dr.; Tinct. aconit., 1dr.; Tinct. hyoscyami, 1dr.; Sp. ether nit., 3dr.; Tinct. gentian, ½oz. Add twenty drops of this mixture to each ounce of the ordinary drinking water, and twenty drops of the compound infusion of senna.

I have saved a great many birds by this treatment after being severely attacked by typhus. Try the receipt first given for mild cases, and if the disease continues to progress, resort to the last prescription.

After the fever has exhausted itself, gentle tonics and egg food should be given. Such tonics as gentian, camomile, and cinchona bark, made into weak infusions, and if during the summer, a small leaf of fresh young dandelion, well washed and partly dried, will be found serviceable in restoring the birds to health.

When the malady has entirely subsided, the whole of the cages, the room, and everything in and about it, must be thoroughly disinfected, including the hoppers, seed and water vessels. First remove the birds and " stove " the room and cages with brimstone for five or six hours, closing up every hole and crevice; the brimstone should be placed in the centre of the room in a strong earthenware vessel or iron crucible; a little oil or paraffin

may be added and set fire to and the door closed as speedily
as possible. After this operation the door and windows should
be left wide open for a period of ten or twelve hours to let out
the fumes, &c.; then the floor, ceiling, and walls should be well
washed with two or three gallons of hot water in which 1lb. of
soda and 2oz. of blue-stone have been dissolved. If the walls
are papered they should be entirely stripped bare and again disinfected by use of the wash; after this process leave the
windows open for a few days, and when the ceiling is again
white-washed add some Condy's Fluid to the whiting. A
temporary abode can be made for the birds by nailing some
half-inch wire netting over a few empty biscuit boxes, and
cutting out a temporary door at the back or side, to be
hung with leather hinges, and secured by a metal button,
the food and water being placed inside to save further
labour or trouble; or a temporary fly cage can be formed
in the recess of a room, or better still the birds allowed to
fly about in a spare empty room, which would be beneficial
to them in every way. After this has been done the whole of
the cages should be gone over again, first thoroughly washing
inside and out with soft soap, soda, and hot water (¼lb. of
soft soap and ½lb. of soda to each gallon of hot water); when
dry, coat them inside and out with the solution of carbolic
acid, or a strong solution of sulphate of copper (2oz. of sulphate to each gallon of water), allowing them to remain
exposed to the open air for twelve hours. Next day they
should be again washed all over with hot water in which a
good handful of common soda has been previously dissolved,
and lastly rinsed off with pure cold water. This process will
thoroughly disinfect both the cages and the room. A basin or
other vessel containing a quantity of chloride of lime placed
in the centre of the room will be found an excellent disinfec-
tant, and will purify the atmosphere. It will be well to expose
the cages in the open air for a few days before again using
them, so that they may get thoroughly sweetened.

All the birds which survive this crucial ordeal should,
before being restored to their domiciles, be well washed in

camphorated water made into a lather with white curd soap, and finally drenched with pure warm water, dried off with a linen rag or old silk handkerchief, and then allowed to completely dry themselves before a fire in a cage or suitable box.

By the early and vigorous adoption of these means the majority of your birds will be saved, and the disease entirely stamped out, but earnest and prompt action is a *sine quâ non* if your efforts are to be crowned with success, for this appalling malady spreads with terrible rapidity, and when it gets a firm footing its ravages are quite astounding. To a new beginner a visitation of typhus is most dispiriting, and causes many eager amateurs to relinquish their hobby.

The symptoms to be observed in diagnosing this disease are: First, the bird sits thick, and looks dull and heavy, and is very listless; it goes searching about the bottom of the cage as if in quest of something it wants but is unable to obtain; it moves in rapid succession, at first between the seed-hopper, the egg drawer, the water fountain, and the bottom of the cage, and in a short time it becomes weak and prostrate, with cold shiverings, and a good deal of thirst, the symptoms developing quickly. The eyes become dull and heavy looking, the bowels distended, the stools fetid, the tongue dry and parched, and if you catch up the little sufferer you will find it hot and feverish, and if you blow back the feathers of the body you will generally find an eruption. This eruption, which in a clear bird often looks quite livid, does not, as a rule, show itself until the second or third day. I consider this a hopeful sign, and with care birds so affected soon recover.

I am thankful to say that I have never experienced this disease in any form among my own birds, but I would recommend those fanciers who may have the misfortune to have a visitation of this terrible malady among theirs to remove those not affected to a separate room by themselves; keep them warm, and feed them upon light nutritious food. Their bowels must be kept open by the use of mild aperients, such as magnesia (20gr. of magnesia and six senna leaves to each

ounce of water), or a few drops of the infusion of senna mixed
with their drinking water; this must be removed once or twice
a day, and fresh water given them, in which two or three grains
of James' Powder must be dissolved, and fifteen to twenty
drops of laudanum added. Condy's Fluid or chloride of lime
should be freely sprinkled upon the floor of the room; the
cages should be thoroughly cleaned out, and a little of the
Condy's Fluid, diluted with water, dashed all over the cages
inside and out. If the weather is mild, let as much fresh
air into the room during the day as you possibly can, but
keep out the night air. Do not open the window if it is
damp or foggy. After the fever has entirely disappeared,
the whole of the cages should be washed out; cleanse them
thoroughly inside and out, using hot water and soap, with a
little common soda or washing powder. After they are dry
wash them out a second time with clean water, to which
must be added a quantity of carbolic acid; after this operation the cages should be exposed in the open air for two
or three days, and then rinsed off with pure water. Lastly,
whitewash them—if they have wooden backs, bottoms, tops,
and sides—with quick lime; but before you use it add a
little spirit of camphor—that is, camphor dissolved in spirit
of wine. This process ought to disinfect the cages and destroy
all contagious matter. The bird room likewise should undergo
a regular process of cleansing and disinfecting, or your labour
might be in vain.

V.

VERMIN.—See Chap. II., on "Breeding and Management,"
p. 52 ("Preparing Breeding Cages"), and also under "Parasites."

VOICE, LOSS OF.—See under "Loss of Voice."

W.

WARTS.—See under "Tumours."

WASTING AWAY.—See under "Decline."

WENS.—See under "Tumours."

WOUNDS.—From a variety of causes, principally accidents, or from an accumulation of hardened matter being forced from the feet of birds instead of being softened by the use of warm water, wounds or sores are engendered. The best treatment is first to cleanse the sore with a little pure spring water, in which a red-hot cinder has been deposited, or, where there is inflammation and irritation, with a little fuller's earth well moistened with water. Afterwards apply, once or twice a day according to symptoms, a little compound tincture of myrrh, with a feather, until the wound is healed, or Friar's Balsam may, in some cases, be used instead of the myrrh, with greater advantage.

I have now, I imagine, enumerated all the principal ills from which canaries suffer, and pointed out, as far as my experience has enabled me, the best mode of treatment and the best means of cure. I hope that those who try them will receive as much benefit from the application of many of the ingredients I have recommended as I have done myself, in which case they will have no cause to regret the efforts they may make to relieve their little suffering friends; but as many of the ailments from which they suffer can obviously be prevented, I must conclude by calling the attention of fanciers to that ever-to-be-remembered adage, " Prevention is better than cure."

CHAPTER V.

MOULTING.

MOULTING SEASON.—The moulting season extends from July to November in each year; in exceptional cases, where birds are permitted to breed so late as the months of August and September, it may last to the end of December, or longer; but when it reaches this advanced period it is regarded as unseasonable, and ought to be avoided if possible. Those birds bred in the spring and early summer months invariably get the best and most satisfactory moult, and appear far more improved by the change than those that are bred later on. Birds which are bred in August and September never appear to shed their feathers freely, and the change of plumage takes place (particularly if the weather is bad) almost imperceptibly.

Some naturalists assert that when birds do not cast their feathers at the proper time they get a new covering without shedding their old feathers; be this as it may, I have noticed that whenever a bird gets a "fresh coat" during cold weather, you rarely see any loose feathers about the cage.

CRITICAL TIME.—The moulting season is always considered the most critical period in the life of a bird; and much depends upon the manner in which it gets through this process or malady for its future well-being. This is strikingly the case with young birds, which, as a rule, are much more difficult to moult than older birds, for with them it is very similar in its effects to what the distemper is in young dogs, and it is quite as liable to be attended with baneful results. Some young hens fail to breed the first season, whilst many of the males are incapable of impregnating eggs; these and similar drawbacks

very frequently result from long and protracted moulting, engendered by cold or by improper diet or neglect, for the greatest
care and attention are necessary at this time.

AGE AT WHICH MOULT COMMENCES.—Young birds usually
begin to moult between the age of eight and ten weeks; those
that are hatched and reared at the commencement of the season
are generally a week or two longer in beginning than those
birds that are "backly bred." There is a very marked difference
in birds for moulting; some shed their feathers with great
freedom, whilst others have great difficulty in doing so.
Much, doubtless, depends upon the health and constitution
of the subject. A strong, healthy, robust bird always gets
over the moult much more easily than a puny, badly-reared
one—indeed, the change that takes place in the system at
this time terminates the existence of a great many such birds.

FOOD DURING MOULT.—Birds ought to be fed liberally
during the time they are moulting, and until they are quite
"fine" in feather; a few dainties may be given them occasionally, but sparingly, such as egg and bread, maw seed, millet
seed, linseed, groats, &c., but little or no hemp seed, the last-
named seed being very injurious to canaries, particularly when
given in unmeasured quantities. A little beef suet and a small
piece of an apple may be placed between the wires of their cages
for them to peck at now and again; and as they approach the
period of a full moult, I would recommend boiled carrots to be
given them fresh, twice or thrice a week, for several weeks in
succession, as it tightens the feathers, and puts a fine gloss upon
them. The carrots should be cut in thin slices, and placed
between the wires of the cages also. It is not advisable to give
canaries green food at this time; a fresh lettuce leaf or a
small quantity of ripe groundsel given judiciously will do them
no harm; but avoid giving them too much chickweed, particularly if it is not ripe, as it is apt to give them diarrhœa.

SYMPTOMS AND FIRST TREATMENT.—When a bird is about
to begin to moult it becomes drowsy and listless, and frequently goes hunting about the bottom of the cage and in the
seed hopper, apparently in search of something which it is

M 2

unable to find. These are unmistakable symptoms, and when observed a change of diet should be given—such as a little maw seed and a few groats, with an equal quantity of linseed and niger seed mixed together, or a few stalks of plantain— well known in Scotland by the appellation of "rats' tails"— will be found very serviceable at this time. In the course of a few days after you observe these signs, if the bird is in vigorous health, several loose feathers may be found lying here and there in and about the vicinity of its cage, and in a few days more you will observe two narrow stripes of feathers, much deeper in hue and more brilliant in colour than its former covering, on each side of its breast; this is a good omen, and the more rapidly these expand and spread, and the more vivid the colour becomes, the better, for it is all the more in favour of the bird getting speedily over it. Let the birds have as much fresh air as you can at this time, and be sure to keep their cages clean and supply them liberally with sand and fine gravel, which assists them to digest their food; but, above all things, be sure to keep them quite free from draughts of cold air, as nothing is so detri-mental to them as cold, for it not only checks, but in some instances it has been known to stop, the process entirely, and thereby caused the death of the birds. Never open the window of the bird room on a cold, bleak day, especially when the wind is from the east or north, or during damp and foggy weather; neither must you give them water to bathe in, except when the weather is hot and dry, and then not too frequently. A bath is very serviceable in promoting the growth of the feathers, but judgment is necessary to regulate its use.

A little magnesia should be given when the first symptoms of moult are observed, say, ten or fifteen grains to a small wineglassful of water; this should be given as ordinary drink-ing water. An old rusty nail, too, acts as a powerful tonic: this should be kept constantly in the drinking trough. A senna leaf or two may be used in preference to the mag-nesia—when thought desirable. A few shreds of meadow saffron placed in the drinking water at this time will likewise be found serviceable. I have found the following of great service during the process of the moult: Dissolve one ounce of Epsom salts in a quart of warm water, and when cold add two ounces of whiskey or brandy and two teaspoonfuls of lemon or lime juice, shake well up, and give this every third day in place of the ordinary drinking water. A pinch of milk of sulphur added to the bath is also useful.

PROTECTION FROM DRAUGHTS.—Sudden changes from heat to cold or cold to heat will be found a good method for inducing birds to begin to moult, when they fail to do so naturally at the proper season: but to change a bird that is already in the moult from a warm place to a cold one, is calculated to check the process and cause the bird, to use a common expression, to " stick in the moult," and nothing tends more to derange the health of a bird than an unto-ward circumstance of this kind. Warmth is a most essential and necessary element at this season, and some fanciers line the inside and cover the outside of their cages with baize or flannel, whilst others have panes of glass fitted to slide in front of them, with the intention of keeping them clean, quiet, and warm. I do not approve of either of those contrivances myself, for experience has taught me that all birds so moulted are very liable to take cold on the slightest exposure after-wards. I prefer a thin calico cover, or a cover of any mate-rial sufficient to keep out a cold draught; and birds moulted in this way are not nearly so susceptible to change of tem-perature as those that are moulted under either of the systems before named.

INFLUENCE OF LIGHT.—Other fanciers, again, moult their birds in dark rooms, gradually accustoming them to this change until they are able to find their food and water in total darkness. This plan is believed to intensify and preserve the colour of the birds, but I think it is frequently overdone. I am fully aware that the direct rays of the sun destroy the colour of birds when they are exposed to it; but if the bird room has a north or north-easterly aspect there is no fear of such an occurrence taking place, for it would only get a reflected light, which would do the birds no harm. My own bird room looks due north-east, and directly opposite to it is a large building used as a chapel. This shuts off a great deal of light, and acts as a protection against the cold winds, consequently I have rarely been necessitated to cover my birds, either whilst moulting or afterwards; and I have exhibited both Cinnamon and Norwich Fancy canaries, moulted in open cages, at several of our best shows, and some of them were never once beaten. I merely mention this fact to show that I am not endeavouring to propound a theory that is impracticable. I may likewise mention that for depth, richness, and purity of colour, they were unsurpassed; and yet these birds were never covered, excepting when the room was being swept or the cages cleaned out.

FORCING A MOULT.—It is a difficult matter to get some birds to moult at all, particularly those that are out of health or permitted to breed to an advanced period of the year. If a bird fails to moult in any year, it will assuredly die in the following spring or sooner. If an old bird shows no signs of moulting before the end of September (which is beyond the proper season) place it in a small box cage, and after it is quite familiar with the arrangement, and knows where to find both food and water, commence to cover it gradually until it can feed in total darkness; then place the cage in a very warm part of a room where a fire is kept burning almost constantly. If there should happen to be a closet by the side of the chimney, and a sufficiency of air can get to it, place it there, as it will require great artificial heat to produce the desired symptoms. Being condemned to utter darkness will most likely cause the bird to fret, and this sometimes effects the change sought for. Before confining the bird it will be as well to give it a little magnesia in its drinking water, or a senna leaf or two, as a slight aperient is requisite. Keep the bird closely covered until it begins to cast its feathers freely, when it may be gradually uncovered and removed to a cooler place, but not into a room without fire, until the return of genial weather in the following spring. If this method fails to bring the bird into the moult, then it must be removed to an opposite temperature, which in nine cases out of ten will produce the effect desired. It is considered a commendable practice to put a small quantity of soot in the drinking water to encourage a free moult. I have also found the following mixture of great service : Vinum colchici, 3dr. ; sp. ether nit., ½oz. ; water sufficient for six ounces. Give a teaspoonful of this to every fluid ounce of water in place of the ordinary drinking water.

MOULTING BOX FOR LONDON FANCY.—I am convinced that much depends upon the health of a bird for reaping the full advantages that are to be derived from moulting, both in colour and feather, and I cannot help thinking that too much close covering is bad for birds and pernicious in its consequences. A fine muslin or thin calico cover, that will admit the air freely, can in no way prove injurious to them, and may be found useful in helping to keep them clean. In moulting London Fancy canaries, it is the practice to place show specimens in cages made expressly for them. These cages have solid wood backs, ends, and bottoms; the top likewise is made of wood, but the front half of it is so constructed as to turn back at pleasure, as it is hung with hinges; the front is wired closely, and a small frame, wired in the same way, is made to fit into that portion of the top that folds back; a framed glass slide is made to cover the front, and after the birds are placed in the cages these slides are put a little way over at first, and closed up until they gradually extend across the entire front; the lids are then propped up a little way when the weather is sultry to let in a supply of fresh air; this is termed "box moulting."

It is doubtless very necessary that birds of this variety intended for exhibition should be kept quiet, and to effect this object they require to be pretty closely covered; but I have a decided aversion to "box moulting," and entertain the idea that a bird of this kind can be moulted quite as well and quite as advantageously in an open wire cage, with a thin calico or holland cover made to fit over it, similar to a nightcap, but open at one side and tied with strings; a piece should be notched out where the seed and water vessels fit on, so that they can be removed without disturbing or frightening the birds. The reason that so much care and attention are required in moulting London Fancy canaries is this: if they happen to get excited and dash about the cage, they are very liable to knock some of their wing or tail feathers out, and these would be reproduced clear, and probably spoil the chance of obtaining a prize at a show.

I have moulted show Lizards in the manner I have described, and nothing could have been invented to moult them more to my entire satisfaction; and, next to London Fancies, there is probably no variety that requires so much care bestowed upon them as Lizard canaries, for if they beat out any of their tail or wing feathers, they become "mooned" at the ends when reproduced, and this detracts from their merits.

MOULTING IN NUMBERS.—Those fanciers who breed canaries on an extensive scale are frequently obliged to draft off their birds in batches of twenty, thirty, forty, or fifty together, and place them in large cages, or in an aviary or room to moult. It is not a desirable example to imitate; but where such an arrangement is unavoidable I should certainly prefer a room or aviary to cages for this purpose, for nothing is more injurious to the health of birds at this critical season than overcrowding; and, unless they are strong and healthy, they are almost certain to succumb, if kept in large numbers in too limited a space. Besides, many birds are of a quarrelsome and mischievous disposition, and appear to delight in plucking the others. More particularly is this the case with cock canaries, and if they should happen to take a dislike to one of their number, which I have known them to do, they chase and peck the unfortunate wretch most unmercifully; and if it is not speedily removed they will probably torment it until they kill it. The only means of preventing these untoward occurrences, when circumstances will not admit of any other alternative, is to keep them in closely covered cages, almost in total darkness; and this is what I object to, for I cannot be persuaded that birds can continue in health very long under this treatment, as it is certain to affect both their bodies and spirits prejudicially. Where a number of birds are kept together in one cage, and it is observed that one of them is bleeding at the top of the pinion or shoulder blade, or elsewhere, remove it at once, for every bird in the cage will have a peck at the injured part whenever an opportunity is afforded of doing so. It is an objectionable practice to place goldfinch and canary mules along with canaries in the same cage, for they are naturally mischievous and meddlesome, and are sure to pluck and harass the canaries.

MOULTING SHOW BIRDS.—In the case of show birds of any variety, it is always best to moult them, and keep them during the show season in cages by themselves; and in the case of London Fancy and Crested Norwich canaries it is absolutely necessary to do so. Two birds, such as clear Norwich Fancy, Scotch Fancy, Yorkshire Fancy (clears), or Cinnamons may be moulted together in the same cage, although they are of that class known as show birds, provided always that they agree, and that the cage or compartment is sufficiently large to admit of this being done—the space should not be less than sixteen inches in height and width, and seven or eight inches in depth from back to front. When birds are not intended for exhibition it is not necessary to be so particular with them. If a show bird is being moulted or kept in an open cage, and is observed to put its head frequently through the wires or "water hole"— *i.e.*, the aperture made to allow it to get readily at its drinking water—something must be done to·break it of this bad habit, or it will in all probability chafe the feathers at the back of its head or on its breast, which would in all likelihood be the means of preventing it gaining a prize, for it would have the appearance of having been intentionally plucked. A piece of cardboard fastened to either side of its cage will generally put a stop to this practice; if not, a light covering placed over the cage will have the desired effect.

Six or eight birds, or more, may be kept in one cage to moult, provided it is sufficiently roomy and otherwise suitable; but it is not a commendable method to pursue, and when resorted to, it will be well to keep the males and females separate—that is to say, so many cocks together in one cage, and so many hens in another, as they will be found to agree much better in this way; for when they are kept all together attachments not

unfrequently spring up between different birds, and this often
leads to jealousy and discontentment on the part of others;
and bickerings and strife are engendered, and other ill consequences ensue, which it is best to obviate when possible.

INFLUENCE OF FOOD ON COLOUR.—CAYENNE MOULTING.—
It is now an acknowledged fact that the colour of birds can be
greatly influenced by the food given them whilst they are
passing through the moult; and in order to reap the full
benefit that is to be derived from this treatment, it is necessary to administer the stimulants required to produce this
change when the birds reach the age of seven or eight weeks,
and it should be continued until they are four or five months
old.   Formerly marigold flowers, beetroot, carrot, cochineal,
saffron, madder (for Cinnamon canaries), annato, and other
compounds were had recourse to for this object, but these
ingredients have been entirely superseded by the use of cayenne
pepper, and this is given to them in the manner following: To
one hard-boiled egg, add two small biscuits (wine or luncheon),
and two large teaspoonfuls of the condiment.   The egg should be
chopped fine, and the biscuits grated ; a good-sized teaspoonful
of this mixture may be given to each bird daily.   Nearly all
birds refuse to eat it at first; but if you remove all other food
from them for a day or two they will ultimately do so, and when
once they get accustomed to it, they devour it most voraciously,
and appear to like it very much.   Whilst they are under this
regimen they should have constant access to canary seed, but no
rape, and a little mustard seed and maw seed should be given
them once or twice a week, as a change of diet, to keep them in
health.   Prior to the discovery of the cayenne process, it was
proved beyond doubt that mustard seed improved the depth and
increased the intensity of colour in canaries.   The credit of
discovering the cayenne feeding is, I believe, due to a weaver
residing at Sutton Ashfield, near Nottingham, although it has
been claimed by other people.   Being a recent invention, it is
difficult to say what effect it may have on the constitution of
birds, but I am afraid not a very salutary one. *Capsicum
annuum*, or, as it is commonly called, cockspur pepper, is an
annual plant, a native of South America, and cultivated in large

quantities in our West India islands, and often in our own
gardens. The pods are long, pointed, and pendulous; first
green in colour, and when ripe bright orange red. The cayenne
pepper sold in shops is an indiscriminate mixture of the powder
of the dried pods of several species of capsicum; but that which
is the hottest of all, and consequently considered the best, is the
variety known as *Capsicum frutescens*, or bird pepper. When
used immoderately it is supposed to occasion visceral obstruction, especially of the liver. Great care should be exercised in
its use, for it is sometimes adulterated with the red oxide of
lead, which is a powerful poison. I am disposed to think that
it has a detrimental effect on the voices of birds, and cannot
therefore recommend the use of it to the canary-fancier with
any degree of confidence.

I may mention here that a number of fanciers give their
birds saffron cake, with the twofold motive, first to promote the
process of the moult, and secondly to improve the colour of the
feathers, though I have little faith in some of these nostrums.
I have found, however, that a few shreds of meadow saffron
immersed in the drinking water is beneficial to a bird whilst
moulting, but it should be used cautiously, as its action varies
very much according to the season of the year it is gathered.
Colchicum combines an anodyne effect with a drastic operation,
as an emetic, purgative, or diuretic, and has in some instances
been known to produce fatal effects.

THE INFLUENCE OF VARIOUS INGREDIENTS ON THE COLOUR
OF CANARIES AND THEIR HYBRIDS.—Since the first edition
of the " Canary Book" appeared, long and rapid strides have
been made in the field of experience with regard to the effect
of cayenne pepper and other ingredients administered to
canaries and their hybrids during the process of the moult, and
much correspondence has taken place in various journals interested in ornithological subjects on the indiscriminate use of
cayenne pepper and its effect on the constitution of birds.

Men of experience in the world of science have entered into
the controversy, and those in the best position to know—surgeons
and veterinary surgeons, who have dissected various specimens
which had partaken of this condiment, and were submitted

to them for their opinion as to the cause of death—appear to be agreed that it is decidedly detrimental and injurious to the health of birds, and calculated very materially to shorten their existence, more especially when given in excess. I do not think that a moderate use of it is so injurious as some people suppose, but unfortunately, there are some men so constituted by nature that speculation seems to be the charm, and, I might say, the very essence of their existence; without it such men would in all probability languish and die. Men of this peculiar temperament who, in addition, possess a considerable measure of ambition as well, are apt at times to do very outrageous and unaccountable things, and their actions betoken them to be, well—I will put it mildly, and say very indiscreet, and their indiscretion leads them to adopt plans and methods that wise men would shudder to think about. The only question is, what will these men not do to carry out their ambitious designs? Such men are to be found in the bird fancy, and such men it is that overdo everything they take in hand, by carrying their schemes and ideas to excess.

From two teaspoonfuls of cayenne pepper to an ordinary hen's egg, and an equal quantity of biscuit—quite enough in all conscience to feed little delicate birds upon—these men have ventured, and have given their birds as much as six and eight teaspoonfuls of the most powerful pepper procurable to the quantity of egg and biscuit mentioned, in order, if possible, to outvie their brother fanciers in obtaining high colour in their show specimens, and some, not content with this piece of gross cruelty, have actually removed all other food from within their reach, and have left the miserable little wretches no choice between eating it or dying of starvation. I have often wished the Humane Society could interfere and punish such unfeeling and heartless beings, and also for the inhuman method now adopted of pulling out the whole of the flight and tail feathers of young birds, when placed in the moulting cage, in order that these feathers, which are never shed by birds at their first moult, may also become steeped in the unnatural colour supplied to them through the circulation of the blood. Others I have known who have gone entirely beyond the cayenne in its normal condition, and have had the oil extracted from the pepper, which is believed to be the active colouring principle, so that they might give it in the highest and most concentrated form; and how many birds have perished through these acts of rashness and folly no living person can tell. Cayenne given in such unmeasured quantities must of necessity be attended by the most baneful results, and those people who have the temerity to purchase such highly fed specimens are sure to suffer for their foolhardiness. The depth of colour in a Norwich canary is not always a guarantee of high breeding, as many circumstances are necessary to bring about a successful issue. Three birds chosen from the same parents, and treated alike, will often vary as much as three birds chosen promiscuously out of a large quantity of mixed birds, so much depends on the constitution of the bird to stand this untoward treatment, and the palest coloured specimen selected will frequently turn out the richest coloured bird at the finish. Sib bred birds will show the effect of the food sooner than those not bred akin, but few of them can stand the treatment.

The method adopted by the most successful exhibitors, who moult large quantities of birds for show, is to have a moulting house built expressly for the purpose; some are built of brick and slated, and others of wood only. When built of the latter material, a double wall or partition is used, these being about three inches apart and filled with sawdust. In any case, the foundation should be a dry one, and the house should have at least one step up to it; and, if built of wood, the roof, as well as being double boarded and lined with sawdust, should be covered with roofing felt to keep out the wet. A ventilator should be placed in the centre of the roof, one that revolves with the wind is best. The only light should be obtained from one or two fixed sky-lights, and a closing shutter should be made to fit over each inside, to be so constructed that the shutters will slide backward and forward, so that, whenever Sol appears in the brightness of his effulgence, his golden and gladdening rays may be shut off, and the poor little prisoners enveloped in utter darkness, as light in any form has the effect of lessening the colour of the plumage of the birds, however deep and intensely brilliant that may be, and each cage from floor to ceiling must be covered with calico, or other material of a like nature. The birds must not be put into total darkness when they are first placed in the moulting house; this must be done gradually during the first fortnight. It is also necessary to have the house heated with hot-water pipes—a double layer of pipes is best. My own experience can testify to the fact that artificial heat and an equilibrium of temperament of, say, from 50deg. to 60deg., are of the greatest possible advantage to those who wish to moult birds for the show bench, and more particularly when very deep colour or good, well-developed crests are required. Those who have no such appliances stand at a great disadvantage against those who use them. The more rapidly a bird moults the better it will appear.

Egg as a medium for the pepper food is not now considered the best vehicle for administering it, and various preparations of farinaceous foods are used instead. The great object is to keep the birds plump and healthy during this trying ordeal, as without these conditions the birds are not likely to make successful competitors. Ground rice, arrowroot, fine oatmeal, ground linseed, and powdered loaf sugar, with port wine and sherry, are among the principal ingredients now used.

The following formula is a favourite mixture; it has been used by some of the most prominent exhibitors of the present day with considerable success, and a high price was paid for the recipe not many years ago: R.—2dr. of meadow saffron, boiled in 8oz. of water and strained; 6oz. of port wine and 4oz. of Maraschino wine; honey, 2oz.; powdered loaf sugar, 1oz. Mix well. Add a teaspoonful of this mixture to the egg and pepper food three times a week.

The latest introduction in cayenne is that which is now known among bird fanciers as "cold pepper" or "tasteless pepper," in place of the pungent sort.

Cayenne pepper can be robbed of its pungent qualities by triturating it with oil; whether the so-called tasteless pepper is procured by this method, or whether it is simply a compound partaking largely of other ingredients containing the desired colouring matter, I am unable to say; but, from my own experiments, I am thoroughly convinced that birds can be produced as high in colour as those fed on the very choicest cayenne without a particle of pepper being used; and if I had been as reckless in the use of some of the articles I have experimented with, as some of my *confrères* have been in the *ad libitum* use of cayenne, it is more than probable that I should have produced specimens quite as rich in colour as any yet exhibited; but I am gifted with a considerable amount of caution, and, I trust, of common humanity likewise, and I must, therefore, feel my way gradually. I am quite satisfied with the result of my experiments so far, and have obtained some beautifully-coloured specimens. For the benefit of those who desire to experiment for themselves, I append a list of the articles which I have used for obtaining colour; they must only be used during the moulting season:

Alkanet root, beetroot, carnation clove, catechu, cardamom (lesser), cochineal, cinchona bark, dragon's blood, infusion of red rose leaves, gum kino, madder, meadow saffron, Parish's syrup, logwood, port wine, sherry wine, and Maraschino wine. I likewise in some cases use some of the mild alkalies to deepen the colours. These hints will enable fanciers to experiment on a somewhat extensive scale, and their ingenuity may lead some of them to extend this field of operation even beyond my own, and I confidently hope and believe that, in a short time, a compound will be discovered that will entirely supersede the use of cayenne, without in any way injuring or prejudicially affecting the health and constitution of birds. Vegetable and alkaline products I find the best. I am not sure whether canaries cannot be obtained of colours never before seen. My experiments have not yet been extended in that direction, my sole object up to the present time being to obtain the colour so much sought after, *i.e.*, deep orange, bordering on red, and orange lemon, without having recourse to cayenne, which is beyond all doubt pernicious in its consequences. It affects the larynx; consequently, it acts as a deterrent to the vocal organs of birds fed with it. It enlarges the liver, and has a very prejudicial effect on birds intended for breeding. It is injurious to health, and, consequently, very materially shortens the lives of birds fed with it. Accum, writing on cayenne pepper, says :

"It is sometimes adulterated with red lead to prevent its becoming bleached on exposure to light. This fraud may readily be detected by shaking up part of it in a stoppered vial containing water impregnated with sulphuretted hydrogen gas, which will cause it speedily to assume a dark, muddy, black colour, or the vegetable matter of the pepper may be destroyed by throwing a mixture of one part of the suspected pepper and three of nitrate of potash (or two of chlorate of potash) into a red hot crucible, in small quantities at a time. The mass left behind may then be digested in weak nitric acid, and the solution assayed for lead by water impregnated with sulphuretted hydrogen. If the suspected cayenne pepper is shaken up in a bottle of clear water, the rapidity with which the red lead sinks to the bottom will give an approximate test of the presence of the poison."

Brande, M'Culloch, Mitchell, Normandy, and others all agree as to the frequent use of red lead, and the last-named chemist mentions finely powdered brick dust as an ingredient used to retain a bright colour, as also red ochre, Venetian red and cinnabar, vermilion, or sulphuret of mercury.

The result of the *Lancet's* analysis of cayenne pepper was that out of twenty-nine samples submitted to examination, twenty-five were adulterated, and only four were genuine. Twenty-two contained mineral colouring matter ; thirteen red lead, often in large quantities; seven Venetian red, red ochre, and brick dust; one sample cinnabar, vermilion, or sulphuret of mercury; six ground rice, coloured with red lead or ferruginous earth ; and two rice only, coloured with red lead.

As red lead and vermilion, or sulphuret of mercury, are powerful poisons, fanciers who give this commodity to their birds in unmeasured quantities little know the risk they are running, and to what dangers their valuable show birds are exposed.

After birds have finished moulting they ought not to have

any more of the cayenne food, or other food for giving colour supplied to them, as it only affects them during the period of shedding their feathers. Those which have been kept covered should also be brought back to the light of day by degrees, and not suddenly, as the change might damage their eyes. The best cayenne to use is Aveper, or sweet pepper.

RED-FED AND YELLOW-FED CANARIES—ALTERATION IN CLASSIFICATION.—At a special meeting held at the Crystal Palace Show in 1890, at which many of the most prominent breeders and fanciers of canaries were present, it was unanimously resolved to abolish the classes known as "Cayenne-fed" and "Non-cayenne-fed," and substitute for these "Red-fed" and "Yellow-fed" classes, as it is well known that most of the winning specimens shown in the so-called "Non-cayenne-fed" classes were really cayenne-fed, but so sparely as in many cases to defy detection; hence it was thought that by doing away with the old titles, which prevented conscientious fanciers from entering, and substituting the new titles, it would leave it open to fanciers generally to use such condiments or colouring matter as best suited them to obtain the colour they really desired. Now the great difficulty to be overcome is to fix a standard of colour for birds to be shown in the "Yellow-fed" classes, as a great many birds were shown last year that were bordering on the orange, which is neither red nor yellow, but a happy blending of the two.

It would be well if the conference were to have another meeting, and decide upon a shade of colour which could be fairly claimed as yellow—either a bright chrome-yellow, a gamboge-yellow, a King's-yellow, a yellow-lake, a yellow-ochre, or a Naples-yellow. The first-named, being the richest and brightest, would doubtless find a majority of fanciers in its favour. If this question were settled, then a freshly-painted piece of wood or cardboard of the proper colour should be placed at the head of each class at every show, for the guidance of the judges and the public. I consider this the only satisfactory method to adopt to prevent disputes. Even

N

with these precautions occasional disputes may arise, for
every one is not possessed of discrimination in shades of
colour, but, under ordinary circumstances, such an arrangement ought to prove satisfactory. The following formulæ
will be found valuable in producing the colours required:

Red-fed.—Formula 1: Linseed oil, 1 pint; dragon's blood
(finely powdered), 1oz. Simmer together on a slow fire for
half-an-hour. One teaspoonful of the compound should be
added to half of a hard-boiled egg and an equal quantity of
crushed biscuit or breadcrumbs, and, lastly, a dessert-spoonful of moist sugar added. Incorporate the whole thoroughly;
this quantity would serve three birds for one day's supply;
it should be given fresh.

Formula 2: Take of red sandal-wood (finely powdered), 1oz.;
the best red Natal pepper (fresh), 2oz.; loaf sugar (powdered),
2oz.; sweet or tasteless pepper, 3oz.; add 1½ teaspoonfuls of
this mixture to the yolks of two hard-boiled eggs and a
table-spoonful of finely-powdered biscuit, and moisten the
whole by adding 30 to 40 drops of the following solution:
Put 1dr. of hay saffron into 2oz. of rum or brandy, let it
digest for six days, then strain through a piece of fine muslin.
During this feed let your birds have red marigolds and the
flowers of nasturtiums to eat *ad libitum*. This is a first-class
colour-feed for the highest colour obtainable.

Formula 3: Red Natal pepper, 4oz.; tasteless pepper, 4oz.;
red sandal-wood (finely powdered), 2oz.; powdered cochineal
(the black bug), 1oz.; moist sugar, 8oz. A teaspoonful to be
added to each egg and moistened with a strong solution of
saffron made as mentioned in last formula.

Yellow-fed.—Formula 1: Nepaul pepper, 2oz.; turmeric,
3oz. Add 1 teaspoonful of this mixture to each hard-boiled
egg, and an equal quantity of powdered biscuit or breadcrumbs. Put 2dr. of saffron in a bottle with 4oz. of sherry
wine; let it digest for seven days, strain through muslin, and
add a teaspoonful of this to every two eggs given. Let the
birds have a mixture of canary- and mustard-seed in equal
proportions and a supply of yellow marigold flowers.

Formula 2 : Annato (air dried and crushed), 2oz. ; turmeric, 2oz. ; salad-oil, 4oz. Triturate and keep in a warm place for three or four days; add 2 teaspoonfuls of this to each hard-boiled egg and biscuit powder (equal quantity) and a tea-spoonful of good brown sugar or honey. Mix into a paste not too stiff. Give marigold flowers freely and canary- and mustard-seed in equal quantities.

Formula 3: Nepaul pepper, mustard, turmeric, and ground ginger, each 2oz.; moist sugar, 8oz. Take 2dr. of hay or meadow saffron, and add to it 4oz. of good sherry wine; digest for seven days, and strain. To one egg and two small biscuits crushed to powder, add a teaspoonful of each of the above compounds; this will be sufficient for three birds. Prepare it fresh every morning, and let the birds have a constant supply of canary- and mustard-seed, mixed in equal proportions. This is said to be a very satisfactory receipt for producing a good bright yellow colour. Give marigold flowers *ad libitum.*

DAMP ROOMS.—Whatever you do, be sure that you do not put birds in a damp room to moult, nor in a room where gas is constantly used, for it is more hurtful than most people suppose, and has, I doubt not, been the means of destroying thousands of birds. It sets them into the moult at unseasonable times of the year, and occasionally causes loss of voice. It matters not how healthy or robust a bird may be, it cannot thrive in a vitiated or frequently overheated atmosphere.

PRESERVING COLOUR.—It is a difficult matter to preserve the colour of show-birds throughout an entire season, especially when they are exhibited frequently, for the action of the light destroys the colour. The best plan to adopt where it is con. venient to do so is to put two or three panes of ruby-coloured glass in the bird-room window, and shut off all the other approaches of light. This can be done by coating over the remaining squares with a mixture of thick glue size and lamp-black, or a board or shutter could be used ; either would do. The ruby glass neutralises the chemical action of the light, and

N 2

consequently preserves the colour of the birds intact; but by all means let them have a plentiful supply of fresh air. It is said by some old experienced exhibitors that it is not possible to keep a bird "up" in colour for a whole season; and that it is necessary for any one to have three or four prize birds to accomplish anything approaching a feat as a successful exhibitor; but I can assure those who feel disposed to try this plan that they will be well satisfied with the result.

CRESTED BIRDS sometimes have a difficulty in throwing off their head gear when moulting; when this is found to be the case, remove the feathers by hand. Do it as gently as you can, a few at a time, day by day, until all are withdrawn; they come off very easily at this time, and do not cause pain to the birds. It is very desirable that the moulting of the crest should not be protracted, or it will appear stunted in its growth.

If a show-bird has the misfortune to damage a tail- or wing-feather, it should be withdrawn as soon as the mishap is discovered.

Cayenne feeding and artificial heat—say about 60deg. Fahr. —especially the latter, are great factors in developing and increasing the size of the crest in Crested Norwich and Lancashire Coppy Canaries.

During the process of the moult it is necessary to feed liberally, and more particularly those birds which appear out of sorts, or those that have been bred with for several months. The process of moulting greatly reduces the strength, and frequently impairs the vitality of birds; so that strengthening and invigorating food, and a plentiful supply of pure air, free from draughts, are of considerable importance at this period. Hard-boiled eggs mixed with bread or biscuit, a few groats, a little hemp-seed, inga-seed, maw-seed, and linseed, together with a bit of sweet apple or a moderate quantity of fresh green food, often will tempt them to eat and uphold their strength. Where a large quantity of birds are kept for stock purposes, one or other of the compounds may be used with advantage and at small expense. A bath during warm dry days will be found of much service.

CHAPTER VI.

MISCELLANEOUS.

DIARY.—Those bird fanciers who intend to breed birds for exhibition or profit should keep a diary or record of their proceedings and success during each breeding season, and also a "Stud Book," to enable them to trace without difficulty the pedigrees and performances of those birds which comprise their studs.

The diary ought to be begun at the commencement of the breeding season, and continued to the end of the year, or longer if desirable—at all events until all the young birds are over the moult and the surplus stock disposed of; every event should be chronicled therein, such, for example, as the full particulars of the birds you breed from, the dates of pairing, laying, setting, hatching, &c. A few minutes should be devoted to this important duty every day, say, immediately after breakfast, if convenient, if not, at some more suitable time of day; but do not procrastinate, neither must an entry be omitted, as this would greatly mar the value of the journal. Each bird ought to have a distinguishing name or number, so that the produce of each individual pair of birds could be easily traced from one generation to another, and their blood-relationship established clearly beyond doubt. The diary should be about 14in. by 10in., moderately thick, and either plain or ruled with horizontal lines only. An entire leaf should be appropriated to the use of each pair of birds for the season. Every

occurrence should be fully recorded in this book, and if properly
and carefully kept it will prove both valuable and interesting
for future reference.   The one kept by myself is arranged as in
the following page.

When a bird dies or is sold, the fact should be duly recorded
in the column headed "Remarks." If a bird dies during the
breeding season, and the survivor of the pair is mated with
another partner, it will be advisable to make a new entry in the
diary, as if it were a distinct pair of birds.   It will be found a
somewhat tedious occupation to keep a journal of this description at first, but after you get accustomed to it, you will regard
it more in the light of a pleasant pastime than that of an
arduous task; and I can assure those who adopt this method
that the perusal of these records in after years affords an agreeable, interesting, and instructive amusement, and the amount
of pleasure derivable from such a source can only be realised
by those people who are themselves ardent and enthusiastic
lovers of birds.

STUD BOOK.—Having given on the opposite page a specimen
entry of my mode of keeping a Diary of Bird Breeding, I will
now proceed to give one of my "Stud Book" as well.   This
book can be compiled from the diaries principally, but whenever
you make a new purchase, or claim a bird at any show, you
must find out its pedigree as best you can; if you fail to do
this, then you must content yourself by entering it with such
particulars as you know, and state such facts as the following :
"Claimed at . . . . Show, No. 301, V.H.C.," or whatever else
may be the state of the case.

If only it would become a general practice to show all birds
with a distinguishing name at our exhibitions, in the same way
as dogs and other animals are shown, it would give a keener
zest to those who are directly interested in them, and a stud
book could be kept much easier, and the pedigrees traced back
for many more generations ; but, as matters stand at present,
few fanciers care to go beyond the performances of the birds
they possess, and that of their parent birds, and few, if any,
attempt to get beyond the performances of their grandsires and
granddams, because it necessitates such a large amount of

Names of Birds.	No. of Cage.	Description or Title.	Bred by	Age of Bird.	Performances, if known.	Date of Pairing.	Hen laid.	Hen set.	Number of Eggs.	Hen hatched.	Number hatched.	Number reared.	Description of Progeny.	Remarks.
BRILLIANT	3	Buff Cinnamon Cock.	Self	Nine months	2nd prize Berwick, v.h.c. Middlesboro. v.h.c. Berwick, only time shown, in 1870.	Feb. 21.	Mar. 10.	Mar. 13.	Set with 3, laid 4.	3 Mar. 27. 1 Mar. 28.	4	3	2 Jonque Cocks, 1 Buff Hen.	One bird died in moulting. One Jonque cock stood 1st Darlington, 1st Stockton, 1st Sunderland, 1st Berwick, only times shown. The other, 2nd Middlesboro', v.h.c. Darlington, v.h.c. Berwick. Sold to Mr. P., Coventry. Kept hen to breed from.
BEAUTY		Jonque Cinnamon Hen.	Self	Eight months	v.h.c. Berwick, only time shown in 1870.		Apl. 18.	Apl. 21.	Set with 3, laid 5.	5th May 3, and on 6th 1. Total 4.	4	4	2 Jonque Cocks, 1 Buff Hen, 1 Jonque Hen.	Kept both hens. Exchanged one cock with Mr. A., Coventry; one with Mr. H., Middlesboro.'

EXAMPLE OF STUD BOOK.

Name, Age and Description of Bird, Name of Breeder, Performances.	Conqueror's Pedigree, also Performances of Sire and Dam.	Pedigree of Sire and Performances of Grand Sire.	Pedigree of Dam and Performances of Grand Dam.	Remarks.
CONQUEROR. Age 7 months, buff cinnamon cock, bred by self, stood as follows:— 1st prize Middlesboro', 1st prize Darlington, 1st prize Scarboro', 1st prize Berwick, in 1872. Bred in May, 1872. Only times shown	By own buff cinnamon cock, winner of following prizes: 2nd Stockton, 1st Sunderland, 1871, Only times shown. Out of jonque hen, v.h.c. at Berwick, only time shown.	Buff cock by my own old jonque cock. 1st Durham, 3rd Berwick, and 2nd Belford, 1870, Only times shown, Out of a hen bred by Mr. J. Stainsby, of Sunderland, from his prize strain.	By Mr. Stainsby's old jonque cock, winner of several prizes, out of a hen from G. Moore's, of Northampton, prize strain.	I bred with this bird in 1873, and sold him to Mr. C. W., Darlington.

writing; but if a bird were famed by a name or title, the record of that name and that of its owner would be all that would be needful to bring it vividly before the recollection of those men who are learned in " birdology," for they alone can properly appreciate the value of a strain of birds that have repeatedly won honours. We should then have the satisfaction of being able to trace any bird of renown and distinction after this manner— Brown's Warrior, Smith's Conqueror, Jones's Beauty, and so on ; and these appellations, or similar ones, would in a short time become just as familar to our ears as are those of Fletcher's Rattler and Pickett's Tyneside, and other celebrities in the dog world.

Mice or Rats in Bird Rooms.—One of the greatest annoyances that a bird fancier has to encounter is when any of these pests make an inroad into his aviary or bird room, for they are not only mischievous and troublesome, but even dangerous and destructive, and when once they get a firm footing in any place they are most difficult to dislodge.

Whenever you discover the presence of mice among your birds, you must not neglect to examine the whole of the seed-hoppers and feeding troughs attached to those cages which contain birds every morning, for I have known numerous instances where mice have literally devoured every grain of seed in a hopper or feeding drawer of a cage in a single night, and the occupants of the cage were left without a morsel of food. Some fanciers do not feed their birds more than twice or thrice at most weekly during the winter months of the year, therefore if an occurrence like the one I have just related should take place, the birds would inevitably perish. I have known valuable specimens meet with an untimely death from this cause, and the owner (a novice of course) wonders what was the matter with them, for the cunning little animals knowingly leave all the husks behind, and this tends to deceive the inexperienced and unwary.

As soon as it has become evident that the precincts of your " sanctum " are infested with mice or rats, a strict scrutiny should be immediately instituted, and their runs found out and traced to their source. Rats are more easily got rid of than

mice, for if you succeed in discovering their runs and fill them
up with old rags, plentifully saturated with coal tar, and
liberally sprinkled over with broken glass throughout the entire
length of their tracks, which usually terminates at or near
a drain—unless it is in the neighbourhood of a water-mill or
other exceptional place—and, lastly, plug up the road of egress
with broken bricks and cement, you will generally succeed
in forcing them to find fresh quarters, unless, as may happen
in rare instances, there is a complete colony of the vermin,
in which case it would be necessary to employ both dogs and
ferrets to thin their ranks before any other precautionary
measures were employed. It would, furthermore, in a case of
this kind be advisable to keep a cat constantly upon the
premises; but cats are almost as much to be dreaded as the
rats themselves, unless they are "broken to birds." "Ha!
broken to birds, did I hear you say?" Yes! Some fanciers
bring up cats among their birds and train them to live among
them on a peaceful footing. For "Catching Rats," see p 204.

BREAKING CATS TO BIRDS.—I have seen a cat which was
allowed to remain in a room where there were no fewer than
sixty or eighty birds flying about loose, and strange to say, she
had kittens a few days old in a corner of the same room at the
time. The birds appeared quite familiarised with the animal,
and took no more notice of her than they did of the water
fountain placed in the centre of the room for their use—I mean,
so far as to exhibit any symptoms of fear or timidity. I have
seen others that were permitted to go in and out of rooms where
birds were kept at pleasure, and to remain there during the
night by themselves, and yet they never attempted to molest
them; the birds, however, were kept in cages, but not beyond
the reach of those feline depredators had they felt inclined
to a little carnage. One fancier, with whom I was intimately
acquainted, possessed a cat that, judging from its actions,
seemed to be not only on terms of great intimacy with the
birds, but actually appeared to have an affectionate regard for
them. I have seen this cat repeatedly drink out of the water
vessels containing the supply for the use of the birds, and then
curl herself up with her face to the cage, upon the cage stand,

and look tenderly towards them. The birds, not the least afraid, would come and give a tug at some of the loose hairs that projected within their reach, and Mistress Tabby would merely wink at them in a blinking sort of fashion. The manner in which those cats are trained humanity forbids me to recommend, as it flavours so strongly of wanton cruelty. They receive their first lesson when they are very young—some eight or ten weeks old; a cage containing birds is placed upon the floor of a room, and "Tom," or "Jenny," or whatever its name may be, is brought and set down in front of them. The kitten no sooner espies the birds than it dashes forward instinctively to seize its natural prey, when its instructor, who is on the *qui vive*, instantly springs forward, and, grasping the would-be assassin by the skin of the neck with a vice-like grip, proceeds to chastise it in manner following: Having, prior to the introduction of the device to allure the poor unsophisticated kitten, heated an ordinary knitting needle to redness, he holds it in readiness for use in his other hand, so that, as soon as the culprit has committed itself, the needle is forthwith placed against the wires forming the front of the cage, and poor little pussy receives a severe scolding, at the same time the operator unceremoniously begins to rub its nose backward and forward violently against the heated wire. They rarely, I am told, ever require a second lesson, if the first has been properly given, and never a third; but by way of a treat those humane individuals (?) (the trainers) sprinkle the first bird they happen to have die, from any cause, very liberally with cayenne pepper, and give it to their unsuspecting pupils, who no sooner get a good mouthful of the profusely seasoned dainty than they drop it as they would a red-hot iron. After this they would as soon think of attempting to catch hold of a live coal as they would a canary.

POISONED GRAIN.—When I have had the misfortune to be pestered with mice and rats—and I have been sorely plagued with both, but not recently, in my bird room, at least—I have proceeded to remove all seeds and food of every description beyond their reach, and, by placing pieces of glass here and there aginst the wall, and nailing tin round the legs of my cage stands, to prevent their climbing, or by securely covering my birds during the night time, I have managed to prevent them from obtaining food and intruding in my cages. In the next place I regaled them with a little provender, prepared expressly for their use, which consisted of grain prepared after this fashion: Get a pennyworth of oxalic acid, or sugar of lead, obtainable from any chemist, and put it in an earthenware vessel of any kind that is of no value; pour over this about a quart of boiling water. As soon as the powder is all dissolved, throw in a few handfuls of wheat, oats, or barley. Stir it up with a stick, and afterwards let it stand for twenty-four hours in a warm place; then pour off the liquid into a drain, or ash pit, or similar place, where it can do no harm. Lastly, dry the grain at a slow fire, and it will be ready for use. It should be sprinkled all about the bird room or place which the little brutes are known to frequent most; but, if you keep pigeons or fowls about your residence, you must exercise great caution in using it; and after you are led to believe that the mice are all destroyed, or nearly so, search out their runs and pour a quantity of gas or coal tar into them; break up a few old glass bottles, and force in as much of the broken glass as you can; having done this, fasten up the entrance to the holes securely from the outside. All the poisoned grain unconsumed should be carefully gathered up and destroyed, either by being burnt or buried.

KEEPING OUT MICE.—If you are troubled with mice, they will probably come through the skirting boards, or in the vicinity of them. Place a stout lath, edge up, and nail it to the skirting or floor. You must likewise nail a stout lath between the stencils of the bird-room door, as close to the door when it is shut as it can be got, and upon the opposite side to that on which it opens, for I have found on more than one occasion that this has been their only means of access to the room.

MICE DESTROYING EGGS.—It very rarely happens that mice have the temerity to attack birds unless they are exceedingly voracious and the birds are weakly or invalids; but they will devour both the eggs and progeny of birds when the latter are only a few days old, should they by any chance happen to get to the nest.

DISTINCTION OF SEX.—"How do you know a cock canary from a hen?" is frequently asked, not only by amateur bird fanciers, but by many people who only keep canaries because they "like to hear them sing." In answer to the interrogatory, I may say that male canaries are, generally speaking, more masculine in appearance than females. Their contour is usually more gallant-like and their carriage bolder and more erect; they are likewise more spruce and lively in their actions, and more dignified and commanding in bearing. Male birds, too, as a rule, are larger and fuller in the head and body, and stand more erect upon their legs than females; beside, their plumage is almost invariably richer and more intense in colour. In addition to these differences, it will be found that the tone of voice in male birds is richer, deeper, more mellow, and stronger than that of female canaries. The male birds are, likewise, more mischievous and quarrelsome in their dispositions. But these are not always to be regarded as infallible proofs, for there are exceptions in rules relating to canaries as well as to human beings; and there are to be found both masculine-looking hens and effeminate-looking cocks in the canary family, the same as there are to be found in the human family masculine-looking women and effeminate-looking men, but they are the exceptions, and not the rule, in either case. A male bird ought to begin to sing, if in good health, and placed in a cage by itself, at a very early age. I have known instances of young birds commencing to sing at the age of three weeks, and it is by no means an uncommon occurrence for them to sing at the age of one month; and when five or six weeks old the majority of them sing with great freedom. The best means to use in order to excite them to a display of their vocal powers is to put something upon a brisk fire to fry—a piece of ham is best, as it creates more noise in the process of cooking than chops or steaks. The grinding of a coffee-mill, or the shaking to and fro of a few grains of seed in a paper bag, or the sharpening of a knife upon a steel, are all more or less powerful incentives, and calculated to awaken within them a spirit of emulation.

It very rarely happens, however, that you can induce them to sing in the presence of strangers; that is, if you make an effort to stimulate them to do so, which is very provoking at times, more especially if you have been lauding your bird to a friend, and he has called purposely to hear it. The best and most appropriate time to hear a young bird sing is either at the early dawn of day, or when the shadows of evening begin to close around, just before the sun sinks in the far west and bids us " Good night ! " It must not be expected that a young bird of a few weeks old will sing vociferously like a bird fully matured. This they never do until they attain the age of from six to nine months, and, in solitary instances, longer. Their first efforts are not particularly symphonious, being a sort of prolonged chirruping noise; the hens as well as the cocks attempt to sing, but herein lies the difference—the male birds pour forth their infantile lays with great energy and vehemence, and in long continuous measure, filling their little throats until they swell and work like the bellows of that unearthly, screeching instrument, the bagpipes; whereas the hens only utter short, sharp, and disjointed notes, and their throats never swell nor work so vigorously as that of a male bird—a practical eye and ear can detect the difference in a moment.

The difference in the sexes of birds is easily distinguished in the spring of the year or during the early summer months, that is if the birds are well and healthy; it is ascertained by examining their vents; the vent of a male bird protrudes, whilst that of a female is broader and flat. If you place a young bird, say, eight or ten months old, that you believe to be a male, beside a well-known hen, say, in the month of March or April, you will not be long in discovering whether your suspicion is correct or not by their movements. If it proves to be a male bird, the hen will very probably turn upon him as viciously as a tigress, unless she is of a loving disposition and pleased with his appearance, when she will sidle up to him and fondle about him in a bewitching manner, and a courtship will be begun at once, unless it so happens that Master Dickey, not charmed by her appearance and behaviour, repels her, and abuses her accordingly. This treatment will lead to a conflict; but if, on the other hand, the bird you presume to be a male should turn out a female, they may, through jealousy, have a fight, but it will neither be so violent nor of such long duration as it would be in the former event.

TIMID BIRDS, &c.—Some birds are so nervous that they never attempt to sing in the presence of any person for a very considerable period of time. I have known instances of amateurs pairing a bird of this description with another male canary, and they have gone through some of the manœuvres incident to breeding, such as billing and feeding and making a nest, &c. I have also known two females paired, by tyros in the fancy, and they laid and sat, but of course brought forth nothing. In one case I heard of both hens having laid in the same nest, and they had ten eggs between them, but they broke most of them through fighting for possession of the nest, both wanting to incubate together. Others, again, will agree and both sit together in the same nest.

BIRDS DECLINING TO SING IN THE PRESENCE OF OTHER BIRDS.—Some birds sing freely enough when left by themselves, but refuse to do so in the presence of other birds. This happens most frequently with birds that have been kept for singing only, and have been isolated for a long time, and probably petted as well. Whenever a strange bird is introduced to the presence of an old bachelor bird, unaccustomed to the company of his brotherhood, he is liable to become peevish and jealous, and is certain to be excited to anger or pleasure on such an occasion, but more frequently the former than the latter, in which case he will sulk and refuse to sing; but, if he takes kindly to a companion, he will most likely sing even harder and louder than before the introduction, through rivalry. The only means of getting a bird of the former disposition to recommence to sing is to remove the stranger or intruder.

CANARIES LEARNING THE SONGS OF OTHER BIRDS, &c.— Canaries readily learn the songs of other birds, more particularly that of the linnet, which is sweet and melodious; but if you wish them to acquire another song differing from their natural lay, you must remove the birds you desire to be taught at an early age, and place them where they can hear the song of no other bird than the one whose notes you wish them to learn. They can be taught to imitate flutes and other musical instruments, likewise an instrument called a bird-organ, which is mostly used for teaching them. One tune only should be played in their hearing daily, until they have acquired it properly, and when a second air is introduced the first one should be repeated at short intervals.

CANARY OR CANARY MULE FOR SINGING.—" Which kind of bird do you recommend for singing—a canary or a canary mule?" This is a question which is often asked. I invariably recommend to all those who appeal to me for an opinion on this subject, a dark mule bred between a goldfinch and a canary, or a linnet and canary, as they are very handsome, lively, and hardy, and when they happen to get smoked or soiled, they do not show the dirt like a yellow or buff or pied canary; beside, their song is more mellow and less shrill. They are usually long-lived birds, not being subject to sexual changes, and this is another advantage in their favour. A male goldfinch mule is easily distinguished from a female by the rich deep orange colour that encircles the beak and emblazons the breast after it has moulted. In the female the colours are much paler.

THE BEST VARIETY OF CANARIES FOR BREEDING FOR PRIZES.—It is often asked which variety of the canary is best for breeding a few prize birds. Good birds of any variety are difficult to breed, and some men are not fortunate enough to breed prize birds until they have had some years' experience, and have succeeded in establishing a strain upon which they can place reliance. So far as the varieties are concerned, it is probably about as difficult to breed prize birds of one variety as another. Cinnamons, Crested Norwich, Lizards, and Yorkshire Fancy are, in my opinion, the best kinds for a novice to select for a commencement, but the fewer varieties a fancier keeps the greater are his chances of success.

AGE OF BIRDS.—"How can you tell an old bird from a young one?" Well, easily enough in an ordinary way, that is to say, provided the bird has not been tampered with. All young birds are free from scales upon their legs or shanks; whilst the legs of old birds are more or less scaled. The legs of some birds, however, scale much more rapidly than others, and hence it is not possible always to fix a bird's age by this criterion alone. I have seen some very old birds with scales upon their legs nearly as thick as their legs were, but some unprincipled people do not scruple to "scale them," *i.e.*, scrape the scales off to make them look young. The marks, or indentations, or rings upon the shanks of old birds are more palpable and more readily seen than those upon the legs of young birds. Their beaks, too, are both longer and stronger, and so are their claws, and the feathers which compose the wings and tails are never so tightly braced together in a bird that has moulted three or four times as they appear in a bird of one or two summers only. Another sign is that old birds very often have dirty feet, and are never so lively and full of "go" as a young bird; these are signs which to a keen observer are unmistakable.

CRIPPLES, OR MUTILATED BIRDS.—Some birds are maimed in the nest by one or other of their parent birds, and others are naturally deformed in their feet, wings, or beaks. These misfortunes or malformations do not always prevent their being reared, but whenever you find a bird with part of its upper or lower mandible eaten off, or one or both of its feet maimed, or the majority of its claws, or part of a wing, it will be found most advisable to terminate its existence at once, for it would be a burden to itself and a source of annoyance to you were you to permit it to be reared.

TAMING BIRDS.—I know some people take a great interest in taming birds, more especially canaries. They accustom them to go about the house from room to room, to alight upon their shoulders or fingers when called by name, to eat out of their mouths, and sundry other amusing little tricks. I have seen a canary that could be sent out of the house into the open air, and brought back again immediately at the pleasure of its owner. I have seen it fly upon the tops of houses at the opposite side of the street, and this, too, in a populous town, where a considerable amount of traffic was being carried on at the time. I have known this bird be away out of sight for several minutes, and the person to whom it belonged bring it back in less than one minute, simply by a well-known call or whistle. This bird was taught, so I was told, by kind treatment alone. There are several methods of teaching birds these tricks, such as clipping some of their wing feathers, and using ingredients to stupefy them; sometimes hunger is resorted to, but there is no necessity to adopt any of those cruel practices in order to domesticate them. If you wish to teach a bird to come and go, to alight upon your finger, to eat from your mouth, &c., procure one about five or six weeks old, and place it in a cage very near to you during the day-time, and talk to it frequently, give it a little green food occasionally, or any little dainty; after it becomes familiar with you, open the door of the cage, and let it range the room at its pleasure. At first it will most likely fly about rather wildly, and against the window panes, but take no heed of this, merely notice it by saying, " Dickey !" " Dickey !" " Pretty Birdie !" Before you give the bird its liberty, secure the window and also the door ; in fact, lock it, lest any one should open it from the outside and let out the bird, for if it got out and you were necessitated to go after it and catch it you would scare it very much, and it would have a most prejudicial effect upon its nerves. Before you give the bird its liberty, prepare a little hard-boiled egg chopped small, and mixed with a little bread or biscuit, or some other tempting morsel, and place it near you upon a plate or saucer ; after a while the bird will have the hardihood to come and partake of it, and if you take no particular notice of it, it will, in the course of a few weeks, or sooner, come and take it quite audaciously, as its confidence will increase rapidly, provided it is in no way molested at first. Do not attempt to catch it to put it back in its cage, as it will be sure to return to it of its own accord if left alone; it is merely a question of time. Persevere with this treatment daily for a few weeks, and it will soon become as tame as could be desired;

place a lettuce leaf upon your shoulder, and after it becomes bold enough to eat it there, coax it to eat out of your hand, or from between your fingers, and thus by patience, perseverance, and kindness, you will ultimately succeed in getting it to do a variety of feats both pleasing and entertaining to you.

CLEANING SEED.—Nothing is calculated to preserve birds in health more than the constant use of good and wholesome food. It is desirable, therefore, where a few birds are kept, to procure a small fine hair sieve to sift the dust out of the seed once a week or fortnight. Where only a single bird is kept it is not worth while to incur the expense, but the seed drawer should be emptied on to a piece of paper or a dish, and the dirt picked out and the dust blown away.

KEEPING BIRDS IN A ROOM WHERE A FIRE AND GAS ARE FREQUENT IN USE. — Most people who keep birds to sing, have them in the room they ordinarily use, and where a fire is almost constantly kept, and the gas often lighted—neither of which is desirable, for both are calculated to have a prejudicial effect upon their health, especially gas, which invariably sets them to moult out of season, and thereby jeopardises their lives, more particularly when they are hung in a lofty situation or from the ceiling, as the intense heat which is generated and accumulated there is most hurtful to them. To avoid this I would recommend the use of plate pulleys— little brass pulleys affixed to plates; fasten one of these to the moulding above the window (about the centre), and the other to the architrave on either side of it, whichever is most convenient—both pulleys must be in a line with each other. Get a piece of blind or picture cord about 10ft. in length, and secure it to the top of the cage by a ring or hook made of wire, and pass it through these pulleys. It will be necessary also to obtain a plated double hook (*i.e.*, two hooks affixed to a brass plate, such as are used for Venetian blinds); this should be fixed to the architrave on the same side as the pulley, and about 3ft. from the ground, so that the cage can be lowered or raised at pleasure; at night, after the gas has been lighted, the cage containing the bird should be lowered to within 4ft. of the ground; this will in a very great measure assist in obviating the baneful effects which must inevitably result in cases where birds are exposed for any length of time to its blighting influences. In the morning the cage can be drawn up. This contrivance is so simple that a child might easily manage it, but the bird must not be neglected or forgotten, especially if cats are kept on the premises.

To know whether Eggs are Fertile.—To ascertain whether eggs are fertile or not, hold them up before a window when the sun is shining strongly. If they are fruitful, and have been sat upon eight days or more, they will be quite opaque, vulgarly termed " black sitting." You can sometimes ascertain the fact at the end of six days, but there is no certainty before the end of the eighth day. If the eggs merely look muddy, and are not quite black, they are what are known as dazed or spoiled eggs. It is a bad practice to molest hens during incubation, as all hens ought to sit their allotted time, thirteen or fourteen days, according to the temperature of the atmosphere. If the eggs are all right they will assuredly be hatched, if not you cannot improve them by looking at them. and I should like to know how many fruitful eggs have been destroyed by this means—some through being let fall, and others by being indented with the finger nails. Never handle a bird's egg when your finger nails are too long.

Impregnating Eggs.—I have very frequently been asked my opinion whether I considered it necessary for a male bird to remain with a female after they had been observed to pair properly, and if they were then separated whether any or the whole of the eggs would prove fruitful. I have heard a great many arguments upon this subject both *pro* and *con*, and for my part I prefer not to offer an opinion thereon. I may, however, cite two cases which bear on the subject both ways, and I will vouch for their authenticity. A friend of mine, a great mule breeder, and a gentleman on whose statement I can confidently rely, related to me that he once sent a canary hen, in full season, to a friend's house, who had a breeding goldfinch, to get the hen impregnated. He sent her by one of his men-

o 2

servants, in a paper bag, with strict injunctions for him to
witness the birds pair, and to wait until they did so, and then
to bring the hen back with him. This was effected in the
presence of the owner of the goldfinch and the man ; the hen
was removed immediately afterwards. He told me that the
man was only away a little over an hour until he returned, his
mission being completed. The hen laid in due time, and the
eggs proved fruitful, and were hatched. I have heard of other
instances very similar. The other case happened with myself,
and is as follows : I once put a young goldfinch with an excellent mule-breeding hen canary, and seeing that she was about
to lay, and not having observed any symptoms of attachment
between them, I removed the goldfinch and placed a male
canary beside her. In the course of a few days after this she
laid four eggs, incubated and hatched, and reared her progeny,
two of which were mules, and two canaries. I have heard of
another case precisely similar in character, so that I consider
it best not to run any risks. I have likewise had a hen lay an
egg without the presence of a male bird. I then introduced
one. She laid five eggs in all, and the last three were hatched.
Another case has come under my observation where a male bird
that had been placed with a hen was removed. Three days
afterwards the hen laid, and out of four eggs laid by her three
of them were hatched. If a hen lays an egg in the absence
of a male bird, and one is introduced immediately afterwards,
as a rule the remainder of the eggs will be fruitful. It has
been repeatedly asserted that cases have been known in which
a hen has been kept in a cage along with a male bird for a
few days, and the latter then removed, and that eggs laid a
week afterwards proved to be fruitful. This is possible, but
success could not be counted upon.

MARKED CANARIES MISTAKEN FOR MULES OR HYBRIDS.—
It is a common error for people to fall into who have a
limited knowledge of birds, to suppose that every pied or
marked canary is a hybrid ; and hundreds of people who
possess common variegated canaries will tell you that they
are mules.

MULE HENS REARING CANARIES.—I have known mule hens pair readily with cock canaries, and have eggs, but they are never fruitful; but if you give them a sitting of fruitful canary eggs they will hatch and rear them. They almost invariably prove to be good foster parents.

BUYING BIRDS.—When a person living at a distance from a well-known fancier or other person wishes to buy some of his birds, it is customary after the bargain is made for the purchaser to send a P.O.O. for the amount before the birds are sent off. Where two fanciers are well known to each other this is not always insisted upon, but, in either case, the birds sent travel at the risk of the purchaser, unless it is agreed that they are sent on approval or return, when they travel at the risk of the vendor, provided there is no agreement to the contrary. If birds meet with an accident in transit, the railway companies are responsible, particularly where an unreasonable amount of delay in transmission has taken place, as they charge 50 per cent. as a risk-rate for all live stock; but, although they do this, they endeavour to repudiate their responsibility, and strive to limit their liability to 5s. a bird; this is simply preposterous. In some cases, railway companies insist upon the senders of live stock signing a Consignment Note to this effect, and refuse to accept and send the birds without this regulation is complied with. I do not think they are justified in this proceeding, and my advice to fanciers is, if compelled to do so, to sign the document under protest, and above the signature write the words: "Signed under protest." Fifty per cent. is a very large risk-rate. For an additional payment of one penny over the ordinary rate of postage, the Post Office authorities guarantee a payment of £5 on all valuable articles duly registered, and for twopence, £10. Surely, then, a railway company, whose least charge for a bird going any distance is 6d.—and, in cases of long distances, 2s. or more, although the packet weigh less than a pound—can afford to pay reasonable compensation, for the risk, if the bird be well packed, is not great. Despite the railway companies' bye-laws, which are not always legal, any unbiased judge or jury will, if the case is brought before them, give the fair value for the loss in all ordinary cases, and where no contributary negligence can be proved against the sender; and I strongly advise any fancier who may suffer through the neglect or carelessness of any railway company to test their responsibility by an action in a County Court. Although birds are delicate and tender-looking little creatures, it is surprising what an amount of knocking-about they can stand - without being injured. Out of many thousands of birds that I have sent away and received, I have only had about four die.

When birds are purchased from a person unknown to you, and he demands pre-payment, send him a P.O.O., payable ten days after date. In order to do this, you must affix a penny receipt stamp, and sign the requisition on the face of the order to that effect. If he fail to send you the birds within a reasonable time, then you can stop payment by giving notice to the postmaster where the order is made payable; but if he give you a satisfactory reference to a banker or town clerk, a magistrate, or a doctor of medicine or divinity, you need not take these precautions. I must not, however, omit to say that an order made payable in this way is not any security to the vendor of the birds, as the remitter of the order can stop payment during the ten days, and get the amount of it refunded to him by the postal authorities.

SENDING BIRDS TO PURCHASERS AT A DISTANCE.—Be very careful always to send birds in small box-cages or in strong boxes, with plenty of holes bored in them to admit air; fix some pieces of wood to the bottom of the box with small screw-nails for the birds to perch on; never place them a little way from the bottom, or the birds may get jammed beneath them, and be smothered with the seed, or hurt. Never put hay, straw, shavings, or similar material inside a box or cage used for this purpose, or the birds will either be hungered to death through not being able to get to the seed, or be suffocated. Always give them a plentiful supply of seed and a little soft, white bread-sop, or a lump of sponge immersed in water inside the cage or box. Cover the cage properly, but do not overdo it. Make holes through the paper with your fingers opposite the holes in the box, or wires in the cage, so that they may get an abundance of pure air; tie it securely, and be very particular in writing the address fully and legibly, and do not forget to write in large characters the words "Live birds—with care—urgent." I have labels printed for this purpose in block type an inch deep, and I generally paste two or three of them on different parts of the cage, where they can be best seen. Before sending them away, acquaint the purchaser with the train that they will be sent by, and send them to the railway station by some person who will wait to see them sent off. If you commit any act, by negligence or otherwise, which may lead to the death of any of the birds you have sold, the purchaser can hold you responsible on the ground of contributory negligence.

GERMAN PASTE.—This can be made by bruising in a mortar, or with a paste-pin, half a pound or a pound of genuine sowing rape-seed; blow away the husks, and add a piece of wholesome white bread, about two days old; roll these well together, reduce the mass to a powder, and keep it in a tin canister or glass bottle with a broad neck (a pickle bottle) and tightly corked to keep out the air, as the rape-seed is liable to turn sour; a little of this, mixed with a hard-boiled egg and a slight sprinkling of cayenne pepper, will be found capital food either for young or old birds. It should be made fresh every twelve or fourteen days. It may be moistened with water for the use of young or delicate birds if required.

SAFFRON CAKE.—Take of fine flour ½lb., sugar 3oz., butter 2oz., and the yolks of two fresh-laid eggs; get a pennyworth of meadow saffron and pour a teacupful of boiling water over it; beat the eggs and the butter together in a basin, next add the sugar and flour, and form the whole into a mass with the solution, after it has been strained through a piece of muslin, and lastly bake. When cold it is ready for use.

MARKING BIRDS.—The method I adopt, and which, I believe, is pretty generally adopted, is to notch small pieces out of the web or fringe of one or more flight-feathers, of one or both wings; this is done with a pair of sharp scissors, and in an angular direction. By means of a little ingenuity in varying the markings, the produce of any number of pairs may be easily traced; but it is equally necessary not only to exercise great care in the performance of this operation, but to use considerable caution in recording the particulars. This I do in the back of my diary in manner following: " Young cinnamons from pair in No. 1 breeding-cage, marked in left wing, first and second flight-feathers; each two notches; placed in flight No. 5 (see diary, p. —)"; and so on with the remainder. Whatever you do, do not place the markings in the tail of a bird, as these feathers are frequently shed or beaten out, and then all trace is lost.

Some fanciers number their birds the same as the cages in which they were bred, and where they breed extensively they put, say, three notches in one wing and four in the other, and multiply them; a bird marked thus would represent the number 12—*i.e.*, three times four and so on.

A CAUTION.—Buying birds from successful exhibitors: Bird fanciers have during the past few years increased at a rapid rate, and many people have taken up with this delightful hobby. On this account some of the more speculative fanciers have found it to be a very profitable business to supply the wants of these new beginners; they have laid themselves out specially to make money by so doing, and have become veritable bird dealers under the designation of "fanciers."

The *modus operandi* pursued by these men generally is to find out a person worthy of trust, in each of the large towns where birds are bred and reared in considerable quantities; the man they employ is termed their agent, and he binds himself not to act for anyone else; and they empower him to purchase on their behalf every bird of the kind they require that is likely to figure as a prize winner on the show-bench at the leading shows; and the agent, who should himself be a good judge, honest and trustworthy, is paid according to the success of his purchases, viz., by giving him a percentage on the winnings of the birds during the first show season. Ten per cent. is the usual sum paid, or 20 per cent. on the amount of purchase money. The birds should be bought subject to approval, but this cannot always be stipulated for, and some breeders will not sell one good bird without selling several inferior ones, as they consider a good bird should sell several, but in this case the price should be regulated accordingly. The time to purchase is in the autumn, August and September. We have known as much as £35 to have been paid for a single Crested Norwich canary, of course, a successful prize winner at the principal shows; and we knew of a case where £50 was offered and refused for a very rare specimen, said to be the best ever seen at that day. He certainly was a grand bird, with an immense crest. I had the honour of judging him at one of the late Crystal Palace shows, and in his class he simply stood alone. Some of the very best specimens out, however, have been bought at prices in first instances at between £5 and £8, before they have been moulted and exhibited, and this is considered a good price with all the attendant risks at that time. I am now speaking exclusively of Crested Norwich canaries, which for some reason, for which it is difficult to account, have of late years brought much higher prices than specimens of any other variety. These speculative fanciers get hold of all the best specimens procurable, principally in the way pointed out, or by attending the first shows of the season and keeping their eyes and wits in full play, and claiming all birds possessed of extraordinary merit at prices up to £10. There are some exhibitors who have written agreements with breeders to have the first refusal of any birds they breed. Some astute exhibitors employ popular judges to look out for "anything good" that is likely to win prizes, and either to purchase for them, or "put them on" the track for securing such birds, and for such services heavy commissions are paid. In

other cases judges look out for exceptional birds and sell
them to successful exhibitors, and the result may be better
imagined than described. I know of my own knowledge that
such things are done, and more than one prominent judge
has acted in the manner described. I do not say that they
have not acted in good faith, but I think the practice is one
that should not exist, and if generally known would be likely
to be resented by those who breed their own show birds, for it
is a method that is likely to cause prejudice in the minds of
exhibitors. The object in getting hold of these birds and
showing them is to create a name, and what can be so
powerful an advertisement? After their name is established
they have seldom any difficulty in disposing of these high-
priced specimens at greatly enhanced prices, after having
bred from them and exhibited them for one or two seasons.
There is always some ardent novice to be found with, as the
Tichborne claimant said, "more money than brains," to snap
up these birds, and it does not do for an exhibitor constantly
to win with the same birds; besides, he generally knows
where to get a better, for less money, at the time he disposes
of one of his "champions," as all prize winners are now
termed.

Young beginners should take warning and not be misled
into the belief that all exhibitors breed their show birds, for
it not unfrequently happens, and that among some of our
greatest prize winners, that they never bred a single specimen
that obtained a first prize, and perhaps not even a second;
there are exceptions of course, but they are exceptions
certainly. It is not the rule by any means. These successful
exhibitors get quite inundated at times with applications for
birds, and they have recourse to buying from less fortunate
breeders their entire surplus stock at a moderate figure, and
retailing them at greatly increased prices. I have heard of
one successful exhibitor who, it is said, can clear as much as
from two to three hundred pounds annually out of canaries,
and I have good reasons for believing that it is not far from
the truth.

Beginners and amateurs must remember that "extraordinary good birds" are not bred frequently; a really grand specimen is a bird in 50,000 of its own variety, or somewhere about that proportion; hence it cannot be expected that one man, however successful, breeds many of these in a lifetime; hundreds and thousands of men never breed one at all, and probably never will. A man is considered fortunate now-a-days who can succeed in getting hold of them even by purchase—so many buyers are on the look out—much less to breed many of them. Purchasers had better, therefore, reflect before they buy, as I can assure them that most of the best birds are bred by men who rarely exhibit, but are tempted to part with their choice specimens at long prices to speculative exhibitors, who soon find out where a good bird is to be obtained.

The same remarks apply to exhibitors of hybrids, and other varieties, but more particularly to the two classes of birds just mentioned (the Crested Norwich and mules).

The best men to purchase from are those who strive to breed prize winners, whose great ambition it is to improve the various breeds, who spare neither time nor expense in doing so, and who never purchase birds to sell again, but only dispose of their own surplus stocks. These are true fanciers, and you are sure to get reliable birds from such men.

Again, if an amateur purchases a prize winner, and he is ignorant or inexperienced in the art of getting a bird up for exhibition, he is sure to be disappointed.

Some of these speculative fanciers cajole young beginners by proffering to prepare their birds after purchase from them, and they may do so for a time, but for how long? Sometimes they offer to lend birds to exhibit at certain shows, local shows generally, with the option of purchase; these are their second or third-rate birds, that in good company will probably get H.C. or V.H.C. at most. By means of these "dodges," young beginners are occasionally led on until they do something rash, such as buying up a few high-class birds, at very high-class prices; after they purchase them they find

they cannot manage to "get them up" properly for a show;
and hence follows vexation and disappointment; the first flush
of victory fades before the non-realisation of their hopes,
and in their anger and indignation they discard their hobby
in disgust, and with an inward feeling that they have been
"taken in and done for"; but pride prevents them from ac-
knowledging the truth, and they suddenly find that "pressure
of business," or some similar cause, prevents them from longer
continuing in the fancy.

This is the old, old story, that has been realised scores of
times, and is likely to be renewed, so long as ambition, instead
of experience, holds sway over red-hot fanciers.

SHOW BIRDS.—Wash your birds but seldom, as frequent
washing makes the feather rough. Keep the birds covered,
and in a place as free from dust and smoke as possible until
the show season is over.

When you show crested birds take care to keep the perches in
your show-cages low down, and also in your breeding-cages if
the birds are very heavily crested. Several cases have come to
my knowledge where birds with unusually long crests have
injured themselves seriously by flying against the perches, when
placed high; and I have known one death result through it.
Besides, in a show-cage birds are seen to much greater advantage when the perch or perches are kept low.

HOW TO CATCH RATS.—Fanciers who use out-of-door
aviaries or stables or coachhouses, or similar out-door buildings
for their birds, are frequently troubled with rats, and how
to get rid of them is often perplexing. They are too cunning
to be caught in ordinary traps; their power of smell can easily
detect where a human hand has been, and poisoned food is at
all times a dangerous experiment to try. Place a tolerably
large tub in the centre of the room, aviary, or building, and
in the centre of the tub put a brick on end, then pour sufficient
water into the tub to cause it to come within an inch of the
top of the brick; this done cover the top of the tub with
stout brown paper, and make it secure. Then sprinkle upon

it some oatmeal, and put a few bits of bacon-rind or toasted cheese as well ; next place a board in a slanting position from the ground to the top of the tub, renew the food nightly for several nights in succession. This treat will soon be made known to all the rats in the neighbourhood and be appreciated. After they get confidence enough to come regularly, slit the paper in the centre carefully in different directions in such a manner that a rat will easily be precipitated into the water when it ventures upon it. The rat, suddenly immersed, will soon recover from the shock, and find his way to the projecting portion of the brick, and will then screech with all his might for help, and in a short time will be joined by one or more of his friends ; in fact all the rats within hearing distance will in a short time rush to the rescue, and getting immersed in the water, and finding their comrade in apparent safety, they, too, will make for the island of refuge; but as there is only room for one rat, the others are repelled, by tooth and nail, by the occupant of the brick, who will not yield his coign of vantage. Then a fight will follow, and the squeals of the combatants will attract more rats, who eagerly rush to the spot; and as rat after rat rushes into the water, the scene becomes more terrible, and the brick is often upset, and by daybreak the following morning the corpses of all the entrapped rats will be found floating round the tub. The next best method that I know of is to catch a rat in an iron spring-trap, tar it all over, and let it have its freedom; some people who are not too scrupulous about the laws of humanity, cut off the tail of the vermin as well. I am told that this method has cleared almost instantly a flour-mill infested with rats for years. Some hundreds were met very early the following morning migrating in a body.

TWIN CANARIES.—On the 8th of June, 1889, Mr. J. M. Wilson, of 15, Lillybank Road, Dundee, had a canary hen that hatched two birds from one egg. I have only known of one other case of this kind, and it was well authenticated.

YOUNG CANARIES FEEDING OTHER YOUNG BIRDS.—Well-attested cases are on record of young birds, six weeks old and upwards, having provided birds of three weeks or a month old with food, when they have been forsaken or neglected by their parents, or where a male bird having sole charge of them has been suddenly taken ill or died. Such cases, however, are rare, although several instances have come under my own personal knowledge. A friend of mine had a young Belgian cock that had never been mated with a hen, who would, if placed in a cage with young birds two or three weeks old, commence to feed them as soon as they pleaded for food, and he was the means of saving my friend several young and valuable birds. I once possessed a cinnamon hen that would do the same thing, and I have known of more than one instance where female mules, and barren hen canaries also, have acted as nurses and reared young birds. I mention these facts so that any fancier in a dilemma of this sort may try experiments, and thereby have a chance of saving young birds which otherwise might perish.

YOUNG CANARIES DEAD IN SHELL.—In the early months of the year (March and April) we usually experience a long continuation of easterly and north-easterly winds. These are prejudicial to sitting-hens, and the severe cold often weakens the young birds until they have not strength to free themselves from the membraneous tissue that lines the shells. If a hen does not hatch at the natural period of incubation, fourteen days, the eggs should be taken out and examined, and if found to be fertile, and there is no appearance of hatching visible, they should be immersed in a saucer of warm water for the space of a minute, then dried and returned to the nest. In most cases this will cause the eggs to hatch. If the shell is discovered to be partly broken, then assistance is required to free the captive from the bonds of nature, but it must be done with care and gentleness, or the young bird may be injured.

YOUNG BIRDS DYING WHEN A FEW DAYS OLD.— Instances have been known of young birds dying at the age of five to seven days, when every possible attention appears to have been given them by their parents. The symptoms observed are enormous swellings of the bowels, and in some instances they have been known to burst, the cause being constipation. This is probably attributable to feeding too freely with hemp-seed or other astringent diet, or for want of a supply of green food.

It is necessary to notice whether the young birds evacuate freely; and if not, a few drops of almond or olive oil should be mixed with the egg food. Biscuits are very astringent as a rule, and for this reason I always recommend wholesome bread being used in preference. I have never had any birds die from this cause, but friends of mine have.

CHEAP FOOD FOR REARING YOUNG CANARIES.—Take 1lb. of the finest oatmeal and roast it in an oven until it becomes of a pale brown colour; keep stirring it repeatedly to prevent its burning, and when cold add ¼lb. of the best Indian-meal and 1lb. of good sweet biscuit, finely powdered, 1 table-spoonful of moist or crushed loaf sugar, and a teaspoonful of salt; mix well together in a mortar, and preserve for use in covered tin canisters in a dry place. When required mix with the above a small quantity of German summer rape-seed, first scalded and washed clean, and sufficient water to make the mass crumbly moist, and it is ready for use.

Another formula is as follows: Take 1lb. of fine oatmeal and 1lb. of good wheat-flour, cook in a slow oven until golden brown in colour, keep constantly stirring to prevent burning, and when cold add ¼lb. of ground rice, 6oz. ground Indian-corn, 6oz. moist or powdered loaf sugar, 4oz. crushed hemp-seed free from the husk, 3oz. crushed maw-seed; mix well together and keep in a tin canister in a dry place. This will keep good for many months. When required moisten with warm water, and make into a stiffish crumbly paste as much as will be needed for one day. It should be prepared thus every morning, and any that is left over may be given to pigeons or sparrows. These mixtures, with a daily supply of green food and canary- and rape-seed, will be found all that is needed for rearing young canaries without the aid of eggs in any form, and is more suitable and invigorating. Young birds grow rapidly when so fed, and when they reach the age of ten days a few wholesome breadcrumbs may be added if desired.

END OF DIVISION 1.

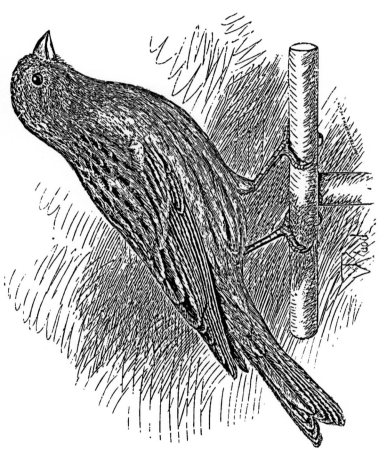

The Original Wild Canary.

The bird illustrated was brought from St. Helena. In markings, it closely resembles the Linnet, yet it is the type from which all the modern varieties have been evolved.

CHAPTER VII.

THE ORIGINAL CANARY—GENERAL REMARKS.

THERE is probably no bird so well known and so universally admired throughout the United Kingdom of Great Britain and Ireland as the canary. It may without hesitation be pronounced the "household pet," as it is beloved and esteemed by all classes, from the humblest cotter in the land, even to Royalty itself, it being a well-known fact that our much-beloved Queen takes great interest in these charming little choristers.

The canary is, without doubt, one of the most charming pets that can possibly be possessed, and, but for the fact that some high-minded people, whose notions are peculiarly aristocratic, imagine that everything pertaining to canary breeding must of necessity be plebeian in character, it would most assuredly hold a much more important position, as a fancy, than it hitherto has done. But why this notion should be associated with canary fanciers more than with pigeon, rabbit, poultry, and dog fanciers, I am at a loss to understand. I have passed through the entire category of these fancies, as a fancier, and despite my most earnest endeavours to solve the mystery I am positively unable to do so. I will venture to say that there is no bird more engaging in manner than a canary; nor any more gay, happy, and cheerful in confinement, and withal so harmonious; their power of memory and imitation is perfectly wonderful, and the attachment of many of those birds to the individuals who supply their daily wants and treat them kindly is widely known, so that, for those who are in pursuit of a harmless and innocent amusement, I know of none where more gratification and enjoyment are likely to be found.

INTRODUCTION.—Hitherto, I have failed to meet with any record giving an account of the first introduction of the canary into England, but Willoughby, in his "History of Birds," states that canaries were quite common in his time; and Gesner, who wrote in 1585, likewise mentions them. Aldrovandus, who published a work on "Ornithology" in 1610, gives a fair description of this bird (*vide* vol. ii., page 355). It is said, on good authority, that canaries were first introduced into England from Italy, and I believe this statement has never been contradicted. There are, however, a great many different varieties of this elegant and charming bird, and since the introduction of the "All-England" exhibitions, the first of which took place in 1858, this fancy has made considerable head-way.*

The canary is to be found in a wild state in some parts of Southern Africa, and also in several of the islands in the Atlantic Ocean, including St. Helena, Ascension, and the Cape Verde Islands, as also in the Canary Islands. It is stated by an early writer on this subject that these birds found their way to the latter islands by accident. A ship, bound for Leghorn, having on board a number of these birds, foundered near the islands, and through this circumstance they were set at liberty. They found the climate sufficiently genial to induce them to breed, and by this means they became thoroughly acclimatised. These birds bear a striking resemblance in size, form, and marking to the ordinary linnet of our own country, but the ground or body colour is green, which is almost the only difference observable. They are frequently brought to this country by sailors from Santa Cruz and Teneriffe. They are much famed for the excellence of their song, which is exceedingly soft and melodious, differing materially from the canaries bred and reared in this country. The bird from which our illustration has been taken was the property of Madame Galeo, of London. It was brought from the island of St. Helena, and although wild when she got it, it became tame and tractable. It is said to have been

---

* I believe the first All England Open Show was got up by Mr. Ruter, Mr. Clark, and myself, at Sunderland, I acting as secretary.

a most charming songster. It was shown in the "Any Other Variety of Canary" class at the Crystal Show in 1875.

VARIETIES.—The common canary is a bird pretty generally known in most countries throughout Europe; in size and shape it is not much unlike a common linnet; its colours are yellow, buff, green, and green pied, or variegated; it is admired chiefly for its song, and may be met with at all professional bird dealers; but by those who are known as "true fanciers," birds of this kind are merely regarded as nurses for rearing the more valued and favourite varieties; consequently they are considered of little value, and may be purchased at a low figure, cock birds varying from 3s. 6d. each upwards, the hens usually being sold from 1s. 6d. to 2s. 6d. each, much depending upon the time of year and other circumstances. Probably the varieties most highly esteemed among the *cognoscenti* are those known as the Crested Norwich and Belgian Fancy canaries, and next to these come the London Fancy, Lizards, Cinnamons, clear and variegated Norwich Fancy, Glasgow Dons, or Scotch Fancy, Manchester Coppies, Yorkshire Fancy, &c., although many of these so-called varieties are artificially produced, and are the result of crossing one variety with another in such a manner as to produce some totally distinct feature or features, differing in some material points from all known and existing varieties; but I need scarcely point out that it requires great care, judicious management, and considerable knowledge and skill to bring about a phenomenon of this description, to say nothing of the time, patience, and expense incurred. I will now proceed to describe the different varieties, and to point out the distinguishing features in each class; the best method of crossing in order to produce those features; and to lay down a standard whereby the different points of excellence may be readily estimated.

CHAPTER VIII.

THE BELGIAN.

ORIGIN—SIZE.—In my descriptions of the different varieties I will begin with that known as the Belgian canary, which, as its name denotes, is a native of Belgium. These birds are bred there in large quantities, and exported to different parts of Europe and America, and several of our colonies. I have in various ways endeavoured to obtain some information bearing on the origin of these remarkable birds, but without eliciting anything reliable; the oldest fanciers in Belgium seem unable to give any satisfactory account of them; I must, therefore, decline to hazard any remarks of a speculative or theoretical nature in regard to them, and will simply treat them in the character of an established variety. This variety of canary has been known and admired in our country for more than forty years, and they are considered, and, I think, justly so, the nobility of the canary race. The principal recommendation of a bird of this description is its peculiar form, its large size and graceful and commanding contour. It is a large bird, and is variously estimated to measure from $6\frac{1}{2}$in. to $7\frac{1}{2}$in. or even 8in. in length, from the point of the bill to the tip of the tail; but few will be found to exceed 7in., which may be taken as an average size. It is a difficult matter to measure a bird of this kind except by the eye, and that is an uncertain and unreliable "rule;" besides, much depends on the health, condition, and season of the year for these birds to show to the greatest advantage; and, although size is an important consideration in birds of this class, contour is much more so.

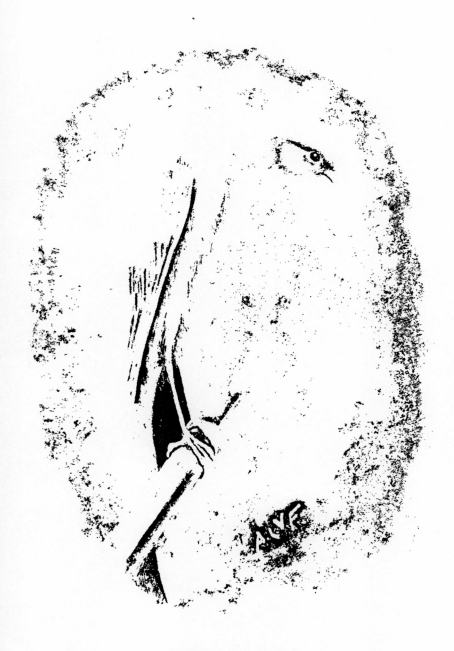

BELGIAN CANARY.

(First Prize, Crystal Palace Show. Owner, F. Reddihough.)

MY FIRST BIRDS.—It is now forty years since I purchased
my first pair of Belgian canaries, and I have a very vivid recollection of the characteristic features that were at that time
looked for by fanciers; they were length and thinness of body,
sleekness, and smartness; and the *beau idéal* of a bird of this
description was one that was so exceedingly slender, that it
gave anyone the idea that it could be passed through a lady's
gold ring. But this particular fancy at that time was in its
infancy in England, and the admirers of Belgian canaries were
groping their way in the dark; the birds then imported were
not thoroughbred, or at least very few of them, and those
that were, were regarded as deformed and ugly. Dealers had
to be resorted to at that time for canaries of this sort, as
very few fanciers, in the North of England at least, were
known to breed birds of this variety, as they had not been
introduced into England many years previously. At that time
I resided in a very pretty village about three miles distant from
a town, which, in a commercial aspect at least, is now considered
one of the chief in the county of Durham. The importer
in this instance was Joseph Greenwell, a man known throughout
the "fancy" thirty years ago, not only as a dealer, but as
a fancier as well. He was in the habit of receiving importations
of these birds during the autumn and spring months of the year,
at stated periods, and they usually arrived on Saturdays, which
I fancy was a good arrangement on his part, seeing that the
majority of his customers were of the artisan class, and these
men received their wages weekly, and generally on the
Saturdays, consequently they would be prepared with the
wherewithal which would enable them to become possessors
of the objects of their admiration, and ready cash is considered
a *sine quâ non* in the bird fancy. Upon one occasion I
called at Greenwell's to purchase a buff Belgian cock, but I
found he had not one to suit me. He thereupon informed me
that he expected a "fresh lot" on the following Saturday
morning. Having ascertained the time of their probable arrival
and other necessary information, I determined, if possible, to be
one of the first in attendance, so that I might have an opportunity of selecting something to my mind. Although I lived

fully three miles from the town, my enthusiasm brought me up to time. When I reached his house I found several men waiting the arrival of the birds, all entire strangers to myself, but apparently eager enthusiasts. I found from their observations that the majority of them were old "practical hands," and being at that time a mere stripling myself, I listened to their conversation in profound silence, in the hope of extending my bird knowledge, which was then somewhat limited. In the course of a quarter of an hour the birds arrived, and I was greatly amused to observe the eager, anxious expression of face that some of these men immediately assumed; all was silence in a moment, and eyes were peering in at every crevice and loophole in the cage in which the birds were, to catch a glimpse of the envied occupants, as Joe, in his usual cool and calculating manner, removed the covering that concealed them from view. This done, a scene of unusual excitement, bustle, and commotion followed, a little confusion, and a terrible clamour of tongues; in the meantime Joe produced two or three smaller cages, and said, "Stand back a bit, and I'll catch them and put them in here, where you can get a better look at them." This request was readily acceded to, and presently out came the enchanters and enchantresses. No sooner had they settled upon their perches and given themselves a "pull up," when several voices were heard exclaiming, "How much for this?" and "How much for that?" In answer to these eager interrogatories came the quiet and patient rejoinder, "How much is it worth?" One replied "I'll give so much," and another would offer so much more, and in this manner what were considered the "pick of the flock" were disposed of.

I lingered by in silence until all appeared satisfied, when I ventured to ask the price of a noble yellow hen with immense shoulders, a nice sleek head, good neck, legs, &c., which had excited the mirth of all present, and not a few were the witticisms that were levelled at the poor unoffending object. One said it was a "young camel," another that it was a "Richard the Third," but all appeared agreed that it was naturally deformed, except myself, and I certainly was the only one who appeared to have the least desire to possess it. Greenwell tried to dissuade me from having it, and said he was sure there was "something wrong with its back." Nevertheless, I had a fancy for it, whether it was maimed or not, and said I would purchase it if it was not a very expensive bird, as I was not sure then but it might possibly be deformed, and consequently of little value. He said I might have it for 7s., and I accepted the offer at once; after I got it home and compared it with my other birds, it occurred to me that this was the "Simon Pure" of a Belgian canary, and the next time I was in town I told him I should like a few more of the same shape, and gave him my opinion respecting it; he smiled quietly, but very significantly, but this did not alter my opinion; some time afterwards I picked up a buff cock similar in shape, but not nearly so good as the hen.

About this time a gentleman with whom I was acquainted commenced to keep birds; he was a manufacturer, and exported goods to Belgium. I suggested to him that it would be a good plan if he were to commission his agents in Antwerp to procure for him a pair or two of the best Belgian canaries they could obtain, and to instruct them to employ some well-known fancier to select the birds; and furthermore to send the kind that was most highly esteemed in that country. He adopted my suggestion, and in due time four birds arrived, and they proved to be the very identical counterparts of my "deformed" hen. The agents wrote to say that they were of the best and most highly-prized strains, and were much dearer than the birds usually sold for exportation. This settled the matter at once, and I was greatly pleased with the discovery; the cross breeds soon gave way to the thoroughbreds, and I had numerous applications for the progeny of my "crooked backed" birds, as they were frequently designated. Three or four years after this some of our most ardent fanciers ventured across the Channel and selected their own stock, and the best birds I have ever seen have been imported birds.

IMPORTING BIRDS.—It is not a long journey neither is it a very expensive one, so that anyone wishing to obtain high-class stock would do well to take a trip to the Continent; those desirous of doing so can embark either at Hull or London. A boat leaves Hull for Antwerp every Wednesday, and returns the Saturday following; the single fare is 15s., return tickets cost 22s. 6d. The passage occupies about twenty-four or twenty-five hours from port to port. The Hôtel de l'Europe is a place where every comfort can be procured; all waiters and servants speak English, and the charges are extremely moderate. Any further information about the boats, &c., can be procured from Messrs. Gee and Co., agents, Hull. No fancier need be deterred by the fact that he is unable to speak the language of the country, as any of the waiters at the hotel I have named will readily get him an interpreter, who, on payment of a small fee, will accompany him to the different breeders, and assist him to make his purchases. Besides Antwerp, good birds can be obtained at Brussels and Ghent, these being the three principal towns for getting the best birds at. Prices vary in accordance with quality and the particular season of the year; the best time to go is probably the month of September, after the close of the breeding season, as birds are most plentiful then, and as a matter of course you have a better chance of selecting something to suit you, and at a lower price than you would pay at a more advanced period of the year. The Belgians set great value upon their best birds, and high prices are demanded for prize specimens, but moderate or faulty birds highly bred can be purchased at reasonable prices. High class birds range from forty francs upwards (£1 13s. 4d. in English money), but fabulous prices are asked for rare gems. Belgian canaries are readily acclimatised in England and Wales, as also in Ireland and Scotland; there is not a great difference in the temperature of these countries. Belgium lies between 49deg. 30sec. and 51deg. 30sec. north latitude, and between 2deg. 30sec. and 6deg. 5sec. east longitude, whereas England including Wales extends from 49deg. 58sec. to 55deg. 46sec. north latitude, and from 5deg. 40sec. west, to 1deg. 45sec. east longitude. These birds, however, do not endure the cold so well as most other known varieties. The Belgian fanciers esteem their own breed of canaries far before all others, and set little value upon some of our esteemed varieties, such as Norwich Fancy, Lizards, and the like.

CONSTITUTION.—Belgian canaries are probably the most do-mesticated of all the tribes of the *Fringilla Canaria*, and on this

account they are great favourites with most fanciers. They soon
get accustomed to and become familiar with their regular
attendants, and display very little of that timidity and nervous-
ness so perceptible in many of the other varieties—I refer more
especially to birds kept in a room set apart for their sole use,
and which are only visited occasionally; and were it not for one
or two important considerations, they would doubtless become
the most popular favourites of all true canary fanciers; the
first of these is that they are naturally of a delicate constitution,
as a rule, and appear to be predisposed to asthma and consumption, maladies not easily curable, and which carry off the
major part of them; they like warmth, and it is a difficult
matter to get birds of this breed strong enough to inure them to
a room without fire during the winter months of the year. If
they were kept in a room where a moderate and regular temperature could be kept up during the coldest period of the year,
and when the north and east winds prevail, by means of hot
water pipes or other contrivances, they no doubt would thrive
well, and ultimately we may produce a race of birds more vigorous and healthy than those of the present day. Another drawback is the enormous price which prize birds of this variety
usually bring, more particularly when you consider that the best
and hardiest bird of its race would be so completely "used up"
if it were sent round to compete at every show during one entire
season, that it would be, literally speaking, worthless for the
purpose of breeding from, if it did not kill it outright. I myself
have known as much as £12 paid for a single bird, but I must
confess that, taking him "all in all," I have not "looked upon
his like again." Great care should be taken of Belgian canaries
during the moulting season, as at this time, more than at any
other, they are likely to contract the diseases before mentioned;
they ought invariably to be kept covered over during this
eventful period in their lives.

BREEDING.—In selecting stock for the purpose of breeding, I
would recommend fanciers to purchase nothing but good birds.
I do not mean all prize birds, or even show birds, but one of the
parents at least ought to be *par excellence*, and for this purpose I
prefer the male bird to excel in the qualities which are most

highly esteemed, although good birds are often produced when the reverse of this recommendation is carried out, but in that case, much, I imagine, depends upon the constitution of the hen; nevertheless, I prefer to adhere to the plan I have already named. Few people succeed in obtaining good birds from moderate parents, even when they are known to be highly bred; but with one good bird judiciously matched with a moderate bird known to be of a good strain the best results are often realised.

If you possess, say a large strong male bird, with great length of body, good legs, fine sweeping tail, and long slender neck, but deficient in shoulder and coarse in feather, you must match him with a hen possessing large shoulders, and close and compact in feather, regardless of all other properties; that is to say, never mind if she is rather small, and somewhat short in the legs and neck; the chief features that you require are those specified to create a suitable match for the cock I have described. If the hen, in addition to the qualities named, possesses other good properties, so much the better, and so much more likely will she be to produce a greater number of good specimens, but if you succeed in breeding one first-class bird of a single pair of birds in a season, you may consider you have done remarkably well.

I do not recommend putting nothing but show birds together, as when birds are too highly bred their progeny are correspondingly tender. Another thing which I wish you clearly to understand is this: never put two birds together possessing the same points of merit, unless they both possess in an equal or approximate degree all the good qualities desired—what I mean, is, never put two moderate birds together; say, for instance, two birds both being deficient in some essential qualities—such as two birds of a diminutive kind, or two birds wanting in development of shoulders, chest, neck, legs, &c.; but always contrive to pair your birds in such a manner that the one bird predominates in the opposite features to the others, as by adopting this method you are pretty certain to get one or two birds at least which will inherit the peculiarities of both parents so blended that the result will, in all probability, prove highly satisfactory to you. It is usual to pair a yellow cock and a buff hen together, or *vice versâ,* as the case may be. It will, however, be found very advantageous to breed from two buff birds occasionally, in preference to a yellow and buff, as it tends materially to improve the size, constitution, and feathers of the birds; but it must not be repeated too frequently, or it will produce coarseness. Some fanciers occasionally pair two jonque (yellow) birds together in order to produce fineness, but the produce are generally deficient in plumage; but a bird bred from two yellows, and mated with one bred from two buffs, or, better still, one bred from double buffs twice over—that is, a bird bred from two buffs, and a second time mated with a buff, the produce of the last cross— very frequently breed the handsomest and best birds.

If you desire to breed variegated Belgians, be sure to select two or three well-marked birds, cocks or hens, not too heavily marked, and pair these with clear birds of the opposite colours and sexes, select from the produce of these birds those which are best marked, and couple them again with clear birds, taking care to pair them in accordance with instructions already given, with reference to breeding clear Belgian canaries, in order that you may effect a general improvement in the *côntour* and *tout ensemble* of your birds. If you happen to breed more clears than you care for, put a marked bird with a clear bird bred from a variegated strain, and by this means you will soon restore the markings. If you put two marked birds together, unless they are both lightly marked, they are very apt to produce young birds too heavily marked, and if this plan is persevered with, that is, the re-crossing of variegated birds, you will ultimately produce them nearly all green together; and occasionally you will get an entirely green specimen.

Be very particular in selecting birds for breeding purposes; satisfy yourself that they are perfectly healthy—this is a most essential consideration, and one which cannot be too rigidly carried out—as much depends upon your first selection of breeding stock for your future success in establishing a race of birds which is likely to reward you for your trouble. Never breed from diseased birds, however good they may be, or you will in all probability propagate the complaints from which the birds suffer—1 refer more especially to asthma and consumption

—and thereby sow the seed of hereditary disease. I know it is very galling, and even tempting, when you possess a magnificent specimen of this variety affected with one or other of these direful complaints, and have to forego the pleasure which you had doubtless looked forward to ere the disease presented itself in outward form, but for all that it is a real necessity, if you want to produce healthy progeny, with vigour and action; you must brook the disappointment manfully, and I am sure you will never regret your conduct in after years. You had far better terminate the existence of a bird of this kind in the most humane manner possible, a thousand times over, than be led to so rash an act as to couple it with a healthy partner and breed from it, as the disease would be sure to show itself sooner or later, in most, if not all, of the birds bred from such parents.

When you are selecting birds to breed from, it will be well to bear in mind that two-years-old cocks are preferable to one-year-old birds, and their produce are generally stronger and more robust. In fact, I think it desirable not to attempt to breed with male birds the first season, for they often fail to impregnate the eggs, or most of them, and it unquestionably weakens their constitutions, which is a material consideration. I do not object to breed with one-year-old hens.

REARING.—A great many bird fanciers will tell you that Belgian canary hens are "bad breeders," that is, bad nurses, but they seldom consider how much they have themselves to blame for this apparent want of maternal affection; their over-anxiety or curiosity frequently leads them to meddle with the birds during the process of incubation, or shortly after the eggs are hatched; indeed, I have known some men so foolish as to disturb a hen every fifteen or twenty minutes whilst she was busy hatching; forcing her off the nest each time merely to ascertain whether she had hatched another egg. How such men can expect birds to perform their duties satisfactorily, under such circumstances, is more than I can say. The majority of canary hens, without distinction of class, instinctively become jealous at this particular time, more especially for the first few days after they hatch ; and if the curiosity of fanciers incites them to such acts of indiscretion they must not express dissatis

faction with the result. I am quite certain that a great many
hens, which doubtless otherwise would supply the wants of their
progeny well enough, are by such treatment completely spoilt.

Always give a hen, and more especially a Belgian canary, a
fair chance, and if she is in good health and left entirely alone,
the probabilities are more in favour of her proving a good nurse
than a bad one. I have repeatedly heard it asserted that
common canary hens are the best mothers, and without doubt
they are as good as any; but experience informs me that they
are little or no better than hens of many other varieties if they
are interfered with. There are no canaries more attentive to
their duties in assisting to rear their broods than the male birds
of the Belgian variety; and I see no reason why the females
should not prove correspondingly attentive. At one time I bred
a large number of these birds; and one season I reared twenty-
six birds from four pairs; three of the hens fed their own offspring, and one pair reared nine birds themselves, but this may
be considered exceptional; still it is not beyond the bounds of
probability to effect a similar *coup de la bonne fortune.* Leave
them alone to their own maternal instincts, treat them the same
as you would birds comparatively worthless, and you will find
that Belgian hen canaries are far better nurses than you were
led to suppose.

If a hen is delicate or out of health, you cannot reasonably
expect her to perform her duties satisfactorily, and in such
cases you must transfer her eggs to another hen on which you
can place reliance; but do not bother her, not even if she is a
"common hen." If a hen has had a difficulty in laying her eggs,
and has been prostrated in her efforts to do so, it would not,
under such circumstances, be prudent to entrust her with the
rearing of her progeny; therefore, if they are at all valuable, it
will be advisable to effect a transfer with some other hen, whose
produce you consider to be of much less importance.

Always bear in mind the following maxim, "That which is
naught is never in danger"—*i. e.*, that which is considered of no
intrinsic value; for, although you may, as most likely you will,
think very highly of some of your birds, and set great store by
them, you will nevertheless find it a golden rule to treat them as

though they were next to worthless. Do not disturb them any more than you can possibly help, and leave them as much to themselves as circumstances will permit, and I am sure the result will be, in the majority of instances, satisfactory alike to the birds and to yourself.

It sometimes happens that the young Belgian canaries are weak and puny, and have not sufficient strength to raise their heads for the purpose of receiving nutrition from their parents during the first two or three days after they are hatched. In the former event you must administer food to them in small quantities, at short intervals, for the first three days, and if the mother appears to sulk, and refuses to feed them afterwards, they must be transferred forthwith to a foster parent.   (For further particulars see chapter on Breeding, page 51.)

As soon as the young birds are able to cater for themselves, place them in large cases, with plenty of length, breadth, and height, so that they will have ample room for exercise, which will be found very beneficial and conducive both to their health and well-being.

RUNNING OUT.—When they reach the age of seven or eight weeks you must begin to train them to "run out," that is, to teach them to go in and out of their usual domiciles, *à la Belgique*, into show cages, as it is a most reprehensible practice to catch birds of this variety with your hands, and a custom which is very apt to scare and frighten them. This performance is easy of accomplishment, and should be achieved in the following manner. First catch the bird you desire to teach, and place it in a show cage with a sliding door, and allow it time to settle down quietly ; then take another cage, a *fac simile* of the last named, and place the doors opposite each other, taking care to raise the sliding doors to their full height, and place the apertures directly opposite each other ; next take a piece of thin wood or lath, previously rounded, and perfectly smooth, like the top of a fishing rod, about two feet or two and a half feet in length—a portion of a penny cane stick will answer the purpose quite well. Put this quietly and carefully through the wires of the cage in which the bird is placed, and endeavour to drive it, in the easiest manner possible, into the other cage. Be sure to

exercise your utmost patience and skill, and above all, do not
irritate or excite the bird. First put the stick above the bird,
and force the latter gently to the bottom of the cage, moving the
stick slowly and dexterously in such a manner as to induce the
bird to approach the entrance to the adjoining cage; but by all
means keep your temper, for if you attempt rough usage you will
most assuredly frighten the bird—an occurrence which must be
avoided if possible. Speak softly and kindly to it during this
operation, and with a little perseverance and careful manipulation you are certain of success. If the bird exhibits symptoms
of fear, leave the cages in the position indicated for a day or two,
and it will become familiar with the arrangement, and pass
from one cage to the other of its own accord. After this you will
have no difficulty in getting it to pass readily in and out of the
cages. If you find that you are necessitated to have recourse to
the latter plan, place a little maw-seed, or a little egg and bread,
or some tempting delicacy, in the empty cage, which will induce
it the more readily to enter. After you are satisfied that the
bird understands what it is required to do, run it into a breeding
cage, and repeat the same treatment until it becomes a proficient
pupil. When a bird is once properly drilled in this manner it
never forgets it, and after it becomes a thorough adept at it you
will find it of the greatest use in assisting you to train other
birds. Having fairly succeeded in your endeavours to train one
bird, place another beside it, and continue the same practice as
before; you will find the other bird soon follow suit, although
it may show a little awkwardness at first, and in this manner
you will be able in a few weeks to teach all the birds in your
possession to come and go from one cage to another.

GETTING INTO POSITION.—As soon as you discover that you
are the possessor of a Belgian canary fit for competition, you
ought to proceed to train it not only to "run out," but to get into
show position; this is done in a variety of ways, and depends
greatly upon the temperament and disposition of the bird. If it is
at all nervous or timid, you will need to exercise great care and
attention and the utmost vigilance, particularly at the commencement; you must approach it with great caution and very
leisurely, chirruping to it with your mouth, or speaking to it

tenderly in low, soft accents—for birds are quite capable of appreciating blandishments and endearments—and by this means you will more readily acquire the confidence of your pupil. As soon as it appears to be on friendly terms with you, lift the cage and move it about in a quiet way, and as soon as it becomes familiarised with " handling," move the cage about more freely, raise it well up and scrape your finger nails along the bottom— not too roughly ; the noise will attract its attention, and it will instantly appear on the *qui vive* ; if it does not dash about or appear too fidgety, you may move the false bottom or draw- board gently to and fro, first slowly, and afterwards more rapidly. As soon as it becomes thoroughly accustomed to this mode of treatment, you may introduce the stick you use for the purpose of a " running wand ;" put it through the wires in the rear of the bird, and push it with the utmost care and gentleness beneath the perch on which the bird is placed ; let it project two or three inches in front of it, and then proceed to move it about slowly and quietly ; if it is not startled it will commence to " pull " itself together, raising its shoulders and lowering its head, and will stretch its legs to the utmost of its ability. This is what you desire it to do, but if you continue it too long it will probably wheel round suddenly, in which case the wand must be withdrawn at once, and after the lapse of a few seconds introduce it again the same as before ; continue this practice for ten minutes or a quarter of an hour, not less than once a week, and not more than three or four times at the most, or you will make it too familiar, which is nearly as much to be deplored as if it were too shy. It is a good plan to place the cage against a wall during this operation. more particularly if the bird is timid or unsteady in his movements. Sometimes it is necessary to pass the wand in a rapid and dexterous manner underneath the cage, allowing it to project suddenly in front or at the side of the bird, but this is only required when the bird becomes too bold. Experience will suggest to the operator other devices for the performance of this necessary exercise.

CLASSES.—Belgian Canaries are capable of being divided into eight distinct classes, *i.e.* : clear yellow, clear buff, ticked yellow. ticked buff, evenly-marked yellow, evenly-marked buff, unevenly-

marked yellow, unevenly-marked buff; although it rarely
happens that they are divided into more than four, and some·
times fewer. ¯ The clears are almost invariably the best birds,
nevertheless it does occasionally happen that a very lightly
marked or ticked bird can be obtained quite as good in standard
points as the very best of clear birds; hence, I think that where
four classes only are provided for this variety of birds, the
ticked and clears ought to compete together, and the evenly-
marked and variegated should be arranged under one head.
Buffs and yellows cannot be shown together on equitable terms,
as the buff birds generally have much advantage in size, &c. It
is likewise a well established fact that the variegated birds are
much inferior in points of merit to the clear birds. This is
somewhat difficult to account for, unless we could believe that
the progenitors of the last named were originally all clear
yellows and buffs, and that the marked variety are the result of
a foreign admixture, and that whenever the birds appear in the
mixed plumage they inherit more largely the properties of this
allied blood. Be this as it may, it is a singular and undoubted
truth that the more heavily a Belgian bird is marked the more
deficient he is sure to be in all the essential characteristics which
constitute a high-class bird of this variety.

POINTS.—The points required to constitute a high-class Belgian canary are as follows : A small sleek head, rather flat on
the crown, well set, with nicely chiselled jaws, a neat, well-formed
beak, a full eye, a long slender neck, delicately formed, and
having the appearance of being chiselled, and which should be
gracefully curved downwards from the junction of the head to the
commencement of the shoulders; the shoulders should be broad,
very prominent, and well formed, rounding towards the back,
with an elegant curved line; the back should be well filled in.
From the termination of the deflection of the shoulders to
the back, the back as well as the tail should be almost perpendicular, with the slightest possible inflection towards an inner
curve; the chest should be prominent and well developed in
front, but flat at the sides; the waist long, small, and finely
formed, with an inward curve towards the thighs; the legs
should be long and straight, and well set, with well-made

Q

substantial thighs and good shanks and feet; the tail should be long, narrow, neat, and compact, and ought to resemble in appearance the shank of a pipe; the wings should be well formed, firmly placed, and hung close to the body of the bird, the tips coming close to the rump; colour and fineness of feather are minor points, but still must be considered. When a bird is in position, he should stand quite straight on his legs with his head well forward and down below the line of his shoulders, the latter being well up. The chief feature to be observed is the form and general contour—the easy, majestic, graceful carriage of the bird—commonly called " standage "— this being most essential, and an indispensable characteristic in a true show bird. There should be a decided appearance of hauteur in its manner and bearing.

SHOW FORM.—In Belgium this variety of bird is called the "bird of position," and the more readily and easily it acquires the position desired the more valuable it is. Some birds are very apathetic, and require a deal of rousing to get them up to show form. This is often the result of too much handling or ill-health; the birds get too familiar with it, and, consequently, treat it contemptuously. Other birds, again, are too nervous, and require to be gently handled, or they will throw themselves out of form through fear; but I will treat of this part of the subject under a different heading.

SYMMETRY.—There is another important consideration in judging Belgian canaries, and one which is too frequently overlooked, and that is proportion, or uniformity of features throughout. For example, picture to yourself a small bodied bird with extraordinary large shoulders, and short stiff legs, and a short neck; why it is simply distorted to ugliness. Again, imagine a particularly slender bodied bird with a huge head, thick straight neck, and a stunted tail. All known standards of beauty, whether of the human form or of animals, or other things, are regulated by symmetry, and it is equally applicable to birds. No doubt it is a difficult matter, if not an impossibility, to obtain a bird possessing all the qualities enumerated. Nevertheless a very close approximation to the object sought after is occasionally to be found, and when it is, we should do all we can to show our appreciation of its many excellent qualities. A very little matter will often disfigure what would otherwise be regarded as a good specimen of a Belgian canary. Take, for example, a long fine bird, with a sleek flat head, long slender neck, well developed shoulders, and short legs—those known as "sickle legged" (hook-shaped); this alone would prevent the bird from assuming that position which is regarded by all connoisseurs as the true line of beauty, and, consequently, its other grand qualities would be seriously counterbalanced by this great drawback.

STANDARD OF EXCELLENCE. — In adopting a standard of points for judging canaries, I think I cannot do better than follow the plan pursued by the · Americans, and that is, to give the maximum of perfection as representing one hundred points, as by the application of this method any person will be enabled to compute the relative value of each individual feature separately :

STANDARD FOR JUDGING CLEAR BELGIAN CANARIES.

Head 6, Neck 7, Shoulders 10	23
Back 10, Chest 5, Waist 6	21
Legs 8, Tail 6, Wings 4	18
Size 7. Colour 3, Quality of Feathers 3	13
Contour or Position	15
Condition	10
Total	100

In judging marked birds I would allow ten points for markings; and, as no bird is perfect, a good margin will always be left to work upon ; consequently it is not necessary to give another table merely to distinguish the single difference, as in all other respects the one already given is equally applicable to the variegated birds as it is to the clear varieties.

PREPARING BIRDS FOR EXHIBITION.—If you are the fortunate possessor of exhibition birds, and you wish to introduce them to the public in that character, it will be necessary for you to prepare them for their *début*.

You must commence, about three weeks or a month prior to the first show at which you have resolved to give them a " run,"

to feed them with a little hard-boiled egg, and stale but wholesome bread—home made preferred—or a little biscuit—either
luncheon or picnic will answer quite well; if you use the latter
it should be crushed to powder. Chop the egg fine, or rub it
through a sieve or piece of perforated zinc ; if you use tin nests
with bottoms made of the material just mentioned, rub it through
one of these; and if you choose bread in preference to biscuits,
it must be rubbed through in the same way, or between the
hands. Mix the ingredients in equal proportions; let each bird
have a small quantity of this food once a day; prepare it fresh
every morning, and in addition give it every alternate day half a
small thimbleful of maw seed—not more—do not give green food
of any kind. You should likewise give them occasionally a little
boiled carrot, cut into small pieces, and placed between the wires
of the cages; this will give a fine glossy appearance to the
feathers, and help to keep the birds in good condition. Show
birds ought to be kept scrupulously clean. Their cages should
be cleaned out at least once a week.

It is an objectionable practice to wash Belgian canaries to send
to shows, and ought not to be resorted to except under peculiar
and pressing circumstances. Colour in these birds is merely a
trifling consideration ; form being the chief characteristic. Still
it is not by any means desirable to send a canary to a show as
black as a chimney sweep when it can be avoided. If you reside
in a large town, and in a locality surrounded by manufactories
washing becomes an imperative necessity; for however good
a bird may be in all points, to see it clad in dirt and completely
begrimed, is a thing which even the most considerate of judges
is very loth to tolerate. Good condition adds greatly to a fine
exterior either in birds or animals; it is one of the things
looked for and generally appreciated, and which reflects
the greatest praise upon those who bestow the attentions
necessary for its production.

If, however, you happen to live in the suburbs of a large town,
or in a small country town almost exclusively of an agricultural
character, or in a village or hamlet, or detached dwelling, you
ought to have little difficulty, with ordinary care and attention,
in keeping your birds sufficiently clean to send them to shows

during the greater portion—if not the entire show season—unless you have the dire misfortune, as some fanciers have, to be the occupant of a smoky house, in which case if you cannot remedy the evil you should have the chimney swept frequently, say once a month, or even oftener if a very bad case, from September to February in each year. You must likewise keep the cages containing the show birds covered with a thin material, close in texture, and, in addition to these precautions, you will find it advantageous to nail some "list"—that is the outer edge, commonly called selvedge, of cloth (which can be obtained of any practical tailor merely for the asking)—round the frame of the door of your bird room; that is, up each side and along the top in such a manner as to make it project over the crevices between the door and the frame, and nail a lath an inch or so thick at the bottom of the door frame; as a matter of course, the latter must be put on inside of the door if it opens outward, but if it opens into the room then it must be outside. These appliances will be found of great service in keeping out the smoke. You might likewise, with some advantage, fasten a broad leather flap over the keyhole of the lock.

With these arrangements it will be necessary to open the window occasionally, to let in a current of fresh air, unless there is a chimney with an open fireplace in the room. By careful attention to these directions your birds ought to require very little in the way of washing; but if their feet are littered up with dirt, or their tails and wing-ends are tinged and soiled, it will be necessary to give them a slight wash two or three days before they are sent off for exhibition. This can be readily accomplished with a piece of clean flannel, a little scented or common soap, and some clean warm water. First make a soap lather upon the flannel, and apply it to the parts that require to be cleansed; lastly, rinse off with pure water, using another clean cloth or flannel for this purpose; dry the feathers as much as you can with an old silk handkerchief, and place the bird in a warm room until he is quite dry: be sure to get the soap thoroughly out of the feathers. Show birds should be supplied with a bath once a week, if the weather is not too cold. Glass vessels, such as preserve or jelly dishes, are best adapted for their use; and

the birds take to them much more readily than they do to dishes
made of earthenware or clay.

PACKING FOR SHOW.—Whenever you send Belgian canaries
to a show, be careful to wrap them well up and make them as
cosy as possible. I would advise you to have green baize or
scarlet flannel covers made to put over the show cages, and
to pack them in boxes or cases specially made for this purpose,
each to contain four, six, or eight birds; but I think one to
hold six is quite large enough to move about with freedom
and ease. The cases can be made with light wood, skeleton
frames, and covered with canvas or thin oil-cloth, or some similar
material; the advantage of using the latter is their lightness,
as they cost less in transit. The carriage of birds to and from
exhibitions is often a considerable item, and amounts to a good
round sum at the end of the year if you send a dozen or twenty
birds to every show of importance during the entire season.

TREATMENT BY SECRETARIES.—You will find it of advantage
to write to the secretaries of shows to ascertain whether the
hall or room in which the show is intended to be held is warmed
by the use of fires or stoves, and whether your birds can be
received a day or two before that on which the birds are to
be judged; but probably it would not be advisable to do this
if the antecedents of the secretary and committee are unknown
to you : but where you can rely upon any individual immediately
connected with an exhibition, it will be found commendable
to adopt this plan, for if Belgian canaries are exposed during
cold weather and become chilled on their journey to a show,
they are certain to lose their best form, and the result is
very frequently unsatisfactory both to the judges and exhibitors.
All birds newly come off a journey should have warm water, and
not cold, given them to drink, and you should request secretaries
to be careful always to give your birds a supply of this about
the same temperature as you would drink tea, as soon as they
receive them; never forget to send along with the birds a supply
of fresh egg and bread, with a sprinkling of maw seed among it,
to be given them as soon as they reach their destination. The
same treatment must be observed as soon as they reach home

on their return journey. Several instances have come within
my own personal knowledge where Belgian canaries have been
sent long distances in cold, bleak, wintry weather, with the
thermometer several degrees below freezing point, carelessly
packed, and badly protected against the bitter, biting winds and
falling snow. When the birds arrived they were "all in a
heap," shivering, and stupefied from the effect of the cold, and,
as might be expected, sat dull and mopish, and would not
"pull" themselves together. No wonder, then, that these birds
arriving only an hour or two before the judges were called
upon to decide upon their merits, were passed by unnoticed.
Next day, after they had got thoroughly warmed up, they might
have been seen "pulling" over everything in the class, to the
great chagrin of both judges and exhibitors. But who was
to blame? How often are judges of these birds subjected to
derision, by the unthinking portion of the "fancy," who hurl at
the heads of those poor unoffending men the most uncompli-
mentary and opprobrious epithets, when in reality no just
censure is attributable to them.

ADVICE TO JUDGES.—A hint here to judges and others
connected with shows may be found useful. As soon as you
enter a show where you have been chosen to act in a judicial
capacity, I would recommend you in the first place to take a look
through the classes for Belgian canaries. If you find a bird
drooping, call the attention of the secretary or other responsible
person to the fact, and request that such bird, or birds, may
at once be conveyed to the immediate locality of a fire or stove,
and there gradually warmed. In a case of this kind, always
leave the judging of these classes to the last; take care,
however, to have the bird, or birds, returned to their place fully
half an hour before you pronounce your final verdict on their
merits, otherwise, if the bird, or birds, had not time to cool
down, it, or they, might possibly get some slight advantage over
their antagonists who had not received a similar privilege.
Committees, too, should invariably place the Belgian classes in
the warmest part of the room. I have always found these
precautions, whether acting in the capacity of a judge, secretary,
or a committee-man, to give satisfaction. In judging Belgian

canaries, the greatest caution and discrimination are necessary, as all thoroughly practical men with ordinary observation must know that some birds, and especially those which have never been accustomed to " handling," are nervous and frightened, and consequently require to be approached with great care and circumspection, or they will plunge and dash about the cage in a panic-stricken manner, like a newly-caught linnet; and it requires some time to get them to settle steadily after this fantastic performance.

Other birds, on the contrary, who have been " over-trained," take an immense deal of energy to raise them to a sense of their duties. In cases of this kind I have invariably found it best to lift the cage containing the bold bird, and, placing it in front of me, have stealthily approached the timorous and fidgety one, taking care to do so in the most gentle manner possible, and by whistling or chirruping, or speaking softly and kindly I have generally succeeded in getting it to steady itself, whilst by a little manœuvring I have managed to get it into position. But birds of this stamp are very unsatisfactory to everybody concerned. If fanciers will only adopt the method of training previously pointed out, their birds will become bold and fearless, but it must not be overdone, or the remedy will be as much to be dreaded as the defect.

RULES OF A BELGIAN SOCIETY.—It will be interesting to English fanciers if I give them a translation of an old copy of rules, which I have in my possession, of a society established at Brussels. More especially at this time when a National Society is considered by most fanciers a very desirable institution.

The following is a literal translation of the rules referred to :

KINGDOM OF BELGIUM.

Central Society of Emulation formed at Brussels for the Societies and Amateur Fanciers of Belgian Canaries.

COMMITTEE.

•   •   •   •   •   •   •   •   •

RULES.

Chapter I —The Society—Its aim.

Article 1. Formed at Brussels, dating from 3rd October, 1854, a central company of emulation for the societies and the amateur fanciers of canaries of the kingdom of Belgium, to be called, The Central Society of Emulation. The society's year to commence on the 1st January and end 31st December of each year.

Art. 2. The institution of the society has for its aim—(a) To bind and consolidate the bonds of brotherhood by which all amateurs are united; (b) to regulate the assembling, and to determine the formation of juries; (c) to form measures of emulation in order to stimulate more and more the zeal and devotedness of all the amateur canary fanciers of the kingdom.

Chapter II.—Admission—Society's Funds.

Art. 3. The election of candidates as members of the society shall take place on written application to the committee, who shall decide on the admissibility of the applicants.

Art. 4. The subscription shall be 75 centimes (7½d.), which shall be paid in advance quarterly, either in money to the treasurer, who will give a receipt, or by P.O.O. in the name and to the address of the president, in which latter case the P.O.O. shall be held as proof of payment.

Art. 5. Any member who, at the expiration of three months from the time fixed for the payment of the subscription, may not have paid, will be considered no longer a member of the society.

Art. 6. The society's funds shall be applied to the payment of premiums, expenses of meeting, and the charges of correspondence, office rent, &c.

Chapter III.—Colours and Insignia.

Art. 7. The colours and insignia adopted as distinctive marks of the Central Society and by its members shall be yellow and blue, with embroidered roses, and a silver medal, having upon its face the emblem of the society in vermilion, encircled by the inscription, "Central Society of Emulation of the Amateurs of Canaries of the Kingdom of Belgium," and on the reverse, two Fringilla canaries, perched on an olive branch, and encircled by the device—Peace—Union—Progress.

Art. 8. The wearing of insignia to be determined as follows: (a) All members of the Central Society may wear at the buttonhole the medal, suspended by a ribbon of the colours above noticed; (b) members of the committee and of the jury shall so wear the medal in saltier, with ribbon of the same colours; (c) the president and vice-president shall wear in addition the colours of the Central Society, scarfwise or crosswise.

Chapter IV.—Meetings—Assemblies—Juries.

Art. 9. A general show of canaries among all the members of the society shall take place about February in each year. To participate in the show it is requisite to have been a member of the society for the whole of the previous year.

Art. 10. The order and locality where the shows shall be held shall be decided by drawing lots. All the members of the Central Society indiscriminately may enter the list, but for a town to enjoy the right to obtain a place it must have a society of ten members at least, being members of this society.

Art. 11. Delegates of societies adhering to the present rules shall meet at least once a year, at a general meeting to be held at Brussels, in order to settle the composition of juries, the basis of shows and the prizes. Societies failing to comply must abide by the decision of the members present.

Art. 12. No society shall send more than two members as delegates to the general meeting. A special regulation determining the basis and conditions of each assembly shall be settled at the general meeting.

Art. 13. The jury shall contain, as far as possible, sufficient elements to represent all the provincial societies. For this purpose the jury shall be composed of active or ordinary members. Members forming this jury to be named at the general assembly of the delegates held yearly, by show of hands. Jurors may participate in the show, but when appealed to for the price of a bird belonging to the class to which they are contributors, they shall instantly be replaced by ordinary members.

Chapter V.—The Committee—Its Powers.

Art. 14. The committee to be chosen and elected from the members of the Central Society, to consist of a president, vice-president, treasurer, secretary, and assistant secretary.

Art. 15. The president to be head of the society, his special functions and those of the other members of the committee to be determined by the bye-laws.

Art. 16. The committee shall meet at least once a month, at the head office, to take into consideration letters and writing, and so to act as they shall judge for the common interest of the members of the society.

Art. 17. The committee shall be re-elected every three years, the members retiring being eligible for re-election.

Art. 19. Any additional rule or thing not provided for by these rules shall be presented in writing to the committee by five members at least, and taken into consideration at a general meeting.

Art. 20. A copy of the present rules to be sent to all the societies and to all the amateurs of Belgian canaries, for their information and approval and convenience.

Made and settled at Brussels, at a general meeting of the fanciers, the 17th Oct. 1854.

* * * * * * ` * *

Our illustration is an excellent representation of a modern Belgian canary of the highest order.

GLASGOW DON, OR SCOTCH FANCY CANARY.

CHAPTER IX.

THE GLASGOW DON, OR SCOTCH FANCY.

I DO not know how it happens, but the tastes and ideas of Scotchmen and Englishmen are so thoroughly at variance with each other respecting canaries—which may almost be said to be national favourites—that any person not knowing the close proximity which exists between the two countries might very readily suppose that the two races were complete aliens to each other. On the one hand, Scotchmen as a rule care nothing for gay, glittering colours; nothing for beautiful even markings, nor delicately tinted pencillings; neither do they attach much value to crests, however good or exquisite they may be. What they admire most of all about canaries is huge size, plenty of bone, sinew, and muscle, combined with a certain peculiarity of form which, to use their own vernacular, they are pleased to term "hoopit," meaning circular in shape. To these birds they appear to be completely wedded, and they uphold them with a zeal and pertinacity that is almost enviable. But this is only characteristic of the people, for Scotchmen are proverbial for adhering, not only to each other, but to everything that appertains to Scotland, and which they are sure to laud, extol, and defend to the very uttermost of their power and abilities; indeed, so much so, that it has become quite an ordinary observation in England to say to any one similar in disposition, "You are as clannish as a Scotchman;" and this singularity of character is just as strongly exhibited among the bird fancying portion of the community as it is among any other class.

Scotchmen think very lightly of any other variety of canary

except the one which is nationalised to Scotland, unless it be the Belgian canaries. There are certainly a few among their number who are able to appreciate these birds; but as for the Norwich Fancy, London Fancy, Yorkshire Fancy, and the like, they set little value upon these varieties, as a rule; and I do verily believe that many of them would not accept the best specimens of these birds that could be found, as a present, if they were given upon the condition that they were not to part with them, so great is their aversion to these varieties of canaries. On the other hand, very few of our English fanciers look with favour upon the Scotch Fancy birds; they regard them as mere " mongrels," and style them half and three-parts bred Belgian canaries, and say, " What is the use of breeding these birds? far better go in for the genuine article at once." But the reason is that they do not understand the criterion of merit in these birds, and consequently they see them from a very different point of view to what Scotchmen do.

I am not quite sure myself but that our far-seeing friends are after all much nearer the mark than we in England are prone to acknowledge. They have evidently discovered by experience that the Belgian birds are naturally so extremely delicate that they are not constitutionally adapted to the severity of our climate; hence they have resolved to cross them with other birds, similar in form, but more hardy and thoroughly inured to this country, and have by this method produced a new variety, which is not very much inferior in point of symmetry, style, and majestic beauty to some of the Belgian birds, whilst they possess the advantage of being so thoroughly acclimatised as to be able to endure all the vicissitudes and hardships that can be borne by the strongest and hardiest of our other varieties. I do not contend that a " Don " or " Scotch Fancy " canary is equal to a high-class Belgian bird in external beauty—far from it—but I hold that they are by far the best substitutes that have been found; and when once you clearly understand the features that are striven to be obtained in these birds, you gradually begin to appreciate them. If the prejudice which Englishmen entertain towards these birds could be overcome, I think they would rank high in general estimation in a short time; but Englishmen appear to

have a difficulty in forgiving the Scotch fanciers for their utterly
ignoring so many of our favourite varieties, and for treating
them so ignominiously at most of their shows, never deigning to
offer a single prize to any of the numerous classes which are to
be found at any of the All England shows. It certainly is a
circumstance to be regretted, and we hope that the fanciers at
"Auld Reekie" (if at no other town) will so far relax their strin-
gency as to offer at least an "Any other Variety of Canary"
class at their shows in future.*

I have tried hard to find out how the Scotch Fancy birds
were originated, but the nearest approach that I have been able to
make in this direction is to trace them back for a period of fifty-
eight years to a breed of birds which, although much smaller in
size and less elegant in form than the "Dons" of the present
day, were nevertheless possessors of the circular form and the
"souple" (supple) tail, which are still the predominating features
in this particular variety of canaries; but a great improvement has been made in their appearance within the past twenty
years, and the "style" of the bird, as it is commonly called,
has been materially improved. At one time, if a bird showed the
least prominence of shoulder it was regarded as unfit for competition, and a good bird was supposed not to exhibit his thighs
when standing in proper position. Now the taste of that period
has completely changed, and good prominent, well-filled shoulders
are considered an indispensable requisite, and if a bird shows a
little thigh it is not considered any detriment, so long as its
general contour is correct.

The old-fashioned Dons appear to have emanated from Glasgow. One of the oldest and most respected fanciers in Scotland†
informed me that he had known the breed for the past forty-
eight years, and described them as "small birds" with "plenty of
action," and "cranked necks" and "crooked tails;" but where
the birds really originated, or how they became the possessors of
these peculiarities my informant did not say. But this is, it

---

* Since the first edition of "The Canary Book" was published, I am pleased to find that
some of our Scotch friends have not only given some encouragement to the English
varieties at their shows, but I am still further pleased to find that some of them
now admire and keep, and exhibit, some of these varieties.
† The late Mr. Robert Forsyth, of Edinburgh, a most honourable and upright man, and
respected by all who knew him.

seems, how they came to be named the "Glasgow Dons;" but they are now better known as the "Scotch Fancy" canaries. The old-fashioned Don of the period just alluded to is rarely to be met with, as much improvement has been made in the breed—first, by crossing them with the Dutch canary, a large strong bird, resembling the old-fashioned Belgian canary in shape, but with a heavily-frilled breast and back, and deficient in shoulders; but latterly they have been still further improved by being crossed with Belgian canaries of a more modern type, but round in form, and having tails inclined to curve inward.

BREEDING.—To breed Scotch Fancy birds up to the mark, good stock birds must be procured of the right shape and style to begin with. These can be further improved by being crossed with Belgian canaries of the shape already mentioned; but they must be smooth birds, as rough-feathered birds are regarded with disfavour by fanciers. From the first cross select those birds only that are of the true Don shape; discard the remainder. These birds ought to be crossed in with Dons again, and occasionally bred a little "sib" to keep the correct contour intact. Young Dons must be trained to travel, and you should commence their education at an early age, say when they are seven weeks old. Great care and caution are needed at first, as these birds are naturally of a wild and timid disposition, and if you once "gliff" them it is a long time before they forget it. Use the same precautions as I have recommended for training Belgian canaries, with this exception, that, instead of getting them to stand steady, you must excite them to action. They are trained to leap from perch to perch rapidly, and in doing this they best display their form, for which they are admired. At first you may use a thin lath or stick, but afterwards your fingers, or even the motion of your hand will be quite sufficient to induce them to display their agility.

CLASSES.—At all the principal shows in Scotland the Scotch Fancy birds are divided into eight classes at least—*i.e.,* yellow cocks, buff cocks, yellow hens, buff hens, flecked or piebald yellow cocks, flecked or piebald buff cocks, flecked or piebald yellow hens, flecked or piebald buff hens; and, in addition to these, there are occasionally classes made for pairs at most of the leading shows, such as Glasgow. It will be observed that separate classes are provided for the females, as it is contended that they do not possess a fair chance when competing against masculine opponents; but our brethren across the border can easily afford to do this, seeing that they rarely give classes for any other description of canaries, unless it be for Belgian Fancy and the common variety. The meaning of the terms "flecked" and "piebald" is that the birds are marked or variegated in colour. In some of the midland counties of England the word "skewed" is used to signify the same thing.

The enthusiasm displayed by the Scotch people for these birds is most wonderful, and the number of entries at some of their best shows is marvellous. I have known as many as fifty-eight buff hens competing in one class. One other fact is probably worthy of note, and that is that Scotchmen like, as the Irishmen put it, " a power o' judges;" for, at the show held in Glasgow, on the 21st of November, 1868, there were no fewer than twelve judges appointed to officiate, the total number of birds exhibited on that occasion being 428.

POINTS.—There is a difference of opinion, even among Scotchmen, as to the "style" of their favourite birds, and this is accounted for by dividing the fanciers into what they themselves have been pleased to designate the "old school" and the "new school." The former belong to that class of people who have a great aversion to changes, hence they still appreciate the little old-fashioned Don, whilst the latter are the go-a-heads that are always striving to get something better than their neighbours. I belong to the latter class, and for this reason I purpose giving the best description I can of the Scotch Fancy canary of the present day, and which is considered to be the *beau idéal* of a Glasgow Don by those who are looked upon as the best authorities on this subject.

Length of bird from 6in. to 7½in.; a few, but not many, may possibly exceed these dimensions; head small and flat on the crown, but full of character, with neatly rounded cheeks; neck long and fine; and gracefully arched shoulders rather prominent; back narrow and long, and well filled up, tapering from the shoulders to the tail; chest full and well formed; waist long and fine; legs long in the shank, with moderately long thighs; tail long, thin, and compact, well " circled," and very free ("souple")ֹ The form of the bird from the crown of the head to the tip of the tail ought to resemble as near as possible the segment of a circle. The tail, which is considered to constitute one of its chief points of admiration, must be supple as supple can be, and should not exhibit the slightest symptom of stiffness; it should be carried well under the perch without touching it. The legs ought to be set far back, and kept well under the bird. The carriage must be bold, free, and majestic, without restraint, and with a certain air of intrepidity about it.

The markings most admired by Scotchmen are, singular to say, those which are almost universally despised by all English fanciers, viz.: An entirely dark head and collar, a breast mark (which, to be deemed really good, must resemble in form a horse's shoe), heavy wing markings, and a feather or two on each side of the tail; but markings go for very little, and only count when two birds are equal in other points. In a case of this kind the markings would be had recourse to to kick the beam; but a dark, badly-marked bird would be placed before a perfectly marked one, if the latter was inferior in "style" to the former.

Next to form of body, which is one of the great essential characteristics in a good Don, come style and carriage, and a well-formed, free tail; for if a good bird possesses the former and lacks the latter qualities, he is looked upon pretty much in the same light as a woman would be if she were of good figure and had thoroughly classical features, but was wanting in vivacity — without warmth, soul, inspiration — a mere cold, phlegmatic beauty. A bird to be completely attractive must be full of life and action, which gives a charm and brilliancy to its external appearance that is lost without it—this is style when combined with correct features.

TRAVELLING.—These birds are commonly trained to pass rather briskly from perch to perch by a motion of the hand. This is denoted "travelling," and unless a bird is a rapid and graceful mover its chances as a prize-taker are sure to be greatly impaired. Whenever a bird travels from one perch to another the motion of its tail is critically observed, and unless it is perfectly free and glib it is reckoned a fault.

STYLE.—The style of a bird is a weighty consideration with Scotchmen. Some fanciers prefer birds with substance about them, although the majority prefer them fine and slender: but if a bird only possesses in an eminent degree the circular form, good shoulders, fine waist, good carriage, activity, and a long free tail, with plenty of length, and compact in feather, the sticklers for stoutness or thinness soon disappear.

STANDARD OF EXCELLENCE.—The following standard has been carefully arranged, and will be found to give the relative value of the different points of merit attributable to each particular feature, 100 points being regarded as a maximum of perfection:

STANDARD FOR JUDGING GLASGOW DONS.

	Points.
Head	4
Neck	6
Shoulders	5
Back	7
Chest	4
Waist	4
Wings	3
Legs	5
Tail	12
Size	8
Form or Contour (circular)	18
Style and Travelling	10
Quality of Feathers	4
Condition	10
Total	100

The bird represented in our illustration is a specimen of the first water.

CHAPTER X.

THE MODERN SCOTCH FANCY.

It is with no inconsiderable amount of pleasure, I observe that this elegant and aristocratic member of the canary family has merged from its comparative seclusion, and now creates a wide-spread interest amongst a large portion of English fanciers.

Before this variety was described in the first edition of the " Canary Book," it was confined entirely to Scotland and the border towns of Berwick, Northumberland, and Cumberland. It is now over twenty years since I became warmly interested in this magnificent production of Scotia, for to our far-seeing and discriminating friends in North Britain are we indebted for this handsome race of birds, so full of grace, beauty, and refinement, elegance of form and contour, combined and blended in a symmetrical whole.

Some eighteen years ago no other variety, with the solitary exception of the Belgian and common canary, were tolerated ayont the Tweed, but since that period great and rapid strides have been made in the endeavour to improve and make perfect this variety. A keen and unerring eye for elegance of form is one of the natural instincts of Scotchmen, and most of them are gifted with critical and refined tastes as well, which guide them in their selection of birds of the most approved type. In the method of judiciously crossing these birds, exhibiting as they usually do much skill and care in producing all the points of merit and excellence observable in high-class specimens, Scotch fanciers have been able to overcome many obstacles, and to breed out the defects noticeable in earlier specimens.

The great advantage of the present improved race over the old-fashioned "Glasgow Don"—the name by which it was originally known, but which I took the liberty to widen and extend when I wrote my book by giving the broader, and I think more effective title of the "Scotch Fancy"—has been accomplished by blending with the old variety the most admirable qualities of the Belgian canary, this cross tending to improve the style, contour, and symmetry, as well as the ease and grace peculiar to these birds, which in reality constitute their chief features and individuality. One of the greatest difficulties to overcome by breeders has been delicacy of constitution, which arose in consequence of the use of the Belgian cross, these birds being naturally delicate and prone to disease, such as asthma and consumption. To a great extent this difficulty has now been overcome by care and judicious selection. The old Dons are a hardy, vigorous race of birds, and the cross with them and the Belgians has added vigour and robustness to the present breed (which some fanciers term the Scotia-Belgian Canary), many of which are strong, vigorous birds, and full of life and vivacity. They have likewise no doubt been greatly invigorated by acclimatisation and a more effectual method of feeding than is practised in Belgium. The groats given by Scotchmen to their birds add to the enlargement and strengthening of frame and muscle—elements that are wanting in the sylph-like creatures that are so admired by the Belgians.

It is now about seventeen years since the first edition of the "Canary Book" appeared, and in it I strove hard to create among all lovers of the canary a special interest in this particular variety, and I feel gratified that my efforts should have borne such good fruit. But our English fanciers have much to learn before they can hope to compete with Scotia's sons on the show bench, as they are not all fully aware of the characteristics most esteemed and valued, neither are they

well acquainted with the mode of obtaining them; that has
to be acquired by deep study and close observation, and it
will require years of practical breeding to insure success, as
Scotsmen do not as a rule believe in allowing their best birds
to leave the country, whatever the temptation offered may be.

I will, in dealing with this subject, endeavour to throw some
light on the *modus operandi* to be observed in breeding, and
I trust it will be the means of assisting and giving renewed
hopes to Englishmen who are desirous of perfecting their
strains, according to the most modern ideas prevalent among
Scotsmen, as to what constitutes a "model" specimen of a
gran' burd.

Besides having lived for nearly ten years at that noted old
border town, Berwick-on-Tweed, where several ardent fanciers
and breeders of these birds reside, and in close proximity to
Ayton, Hawick, Galashiels, and other border towns, where
high-class specimens have at different times been produced,
I have been in close communication for several years with
many of the most eminent breeders in some of these towns
and in Edinburgh, and have bred and successfully competed
with birds of my own breeding against the most distinguished
exhibitors in Scotland at that day. I hope, therefore, to be
able to assist those who have not had the same opportunities
of extending their knowledge.

I have already, in the previous chapter, given full details
of the old variety of the "Glasgow Don," and I will, in
dealing with the new type, endeavour to set forth clearly and
tersely the principal methods adopted by the best breeders of
the day in obtaining, developing, and perfecting the high
qualities possessed by the birds of the present day. It must,
however, not be forgotten that there is even now a great deal
of difference of opinion among the Scotch fanciers themselves,
and a goodly proportion of those of the old school condemn
the using of Belgian blood too freely, which they consider an
innovation, and some even go so far as to say that the "grand
old breed is being ruined by young go-a-heads."

It is a common and prevalent idea among amateur bird

fanciers that experienced breeders will spontaneously divulge the best and .most approved methods whereby show specimens of any and every variety of canary may be produced; but a little reflection ought to convince them of the absurdity and the unreasonableness of such a notion, as it can scarcely be expected that men who have spent large sums of money and years of labour and study in producing and perfecting certain features and characteristics difficult of attainment by which they hope to reap some advantage, either pecuniary or by making a name and becoming famous, are likely to stand at the corners of streets and proclaim to the world at large their hard-earned knowledge. Amateurs must therefore climb the ladder of fame for themselves; long purses and advice obtained from experienced people aid beginners and novices very considerably, and save them much time and labour, but they must not expect experienced breeders to give advice without receiving from them a *quid pro quo* in lieu thereof. As a rule, breeders are very reticent in imparting information which has cost them much labour to obtain, and few will blame them for their silence on a subject which has cost them so much time and money. But my ideas differ widely from that of the majority of fanciers, inasmuch as I think that by the general dissemination of knowledge, and by giving brother fanciers a helping hand up the rugged path that leads to fame, we multiply the number of bird lovers and bring within our ranks men of probity and intelligence, thus at once extending the fancy and raising it to a higher standard. Personally, I consider that any man who is not willing to render all the assistance he can to his brother fanciers by imparting any discovery he may have made is hardly worthy of the name of a true fancier.

Any person who possesses large means can claim at exhibitions or purchase from the exhibitors some of their most successful specimens, for the purpose of breeding or exhibiting; but this is only a preliminary step in the right direction for a beginner, for much has to be learnt of the methods of selection and crossing, as well as how to feed and prepare birds· for exhibition in order to achieve success, and this must be a matter of time and much vigilance. The "Dons" of half a century ago were described to me by an old fancier as "smallish birds, vara hookit in shape (circular in form), and had vara thin sma bodies and gleg tails, and as souple as eels"; and further that they were "vara sma as compared we burds ye see the day," referring to his own birds, we being in his bird-room at the time. He said they were "real bonny and nicely shapit." Those in his possession had, I observed, a goodly supply of the old Belgian canary in their composition, but nothing as compared with the birds of the present period, which, for head, neck, and shoulder properties would compare favourably with high-class birds of this variety. I mentioned this to my friend, and his reply was, "That's richt, they are weel crossed wi the richt stamp o' bird, and that's hoo they are sae muckle improved, but it wadna dae to use these straight-backed anes wi high shoulders and stiff tails, as are sae fashionable the noo," referring to the modern straight-backed Belgian birds with high shoulders and long drooping necks. But even the taste of that day has been modified, and birds of this description have been used in order to gratify the modern taste of fanciers. In the specimens published by *Poultry*, February 27th, 1891, Mr. G. Lawson's buff Scotch Fancy cock, drawn by Mr. Harrison Weir, shows as much Belgian blood as that of the Scotch Fancy.

The idea of the present generation of fanciers is to get the Belgian head, neck, and shoulders planted on the Scotch Fancy body. Mr. Lawson's bird was specially referred to by Mr. Thos. Smith, Vice-President of the Glasgow and West of Scotland Association, and Secretary to the Glasgow Southern and Glasgow Southern Albert Societies, at the annual meeting and social gathering of the Glasgow Ornithological Association, held on the 6th of March, 1891. Mr. Smith said, in reference to arriving at a definite understanding as to what is really a Scotch Fancy canary, "The latest was Mr. Lawson's buff cock, which is a near approach to the best of the proposed models."

The friend to whom I have already referred once said to me, "We mun hae the circle and the gleg tail; these canna be dispensed with at nae price." And these characteristics are still preserved, and in my opinion constitute the most important feature in a bird of this variety. The origin of these birds was probably a cross between the old French and Dutch canaries, and then with the old type of Belgian canary, which was more circled than those of the present day. Twenty years ago a "Don" was required to be slim, very circular in form ("half mooned" as many Scotch breeders term it), fine in feather, with great freedom and grace of movement, and quick action and celerity, known as "style," which is obtained by training the birds to move rapidly from perch to perch by a motion of the hands. In the old-fashioned "Don" prominence of shoulder was not admissible, as it was considered to break the circular line; an exhibition of thigh was looked upon as a grave defect, and a stiff tail as most objectionable.

Such was the ideal Scotch Fancy a quarter of a century ago, and even less; but comparing a bird of this description with one of the present period, it might truly be said, in scriptural language, "Behold, old things have passed away, and all things have become new," for the ideal bird of the present generation of fanciers is a widely different creature in its general *tout ensemble* to the bird we have described, and some of our English fanciers are difficult to persuade that the modern birds are Scotch Fancies at all. They regard these more recently produced specimens as Belgians pure and simple, as they do not discover the difference between the round back and tail of the "Don" and the square back and straight tail of the Belgian bird.

From what we have said, it will be readily understood that the only way to obtain birds that are likely to meet with approval is to breed freely between the long circular Dons and the big-shouldered, long-necked, fine-headed Belgian birds, selecting for future use all birds that possess the best points required; the object being to get the fine head, neck, and shoulders of the Belgian canary planted on the circular free-tailed Don, and so modelled as to have the upper part of the bird a good Belgian, and the other part a good Don.

To a well-circled Don hen, with good length of side, plenty of neck, and a long sweeping free tail, and well hollowed out in front, put a Belgian cock with a fine head, long drooping neck, and prominent well-filled shoulders, and if possible with a back and tail inclined to the circular form. From this pair you must select birds nearest to the " model" and dip in again to the Don on one side, and the Belgian on the other as circumstances· require, carefully selecting and pairing your stock until you obtain birds as near the ideal model as possible, then breed brother. and sister together to establish the features you have gained, and breed out from these again in the direction most needed, and again resort to in-breeding from first cousins, the result of your next cross, but do not overdo this sib-breeding or you will weaken the constitution of your birds. It will take years of careful breeding to produce the stamp of birds you want.

You may, by buying birds from experienced breeders, save yourself some time in crossing, but you must be careful not to be misled, and the safest method to adopt will be to begin on the plan indicated. I must not, however, omit to warn the beginner against trusting to Scotch Fancies to rear their own progeny, as they are as a rule indifferent feeders, and therefore the breeder must be prepared with some reliable foster mothers, and for this purpose I would recommend Cinnamon hens in preference to all others, the majority of them being very reliable feeders.

Even markings are not cultivated among the Scotch fanciers, who do not pay much regard to markings, but go on the principle that "a good horse is never a bad colour." It is form and style that they esteem most. I have seen several very good specimens of the Scotch Fancy, both Cinnamon, and Cinnamon variegated (hens of course), but it shows that at some remote period a dip of pure Cinnamon blood has been mingled with the blood of these aristocrats of the north, as this is a colour that will make its appearance in future generations, when once it is implanted in the blood.

The object of the modern breeder is to get a bird with a fine sleek head, a neat back, and long well-tapered neck, with plenty of forward reach, and tightly fitted to the shoulders. The shoulders should be prominent, nicely rounded and well filled up, leaving no hollow; the back should be round, or circular and narrow; the wings should be long, well formed, close fitting to the sides, and meet at the tips; the chest should be well hollowed out, showing no prominence; the under-body from neck to vent should be perfectly concave, or as it is more generally termed, "well scooped out"; the legs should be set well back on the body, and not show too prominently; the tail should be long, thin, and tapering to a point, not fish-tailed, well padded at the vent, and brought well under and around the perch. The bird should display much nerve, and travel from perch to perch with a rapid and graceful motion, pulling itself into position each time it alights on the perch, and displaying all its best qualities in the fullest perfection.

The faults in a bird of this variety are here summarised: A prominent thick forehead, wide skull, a thick or short neck (which causes the bird to elevate its head too high), a heavy or pouter chest, a too heavily feathered breast, flat shoulders, a straight back, or back too broad, or a hollow between the shoulders and forming a sort of channel, short thick-set wings, or wings that cross or hang loosely, a tail that is short, straight, stiff, or badly filled up at the vent, or loose and untidy or deficient in feather at the base, too much thigh or a want of feathering on the thighs, a short reach, a want of nerve or action, and a stiffness or sluggishness in motion.

The feathers on the body should be smooth and tight, and it is scarcely necessary to remark that the health and condition should be perfect in a show specimen.

POINTS FOR JUDGING.

	Points.
Head, for sleekness and neatness, including bill	7
Neck, for length, fineness, reach and set on	12
Shoulder for prominence, roundness, and finish	15
Back for roundness, narrowness, and being well filled-up	10
Wings for length, tightness, and carriage	5
Tail for length, form, and suppleness	15
Chest, well hollowed out	8
Legs	5
Size, length and reach, general form, contour, feathering, and condition	15
Nerve and travelling	8
Total	100

ADVICE TO BREEDERS.—I would advise all amateurs, as far as possible, to eschew birds possessing any of the worst faults I have enumerated, that is, if they desire to breed show specimens, for the faults as well as the good properties are sure to be perpetuated, if birds possessing them are used for breeding purposes. Minor faults may be overcome by judicious breeding and selection, for no bird is perfect, and if a bird has many good properties, and only a few faults, these in time may be bred out.

LANCASHIRE COPPY CANARY.

CHAPTER XI.

THE MANCHESTER COPPY.

SINCE the publication of the first edition of "The Canary Book" a marked improvement has taken place in the estimation of fanciers with regard to this variety. Instead of this breed of birds being confined, as heretofore, almost entirely to the county of Lancaster, and few or no classes being provided for them at some of the principal shows in the United Kingdom, now a very extensive and active demand for them has been created in all parts of the country. This is owing in a great measure to the fact of their now being much used to cross with the Norwich crested variety to gain size in body, and to increase and improve the form of the crests of the birds, and classes for "Coppies" are now made by the committees of all shows with any pretension to be considered "leading shows."

The true Coppy is a large, noble looking bird, and very commanding in appearance. It had its origin in and around the town of Manchester, and was first introduced to public notice under the name of the "Manchester Coppy." These birds are extensively bred in the town just named, and likewise at Oldham, Rochdale, Ashton-under-Lyne, and Stalybridge, and from these towns the best specimens are derived.

ORIGIN.—The Coppy canaries originated from the old Dutch variety, now almost extinct, and which they very greatly resemble in size and general conformation. The crest or "coppy" has no doubt been the result of an extraneous cross with some other variety possessing this appendage, as we never remember having seen a specimen of the old Dutch variety adorned with a crest, and hence has arisen the appellation or title of the " Manchester " or " Lancashire Coppy." It is now thirty-four years since we first saw a bird of this kind, and those we saw were the property of a very spirited fancier who always made it a rule to purchase the best description of birds of the varieties he kept that money could procure; hence we presume that the birds we then saw were good specimens of the variety at that day; they were, however, much inferior to the birds of the present day in size and contour, and at that time I thought they were a cross between a Dutch canary and one of the common crested variety, and I dare say I was not far from the mark in my conjecture.

POINTS.—The Coppy is probably the largest and most massive of all the members of the canary family, and a good specimen should measure fully eight inches in length from the tip of the bill to the end of the tail, and some birds may be found to exceed these dimensions. I have one in my possession now which is considerably over eight inches.

The principal points of admiration in these birds are size, length, and stoutness, and crest. The head should be large, long as well as broad, the beak small and neatly formed, and clear in colour, the neck long, straight and massive, the body should be of great length and very full throughout, with a deep broad chest, large expansive shoulders, square, but not prominent like a Belgian or Scotch Fancy canary, and should exhibit great substance throughout the entire body, the body should likewise extend considerably behind the thighs and appear thick and full to the seat of the tail. They should have good legs, long and massive, showing plenty of thigh. The bird should be erect in carriage, and graceful in its movements, and appear straight in the back from the base of the skull to the rump, but having a gentle but clearly defined curve from the throat to the vent on the under side of the body; the tail should be long and straight, rather massive but compact, and slightly drooping from the tips of the wings; the wings should be closely braced and meet at the extremities or nearly so, although Coppies are very frequently cross-winged, the result of breeding too frequently from two buffs. The crest or "coppy," which is a very distinctive feature in this variety, should be round in form, full, flat, and very closely and densely packed, without the least appearance of a break or split in any part of it; it should come well over the eyes and beak of the bird, drooping all round, and finish off at the back of the head without showing deficiency of feather. No part of the skull of a good bird should be visible at the back of the head or termination of the lateral crest. The crest should have a clearly defined but close and compact centre, and the feathers should radiate from this point in a uniform manner all round, giving it the appearance of a daisy in full bloom. The position of the bird when placed in a show cage is very important; it should be erect, easy, and elegant, and not cowering or timid; the feathers profuse, but fitting close to the body, not rough, and showing a frill on breast, or coarseness in other parts of the body, wings, or tail; the crest or "coppy," as well as the under body feathers, should be perfectly clear in colour, free from any dark tinge, and should blow as white and soft as floss silk. Some Coppies are quite plain at the back of the head.

The natural colour of these birds is pale, whether yellows or buffs. The "Plain Heads" should be possessed of the same points of excellence in conformation of body, size, &c., as the crested variety, and the feathers forming what is termed the bird's eyebrows should project over the eyes, called by some fanciers "over-hanging eyebrows," and the more a bird shows this peculiarity the better it is considered to be bred for crest. Some of the most experienced breeders, in order to improve the crests of these birds, frequently breed them "double crested"—that is, two crested birds together, but in doing so two birds are chosen that are deficient in crest properties—for example, one bird is selected with a short or a split frontal crest, and the other showing a sparsity of back crest. Sometimes a good bird is obtained in this way, but the Plain Heads which are bred from breeding with two Coppies are the most highly esteemed for re-crossing with Coppy birds again, and I am assured by a successful breeder and exhibitor of these birds that this is the best plan to improve the size and form of the crest.

There is at the present day a great rage for this variety of canary; but for some reason or other prime specimens appear to be getting very scarce. I imagine this has arisen in consequence of the great demand during late years for crossing with the Norwich variety to obtain increased size of bodies and crest properties; and the majority of the Lancashire breeders appear to have unwittingly disposed of their best birds at tempting prices, and kept inferior stock to breed from themselves. It is the greatest mistake a fancier could possibly commit, for in addition to the best blood procurable, you require the best specimens you can obtain to produce high-class youngsters. Never forget this.

In Rochdale, Oldham, Manchester, and other Lancashire towns, this variety of canary is still held in the highest estimation, and nowhere else can be found birds of greater merit than have been produced at one or other of the towns named. The Lancashire Coppy is to a Lancashire man what a Scotch Fancy is to a Scotchman, the beau ideal of his highest fancy, the concentrated reality of his keenest imagination.

BREEDING.—In order to breed A1 specimens of this variety you must first procure a high-class Coppy cock, a bird of great length and substance, a strong, bold, upstanding bird, with a massive head, and an abundance of crest, well arranged, expansive, and of good quality and form, and in addition to these properties you want a good constitution, for it is useless to breed from diseased or unhealthy birds, however good they may be. Pair this bird with a thoroughly well-bred hen, a crested plain-head, large in body, with plenty of length, broad in back and shoulders, with a massive skull, a neat beak, a stout neck and full breast, good substantial legs, and a long strait tail set well on, and with an abundance of head and body feather; but the first-named is most essential, it should, when turned back, almost reach the end of the beak, and should hang well over the eyes and the back of the head, almost like a tight-fitting crest. You may if you choose put two such hens with the cock. This is pair one, but you want about ten pairs at least if you hope to be successful. You may if you choose use a plain-head cock and a Coppy hen possessing the points already named. The reason that I prefer a Coppy cock is that he can be run with two plain-head hens and produce crested birds from both, whereas if a plain-head cock is used you would require two Coppy hens to produce crested birds from both pairs, and crested or Coppy birds when good are much more expensive than plain-heads. Another advantage in this plan is a saving of expense, as there is a much greater risk of losing hens than cocks during breeding operations, as hens frequently become egg-bound, and occasionally ruptured in the act of laying eggs. Apart from these considerations, I am of opinion that the cock bird, as a rule, has the greatest influence on the progeny. At most of the Lancashire shows they have as many as eight classes for this variety of bird, which are divided as follows: 1. Clear Yellow Coppy; 2. Clear Buff Coppy; 3. Clear Yellow Plain-head; 4. Clear Buff Plain-head; 5. Ticked Yellow Coppy; 6. Ticked Buff Coppy; 7. Ticked Yellow Plain-head; 8. Ticked Buff Plain-head.

Clear and ticked yellow birds of superior quality are much more difficult to obtain than good buffs, as they are not nearly so plentiful. The ticked birds are invariably the best, and these are the kind that Norwich breeders should purchase.

Lancashire men, however, regard their clear birds most highly; but in order to improve them in size and crest it is necessary to have recourse to the ticked birds occasionally. Some breeders put two ticked birds together, and keep all the clear birds bred from them, and pair these with clear birds again, for it is well-known that the best crests are obtained by using this cross, as it is also the best for increasing the size and substance of the birds. The plan mostly followed is to mate a ticked Coppy with a clear plain-head, and to pair the produce of these birds with clears, the ticked blood only being resorted to once in two or three years, as many of the Lancashire breeders are greatly averse to the ticked birds, but for what reason it is difficult to say, except that clear birds are most highly prized. The ticked birds have become more plentiful of late years, and this, no doubt, has arisen from the fact that some breeders have had the temerity to introduce a clear- or grey-crested bird of the modern Norwich type into their strain to improve the head of the Coppy, but many of them would now be glad to expunge it, as it has led to smaller sized birds being produced. It is also recommended by some breeders to put two Coppies together, say once in four or five years, to increase the size and fullness of the crest and width of skull, but it is rare to breed a show bird in this way, although occasionally a good specimen is produced; but it is singular, as well as true, that breeding after this fashion produces loss of length and size generally, and to overcome this drawback it is considered necessary by some of the most successful breeders of this variety to put two plain-heads together and mate the produce of these with the double-crested bred birds, as the produce of the latter frequently have rough mop crests, or are bald at the back of the head, and by crossing with double-bred plain-heads, these defects are most quickly remedied. In breeding from two Coppy or crested birds both should be of good quality, with moderately large crests, but free from baldness at the back of the head, bareness at the upper part of the neck, and open centres; neither bird should be too full in body-feather, or coarse offspring will be the result. The best birds to select for this purpose are a yellow Coppy cock and a buff Coppy hen; under no circumstances should a Coppy bred from two Coppies be mated with a Coppy again, or the produce will be most unsatisfactory.

To pair a buff plain-head with a buff Coppy, or a buff ticked Coppy, is a plan often resorted to by the best breeders, as it has a tendency to increase the length and bulk of the body of the produce, and it also increases the length and density of the feathers, but it should only be adopted at intervals of two or three years, or the birds will be produced too rough, and will deteriorate in colour and quality of feather likewise. In following out this plan of breeding the best coloured birds should be selected. Some fanciers breed from two buff Coppies, in place of a buff and a yellow, and the result is generally the production of rough- and slack-feathered birds. Discard all birds to breed from that inherit grave faults, such as open centres, split side or frontal crests, bareness at the base of the skull or neck, with back and tails inclined to be circular, cross wings, loose ungainly tails, or birds that are narrow in the head, and with thin scraggy necks or weakly legs, or birds that do not stand erect on the perch. As soon as you succeed in producing birds of a good stamp you must adopt the plan I have frequently recommended for many years in breeding birds of other varieties, viz., consanguinity or in-breeding, for there is nothing to equal it when used in moderation for perpetuating the features you desire to retain.

Lancashire birds, like their progenitors, the Dutch and Belgian canaries, are not reliable nurses; very few of them excel in this respect, and the males I have generally found to be worse than the females. Therefore, if you decide to breed birds of this kind, by all means obtain a few good reliable foster parents, either German, Cinnamons, Greens, or Crossbreds (between the Yorkshire and Norwich variety), all of which as a rule are good nurses, otherwise you will not succeed in your endeavours, although you may put up several pairs to breed from. Another great drawback to these large and noble birds, the Lancashires, is their great lack of stamina; they are far from robust and vigorous birds, taken as a whole, and they are prone to be affected by those terrible maladies, asthma and consumption, which are probably the most troublesome and fatal complaints that affect the canary.

Some of the specimens I have seen have evidently been crossed with the Belgian canary, but these are much thinner in the body, considerably narrower in the head, and flat at the sides; furthermore, they exhibit a little of the Belgian shape in the curvature of the back, and are never possessed of such expansive crests as those which are full of the old Dutch canary.

s

STANDARD OF EXCELLENCE.—100 points to be taken as a maximum of perfection.

STANDARD FOR JUDGING LANCASHIRE COPPIES.

	Points.
Head and Beak..	8
Neck...	6
Back...	8
Breast...	8
Legs...	6
Wings...	8
Tail...	4
Feathers for Closeness and Quality..............	6
Colour..	3
Size of Bird..	10
Contour and Position...............................	8
Crest...	15
Condition...	10
Total...	**100**

The Evenly-marked Yorkshire Canary.

This variety has been produced chiefly by crossing the Belgian with the
Lancashire Coppy, the Cinnamon Variegated, and other kinds.

CHAPTER XII.

THE YORKSHIRE FANCY.

THE bird fanciers in London, Norwich, Scotland, and other towns and countries, each have a special and distinct variety of canary of their own; and Yorkshiremen, actuated, no doubt, with the laudable desire to aim at originality, and to emulate the example set by their *confrères*, have attempted to establish a variety of canaries peculiar to the county of "broad acres." With this object in view, they have striven to produce a breed of birds differing in some respects from all known varieties, and, to some extent, their endeavours have been crowned with success. At the present moment this breed of birds may be regarded as being in its infancy, but no doubt in the course of a few more years we shall see a marked progress and improvement in them.* Improvement always takes a considerable time to develop—in anything appertaining to perfection—a new variety of any description, whether it be birds, animals, plants, flowers, or what not, for in point of fact there is invariably a diversity of opinion, even among those who are considered best able to judge of their merits or demerits, as to what ought to constitute an essential quality and what a disparagement; and until these differences are finally set at rest onward progress is sure to be retarded.

BREEDING.—The Yorkshire Fancy birds are produced chiefly by crossing the Belgian Fancy and some other varieties of canaries together, such, for instance, as the Manchester Coppy,

---

* Since the foregoing was written a marked improvement in the contour of these birds has taken place.

the Cinnamon variegated, and the common breed of canary; and some breeders, who are fond of rich bright colours, have ventured to introduce a cross of the Norwich Fancy blood as well; but the majority of them—and among these may be counted their most ardent admirers—entirely ignore both the colour and shape of the Norwich variety, and regard all specimens inheriting any of the properties of the last-named breed with much disfavour.

To breed Yorkshire Fancy canaries successfully and fit for competition it will be necessary to procure a few long, thin Belgian canaries, or, to be more accurate in my description, I probably ought to say three-quarter bred Belgian canaries, select those that are very deficient in shoulder and as straight in shape as they can be obtained—in fact, to speak plainly, birds known in the "fancy" as "bad Belgian canaries,"—those least esteemed and of little value except for breeding purposes of this sort. In addition to these you should get a few plain-headed Manchester Coppies and a few half-bred Dutch or French canaries—I prefer the latter for my own fancy—always keep in view great length of body and tail; the recognised shape and fineness of feather as well. Cross the different breeds of birds already enumerated in such a way as you consider best calculated to obtain the qualities most desired, always eschewing all birds to breed from that show the least inclination to curves whether in the back or tail. After you succeed in producing a race of birds to your mind, adopt the method of "sib" breeding (in-and-in), and this may be indulged in pretty freely at first, as it is the safest plan to follow, and the only one that can be relied upon with certainty for reproducing, establishing, and perpetuating certain features with accuracy, but, as I have before pointed out, in treating of other varieties, care must be taken not to overdo it, or your birds will degenerate in size and stamina, and become puny and delicate. Experience, however, will prove the best and most trustworthy tutor in this respect. The observations I have made relate to the clear varieties only. If you desire to breed evenly-marked birds or unevenly-marked birds, you must observe strictly the same rules for crossing as those laid down for breeding the marked varieties of Norwich Fancy canaries.

Some slight alterations have taken place in the style and type of these-birds since I wrote my former account of them. At a conference held at Bradford, Yorkshire, in 1890, it was agreed that the length of a bird of this variety should not exceed 6¾in. in length, to be eligible for competition at any show. This regulation is to prevent too free a use of the Lancashire cross, and to preserve the type from running in that direction. The head of the bird now should be slightly arched at the crown, and colour is more keenly sought after than heretofore; but this addition to their appearance is most frequently obtained by artificial means, *i.e.*, "colour feeding," in the same manner as that applied to the Norwich and Cinnamon varieties, breeds in which colour is a great desideratum. For my part I do not think that a bird should be rejected that measures 7in. in length, and I had hoped that this length would have been allowed.

The Lancashire cross has been freely used in the manufacture of this variety to get the birds into the form most admired, viz., straight, and to take away the slight curvature of the back, resulting from the Belgian alliance; but only those Lancashires are used that are long, straight, and slim, and sparse of feather, a class of birds that Lancashire breeders sell as "weeds" and "stragglers." Careful selection is one of the great sources of success in building up a good reliable strain of Yorkshires, or in fact of any other variety; but to this breed it is particularly applicable.

There will no doubt be bickerings and wordy disputes about measurements, as it is doubtful whether any two judges can measure a bird to a-quarter-of-an-inch. The measurement is usually obtained by placing a bird on its side, on a 2ft. rule, such as is used by carpenters, and I contend that a judge may, if he be so disposed, stretch a bird fully a-quarter-of-an-inch; but to be perfectly fair no bird should be subject to this operation. The usual method is to take the length from the point of the bill to the end of the tail, and to ensure exactness a padded frame should be used, with an upright piece of wood at one end and a sliding piece at the other,

similar to that used by shoemakers in taking a measure for
boots; the contrivance should be made to work backwards
and forwards, and if a wood bottom were used with a scale
of 8in. divided into eighths, it would probably be considered
satisfactory, but until something of the kind is used the
measuring of birds is likely to lead to · very unsatisfactory
results.

With these alterations I am disposed to make a slight change
in, the standard for judging the clear and ticked birds, as
follows :

STANDARD FOR JUDGING CLEAR AND TICKED BIRDS.

	Points.
Head and neck	10
Back and shoulders	15
Chest and waist	10
Legs	7
Tail	7
Size of bird	8
Colour	8
Quality and feather	10
Contour, position, and style	15
Condition	10
Total	100

There is a difficulty as to what constitutes a ticked bird,
and some judges disqualify a bird in a clear class because
a dark under-fluff feather may be discovered on the leg by
handling.

This is carrying the matter a little too far, as it is not at
all improbable that if the bird were shown under another
judge as a ticked bird it would be disqualified or passed
over as being a clear bird; such a slight blemish might be
considered by a judge in giving his award between two birds
of equal merit in all other respects, and this would only be
fair and right. I have often regretted having classified ticked
birds with unevenly-marked birds, as I am now of opinion
that ticked birds should either form a separate class, or be
allowed to compete on equal terms with clear birds, and that

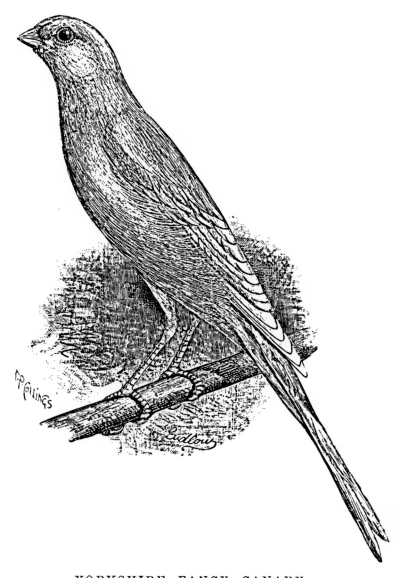

YORKSHIRE FANCY CANARY.

no birds should be allowed to be shown in an unevenly-marked class with less than two distinct and visible marks or patches of a dark colour. When ticks are so slight as to be almost invisible to the naked eye, there can be no valid objection to their being shown in a class for clear birds, and such birds are almost invariably bred from clear birds.

CLASSES.—There are six classes of Yorkshire Fancy canaries, and these are generally divided as follows: Clear yellow clear buff, evenly-marked yellow, evenly-marked buff, ticked or unevenly-marked yellow, ticked or unevenly-marked buff.

POINTS.—The principal attractions about these birds are their size and shape, more especially the latter. Another desideratum, and one which ought not to be overlooked, is great length in body. The longer you can get a bird, provided always it is correct in shape, the more valuable it is on this account.

The form mostly admired is that usually termed "straight," *i.e.*, running level all over, from the crown of the head to the tip of the tail. The head should be small and sleek (the cheeks having the appearance of being chiselled) and somewhat flattish on the crown; the neck long, straight, and thin; the shoulders ought to be moderately broad, but not prominent; the back well filled up, but flat and level throughout. The wings are required to be long and well braced together, meeting at the tips, but they must not overlap each other—this is a fault in a bird of any breed; the waist should be long and rather slender; the body inclined to be thin, and flattish at the sides; the tail must be of good length, close and compact in form; the legs long, substantial and inclining to be straight, with good thighs; there should be no appearance of a frill on the breast; and a good bird ought likewise to be very close in feather, and look as if it had been carved out of marble, a real model; colours, pale brimstone, yellow, and pale buff. The attitude should be a little dignified and commanding, but withal easy and graceful. By far the handsomest birds, however, of this particular breed are the evenly four-marked variety.

The evenly-marked birds are rarely so good in shape and style as the clear birds, but this could not reasonably be expected, seeing that the markings, which are far more difficult to produce than shape, must be preserved intact. The most beautiful specimens of these very charming birds that I have ever seen have been bred in the North and East Ridings of Yorkshire, and in some parts of Lancashire, where they are highly esteemed and greatly prized. The eye markings should be elliptical in form, or in two parallel lines at the front and behind the eye; the wing markings should be even, about seven, eight, or nine feathers in the secondary flights.*

STANDARD OF EXCELLENCE.—The standard for judging the clear varieties—computing 100 points as representing the ideal of a perfect specimen—is considered as under:

STANDARD FOR JUDGING CLEAR YORKSHIRE CANARIES.

	Points.
Head	5
Neck	6
Shoulders	5
Back	10
Chest	4
Waist	8
Legs	8
Tail	8
Size of bird	10
Colour	3
Quality of feathers	8
Contour and position	15
Condition	10
Total	100

The foregoing criterion is equally applicable to the unevenly-marked classes, with the only exception that fifteen points should be allowed for markings, the other points being proportionately reduced to admit of this being done. In the unevenly-marked class a bird with evenly-marked wings and an oval cap is unquestionably the "pick of the basket," so far as markings are a consideration. Next to this in point of perfection is a bird similarly marked, with the addition of eye or

* Some fanciers like a dark feather on each side of the tail; I prefer them without it, and like a four-marked bird better than a six-marked one.

cheek markings, and for a third choice I should prefer a bird
with regular wing-markings and a solitary eye mark.

The standard for judging the evenly-marked classes differs
materially from that given for the other varieties, as the
markings are considered of the first importance in this variety.
The subjoined criterion, therefore, will be found applicable to
these birds:

STANDARD FOR JUDGING EVENLY-MARKED YORKSHIRE CANARIES.

	Points.
Head and eye-markings	15
Neck, shoulders, and back	10
Chest, waist, and legs	10
Wing-markings and saddle	20
Tail	6
Size of bird	8
Colour	3
Quality of feathers	8
Contour and position	10
Condition	10
Total	100

The illustrations are taken from birds of the true typical
highest-class Yorkshires.

CHAPTER XIII.

THE CINNAMON.

THESE birds have derived their name from their peculiar colour, which greatly resembles that of cinnamon bark used for culinary purposes, although it is much deeper and richer in hue. It is an old-established variety, and its origin, like that of the Lizard canary, is beyond the knowledge of the present generation. It is a breed that has always been regarded with much favour among what I may call the educated fanciers; by this term I mean men who have made canaries a daily study for years. There is something about them quite uncommon in appearance—something totally unlike any of the other recognised varieties in the colour of their plumage; and, although the tint is somewhat quiet and sober, it is nevertheless peculiarly pleasing and attractive. Some twenty years ago the colour of these birds was much less brilliant than it is found among those of the present day, as a rule, for since the introduction of the Norwich Fancy blood into their veins their charms have been considerably enhanced. Indeed, so grave and sombre-looking, so thoroughly drabby were these birds in appearance at one time, that they gained the names of "Quaker" and "Dun" canaries.

If I were to begin to extol the variegated Cinnamons as much as I consider they deserve to be, the probabilities are that some person might feel disposed to remind me that they were merely cross-breeds. Just so; but it is well to remember that some cross-bred animals are highly prized, and to give an instance in point

I might mention the cross between the bulldog and terrier, which is, in most cases, a much handsomer dog than either of its progenitors, and a breed greatly valued by the *cognoscenti* of the canine race.

A reason which militates greatly against this particular breed of birds is that there are so few shows that make separate classes for them; and this is more easily explained than remedied. The north country fanciers, almost without exception, cross the Cinnamon and Belgian Fancy canaries together, as they prefer symmetry to colour; whilst the south country fanciers give precedence to the latter, and for this reason they cross the Cinnamon and Norwich Fancy varieties with each other; the consequence is that, whenever the two distinct crosses of birds meet together in the same class for competition, the awards of the judges very rarely give satisfaction to all parties. Most of the secretaries and committees of shows are fully aware of this bugbear, and rather than run the risk of bickerings arising at their shows, they prefer to make an "any other variety class," instead of giving a special class to the variegated variety.

In some parts of Yorkshire, Lancashire, Durham, and Northumberland, many elegant specimens of the Belgian cross are to be met with—large slender birds, graceful in form and commanding in appearance, with sleek flat heads, exquisitely chiselled, and long slender necks, with good substantial legs, well formed, and a fine erect carriage. Add to these properties a pair of evenly-marked wings and two delicately and beautifully pencilled eye-markings, and you have what I consider a gem of a bird to behold. "There is no accounting for taste," for the cross between the Cinnamon and Norwich Fancy canaries are very diminutive birds, displaying nothing beyond the form of the commonest type of canary, and having no other recommendation beyond their superior colour over the class of birds I have endeavoured to portray; but whether high colour in this case really is an advantage is purely a matter of opinion; for my part I think that the infusion of Norwich blood, giving the colours a brighter and a deeper hue, detracts rather than adds to the appearance of these birds, for I have always considered that one of the most pleasing features about them is the great contrast in the colours, which is so readily apparent in the cross with the Belgian canaries, but which is not nearly so perceptible in birds bred between the Cinnamon and Norwich Fancy varieties. Indeed, whenever I look upon a superb specimen of an evenly-marked buff Cinnamon—a cross between the Belgian Fancy and Cinnamon varieties—it invariably reminds me of that beautiful bird the turbit pigeon. It may be thought by some a rather singular comparison, but such is the fact, nevertheless; there is something so serenely pure, so mild, affectionate, and innocent-looking about them (when clean and in proper condition) that I often wonder how any person can look upon them without admiring and esteeming them.

It is greatly to be regretted that any difference of opinion should exist among fanciers in regard to this variety, as it undoubtedly has been the means of preventing, to a considerable extent, the propagation of one of the most beautiful and charming of our cross-breeds.

Cinnamon, as well as most of the Cinnamon variegated, birds, have eyes of a pink or palish red colour, and they can be distinguished by this peculiarity when they are only a day or two old, as the pink shows through the thin film which covers the eyes of the young birds.

BREEDING.—It is a little singular, but none the less true, if you cross a Cinnamon canary with one of any other colour or breed, you may rest assured that the cinnamon colour will predominate eventually, if it does not in the first instance. To illustrate my meaning more clearly, we will suppose that you have mated a Cinnamon and a Belgian canary for the purpose of a cross, we will likewise presume that among the progeny obtained from this pair of birds is one perfectly clear in colour. The following year you mate this bird with a Belgian canary again, or one of a similar breed, and you will find that some of the produce of the latter cross will be Cinnamon or Cinnamon Variegated, but most probably the last-named kind. I have known instances of this occur in the fourth and fifth generations, when the Cinnamon bird first used was well bred and free from any other cross or admixture of foreign blood. The colour of the cross breeds is, as a matter of course, much paler and more dingy-looking than the standard colour recognised in the genuine article; still it is for all that an unmistakable cinnamon hue.

A few years ago I mated a good jonque Cinnamon cock with a jonque Lizard canary hen—both being odd birds, but of first rate quality. I thought they would do for feeders if their produce proved worthless. . They bred nothing but pure greens and Cinnamons, but chiefly the latter, and all were very rich in colour, and were much admired by everyone who saw them. A friend of mine had a young green cock from this cross, and the following season he mated him with three hens of different breeds, as an experiment, and in every instance good average specimens of Cinnamon canaries were produced.

Some people will tell you that Cinnamon canaries are bred by crossing a green canary with a clear yellow one, but, unless one or other of the parent birds has some of the genuine Cinnamon blood in its composition, you may depend upon it such a circumstance will never happen. I have known people who have put jonque green birds to clear yellows, and buff green birds to buffs, over and over again for this purpose, and I have done the same thing myself many years ago, but all to no use. That some people have succeeded in breeding them in this way I do not for a moment doubt, but I am quite confident the Cinnamon blood existed in one or other of the progenitors.

Those fanciers who are desirous of breeding birds of this variety, fit for any competition, will need to procure a few high-class birds to begin with. The best plan to obtain them is to claim a few good male birds at the Crystal Palace Show at Sydenham, unless you are acquainted with any fancier who is reputed for having a good strain, but, even in this case, I should prefer to get the hens from him and claim the male birds as advised. Nottingham was famed for the production of Cinnamon canaries thirty years ago, but latterly Northampton has borne the palm, and perhaps there is no other town in the United Kingdom where so many of these birds are bred (and good ones, too), although it has had to lower it colours to towns of less importance within the past few years, but, for all that,

there is no better blood to be found to breed from than can be
obtained within its precincts.

When you commence to breed Cinnamon birds, put together,
the first year, two. pairs of pure bred birds, without- spot or
blemish, and in no way related to each other; at the same
time mate a good jonque Cinnamon cock with a well-bred
yellow variegated Norwich Fancy hen, the latter possessing
good colour, form, size, and quality, and not too heavily marked,
or one pure green, if obtainable. Be sure that the Cinnamon bird
used for this cross has been bred from self-coloured birds for at
least three generations. From the produce of the last-named
pair keep the richest coloured hen, of good size and feather, if
not the second best in colour, provided she is best in other
respects; a Cinnamon or Cinnamon variegated bird to be preferred. Second year: Keep the best birds bred from the two
pairs of Cinnamons, and cross them together to the best of your
judgment; one pair, however should be buff birds. Purchase a
good buff Cinnamon cock of a different strain, and put him with
one of the cross bred hens (jonque). Third year: Pair the produce from your pure Cinnamons together again, always keeping
the best birds to breed from. These birds will be full cousins,
but it is necessary to breed them a little akin occasionally, as it
keeps the blood pure. Take a young cock, bred from two pure-
bred buffs, and put with the best jonque hen bred from the other
pair containing the Norwich cross. Fourth year: Introduce
new blood by pairing a pure Cinnamon bird with the best bird
bred from your own breed of Cinnamons, and another with the
best bird from the other pair, which will now be almost pure
again. The following year mate the produce from the two last
named pairs, and you will find the colour perceptibly improved.
Continue the same process, introducing the Norwich cross every
third or fourth year; by this means you will vastly increase the
colour of your birds without detracting from their other qualities.

Avoid breeding from pied birds as much as possible, but a
single white feather, or even two, in the tail of a bird, if good in
all other points, is not a serious objection; at the same time, it
is commendable to avoid it as much as you can, as the defect is
very likely to be perpetuated if too much use is made of birds

with a blemish of this kind. I have purposely confined my remarks to as few pairs of birds as I could, in order to elucidate the system of crossing herein recommended, so that I might be able to make it all the more easily understood; but I must not forget to point out to those who desire to climb the pinnacle of fame as breeders and exhibitors of canaries that it will be advisable to put double, or even treble the number of birds mentioned together if they wish to stand a reasonable chance of success as prize takers. Another injunction I think it desirable to give, and that is, do not attempt to breed too many varieties at the same time, for those who do so very rarely succeed in attaining eminence either as breeders or exhibitors.

To breed *Variegated* birds you must begin by crossing the Belgian and Cinnamon varieties together, or the Norwich Fancy and Cinnamon birds, whichever kind you desire to cultivate. The following year select the best and most evenly-marked young birds, the produce of the first cross, and mate them again with the Belgian or Norwich varieties, as the case may be. For further particulars in regard to crossing in order to obtain evenly-marked birds, I must refer you to the chapter upon evenly-marked Norwich Fancy canaries.

If you are desirous of breeding evenly-marked and *Crested* Cinnamon canaries, which are particularly pretty, you must couple a pure Cinnamon canary with a clear or grey-crested Norwich Fancy canary, or, presuming that you desire to possess shape in conjunction with the crest in preference to colour, then you must use a Manchester Coppy canary in place of the Norwich Fancy bird. From the produce of this cross you must keep the crested birds—those that please you most—and mate them again with plain-headed birds bred from crested strains, either Norwich Fancy or Coppies, whichever you require. By this means you will be able to propagate birds that will be likely to please you, and repay you for your trouble and outlay as well. Whenever the markings begin to get too light, take another dip of Cinnamon Fancy blood, which will speedily counterbalance the superfluity of the blood of the clear strains.

Some of these crosses are extremely handsome, and it must not be forgotten that the clear birds bred from them, with pink.

or palish red eyes, are valuable for crossing to obtain hens for breeding canary and linnet mules.

CLASSES.—There are only two classes for *pure* Cinnamon canaries, viz., jonque and mealy; the former being more deep, intense, and brighter in colour than the latter variety; but the last-named is more largely endowed with that beautiful silvery-grey light which pervades the outer surface of the feathers, and which is so much prized by fanciers as an indication of high breeding and rare quality.

There are a great many varieties of Cinnamon *Variegated* birds; indeed, they are capable of being divided into the same number of classes as the marked Norwich Fancy birds; but they never are, as they are not nearly so popular at present as that world-renowned variety. Hitherto there have been but two classes set apart at any show for birds of this kind, and they are principally given under the designations of "variegated yellow Cinnamon" and "variegated buff Cinnamon." Now, what constitutes a variegated bird is simply a bird with a diversity of colours; consequently, both evenly and unevenly marked birds can compete together under this head, but the evenly-marked are sure to take precedence. The other varieties are generally to be found at shows which wind up their schedules with that most useful and needful class, the "Any other variety of canary," and in it they figure very prominently in most cases.

POINTS.—The *true* Cinnamon canary resembles in form and size the Norwich Fancy birds—perhaps, if anything, they are a little larger; that is, taking the general average of the two varieties. The distinguishing features in these birds are colour and form, but more particularly the former. The colour most prized is a deep rich mellow orange cinnamon, and this should be distributed as evenly as possible all over the bird. A light-coloured throat, belly, or rump, or even light-coloured thighs, are considered blemishes. Next in point of esteem to the birds just described are those of a yellowish tint; but avoid the green and the dusky, smoky smut-coloured birds, as they invariably possess bad blood. A stripy appearance is bad; the more nearly a bird looks all over one unbroken colour, the more prizable it is.

The best wing-markings of the *Variegated* birds are those
which are perfectly even—that is to say, the same number of
cinnamon feathers in each wing, and the corresponding feathers.
The eye-markings should either encircle the eye completely or
extend backward or forward, or both, from the centre of the eye,
these being called " front " or " back centre " eye-markings,
whichever they may happen to be; but those that envelop the
eye and which are known as " spectacle " eye-markings, are most
prized—a white feather intermixed with the dark feathers in the
wings, or a dark feather with the clear feathers, is regarded as a
fault. The wing coverlets, saddle and rump feathers, as well as
those on the body of the bird, barring eye and wing markings,
should all be perfectly clear externally. The underflue feathers
about the vent frequently blow dark, and those on the thighs as
well, but these are not considered serious blemishes. Neither
are dark legs and beaks. I prefer a four-marked bird to a six-
marked bird, as I do not consider a dark feather on each side of
the tail an acquisition but rather the reverse.

STANDARD OF EXCELLENCE.—The following standard will be
found to give the relative value of the different points of merit,
100 points to be assumed as representing the highest excellence :

STANDARD FOR JUDGING CLEAR CINNAMON CANARIES.

	Points.
Colour, for depth, clearness, purity, richness of tone, brightness and regularity throughout	40
Quality and Sheen	20
Size, for length and substance	15
Condition and Feather	10
Contour and Carriage	8
Saddle	7
Total	100

STANDARD FOR JUDGING VARIEGATED CINNAMON CANARIES.

	Points.
Size, Contour, and Carriage	20
Wing-markings	25
Eye-markings	20
Colour	10
Condition and Quality	10
Saddle	5
Feathers	10
Total	100

T

CHAPTER XIV.

THE MODERN CINNAMON.

THE innovations that have been practiced in late years by
many breeders of canaries, in order to increase the size of
their birds, have been extended to the Cinnamon Canary, and
carried to such an extent as to greatly imperil the chief
characteristics of this truly lovely variety of the Canary
family. In place of the beautiful Norwich type of Cinnamons,
with their peculiar coats of rich orange brown, or deep reddish
mahogany hue, we have had established a race of great overgrown
mongrels, many of which show almost every point that is
objectionable in a good specimen of this breed. A true
Cinnamon is a beautiful bird, and its chief and most valued
properties are purity of colour and richness and evenness of
tone, pervaded by a bright sheeny surface, which should be
evenly distributed over the entire plumage; it should be free
from stripiness both on the back, breast, and sides of the
body.

The true colour may be characterised as a reddish-orange
brown, with good under colour, and in the jonques of high
merit there should appear a sort of rich ruby colour peering
through the ground colour; and in the buffs, or mealies, a
rich orange yellow should glint radiantly on the upper surface
of the body colouring, almost dazzling in its intensity; particularly when daylight is fading is this peculiarity observable,
and it may be held as a sure sign of high breeding. It is in
the evening, or on a dull day, that a good Cinnamon bird is

seen in its full beauty; and it is really a bewitching sight to a true lover of this variety.

But those great overgrown, dusky, murky, indefinite-looking objects, with their natural greeny, drabbish, smoky-looking hue, and ·coarse feather (the worst points that a Cinnamon bird can possibly possess), together with light-coloured throats, pale washy-looking breasts, sides, vents, and rumps, with long greenish, dusky stripes displayed on their backs and sides, fill a genuine admirer of this variety with disgust and loathing. Why sacrifice every quality that a good specimen possesses merely to obtain size? To me it seems simply madness. Size can only be obtained by crossing with the Dutch or Lancashire birds, and the latter are the lineal descendants of the old Dutch canary. In every other feature except size, such a cross tends to detract from the chance of producing a high-class representative of the Cinnamon proper. Get size by all legitimate means that you possibly can, by selection, by breeding from double buffs, by the introduction of an exceptionally good crested-bred bird, inheriting in a large degree the rich colour and fine feather of the Norwich plain-head, but eschew the direct use of the Lancashire plain-head to obtain your object. But the present mode of breeding is first to put a plain-head Lancashire cock with a Norwich Cinnamon hen, and from this cross to obtain green and variegated green cocks, and clear and variegated hens, and Cinnamon variegated occasionally, if the Cinnamon blood be reliable and pure. These birds are crossed with Cinnamon birds again, and green and Cinnamons are produced, but "size! size!" is still the cry, and the Lancashire bird is again resorted to, and this process is continued until ultimately a three-parts bred Lancashire Cinnamon is produced, with all or most of the faults I have specified, and then cayenne is resorted to, to cover all these defects. Oh, this cayenne! It is really the bug-bear of the fancy, if not the curse of it, and has done so much harm to some breeds that ten years of careful and honest breeding would not suffice to eradicate all the evils which have followed in its train. There is no kind of science in this kind of breeding, no skill required, no foresight, no brains. It is almost a matter of chance; then why resort to it? Be warned in time, do not destroy one of the loveliest of our varieties for the sake of a whim. Besides, fanciers forget that the Lancashire bird is descended from the Dutch and Belgian birds, and I am sorry to say that many of them have inherited in a large degree the delicacy of constitution inherent in these varieties, such as asthma and tuberculosis, and thus they are unconsciously propagating these disorders also. The original Norwich Cinnamons had the most robust constitutions, but how many of those modern birds are to be found that have sufficient stamina to carry them through three years of breeding operations to say nothing of exhibition specimens? I should say very few. I am a great stickler for type, but the true types of several of our varieties are becoming lost owing to the riding to death of this rampant mania for size, and ere long a new classification will be needed unless the craze can be abated.

If fanciers really do want and admire large mongrel Cinnamons, by all means let them have them, but they should be shown in the "Any other variety class," and not as true Cinnamons. The colour of the genuine Cinnamon canary is so powerful and vigorous that with care and judicious breeding it can be produced in any breed, and Cinnamon Belgians, Cinnamon Scotch Fancies, Cinnamon Lancashires, or Cinnamon Yorkshires could be easily manufactured, but the colour would neither be so fine nor so rich as that found in the Norwich Cinnamons, which after all is the true standard.

At the present time there are first-class specimens of the Scotch Fancy of a Cinnamon colour, and I saw one exhibited at Birmingham, by Mr. Greame, of Brough, Yorkshire, in 1890, a bird, I believe, he purchased in Scotland, and a bird of considerable merit, and in England would be, if properly judged, difficult to beat in a class set apart for Scotch Fancies; but singular to say these sports in colour are all hens. About twenty years ago, or perhaps a little more, I bought a large buff-crested cock, almost a thoroughbred Lancashire, with immense body and a good crest, one of the sturdy thick sort. I put him with a very high-class Cinnamon hen, my object being to breed evenly-marked and crested Cinnamons, and eventually I succeeded in breeding two splendid specimens, almost perfect, and both out of the same nest. These were the first birds of this variety I had ever seen or heard of, both hens, and probably as perfect as they could possibly be bred. It occurred to me to use some of this blood to get more size into my Cinnamon birds and to increase the head properties, and I succeeded, but at a great sacrifice in colour. I remember sending a bird from this cross to a show at Darlington, and with it two other Cinnamons, in the same class, one a gem of the first water; and to my horror and disgust this big mongrel, as I considered it, was placed first prize, and the best bird second. I put £3 on him as his value, and received a telegram from Mr. Cleminson, of Darlington, asking the lowest price I would accept for him. I declined to accept a less sum, as I wanted him to run with a hen of my best strain of Cinnamons to increase the size; he was claimed, and to this day the bird is known and referred to among the old-fanciers in Darlington as "Telegram," that title having been given to him after the event; this happened a good many years ago. I often regretted afterwards that I sent him, as it appeared to awaken a desire among fanciers to have a race of big Cinnamons, to the detriment of the more admirable features possessed by birds of the pure race.

I consider that the Cinnamon canary is essentially a bird of colour, as much or even more so than the Norwich plainhead, and deprived of this special feature it loses its most fascinating charm. True, the colour can be sustained to a great extent by artificial feeding, but it can never be obtained so pure as that produced by high breeding.

I do not desire to be considered so conservative as to be an opponent to improvements, decidedly not; but I must first be convinced of the advantages that are to be gained by crossbreeding. If an increase of size is to be obtained by the sacrifice of points which are far more essential, then I feel myself bound to oppose the innovation. Some limit should be placed on the length of this breed, and I think 6¼in., or at the very most 6½in., should under no circumstances be exceeded, and even then it will take years of judicious breeding to bring up the quality and colour in a bird of these dimensions. This should be accomplished by selection, by breeding from double buffs, and an occasional dip into crested-bred Norwich blood. Green birds should be avoided as much as possible in the attainment of this object, as this shade of colour in a Cinnamon is most objectionable. It will certainly take a year or two longer to breed up from clears and Cinnamon variegated birds, but in the end the result will be much more satisfactory. I prefer substance to great length. We want the Cinnamon of the thick, deep-set, bullfinch shape, and not of the thin spare Yorkshire type.

I would recommend amateurs who desire to attempt to improve this variety to first obtain a pair or two of the pure Norwich Cinnamons of the old school, birds that have been bred pure for several generations. Take one pair of these and cross them with a pair of large-crested bred plain-heads. Let them be pure in colour, rich in tone, and fine in feather; big-framed birds, as bulky as possible, but free from coarseness, and destitute of the overhanging eyebrows, and with thick necks, short legs and tails, but deep broad chests, and wide backs, and good shoulders. Pair a buff Cinnamon cock, of a deep pure colour and level throughout, with a large yellow hen of this kind, and a jonque Cinnamon cock with a buff hen of the character I have described. It is advantageous to use Cinnamon cocks in preference to Cinnamon hens and hens of the crested-bred strain, as the colour is more influenced by using Cinnamon cocks, and the colours obtained in the young are brighter and clearer. Select from the offspring of these the clear birds with pink eyes and the Cinnamon variegated hens, and cross these again with Cinnamon cocks bred from a pure strain, putting a buff and jonque together as before. From this second cross there should be some nice Cinnamons. Put a cock of this cross with a Cinnamon variegated hen bred from the first cross, and another with a pure Cinnamon, and the following season breed from birds the production of these crosses, always selecting the largest and best. From the last pair run two buffs together, but never two jonques; avoid all kinds to breed from that show too much of a green tinge, or with light-coloured throats, breasts, rumps, or bellies. Select those that are pure and level in colour throughout and free from stripes, if possible, for future operations, and proceed on the same lines; but occasionally, say, once in three years, breed them akin, and a strain of Cinnamons will be built up that will do the breeder credit, but if he tries to progress too rapidly he will assuredly fail to produce a race of birds that will stand the test of time.

In the standard for judging the new type I would make a little alteration from my former standard, as follows:

	Points.
Colour for depth, purity, and richness of tone	40
Quality and sheen	15
Size for length and substance	20
Condition and feather	10
Contour and carriage	7
Freedom from stripiness	8
Total	100

I only give these standards as showing to what extent I regard the various properties. I do not advocate judging by points, as the process is too tedious, and would be more unsatisfactory than the usual method of judging by sight. Still it is of the utmost importance that all judges should bear in mind the relative value of the various points, as held in the estimation of breeders and fanciers, to enable them to make their awards satisfactory to exhibitors and critics alike.

CHAPTER XV.

THE CINNAMON CRESTED.

THERE is probably no member of the British *Canaria* family more interesting than this, and I am pleased to find that the variety is coming more into favour every year, and that classes are now provided for it at all our best shows. The reason for this breed not being so popular as the Norwich Crests is that good specimens are more difficult to obtain, and require a much longer time to bring them to a state of perfection. I bred the first specimen of this variety that I ever saw, some thirty-six years ago, but it is quite possible that someone may have bred them before me.

I have also been fortunate enough to breed some of the best specimens of this variety that I have ever seen, and one of these, a young cock, evenly-marked and crested, which I sold to a Mr. Hillyer, of Leicester, took, amongst other honours, first prize at the Aquarium Show in London, and also first prize at the Crystal Palace, at Sydenham, and he is the only male bird I have seen that approached anything like perfection.

His mother was a Cinnamon variegated plain-head, bred from a green hen, the produce of a pure well-bred Cinnamon hen and a crested-bred Norwich cock. His father was an even-marked and Crested Norwich bird, whose mother was bred between a Cinnamon canary and a Lancashire Coppy. The crested blood in him was all of high-class quality.

There is no difficulty in breeding Cinnamon crests, especially self colours. Put a Cinnamon cock bred for a few generations from pure Cinnamons with an evenly-marked and crested Norwich hen of good quality; at the same time put another Cinnamon cock with a good pure Lancashire crested hen, and select from these pairs the best of the crested and plain-head youngsters, picking out all those that have pink eyes or are Cinnamon variegated, and mating them with pure greens, as some of the progeny are sure to be. Be sure to select and keep the best of the crested birds. The following year keep the best crests and those that show the best Cinnamon qualities, and cross them with Yorkshire Cinnamons, as these birds inherit a lot of Coppy blood, and it will help you to get size and crest, the latter being the most difficult thing to obtain, as the admixture of Cinnamon blood tends to shorten the crest, and this is the greatest difficulty you will have to overcome.

If you prefer the self-coloured Cinnamons, select the greens or heaviest variegated from one pair, and run them with the self Cinnamons or heaviest variegated Cinnamons bred from the other pair, selecting as a matter of course, one a plain-head and the other a crest; from the later cross select the best-crested birds, and mate them with pure bred Yorkshire Cinnamons the following year, and so on, going back to the crested Norwich and Cinnamon alternately as required for the improvement of crest and colour. But if you prefer to breed evenly-marked and crested Cinnamons, which are by far the handsomest birds of this variety, instead of whole Cinnamons, select the best of the Cinnamon variegated plain-heads, and put with them marked and crested Norwich birds for first cross; from the produce of these choose the best of the crested birds, and pair again with the best of the Cinnamons variegated, the produce of the other pairs. Choose hens with Cinnamon marked wings and caps, or the nearest approach to such. In the following year you must exercise your judgment in selecting birds bred from the pairs named, and if you succeed in breeding any evenly-marked and crested, which you ought to do with ordinary luck, keep them, and pair with hens or cocks closely related to them, and in a few years you will be enabled to breed them more frequently. Of course, you will breed birds at first that are not what you require, these must be discarded, and sold for what they will bring in the market. You may pair brothers and sisters or first cousins, but do not continue this in-breeding too long, or the birds will deteriorate in size and feather.

In selecting Cinnamons for these operations you must have large birds, with plenty of substance and good broad skulls, and if they have heavy eye-brows, so much the better, as the greatest difficulty you will experience will be to get large well-formed crests, as the admixture of the Cinnamon blood most undoubtedly has a tendency to circumscribe the crest; therefore, to breed a really well-crested Cinnamon variegated bird you want no more Cinnamon in its composition than will give the required colour. On the other hand, if you pursue the improvement in crest too far you are apt to sacrifice the colour; it requires patience, perseverance, and sound judgment to obtain what you really want, but when you succeed you will be well repaid for all your trouble, for a good bird of this variety can always command a good price and plenty of customers, and there is a more open field for obtaining success than there is in breeding Norwich crests, where you have thousands of breeders to contend against, whereas the breeders of crest Cinnamons are confined to comparatively few. In a few years these classes will be extended, and the demand for them will increase accordingly. These birds should be bred and judged by the same methods and standards as are applied to the crested Norwich canaries.

CHAPTER XVI.

THE EVENLY-MARKED CINNAMON.

THESE birds are shown in the "Any other variety class," and are generally of the Yorkshire type of bird. Of late years some very handsome specimens have been exhibited, and with great success. They can be produced by careful breeding and selection between the plain-head Cinnamons and the Lancashire Coppies. Some go for the Yorkshire type, and in this case long thin Lancashires should be used for crossing purposes; others prefer them with more substance, and use stouter and fuller-bodied birds. The great thing is to get them well and evenly-marked, and to obtain this it will be necessary to cross with the evenly-marked Yorkshire birds. I also advise readers to follow the plan recommended for breeding evenly-marked Norwich canaries, and also to resort occasionally to in-breeding to fully establish the essential points required, *i.e.*, size, colour, markings, feather, and shape.

CHAPTER XVII.

THE NORWICH FANCY.

ORIGIN.—The Norwich Fancy canaries doubtless owe their existence as a distinct variety to the town of Norwich, and have derived their origin, I believe, from crossing the London Fancy or Lizard canaries with the common stock; and by further judicious pairing, feeding, and careful moulting they have ultimately attained that exquisite colour for which they are so widely famed.

The method of breeding and rearing clear Norwich, in order to produce and retain their rich dazzling plumage throughout the show season, was held in such profound secrecy among the breeders and exhibitors in Norwich at one time that it was publicly asserted by a gentleman of position, then in the "fancy," that one hundred pounds would not extract the secret of obtaining the high colour in these birds and the genuine process of crossing them and moulting them in order to obtain perfection, at least so far as it was then known. Without doubt, there was a wonderful amount of freemasonry existing among the craft in Norwich some years ago, and they kept their secrets remarkably well; but the bubble burst at last, to the chagrin of many, I dare say, and the secret of high colour became common property.

VARIETIES.—Of the Norwich Fancy canaries there are the clears, the evenly marked, the ticked, the unevenly-marked, the green, and the crested varieties.

The *Clear* birds have hitherto been held in considerable

estimation by a great many fanciers, and more especially by ladies and amateurs, their gorgeous and brilliant plumage being their principal attraction; but now that it has become so extensively known that those vivid hues can be readily procured simply by administering cayenne pepper, mixed with egg and biscuits, and given as food during the period of moulting, it is a question whether this knowledge will not dispel the fascination that has hitherto hung around these birds. That it will very materially affect their value commercially I think there can be no shadow of a doubt. Meanwhile, I believe that the best bred birds will reap the greatest advantage from this novel *régime*, and that they will continue in a proportionate degree, according to breeding, to bear the palm over all their competitors of a more lowly origin, but it is just possible that I may be wrong in my assumption. However, apart from this, there can be little doubt now that, even prior to the discovery of this ingenious method of using cayenne, many of the most highly coloured specimens exhibited owed in a great measure their gaudy glistening colours to some particular mode of feeding, for it seems to have been long known to the principal breeders in Norwich that the exterior grandeur of these birds could be materially improved by giving them certain ingredients, mixed with their food and otherwise, during the moulting season, and numerous and various have been the devices resorted to for this purpose. Among other things which have been tried to influence and improve the colour in these birds are : Marigold flowers, cochineal, meadow saffron, annatto, beetroot, carrots, madder, turmeric, mustard seed, &c., but the whole of these ingredients appear to sink into utter insignificance, so far as effect is produced, when compared with the magical results which have been achieved by the use of the cayenne pepper. See chapter on " Moulting " (p. 162).

In addition to the nostrums already specified, and which are intended for internal use only, some unscrupulous persons have had the temerity to resort to external embellishments as well, and to accomplish their object they have applied such compounds as " Judson's Dyes " and similar preparations. Where these artifices have been detected, the perpetrators have been in most instances justly exposed, and likewise excluded from competing at those shows where their impostures were brought to light.

The *Evenly-marked* variety of Norwich Fancy canaries is much admired and greatly prized by the " talent " or bird critics, and is also regarded by many people of taste and discernment as being superior in most respects to the much vaunted London Fancy variety. One decided advantage the Evenly-marked bird certainly has over the last-named breed is this: if it happens to shed one of its dark pinion feathers prematurely, it is reproduced by a *fac simile* of the lost feather; whereas, it is otherwise with a London Fancy canary. Another and still greater advantage is possessed by the Norwich birds, for they can be exhibited for several years in succession, if carefully moulted and preserved in good health and fine condition, whilst the London Fancies invariably lose their show plumage after the second moult.

Of all the different varieties of Norwich Fancy canaries, there are none more beautiful or interesting than the *Crested* birds, for they not only combine—when highly bred—the rich and brilliant plumage of the clear varieties, but the evenly-marked and crested classes possess the much admired wing-markings of the evenly-marked or variegated birds, and in addition to these advantages, they are adorned with an elegant ornament on their heads in the form of a crest; this is designated by some fanciers a " Top-not," by others a " Crown," a " Coppy," a " Toppin," and by a few a " Tassel."

There can be no doubt that the crest is an innovation among the Norwich Fancy canaries, and has doubtless been produced, in the first instance, by crossing with the ordinary or common crested canary, and the introduction of this extraneous blood, whilst imparting the coveted ornament, has greatly detracted from the glowing colours that the best specimens of these birds so largely inherit. This drawback might by judicious and careful crossing be overcome in a few years; but, unfortunately for experimentalists, there are more weighty considerations in breeding these birds than the mere attainment of brilliant plumage. Good crests are not produced easily, and unless they are bred in a prescribed manner — which I shall point out presently—they soon deteriorate both in size, form, and colour.

TRIMMING.—There is an amazing amount of trickery carried on with marked birds by exhibitors whose conscientious scruples are so infinitesimal as in no way to disturb their equanimity, so that honest fanciers have but a very meagre chance of success, for those who are experienced manipulators in doctoring these birds can make a moderately good bird almost faultless. Eye-markings can be put on or enlarged as occasion requires by using a preparation of the nitrate of silver; foul wing and tail feathers are extracted and substituted by others. This is done by cutting the feathers short off through the quill, leaving a socket; corresponding feathers from other birds (not good enough to show) are extracted and fitted in, and secured with a little thin glue or solution of gum arabic. These and other similar devices are frequently resorted to, so that judges require to be on the alert; but many of these transformations are so skilfully and dexterously accomplished as to defy detection.

MARKING BIRDS.—Breeders of canaries on an extensive scale are sometimes necessitated to place birds of the same variety, but of distinct breeds, in a large flight cage together. When this happens, each bird should be marked in one or other of its wings, separately, and a record of such markings should be kept in the diary. Say, for example, all birds of No. 1 pair are marked with a notch made in one of the webs of the two first flight feathers of the left wing; the produce of No. 2 pair, two notches in each feather; those of No. 3 pair, three notches, and so on, making use of both wings if required. These marks are made with a pair of ordinary scissors; but, as much depends on being able to identify the different birds for crossing, the greatest care in the performance of this duty is necessary. Never resort to any part of the bird other than the wings for making these marks of identity. The tail feathers are so easily knocked out.

BREEDING.—In selecting stock to breed *Clear* Norwich from, you ought to procure a few superior birds; be sure to purchase them from well-established fanciers of good repute and integrity; by this means you are more likely to succeed in getting such birds as you need. You will require both clear and marked birds to breed clear birds frcm, and rather heavily-marked birds too; indeed, one entirely green, if of good colour and quality, is by no means to be despised. I think I cannot do better than relate here the method of crossing pursued and recommended by one of the oldest, most experienced and successful breeders in Norwich, after which I will detail my own experience. The method recommended by the breeder referred to is as follows: First year: Put a clear yellow cock with a marked buff hen; be sure that she is bred from greens (pied birds) and not from " fancy"—by the last-mentioned term he explains that he means Lizard canaries—"because," says he, " Fancy must not be used except at the proper time, as I shall tell you." Second year: He recommends the young birds ("clears") to be crossed with clear birds from a second pair mated in precisely the same way as the first-named pair. Third year: He says, "Take the best clear birds bred from the last cross and pair with a clear bird bred from the 'Fancy,' and you will find the best birds are got from this cross;" he explains that, to obtain a bird such as he describes, you must put a Norwich Fancy and a Lizard canary together; from the produce of this pair you are to select those birds which are the least marked, and pair them with the Norwich Fancy again—I presume with clear birds of the last-named variety, but he does not say so. He adds, " In three years you will breed clears." " In selecting the final pair to breed from they should blow clear all over; the produce of this cross are only for show, and are of no use to breed from." He adds significantly, " No honest man would sell you birds bred thus to breed from again, nor would I buy a bird to cross with except I knew the man I bought it of." See "A Caution" to beginners in buying birds (p. 200).

My own system of breeding clear Norwich canaries is as follows: First year: Put a London Fancy and a Lizard canary together. At the same time mate two clear buff Norwich canaries, and likewise two clear jonques, or yellows; both the last-named pairs must blow clear all over, be close in feather, and full of quality. This makes three pairs of birds in all. To hope to be successful as an exhibitor, it would be necessary to put together several more pairs on the same plan; but those I have selected are sufficient for me to illustrate the principle of crossing I advocate myself. Second year : Select a bird from each of the clear pairs of Norwich Fancy, and mate them with birds bred between the London Fancy and Lizard canaries. Always choose those nearest clear from this cross. Third year : Select the lightest marked birds, buff or yellow, from the last crosses, and mate again with clear Norwich Fancy birds bred from "double buffs" or "double yellows," but, be sure, in the final cross, to mate them so that the ground colours of each are of an opposite hue to each other, *i.e.*, the buff or buff-marked birds must be put with clear yellows, and *vice versâ*. The result will be found satisfactory. The reason I advocate this cross is that birds so bred are greatly affected by cayenne and other foods for obtaining high colour.

To breed *Unevenly-marked* or *Variegated* Norwich canaries : Put a clear yellow and a yellow marked bird together; select a clear yellow bird from this cross, and mate it with a buff-marked bird bred from the last cross in breeding for clear birds, bred according to my own method. The produce of this cross will be found mostly very rich in colour. The reason alleged for breeding from the green varieties is that it strengthens the colour and makes it more lasting, and that for introducing the Lizard canary cross once in three years with the green birds is because it gives a softness to the feathers, and makes them have a silky appearance; but if you breed too long in with the "green" the feathers get long and rough.

The *Ticked* birds are obtained in breeding for clears, and like-wise for marked birds. They are simply birds that are not quite clear in colour, but have a slight tick, speck, or mark on some part of their bodies. The points required are the same as those aimed at in breeding clear birds.

The *Green* variety is produced by crossing heavily marked birds together several times in succession, but two jonques (greens) should be put together, say, once in three years, to prevent the feathers from becoming too coarse.

There are probably no breeders of canaries that have so many difficulties to encounter in attaining their object as those who

U

pursue the somewhat tantalising occupation of breeding *Evenly-marked* birds; consequently those who have made up their minds to embark in this particular branch of bird-breeding must be fully prepared to meet with hopes kindled only to be blighted and disappointments innumerable. To breed evenly-marked Norwich canaries fit for exhibition, and in the most expeditious manner possible, it will be necessary, in the first place, to procure a few good evenly-marked birds to begin with, and in selecting them I would advise that birds with dark caps be avoided. It is absolutely necessary to obtain birds of distinct breeds, free from blood relationship, to begin with. Mate two " four-marked " birds together; both should be rather lightly-marked than otherwise, and one of them at least should have white or flesh-coloured legs, and clear under flue feathers (the small feathers next the skin); this pair, for the sake of distinction, I shall afterwards refer to as " No. 1." Next put another evenly-marked bird with a perfectly clear one, the latter being bred from a clear strain; it should be large in size, rich in colour, and of undoubted quality; this bird should be perfectly clear in colour all over, which fact must be ascertained by taking it in the hand and blowing back the feathers over and under the body; this pair I shall call " No. 2." The following year select the two best marked birds, the produce of No. 1 pair, and mate the heavier marked bird of the two with a clear bird, the produce of No. 2 pair, and the other with the lightest and most evenly marked bird, likewise bred from No. 2 pair. These pairs it will be necessary to designate "No. 3" and "No. 4." The following season select from the produce of No. 3 and No. 4 the best birds, and pair in the manner already pointed out; the young birds from the last named pairs will be first cousins, but this is just what is wanted, for breeding them in-and-in occasionally is one of the secrets for obtaining regularity in markings, but it must not be resorted to too frequently, or the birds will soon become small and scant in feather. To improve the colour in these birds and to preserve the markings, I have found it advantageous to cross with a London Fancy bird, say, once in three or four years; couple a bird of the last-named variety with a clear bird, bred by yourself from an evenly-marked strain, and keep the clearest birds, the produce of this cross, or those only marked in the wings, to breed from. When the birds get all related through this system of crossing, it will be necessary to purchase, from time to time, as they are required, one or two good evenly-marked birds from some fancier who is reputed for breeding good birds of this variety to cross with them. If two evenly-marked birds are put together too often, the produce will be heavily marked; this must be regulated by resorting to clear birds bred from an evenly-marked strain. The great secret in obtaining good evenly-marked birds lies chiefly in the following rules : First, in breeding from birds which are evenly-marked, and clear birds the produce of an evenly-marked strain; secondly, in the process of consanguinity, or blood relationship; and thirdly, in avoiding all birds for breeding purposes which are irregularly marked; no matter how well they may be bred, all such birds must be sent to the " right about."

It will be seen by the foregoing remarks that I have confined myself to as few pairs as possible to elucidate the system of breeding I advocate; but ere you can hope to be successful in producing a few birds fit for competition, it will be necessary to breed from several pairs of birds, and if you persevere in following the instructions I have given, you will find in the course of three or four years that you will be able to produce the even markings with wonderful precision and regularity; but be very careful about the introduction of new blood, for if you happen to introduce a bird bred from irregularly marked birds, it will cause you a great amount of trouble and vexation. I might have advised you to put two clear birds, bred from No. 2 pair, to the two evenly-marked birds known as No. 1 the second season, but I have purposely avoided doing so for fear it might confuse beginners.

For breeding purposes, be sure to keep all the clear birds with eye-marks ; these you can utilise where clear birds are required with greater advantage. You may likewise preserve all the birds with evenly-marked wings and one eye-mark, or birds with two eye-marks and one wing-mark, as all birds of this description are choice stock birds : birds marked on the head, neck, chest, or rather heavily in the tail, as well as all irregularly-marked or pied birds, you must dispose of at the first opportunity. If you breed a bird with heavy wing markings, but slightly marked about the eyes, mate it with a bird that is clear in the body, with eye-markings only. If you have a bird with heavy eye-markings and lightly marked wings, pair such a bird with one that is marked in the wings only, and so on. With these instructions you only require experience to enable you to breed evenly-marked birds with undoubted success. Birds bred in this way for four or five years are very likely to produce evenly-marked mules ; choose the clear or very lightly-marked birds for this purpose.

It will be necessary to pair two buff-marked birds together sometimes, or a buff-marked bird and a clear buff bird from an evenly-marked strain, as this tends not only to improve the size of the bird, but it increases the quantity of feathers, although, as a rule, you should breed from a jonque and mealy (yellow and buff).

If you desire to breed *Crested* Norwich canaries (old type) for exhibition, you must first procure a few good crested birds, either males or females. I prefer the former, as I find that the progeny more frequently favour the male parent than otherwise. They must in all cases be good specimens, or of undoubted high breeding, and you will find it advisable to claim a few prize winners at some of our best shows—the Crystal Palace at Sydenham is probably the best for this purpose. It is held usually in the month of February, which is, or ought to be, the end of the legitimate show season, and hence exhibitors are disposed to put a selling price upon them if they wish to part with them. If you cannot attend the show yourself, the Secretary—whom I have always found exceedingly obliging at all times—will claim for you such birds as you require, if you send him a P.O.O. in advance and instructions what to do. To an evenly-marked and crested cock you should put a clear, or very lightly-marked plain-headed hen, bred from a crested strain. You should purchase your hens from some respectable, well-known fancier, who has made his mark as a breeder of crested birds, to begin with; afterwards keep hens bred by yourself. If the cock or hen is a clear bird with a dark crest, then it ought to be

paired with a plain-headed bird of the opposite sex with a dark
cap and wing markings, or a clear bird from a dark-crested
strain; but by crossing the clear and marked birds together you
have a chance of getting young birds of both varieties in the
same nest. In order to improve the colour and quality of your
birds it will be necessary for you to cross them occasionally with
clear birds, not of the crested strain; in this case you should
mate a marked and crested bird, or a clear bird with a dark
crest, with one as evenly marked as you can procure of a high-
coloured strain, for if you cross with clear birds you may expect
to get more grey and clear crested young birds than dark-crested
ones. Select from this cross the best crested and heaviest marked
birds, and mate them with clear birds bred from a marked and
crested strain; or, better still, if you can procure them, with clear
bodies with dark caps. Whenever you breed birds of the description just named be sure to keep them; they are invaluable for
breeding purposes, and far more difficult to procure than crested
birds. To improve the evenly-marked and crested birds in their
markings, you will be obliged to cross a clear bird with a dark
crest, or one lightly wing-marked, with an evenly wing-marked
bird of the plain evenly-marked strain (four marked), and if
marked about the head it is so much the more to be preferred,
but must be marked nowhere else; this should be done about once
in three or four years. It is the regular custom to couple a
jonque and mealy bird together (yellow and buff), but if you wish
to breed large birds, close in feather, with large well-formed
crests, you must frequently breed from two buffs or mealies, but
be sure that one is crested, and the other crested bred; this must
not be overdone, or the produce will be coarse. I sometimes
select a bird nearly all green, with a crest, and cross it with a
clear bird, as it improves the colour both of the body feathers
and the crests. When you have succeeded in producing a race
of birds with crests and markings to your liking, breed them
together occasionally a little "sib" (consanguinity), say, first
cousins, but be careful not to overdo it, or the produce will
become small, weak, and puny. By the adoption of this method
you will perpetuate the features you require.

If you pair two crested birds with each other, their progeny, as a rule, will be bald at the back of the head, or have mop crests, which is a great disfigurement in either case. The majority of crested birds are more or less bald behind the crest; but by breeding two buffs together you will soon overcome this defect.

A crested bird can be identified when it is only a few days old by its peculiar formation of the head, and a very small smooth spot is generally visible on the top and at the back of the cranium. As soon as you discover that you have an unusually good crested bird, place it by itself as soon as it is able to feed on seed; and be sure that the cage in which you place it is provided with good sized holes to get its head through when feeding or drinking, or the crest will get chafed and disfigured. After a crested bird has moulted it should not be placed with another bird until the show season is over, because the other bird is pretty certain to pluck its crest, and the feathers will not grow again until the bird moults.

Before concluding this subject, I would strenuously advise those who are devoted to the Norwich Fancy canaries not to neglect the methods of crossing pointed out to improve the breed, as I am convinced that it will in the end prove more satisfactory than the newly-discovered system of feeding to produce high colour, and which, I think, must of necessity be attended with baneful results, as such a powerful stimulant as cayenne pepper cannot but be injurious to the health of canaries. See " The Influence of various Ingredients on the Colour of Canaries and their Hybrids " (p. 171).

CLASSES.—The clear Norwich canaries, as well as the evenly marked, the crested, the ticked, the green, and the unevenly marked, are each divided into two separate classes, i.e., jonques and mealies.

In the *Clear* varieties there are the jonques and mealies, better known as yellows and buffs, but "orange" would be a much more appropriate and fitting name for the first-mentioned variety, and "orange mealies" for the latter, as these appellations are more truly descriptive of their real colours.

There are only two classes for *Evenly-marked* birds, which are arranged thus: Evenly marked yellow Norwich canaries and evenly-marked buff Norwich canaries, and these may consist of

" two-marked," " four-marked," or "six-marked " birds ; for, with all or any of these markings, a bird is eligible for competition; all being entered in the same class, under one or other of the names just referred to.

The *Crested* canaries are divided into six classes as follows : Clear buff, clear yellow, evenly - marked buff, evenly-marked yellow, unevenly-marked buff and unevenly-marked yellow ; although it is seldom that committees of shows set apart more than four, and more frequently only two classes, for these varieties, which is unsatisfactory alike to exhibitors and judges. The evenly-marked and crested birds are considered, by most fanciers, as the first of the crested varieties, and next to those the clear bodied and dark crested are held in the highest estimation.

POINTS.—In size, shape, and general appearance, the *Clear* and *Ticked* Norwich resemble the marked and crested varieties, the chief distinction being that those under consideration are quite plain; that is to say, destitute of ornament in the shape of even markings, crests, &c., but they ought to excel the other varieties in richness, depth, and brilliancy of colour. Despite the efforts that have been made by a few fanciers, who are deeply interested in these birds, to overrule this hitherto universally acknowledged chief feature, as the principal charm, and to set up a new theory of qualifications, it cannot succeed, for the merest tyro in the " fancy " knows quite well that colour has always been considered the ruling characteristic in these birds. This refers to the old type of crested Norwich. See chapter on the new type (p. 314).

The choicest specimens of the *Unevenly-marked* varieties are unquestionably those with perfectly oval caps and even wing markings; indeed, it is a matter of opinion as to whether birds marked in the manner described are not entitled to be considered evenly-marked. For my part, I contend that they are, for the simple reason that canaries only possess one head each, and hence an oval cap should be regarded as a regular marking; but as birds of this description are permitted to be exhibited in the unevenly-marked class, without complaint, I have no desire to disturb this arrangement. When the cap is well formed and the wing-markings even, a bird of this sort presents a very attractive appearance, and has a host of admirers. Next to a bird marked as described, I should prefer one with dark cap, eye-markings, and wing-markings, or one with evenly-marked wings and eyes, and one dark feather in the tail, and next to these, a bird with one eye mark and evenly marked wing. Colour and quality, however, in this class of birds are indispensably requisite.

The principal features which entitle *Evenly-marked* Norwich canaries to the distinguished position which they hold are their gorgeous colours and regular and artistic markings, but more especially the latter, as they are most difficult to obtain, even to an approximation of the criterion of excellence.

The first and most important of the markings in the evenly-marked birds are those of the wings. A bird may have two, four, five, seven, or any similar number of dark feathers in each wing, or it may have five in one wing and seven in the other, or any similar or other number, and still be considered a legitimate candidate for this class, so long as the wings appear even to the unaided eye; but a bird so marked will show to disadvantage if shown against a bird with perfect wing markings—that is to say, if a judge is careful, and handles the birds when performing his judicial functions, which too many of them neglect to do. There are very few birds perfect in this respect, even among those which figure prominently as winners at our best shows. Some judges prefer a bird lightly marked in the wings; others, again, prefer them heavily marked rather than otherwise; but a bird with the first nine pinion feathers white, and the remaining nine, or the secondary pinions, black, corresponding exactly on each side, is, without doubt, the most perfect of all, and those nearest to this standard come next. Many birds, and birds of great merit, too, very frequently are possessed of a "mixed" wing, that is, one or two white feathers intermixed with the black ones or *vice versâ*; both are regarded as grave faults, but more particularly the latter, as it is more readily detected by the naked eye.

The next markings of importance are those of the eye. Some birds are pencilled in front of the eyes only, and others behind the eyes, whilst others again are pencilled both in front of and behind the eyes, which is preferable to being marked on one side of each eye önly; but the most approved and perfect eye-markings are those which encircle the eye completely, and these are known as " spectacle " eye-marks; they should not be either too large or too small, but proportionate with the size of .the bird, and in keeping with the wing-markings; when well formed they ought to be elliptic, or egg-shaped.

Symmetry in marking is an important consideration, and one which is too frequently overlooked or ignored. The other recognised markings are one or two dark feathers on each side of the tail; but these must be the extreme outside feathers, and none others. Such markings may·be regarded as doubtful acquisitions, although a few of the " old school " profess to cherish a liking for them. Nevertheless, there can be no question that a perfectly " four-marked " bird is the beau ideal of a bird of this variety—I mean a bird with good wing and eye markings, and a clear tail. " Two-marked " birds may be possessed of wing markings only, or of eye-markings only, with a clear body, but a bird having a clear body and a dark feather on each side of the tail only, is not so recognised. Many good judges prefer a bird with evenly-marked wings and a clear body to a " six-marked " bird, as they look upon the tail markings as a detraction and not as an embellishment, but those with eye-markings only are the least valued of all except for mule breeding.

It will be found, on closely examining an evenly-marked bird, that its eye-markings do not exactly correspond; at least, I never saw one with both eye-markings precisely alike, and I have scrutinised hundreds. Those birds with eye-markings most closely resembling each other are to be preferred. A good saddle is an indispensable requisite to an evenly-marked bird, and a point deserving of attentive consideration, as a finely formed, full, flowing saddle greatly enhances the appearance of the wing-markings. Some fanciers term evenly-marked wings V shaped, but I fail to see the force of this, as a V is much thicker on one side than the other, and therefore, a bird to be V wing-marked must have one wing more heavily-marked than the other, hence it would not be even.

With the exception of the markings already described, a bird of this variety should be clear in all other parts of the body, and it is desirable that it should be free from dark feathers in the saddle and coverlets, whether of wings or tail. The greater portion of marked birds are dark in their under-flue feathers, and others again are tinged on the thighs, vent and rump, and have dark legs and feet. These are only regarded as minor considerations; but where two birds are equal in merit in all other respects, the bird that possesses the fewest of these blemishes is undoubtedly entitled to bear the palm.

The evenly-marked Norwich canaries are about five inches and upwards in length. In form they resemble the original, or, as it is more frequently named, the common canary. They should have round, full heads; necks medium in length, and rather stout; bodies full and plump, with deep, broad, well-developed, and prominent chests; broad, well-filled backs, and substantial shoulders; legs rather short, but well set; carriage easy and commanding, with plenty of vivacity.

The *Crested* Norwich birds in size and general conformation resemble very closely the foregoing variety. The head should be round, broad, and full; the neck moderately long, and gradually increasing in thickness from the junction next the head to the shoulders; the body should be full and plump, and of a demi-semi-circular form from the throat to the vent; the back broad at the shoulders, tapering towards the tail, and slightly curved outwardly; the tail projecting in an obtuse manner from the body, although it is usually termed "straight" by fanciers. The chest should be deep, broad, and full. The body colour clear, bright, vivid and level throughout, except the shoulder blades, or pinion covers and rump, which are always more intense in colour in highly-bred birds—this is termed "quality" by the *cognoscenti*. The flights, tail feathers, and vents of all birds are invariably paler, but more so in some birds than in others. Closeness and firmness of feather are advantageous, and likewise denote quality; and a full well-formed circular saddle is a great acquisition, especially to a marked bird, for it shows the wing markings to much greater advantage, and makes them appear more angular, or, as it is generally termed, "cleaner cut." The feathers should be silky in texture and appearance.

The crested birds are generally a little inferior in colour, when compared with the choicest specimens of the clear varieties, but it is amazing what amount of improvement has taken place in crested birds in this respect during the last few years.

The crest consists of a tuft of feathers which cover the upper portion or crown of the head, and it is formed in many respects like a flower, as it appears to converge to a point or centre, and the feathers overlap each other like the leaves or petals of a rose, or marigold, falling or drooping partly over the beak, eyes, and back part of the head of the bird, and this feature constitutes the chief point of beauty in this variety of canary. The crest varies in shape, size, and colour. There are the elliptic or oval crest, the round or circular crest, and the shield crest (so called from its resemblance in form to the escutcheon); the last is rounded in front, and as it extends backward from the centre or orifice it expands in breadth, and terminates in an almost horizontal line, except at the extreme outer edges, where two small elongated tufts of feathers (one on each side corresponding) project like two diminutive horns; these are termed by some "pheasants' ears." A well-formed crest of this description is exceedingly handsome, more particularly when it is adorned with a hood—that is, with a dark patch of feathers extending from behind the eyes of the bird, and down the back part of the neck for some distance, and partly over each side of it as well. In shape it is like a monk's cowl, and is frequently termed a "hood crest," and sometimes a "curtain crest," and when perfect in form it is considered by connoisseurs as the *chef-d'œuvre* of crests.

A good crest of any form should have a clearly defined but well filled centre, from which the feathers should fall gracefully in every direction over the head; it should likewise be well filled and closely packed, without a break or split in any part of it. It ought to come well over the beak, eyes, and base of the skull; the longer and thicker it is the better, provided it is well formed and well proportioned. It should be as flat as possible on the top, and have the appearance of having been pressed with a flat iron. The colour most admired is dark green, approaching to black. Next to green comes grey or mottled, called by some fanciers "grizzled;" clear crests are held in the least esteem of all, so far as colour becomes a consideration. You cannot get a crest too dark, nor too large, provided it is well-formed and densely packed. The formation of the crest is the chief consideration, next size, and lastly, colour. It is not customary at shows to make separate classes for the different forms of crests; all are shown together, and each fancier has his opinion as to which he considers best.

I know from experience that the most difficult form of crest to produce in anything like perfection is the shield crest with the hood; and those who have made crested birds their particular study will acknowledge that this is by far the handsomest.

The *Evenly-marked and Crested* canaries look best, I always think, when they are not too lightly wing-marked. I prefer a bird with the first six or seven large flight feathers clear and the remainder dark. The darker and more defined they are, the more valuable the bird possessing them becomes. In a really first-class specimen of this variety none of the wing coverlets or saddle feathers should be dark, only the flights specified and the crest; a mixed wing is a fault, that is, a white feather intermixed with the dark ones, and this frequently happens. A self-coloured tail, whether dark or clear, and even a mixed tail, provided the dark feathers are at the outer edges of the tail, and correspond, is admissible, but a clear tail is without doubt most esteemed. A black feather or more on one side of the tail only, although the bird has evenly-marked wings, is considered a disqualification in an evenly-marked and crested class, and a bird so marked should be entered in the "unevenly-marked," or "any other variety" class. For my part, and many fanciers are of the same opinion, I should be disposed to admit a bird of this description into the evenly-marked class, and count three points against it for the defect, as it is birds of this stamp that tempt unscrupulous fanciers to tamper with them.

STANDARDS OF EXCELLENCE.—The following tables will be found to give accurate estimates of the relative points of merit in the different varieties, 100 points to be regarded as a maximum of perfection :

STANDARD FOR JUDGING CLEAR NORWICH CANARIES.

Points.

Colour, the principal considerations being vividness, clearness, and purity, the tint mostly esteemed being deep orange, and distributed evenly and regularly over the breast, back, vent, &c., of the bird	45
Quality, for extra brilliancy and sheen, particularly on the crown of the head, pinions, or shoulder blades and rump, and for having a fine silvery luminosity pervading the head, neck, breast, &c.	20
Size of birds, for length and substance	8
Condition and feathers	15
Contour and carriage	6
Saddle	6
Total	100

For the *Ticked* and *Green* varieties the same standard as that given for the clear birds will be found equally applicable; but with regard to the *Unevenly-marked* birds the markings, which form an interesting feature in this class, must be taken into consideration. I therefore give the following as a standard of excellence :

STANDARD FOR JUDGING UNEVENLY-MARKED NORWICH CANARIES.

Points.

Markings	20
Colour	30
Quality	15
Size (length and substance)	8
Condition and feathers	15
Contour and carriage	6
Saddle	6
Total	100

The following is the Standard of Excellence for *Evenly-marked* Birds :

STANDARD FOR JUDGING EVENLY-MARKED NORWICH CANARIES.

Points.

Colour—for richness, intensity, and regularity throughout	25
Marking and pencilling, 35 points, sub-divided thus:	
Wing-marking	20
Eye-marking	15
Saddle—for fulness, shape, and closeness	8
Condition and quality (meal or floss)	10
Size (length and substance of bird)	8
Feathers—for firmness and sheen	8
Contour and carriage	6
Total	100

The Standard of Excellence for *Crested* Norwich is as follows :

STANDARD FOR JUDGING CRESTED NORWICH CANARIES.

	Points.
Crest 45 points, sub-divided as follows :	
Form and size of crest...........................	30
Colour of crest.....................................	7
Centre of crest	8
Total...........................	45
Colour of bird—for depth, evenness, and brilliancy ..	10
Wing-marking	10
Condition and quality	10
Feathers...	1C
Contour and size of bird..........................	10
Saddle	5
Total........................	55
Grand Total	100

All show birds ought to have good sound legs and feet; the wings ought not to overlap each other at the tips, nor droop from the shoulder like a "slip wing."

An otherwise good bird might, through an accident, lose a claw, or cross or droop its wings more than is natural. I do not think it would be right to disqualify it as a show bird on this account; but all such imperfections ought to be carefully looked for by judges, and, when discovered, should be fully considered and well weighed ere the awards are made, and for each defect so many points should be deducted from the qualities of the bird so maimed as they considered right and just to all parties concerned.

The standard for judging the clear and unevenly-marked *Crested* varieties, with the exception of the wing markings, is the same as that already given. At those shows where the three classes are merged in one it is for the committees to say whether the wing markings of the evenly-marked birds are to count, as judges, not being instructed to the contrary, should adhere to the standard.

WHAT IS AN EVENLY-MARKED BIRD ?—This question has frequently been asked of late, and there appears to be much difference of opinion on the subject. I will endeavour to explain the matter clearly and tersely.

A bird marked with a round spot in front of each eye is known as a "pea-eye-marked" bird; other eye markings consist of a line in front or behind the eye, and frequently both; and in other cases the eyes are surrounded with oval or roundish dark markings, known amongst fanciers as "spectacle eye marks." These last-named are considered the most perfect, and consequently are most esteemed. When a bird is possessed of any of these appendages and a perfectly clear body in other respects it is considered evenly-marked, and is termed a "two-pointed" bird. If, however, in addition to these marks it has a dark feather clearly visible in either wing or the tail, then it is classed with the unevenly-marked or variegated birds. If a bird is marked near one eye only, and is quite clear in colour on all other parts of the body, it is known as a ticked bird.

A bird marked in each wing, although it may have five dark feathers in one wing and seven in the other, or seven in one and nine in the other, or similarly marked, but appearing even to the unaided eye, is considered an evenly-marked bird, and is designated a "two-pointed" bird also; but if marked at one eye only and on any other part of the body including tail in addition, then it becomes an unevenly-marked bird. A bird marked at each eye and in each wing and nowhere else, is undoubtedly the most perfect type of the evenly-marked variety, and is termed a "four pointed" bird. I consider a bird with well-formed spectacles or oval eye-markings, and the nine secondary flying feathers in each wing coloured, the beau ideal of an evenly-marked bird. Again, a bird marked at each eye and each wing, and with one or two dark feathers on each side of the tail (being the extreme outside feathers) is also an evenly-marked bird, and is known as a "six pointed" bird; but if it has only a dark feather on one side of the tail it is not eligible, but with two on one side and only one on the other it is still regarded as an evenly-marked bird. The dark tail feathers are, in my opinion, a drawback rather than an advantage, although I know that some fanciers differ with me on this point. I have never seen a perfect evenly-marked bird, nor do I believe one has ever been bred by any fancier. Some years ago I made this variety of bird my especial study, and I bred some of the most perfectly marked birds I have ever seen, and some of them were never beaten when exhibited in the best of company. It is rare to get the eye-markings nearly equal, and in the wings there will generally be found one or two more dark feathers in one wing than in the other, and one or two white feathers mixed up with the dark, or a few dark feathers in the saddle near the junction of the wings may occasionally be found just above the rump, or on the rump, vent, or thighs.· These blemishes do not entitle the birds to be shown in any other class than the one for the evenly-marked. and when allowed to remain they count as points against them; but I am sorry to say many exhibitors manipulate birds showing such blemishes to a considerable extent. It is not uncommon for an otherwise perfect bird to have a few dark feathers at the butts of the wings, which is a great blemish, and when judging a class of this sort I have frequently had to disqualify birds for being "faked" (trimmed)—many of them even by some of our most successful exhibitors. I need not say that the practice is a dishonest one and a robbery from honest fanciers.

WHAT IS A VARIEGATED BIRD?—This is another bone of contention among fanciers, but one that is not, in my opinion, difficult to settle. A variegated bird is simply a bird diversified in colour, and whether these colours appear in the shape of even- or uneven-marking, it is to all intents and purposes a bird diversified in colour, and consequently a variegated bird. You cannot go beyond the definitions given by the compilers of our dictionaries. I am aware that many bird fanciers do not regard an evenly-marked bird as a variegated bird, but it is so nevertheless. To prevent any misunderstanding, the Committees of Shows should exercise the utmost care in compiling their schedules of prizes, and state precisely what variety of birds are intended to be allowed to compete in certain classes, and this should be done in the clearest manner possible. The word variegated has proved· misleading to many exhibitors,·

and, therefore, I would suggest that the most straightforward plan would be to state clearly and emphatically what is really meant. For instance, supposing you wish to include in one class all variegated birds, whether marked in regular or an irregular manner, the schedule should read thus: Evenly-marked, Unevenly-marked, or Ticked. If you wish to exclude the Evenly-marked, then the words, Unevenly-marked or Ticked should be substituted. But what are you going to do with the evenly-marked birds, which are really the gems of this variety? You surely would not relegate them to the other variety class, as it would be an undoubted injustice to do so. At some shows, in fact at most of the best shows, separate classes are given for evenly-marked specimens, and this order of things I consider much the best, but at small shows, such liberality cannot be exercised on account of the expense. Therefore, when judges find that evenly-marked, unevenly-marked, and ticked birds all compete together, every allowance should be made for size, shape, colour, quality of feather, and condition; and as the evenly-marked birds lose considerably in colour and frequently in size and form, the contest is often keener than many suppose; for it must be remembered that all birds not eligible for competition in an evenly-marked class must of necessity be eligible for an unevenly-marked class, and this would include all birds marked in each wing and with a dark cap; all birds evenly-marked in the wings and at the eyes but with one dark feather in the tail, or with evenly-marked wings and one eye mark; and those marked at each eye and in each wing but with a small spot or speck on the crown or centre of the head. These, of course, are the perfection of unevenly-marked birds so far as markings are concerned, and in a class including both varieties these birds frequently make the contest very warm, as a little extra size, or superior colour or contour, may easily cast the balance of points in their favour.

Some fanciers would like to have three and five pointed birds relegated to the evenly-marked classes, but this I regard as nonsensical. I would rather see all marked birds come

x

under the simple head of "Variegated," for by no rule of
logic or common sense can an unevenly-marked bird be
classed as an evenly-marked one. Birds that are heavily or
badly marked require to be possessed of some extraordinary
merit beyond their markings to have even a remote chance
of success as a prize winner, when competing against such
birds as I have described.

WHAT IS A TICKED BIRD? There's the rub! A *bonâ fide*
ticked bird is a bird that possesses one clear and distinct
dark tick or spot on some part of the body, that can be
discovered without the aid of a magnifying glass, or straining
the sight for the space of ten minutes to find its where-
abouts. I do not consider a clear-bodied bird with a little
dark under-flue feather on the thigh or at the vent a ticked
bird. Birds with these slight blemishes are eligible to compete in clear classes, and such trivial defects should be taken
into consideration in awarding the prizes. I do not place
much weight on these defects myself, and would only count
two or three neutral points against birds so marked.

Evenly- and unevenly-marked Cinnamons of the Norwich
type are never shown in classes for Norwich birds, but are
invariably entered in the A.O.V. class; the same remarks are
equally applicable to Cinnamon-marked birds of the Yorkshire varieties.

For my part I see no reason why Cinnamon-marked birds
of the Norwich type, or the same variety of birds of the
Yorkshire type, should not compete against green-marked
birds of the same varieties, and where committees decide on
this the fact should be specially mentioned in the schedules.
No doubt this opens up another question, and that is, why
should not Cinnamon crests be made to compete in the
Crested-Norwich classes? My answer is, that this may be
regarded as quite the exception to the rule, from the fact
that the introduction of Cinnamon blood stultifies the crest
properties, and, therefore, a Cinnamon-crested bird would
have no possible chance of competing with success in this
class. But with marked birds it is otherwise, as the

Cinnamon colour does not interfere with regular marking, as may be proved from the fact that some of the best of the evenly-marked Yorkshire birds of the day are Cinnamon-marked.

In a mixed class of variegated birds, an evenly-marked bird has undoubtedly a greater chance of gaining a prize than a patched-about bird, or even a ticked bird, as great weight is always given to regularity of marking. On the other hand, to preserve these features, in-breeding has to be greatly resorted to, and this has a tendency to deteriorate qualities, such as size, colour, feather, form, and robustness, and these points can always be obtained in greater perfection in a ticked or irregular-marked bird. Judges officiating at shows where mixed classes prevail, have to use their best endeavours to balance all the points enumerated in a fair and impartial manner; and then in the absence of one or two high class specimens of evenly-marked birds, there is a greater chance of success for the exhibitors of ticked and irregular-marked specimens than many exhibitors believe. Still, I have no desire to allure the owners of these birds into the belief that a chance of winning a prize with a moderate specimen is not remote; on the contrary, I say that it would be useless to expect to take a prize in such a class as this with a ticked or unevenly-marked bird, unless it excelled greatly in size, form, colour quality, and condition.

CHAPTER XVIII.

THE MODERN PLAIN-HEAD NORWICH.

As prognosticated by me in the last edition of this book, a great and marked change has taken place in the style and type of this variety of canary.

Owing to the introduction of cayenne and other ingredients for producing deep, bright colour (which is regarded as the chief feature in this class of birds), the original small, active, dapper little Norwich bird of former days, famed for its rich, natural mellow colours, its lovely silky feathers, its close-fitting coat, and clean-cut appearance and active movements, has now been superseded, by a larger, more heavily feathered and bulky bird, created between the bird last described and the Yorkshire and Lancashire varieties mixed, to obtain greater length and substance of body. A great deal has been written and said on this subject by many of the leading fanciers of this variety. In 1890 a conference on the subject was held at the Crystal Palace Show, and a meeting formed of some of the principal exhibitors, dealers, general fanciers, amateurs, and judges, and a standard to breed to was agreed upon. The birds, according to this, should be thick and cobby in shape, and should measure so much as six-and-a-half inches in length, whereas the old style used to measure from five-and-a-quarter to five-and-three-quarter inches, and an inch added to the length of a bird is equal to twelve inches added to the height of a man; so the plain-head Norwich are enlarged almost beyond recognition. Of course, to obtain this style of bird

THE NORWICH PLAIN CANARY.

(First Prize Crystal Palace, 1899. Owners, Messrs. Angus and Crane.)

the type is considerably altered owing to the infusion of so much foreign blood—the beautiful rich, natural colour and silkiness of feather are considerably sacrificed. But for the use of condiments to produce the required colour no such change would have been tolerated, so that it is doubtful whether the discovery of this method of obtaining artificial colour is of any benefit whatever to bird fanciers generally.

I think that six inches should have been the utmost limit allowed to birds of this variety, and if the same free license is continued to be allowed to breeders, it will soon become a difficult matter not only for amateurs, but even for judges, to distinguish the plain-head from the crested-bred, and, in some cases, these latter from thick-set Yorkshire birds. It is a great mistake, in my opinion, to bring the type of these varieties so closely together. Of course, we know that a Yorkshire bird should be slimmer, lighter, more graceful, and more erect than a Norwich bird, and that a crest-bred should be fuller in the head and body, and have the overhanging eyebrows which, in a plain-head, would be esteemed a fault; but according to the present method of producing these varieties, a plain-head Norwich is often difficult to distinguish from a small Yorkshire bird, and another, probably out of the same nest, may just as nearly resemble a crest-bred; and if this tendency to increase the size in these varieties is cherished, I contend that in a short time it will be possible to breed specimens of Norwich plain-heads, crest-bred plain-heads, and Yorkshires, from the same pair of birds. This possibility, in my opinion, ought not to exist; but since the rage for large birds has become a craze of the present generation of fanciers, and many of the most attractive qualities are more or less ignored, I fear that in a short time we shall entirely lose some of the best features of the old and beautiful bird which so greatly charmed our predecessors.

The question may some day be asked, who is to blame for these things? My answer would be, the judges. These are the men who ought to lead and guide exhibitors, instead of, as at present, pandering to the whims and fancies of inexperienced breeders.

Where this craving for size, to the detriment of all other qualities, will lead, I do not pretend to know, but I think it has already done an incalculable amount of mischief. Amateurs desirous of breeding these modern plain-heads should, if possible, procure hens of the old original strains, and mate these with large specimens of the crest-breds, with long stout bodies, broad deep chests, wide substantial backs, small narrow heads, and short tails; or they may pair a hen of the description named with a Lancashire plain-head cock, and select from this cross the shortest and stoutest birds (many of which will not exceed six or six-and-a-half inches in length), and pair these again with small, short, thick-set, crest-bred plain-heads; or a bird bred between a Lancashire and a Yorkshire first cross may be put to a bird of the original Norwich type to breed these modern varieties from. It is all a matter of taste and judicious selection. The colour can be obtained by feeding during the moulting process, but those birds which show richest in natural colour, and which have favoured the primitive type, will assuredly show up best, so far as colour is concerned, at the end of the process. If you first cross the plain-head and crest-bred together, in some cases too much skull and eyebrow will be produced, but if these birds are again crossed with a good specimen of the small Yorkshire variety, the present admired type will be obtained. As soon as you succeed in getting the birds up to the required standard of size and shape, breed them sib—*i.e.*, in and in—for a generation or two, and then introduce fresh blood from some other fancier, who has a similar type of birds to your own. It takes a few years to produce in anything like perfection a new style or type of canary.

The only thing further that will be needed will be to feed according to the methods we recommend to obtain colour, but it will be found that birds bred in this way will be better adapted to the yellow than the red-fed classes for shows. Of course, it will be necessary to exercise care and judgment in selecting your breeding stock; broad-headed birds showing too much eyebrow must be discarded; symmetry, colour, and compact tightly-feathered birds must be chosen, if you expect to succeed in breeding prize specimens. The large-headed, thick-set, long-feathered offshoots should be crossed with Lancashire plain-heads, to obtain birds to show in the crest-bred plain-heads; but unless they have big, broad heads, heavy drooping brows, deep broad chests and heavy shoulders, with a profusion of body feather of good length, they will not be suitable.

Birds bred in this way are useful to cross with Cinnamon birds to obtain size and shape, but it must not be overdone, or you will lose too much colour, which, in my opinion, is the greatest feature in a Cinnamon canary. As the Norwich canary originated in the city of that name, the name is still upheld, but the present type of bird owes its origin as much or more to the Yorkshire and Lancashire crosses than it does to the bird so called. It is known that Norwich fanciers and exhibitors have had to go to Yorkshire to obtain fresh blood both for breeding and exhibiting this modern variety, but this will only be for a limited period, for there are no keener or more spirited fanciers of canaries in the world than are to be found in Norwich.

Some twenty-six years ago, I, with Messrs. Jno. Rutter, Thos. Clark, C. J. Ayre, Geo. Shiel, Edwin Mills, W. Rogers, Snaiton Hall, and a few others, got up an open all-England show in Sunderland, and I was much astonished to find that Mr. Richard Mackley and Mr. G. Collinson came all the way from Norwich with their show specimens; Mr. W. Walter, from Winchester, Hants, and Mr. Howarth Ashton (with his man, Jones), from Manchester. I made all the preliminary arrangements for this show up to the time of opening, but being held at Christmas-time I could not see my way clear to continue as acting secretary, and I tried to get Mr. Mills to take my place. He objected, but said, "I can find you a man that will do the work admirably, but he knows

nothing about birds; nevertheless, he will do everything in
his power to carry out your wishes." This man was the late
William Anthony Blakston, and he proved a very useful
adjunct, and this was the means by which he was brought
into the "fancy." He was an astute and intelligent man,
and one that could readily pick the brains of most men, but
as a practical breeder his experience was very limited;
his knowledge was gained from other men, such as Rutter,
Clarke, Wilkinson, and others. I do not say this in disparagement of Mr. Blakston, whom I have always considered as
a shrewd, clever, and ingenious man, and a fluent writer, and as
such I have always admired him, but I believe that many
people who did not know him intimately run away with the
idea that he gained his knowledge from practical breeding
and observation, which was not the case. He could truly
have said with Wotton, " I am but a gatherer and dispenser
of other men's stuff."

The interest taken in birds now, as compared with the bird
fancy thirty years ago, may be taken from the fact that
Messrs. Mackley, of Norwich, alone dispose of something
like 20,000 birds in a year, whereas thirty years ago the
sale out of Norwich would probably not reach 1000, spread
over the whole of the breeders in that city, whilst I should
think that more than 40,000 birds were sold in Norwich
during the year 1890.

The bird selected as a model for the modern type is thick-
set, or very stout in body, a deep broad chest, broad back,
substantial shoulders, a neat round head, plenty of feather,
close-fitting wings, and a moderately long tail—a tail in every
way proportionate to the size of the bird, and the lighter and
more compact it is the better—a broad spreading tail is an
eye-sore. The bird should stand semi-erect, and well over the
perch, and there should be no loose feathers about the breast,
thighs, or vent, and no appearance of eyebrows. The entire
covering of the bird should be tight-fitting, the colour rich,
level, deep in tone, bright in hue, well fringed with meal, and
soft and silk-like in texture, which denotes high quality. It

takes some time to breed a truly typical bird, and hence high-class specimens are rare and costly, both for exhibition and breeding purposes. Even the best known specimens at times breed inferior stock; still prize winners generally come from the best birds.

CHAPTER XIX.

THE MODERN CRESTED NORWICH.

Some thirty-seven years ago crested birds were despised, and I have laboured all these years, not only in cultivating the breed, but also in encouraging a taste for it in others, and I feel fully satisfied with the result of my labours.

I have now in my possession the first evenly-marked and crested yellow Norwich canary I ever saw. I need hardly say that it has been under a glass shade for at least a quarter of a century. I bred it some six-and-twenty years ago, and at that time it created quite a sensation in the bird world. I have also one by the side of it which I bred some seven years ago, a bird that could win at this day, and the difference is very marked between them, and shows at a glance the wonderful improvements that have been achieved in the last twenty years towards perfecting this variety.

The modern crested Norwich has been produced by crossing the original and true type of crested Norwich Canaries with the Lancashire Coppies; and I believe I am not far from the truth when I say that the first attempt to introduce this cross, of course, in a surreptitious manner, was made at Northampton some eighteen years ago. Since the first introduction of the Coppy, which was done in a stealthy manner, breeders have become emboldened, and latterly no secret has been made of it, as judges instead of putting their veto upon it, have openly encouraged it, not only by awarding the whole of the prizes in the crested classes to birds of this type, but by lauding them when writing the accounts of the shows where they judged, and some going so far as to tell the fanciers that it was "a step in the right direction." Being thus encouraged, the breeders have gone on, step by step, introducing the Coppy from one generation to another, until some of the birds of the present day are so fully impregnated with that blood, that if it were not for the body markings and dark crests which Coppies never possess—and the cayenne feeding—it would be a difficult matter to distinguish some of these birds from genuine Coppies. I have seen specimens, yea, and successful prize winners too, that in conformation of body and crest bore no resemblance whatever to the real, true type, the original. Crested Norwich birds and the last-mentioned variety, however good they may be in all points, have no chance whatever of taking prizes when competing against this modern variety. The breeders in Norwich, however, have no just cause of complaint against this comparatively recent innovation, as they themselves were among the first to impart this foreign admixture into the old breed, and some, if not the very best specimens of this new variety have been produced in that town, although not necessarily exhibited by Norwich men. I have been behind the scenes, and know where most of the best birds came from that have been exhibited by different fanciers since their first introduction to the public. I am free to admit that I consider the cross an immense and beneficial improvement in many respects, but I certainly would like to see them distinguished by a more appropriate and fitting title, and I imagine that ere long they will come under the more apt and truthful designation of Marked or Variegated Coppies, or Lancashire and Norwich Union Crest, and it would doubtless be to the advantage of fanciers themselves if this were so, as no restraint would then be felt by either breeders or judges, and a still further improvement would doubtless be effected in their appearance and general contour. No one who is acquainted with the different varieties of these birds can doubt that the present appellation is entirely anomalous and utterly misleading.

To breed this variety successfully it is necessary to obtain Coppies of the very best type procurable, and cross them with Norwich birds of the best crested strains obtainable, but-it will require years of judicious crossing to obtain birds as perfect as can be found at the present day and in the hands of practica¹ breeders only. Anyone desirous of experimenting on his own account I would recommend to begin with crested Norwich hens, and plain-headed Lancashire Coppy cocks, always being careful to choose the latter birds short in tail and massive in body, with well-developed craniums. The Norwich hens should be evenly-marked, or green birds from an evenly-marked strain; be sure they are of good quality and type, and always procure them from well-known breeders, not exhibitors, in all cases, as most of these people purchase their show birds from other fanciers more successful and experienced than themselves. Always keep the heaviest-marked birds, the greens, and those with dark caps and wing markings, to cross into the Coppy blood again, as the latter variety, being bred for purity of colour for so many generations, have a great influence on the colour of the cross breeds, and birds with clear or grizzled crests are not nearly so valuable as the dark crested birds.

I am very particular myself about having birds from an evenly-marked strain to begin with. Though no one can breed these birds with regularity, I endeavour as far as I possibly can to retain this blood, and I get my share of evenly-marked young ones.

I choose all my hens with great substance, and large broad heads, very full breasts, short legs and tails; in fact, Norwich in shape, and Coppies in substance, a sort of condensed Coppy. When I get them as large as I can, full of Coppy blood and the Norwich Fancy shape of body, I breed them together, and invariably choose two marked birds, as this establishes the markings, increases the green colour, and intensifies it as well. The object is, in fact, to establish the points and markings already obtained. I do this for two generations and then dip into the Coppy blood again, always choosing those birds which show the best blending of the two varieties and the nearest to the Norwich birds in contour and colour.

It is astonishing to observe how these crosses sport at times, some taking after the Coppies, and others entirely after the Norwich varieties, whilst others show a happy blending of both. The latter are the birds which should be selected for further experiments. Eschew long tails, and long thin bodies ; all birds resembling the Yorkshire Fancy in shape should be discarded.

I have sometimes bred three distinct types of birds from the same parents, and no one could have believed, excepting only those who know by experience, that these birds were related, much less brothers and sisters, and reared in the same nest.

I have had specimens that were more than half-bred Coppies, that no one could have distinguished from the pure Norwich breed, and others which would have passed for Coppies if they had been clear in colour, whilst the third would show the admixture of the two varieties thoroughly blended, and these are the birds that are most valuable.

Some birds show it in only two ways, size of body and form of crest—the true Norwich shape, and this is what breeders aim at. A true Norwich crest is broader at the back than it is at the front, and the best specimens are finished off at the back of the neck with a curtain or hood like a monk's cowl. Coppies never have this appendage, and most of the Coppy crosses are also destitute of this ornament, and have a round or elliptic crest which appears clean cut all round, and which is strongly indicative of Coppy blood. It is no uncommon occurrence for two birds from the same nest to be exhibited in the same class, the one to receive high honours and the other to be disqualified for showing "too much Coppy." Several instances of this kind are within my own personal knowledge, and I consider it the strongest argument that can be brought forward to show that the present designation of these birds is a misnomer.

A bird of this variety should be large in size, and should resemble the Norwich Fancy in shape, being full in the body and head, deep and broad in the chest, short in the legs, wide across the shoulders, and not too long in the tail. The crest, however, is by far the most important feature, and next to this, contour, colour, quality of feather, and condition. The crest should be round, oval, or shield-shaped, that is wider at the back than the front; the latter being the true Norwich type of crest.

Some fanciers, as well as judges, prefer one kind and some another. All of them look well, provided they are properly formed, free from faults, and are well and artistically finished. I think, however, that those which are full and round in the front and square at the back with the cowl are the most telling, as they appear much larger than a round or oval crest finished close off at the back of the bird's head. A good crest of any form should be broad and long in the front, come well over the eyes, and drooping with regularity all round : some crests stand off and do not droop, and are in the form of a flat button; this makes the crest look very wide. I do not despise a bird with a crest of this sort, if it is perfectly flat and well formed.

Those who have had much experience in breeding crested birds must know that it is quite as difficult to get a good well-finished back crest as it is to get a long broad-frontal crest; hence, when a bird is possessed of both these qualities, it must be of greater value than a bird which possesses only one of them. For my part, I breed both kinds, and can, therefore, readily appreciate the difference.

A bird shown by the Messrs. Mackley, of Norwich, in the year 1883, at Dudley (in the Evenly-marked class), where it obtained second prize, and at the Crystal Palace (in the Unevenly-marked class), where it obtained first prize, was a grand example of the type of crested birds I advocate, and unless he has been beaten since, is probably the best crested bird living, including every variety of crested Norwich canary. His crest is, in my opinion, simply perfection, and his back crest prodigious and exquisitely finished, and I consider it gives him an undoubted advantage over any bird not adorned with this appendage.

To obtain size of body and profusion of feather, breeding with two buff birds is much resorted to; but this should be done with care and judgment, as it is apt to produce coarseness of feather both on the body and crest of birds. Others, again, to enlarge and improve the size and form of the crests, put two crested birds together, and if these are not properly matched, the result is either a large mop crest, without quality or proper form, or it may result in a sparsity of crest; but when two crested birds are judiciously matched, a good crested bird may occasionally be bred in this way. If ever you breed from two crested birds, be sure to select two which are undoubtedly well bred and not deficient in crest properties, and keep the plain-heads bred in this way and put to crested birds again, as this is a sure method of improving and enlarging the crests; but this, too, must be done with care and caution, or you will obtain birds with faulty crests.

A good crest must, in the first place, be adorned with a good centre, distinct but closely filled in all round, appearing like the head of a small pin. It should be placed about the middle of the head of the bird, for, if placed too near the beak, it gives the appearance of a short and narrow frontal crest; and I have seen good birds spoiled through having the centre placed in this way, although it makes such birds show a greater profusion of lateral crest; but a properly balanced crest is unquestionably the most prized. From this centre the feathers should radiate in a uniform manner, and be placed as close as they can be packed without the slightest appearance of a break in any form. The crest should lie quite flat to the head of the bird, and appear smooth and unruffled. It should also be broad and expansive, thick and solid looking, with a good droop, giving it something of the appearance of a mushroom. A thin hairy looking crest is objectionable, however good it may be in other respects, and such crests are easily disarranged.

A flaw or opening in the front or at the side of a crest would be fatal to the chance of any bird on the show bench in good company; but there are a class of exhibitors who can patch up and trim faulty crests in a wonderful manner, and this is practised by some of them to a great extent; the loose feathers that have an aggravating and defiant method of standing erect are cut off short, or if very few in number are occasionally plucked out. A system of grooming is likewise resorted to; the bird is caught regularly every morning, and he is toileted like a baby; his crest is brushed with a soft tooth-brush, dipped in water when necessary, and if this operation does not succeed in bringing the stray and wayward feathers to subjection, a mixture is used in the final preparation before the bird is exhibited; bandoline* is one of the compounds used, and a weak solution of gum and spirits of wine, diluted with water; gum arabic or gum mastic are preferred for this operation, but it must be used very weak, 'or it will be detected. It requires skill and practice to use these artifices properly; and I only mention them to put those unacquainted with such devices on their guard, as I have heard of amateurs claiming such "faked" birds at a show, and after moulting them, they could not understand how they had deteriorated so much through, as they supposed, not getting a good moult. Such practices are not only highly reprehensible, but they are dishonest, and the perpetrators of them deserve to be exposed. As a safeguard against such birds being claimed, it is usual to place a fabulous price on them, but not in all cases. Those birds which need no grooming are much to be preferred; but high class birds of any variety, free from faults, are scarce, and consequently very costly. Good crested birds should be carefully handled, and not washed oftener than is absolutely necessary; the same remark applies to all other show specimens, but more particularly to crested birds than most other varieties. Every care should be taken to preserve them from dust and smoke, and they

* A preparation for the hair.

should always be kept in single cages by themselves so long as they are required to be exhibited.

One of the chief secrets of getting large crests is in obtaining a superabundance of feathers, and these should be long as well as profuse.

In selecting birds to breed from, fanciers should examine them minutely before purchase, when this can be done, to see that they possess this property; pass one of your fingers over the head of the bird from back to front, turning over the feathers, and, if good, they should come down to nearly the end of the beak; then blow the body feathers back; if a bird is full of feather, you will have to blow hard before you can obtain a sight of the under body; and if they are of good length as well as dense in quantity, that is what is required. As I have previously remarked, the quantity of feathers is greatly increased by breeding from two buff birds, instead of the recognised method of a buff and yellow; but when this is resorted to frequently, a coarseness of feather is produced, which is objectionable, and to counteract it, crossing with yellow birds is necessary. Yellow birds are never so full of feather as buff birds, and they are more silky in texture.

All show birds containing the Coppy crosses ought to be fed with cayenne, or other ingredients, to influence the colour during their moult, as they suffer much in loss of colour through the Coppy crosses; and high colour, next to a superb crest and contour, is the next thing to arrest the eye of a judge; and when you succeed in obtaining rich and brilliant colour in these birds, the judges are generally nonplussed and deceived as to the actual amount of Coppy present in the specimens.

I object to an immoderate use of cayenne pepper, but other ingredients can be used for this purpose which are harmless in their action.—See " The influence of various ingredients on the Colour of Canaries " (p. 135).

When a bird is satisfactory in all other respects, but has a long " Coppy tail," it is the custom of some exhibitors to draw it out about a month before the date of the show to

Y

which it has to be sent; it then appears with a three-parts grown tail, which completely hides the defect.

An open badly filled-in centre is a great drawback to an otherwise good bird, and this is one of those faults for which no remedy can be discovered; but in order to prevent such a fault appearing conspicuous, some exhibitors have recourse to dye, a subterfuge which frequently deceives a judge; and how few of these men there are who, when they do detect these fraudulent practices, have the moral courage to expose them, and more particularly so when the birds are the property of a professional exhibitor — and these are invariably the offenders.

The question may be asked—How are the judges to know? Very easily; show cages tell tales; and after a judge has had a bird through his hands at three or four different shows, it presents what they term " an old familiar face."

The points for judging this variety should be the same as those given for adjudicating on the original variety of Norwich-Crested Canaries.

The illustration is taken from my bird " Titan," and he is an excellent representative of a true Norwich-Crested Canary of the modern variety, fined down.

In this year of grace, 1891, we have reached a climax in the breeding of this much esteemed variety. The old type of Crested Norwich has now entirely disappeared from the show bench, as it would in these days of " Giants " stand a meagre chance of success, for the modern type are such " monsters," as some of their admirers are pleased to term them. The fact is, that the new variety is so thoroughly impregnated with Lancashire Coppy blood that there is a great deal more of the Lancashire in their composition than that of the Norwich, by which name they are still known; but this I consider very unfair to the Lancashire breeders, and I hope some day that they will be known and recognised under the title of dark-crested Lancashires. I do not condemn the innovation of the Lancashire blood, as it has greatly improved the Norwich in many respects, and more particularly in the size and formation of the crest, which, after all, is doubtless the most distinguishing feature of this variety of canary, and has remedied many of the defects observable in the original Norwich birds, such as baldness at the back of the head, the result of too much in-breeding and double-crest breeding. It has also been the means of improving the shape of the crest; producing more round and oval crests. The old Norwich type were full and square in the back crest, whereas the Lancashire birds are deficient in this respect, but they fairly surpass the Norwich birds in length and width of frontal and side crest owing to the great length of feather inherited from their ancestors, the old Dutch canary. Thus the cross has proved most beneficial and advantageous by blending the properties possessed by each variety. That this variety has been vastly improved is indicated by the fact that many modern specimens have realised nearly as many pounds each as the best specimens of the crested birds a quarter of a century ago would realise shillings. One of the best specimens of the day is the " Prince of Wales," a bird purchased by Messrs. Mackley Bros., of Norwich, from a breeder at Plymouth, for £20; others we could mention that have been sold for similar and even higher sums, such as £30, £35, and £40, and I know of one case where £50 was offered and refused for probably the best bird of his day, £60 being asked for him. I, myself, offered Mr. G. E. Russell, of Brierley Hill, £30 for probably the best bird he ever possessed, and for which he paid, I believe, £20 to a firm in North-amptonshire. I have bred several birds that have realised £5 and £10 each, and some of these, after winning prizes in first-class company, have been re-sold at much higher figures I enumerate these facts to show that the successful breeding of this variety is a source of profit as well as pleasure, but such birds are not bred every day—not by the most successful of breeders—neither can they always be obtained from the best-breeding stock procurable. I have known a pair of birds produce high-class specimens, and yet when ·these birds were separated and mated with other birds equally well bred, the offspring from both parents proved most disappointing, so that whenever you find a pair of birds produce young of a superior class, do not separate them; and in order to keep the blood pure breed them occasionally nearly allied, say, brother and sister, or uncle and niece, and so on. I also recommend fanciers who breed extraordinarily good birds, if they desire to keep up their name and fame as successful exhibitors, to keep the best of their specimens to breed from, and not to sell them even at "fancy" prices, for in the long run it will pay best to keep them, for good specimens can only be bred from typical parents as a rule.

There is also a great deal depending on selection. Choose birds that possess the best points; you must have very stout full-bodied specimens, with wide big heads, thick necks, and a profusion of long feather, especially on the head, which, when turned back, should reach to the end of the bill, and with thick drooping eyebrows also; only you must not discard a really well-bred bird simply because it does not happen to inherit all these qualities. I have great faith in good blood, and I have known grand birds bred from hens that were undersized and rather small in head and body, but of un-doubted quality as regarded breeding; hens not at all such as I would have selected had I not known the strain. On the other hand, I have seen miserable specimens produced from birds possessing all the qualities I have named—I refer, of course, to crested-bred plain-heads—but which were not the produce of high-class parents; so that it behoves an amateur to be careful in the selection of his breeding stock.

My advice is to keep your own plain-head hens, and buy crested cocks that have taken honours or prizes at the leading shows, and the more strains of high-class blood you can get into your birds the more reliable and profitable they will in time become, and the more certain you will be of producing typical specimens. The Lancashire fanciers are now very loath to part with their best birds. A few years ago some spirited breeders of the Crested-Norwich variety offered them tempting prices, and in many cases succeeded in obtaining

The Modern Crested Norwich Canary.

This bird has been produced by crossing the old type of Crested Norwich with the Lancashire Coppy. Size, form, colour, and droop of the crest are the principal points.

their very best specimens, and the result is that the Lancashire birds have in many respects deteriorated, and some of
the cross-breds, passing under the name of Crested-Norwich,
could beat them on their merits on the show-bench in Lancashire points alone, and in a few cases I have known this
done with clear crested birds. Another reason why the Lancashire birds have lost in size and fullness of body is that
some of the most prominent breeders of these birds have
introduced the modern variety of Crested-Norwich blood (clear
crests, of course), to improve and enlarge the crest of this
variety, and it is doubtful if, in so doing, they acted wisely.
I think not. Neither do I think that the breeders of the
modern Norwich have shown sufficient discretion in dipping
so deeply into the blood of the Lancashire birds, foi it
must be remembered that this variety is the produce of the
old Dutch and Belgian birds, mixed with the blood of the
common old-fashioned English canary, and as the Dutch and
Belgian blood vastly predominates, the breed has inherited
all the delicacy and weakness of constitution of the varieties
named ; and in consequence of the unlimited admixture of
this blood with Norwich crests, the modern Norwich has
become much more delicate than birds of the old type, being
subject to tuberculosis, asthma, and kindred complaints.
Many fanciers who strive to keep in the front rank of successful exhibitors have found to their cost that it is rather
an expensive " game " to keep up, for some birds costing
large sums have not lived more than two or three years when
exhibited regularly, and were bred from, as they speedily
became affected with diseases of the lungs or liver and
succumbed during that trying ordeal, the annual moult.

It seems to me strange that this craze for size in body
and crest should lead fanciers and judges alike to ignore
other qualities which are most desirable in a perfect specimen, such as even marking, rich colour, silky feathers, and
above all robust health ; all these might be attained in time
with judicious breeding and care ; but in order to do this,
some limit as to length should be agreed upon, and I think

that in time a model bird, possessing the much admired substance of body, and with a crest that nothing could excel, might be produced in a bird limited to a length of .6½in.; and to obtain a bird up to this standard, it would have to possess at least one-half · of Coppy blood, for this is the medium of length between the original Crested-Norwich and. the Lancashire bird.

Size is certainly a fundamental property, but with it ·you require refined shape, and either a clear body or evenly-marked wings, rich colour, sound soft silky feather, a nice carriage, a lively gait, and a general healthy appearance. Then the crest should be round or oval, the centre should be well set, close, and well filled in all round; the frontal crest should be broad and semi-circular, and come well over the beak; the side crest should be full and descend below the eyes; the back crest should be profuse and come well over the hind part of the head, and be neatly rounded off at the extreme base of the skull, or it may extend a short way down the neck, but should lie close and flat all over. There should be no upstanding wayward feathers in a perfect show bird, every feather should be smooth, close fitting, and firm, and with as much density as possible, so that it cannot easily be disarranged; and in addition to these qualifications you want a short beak, a thing difficult to obtain. A large bill is a great detriment to an otherwise good bird, and makes the frontal crest appear shorter than it actually is.

A bird possessing all these qualities would indeed be a *rara avis*, and few birds, even among the chief prize takers, can boast of three-fourths of them; but some excel in one feature and some in another, and hence the art, and science, and pleasure lies in the successful endeavour to create by skilful and judicious crossing, a bird as near the standard of perfection as it is possible to obtain. I have noticed that some large-crested prize-winners have been wide in the back crest, and narrow at the front, and others in the opposite direction, not well balanced, even, and regular; and in the same class might be observed a bird with a beautiful round or oval crest.

of good shape and, quality, but not profuse, that would be passed by or receive a simple H.C. or V.H.C. card. This is too bad, and ought not to be. I have frequently been struck in looking over the prize-winners at a show to find how widely divergent in type and quality the first, second, and third prize-winners often are, even in the same class, and I have heard young fanciers say, "How are we to know what to breed to when the judges themselves don't seem to know?" and I think they were quite justified in their remarks. This sometimes happens for want of an extended classification, which, I think, in the case of crested birds, might be made at many shows with beneficial results. There ought to be a class for clear bodies and dark crests, another for evenly-marked and crested, a third for unevenly-marked and crested, and a fourth for any other variety of crest. At all shows this could not be expected, but it might be carried out at the largest and best of them, and I think it would be a means of preventing degeneracy in quality and type. If things continue as they have of late the present title of Norwich will have to be modified or altered, in which case I would suggest that the word Norwich be expunged, and that the following classification be substituted : Dark-crested canary (clear body); evenly-marked and crested canary; unevenly-marked and crested canary; any other variety of crested canary. This arrangement would clear the way for amateurs, and give breeders the opportunity of gratifying their various humours as to size, type, &c., and the judges would hold a free hand to deal with them as they think proper. I am, of course, opposed to such a change, but I think it high time something was done one way or the other.

I have frequently been amused to find a bird entered in an " Any other variety class " as a " First cross Coppy and Norwich," whereas at the same show there have been birds, and some of them prize winners, exhibited in the Norwich classes, that were fully three-parts bred Coppies. It is too funny to contemplate, far too funny, by half. Open the gates by all means, if fanciers cannot agree to a standard type, and let the birds be classified as I have suggested, and in a few years the difficulties at present experienced will solve themselves, and I have no doubt in the manner first suggested.

In moulting crested birds for the show bench, artificial heat is an essential, and it should be applied both internally and externally, in order to ·fully develop the crest properties. By internally, I mean ·by cayenne feeding, and by externally, to being moulted in a room at a temperature of not less than 60 deg., nor more than 70 deg.

Where the Lancashire cross is freely used it is of importance to breed from green or heavily variegated birds on one side, otherwise grey or clear crests will predominate, and they are of much less intrinsic value than dark ones, however good they may be in size and quality.

In mixing up two varieties of birds, such as the Norwich and Lancashire varieties, where many of the chief features are widely divergent, such as type, colour, and feather, to create an improved breed there are always a number of difficulties to be overcome, and it takes a long time to discover where the improvements are to be continued or diversified to suit the classification at shows and the views of particular judges. An occasional cross with double crests is believed by many to be a good method of increasing the size and fullness of the crests, but it has so many drawbacks that I do not as a rule advocate it.

Too many mop crests result, and some of them stand up as defiantly as the quills on an enraged porcupine, and to breed this out you must have recourse to plain-head blood, so that the supposed advantages to be gained are somewhat problematical in cases of this sort. Occasionally a good result is obtained, but this is only the exception and not the rule. I prefer to use plain-heads bred from two crested birds; these are undoubtedly an acquisition for breeding purposes.

If you desire to breed high-class birds of this kind you must be very particular about the plain-heads; the crested birds there is no difficulty about, for good crests are not produced from inferior birds. There is a great outcry for birds with broad skulls and plenty of feather, but you must have the right sort of blood as well. I have bred some splendid birds from hens of medium size, and some with rather small heads, but I knew that they possessed the blood of several prize winners. I certainly like length of feather on the head, and good drooping eye-brows are indicative of high breeding, but I am not such a stickler for long body feather as some fanciers are; at the same time I like dense feathering of the body. Some of the best crested birds I have ever seen were produced from parents with medium length of body feathers and long dense head coverings; whilst some of the worst crested birds I have bred were the produce of birds with immense body feather, both long and profuse, so that there is no golden rule to be followed on these lines alone. Blood, gentlemen, blood! Nothing tells like it, whether in breeding birds or animals, and unless you can get the right strains to breed from, all your efforts will result in nought. I not only recommend the best - known strains to breed from, but good specimens must likewise be obtained. To ensure success this rule must be closely followed. Moral: Never dispose of your best birds whatever the temptation may be.

This rule rigorously carried out was the secret of the success of Robert Ritchie, of Darlington, who for years carried all before him in the Lizard classes, and only when illness and misfortune overtook him, and he let his best birds go, did he lose his position as a successful exhibitor.

It is customary before pairing crested birds to cut the crest and tail feathers short, and to thin the long feathers which surround the vent. I think it a commendable practice to cut the crests of show birds as soon as the show season is over in order to preserve the sight, as I am certain that long side crests, covering the eyes, is the cause of birds losing their sight from cataract.

A really good crest cannot be covered by a florin, and it should be of deep sound colour, with a blackish-green margin, and a black mid-rib, commonly known as a veined crest.

Breeders should avoid birds with faulty - shaped crests to breed from, and those with narrow or short frontals and peaked backed crests, split sides, fronts twisted and warped, and curled backs, and more particularly rough mop crests.

The standard for judging the present breed of Crested-Norwich I would place as follows:

	Points.
Crest, for form, size, centre, colour, and droop	55
Size of bird	15
Feather	10
Type, contour, and condition	20
Total	**100**

The Lizard Canary.

The bird from which this illustration was drawn won high honours in the Exhibition World in its day, and is an excellent example of the variety.

CHAPTER XX.

THE LIZARD.

THIS very beautiful and unique variety of canary stands pre-eminent, in the estimation of nearly all true fanciers, among what may be considered the real English Fancy canaries. There is no means of tracing the origin of these birds, but they have been known and esteemed among fanciers in this country for a great many years, and I think there is little doubt that they are the real source from which some other known varieties have been derived. They are great favourites in some of the midland and northern counties of England, especially Lancashire and Nottinghamshire; and it is in these counties that the best specimens are usually bred, although the county of Durham has, within the past few years, produced specimens which have successfully competed against all comers.

TRIMMING.—Lizard canaries are more frequently tampered with than any other variety by unprincipled exhibitors, hence it behoves judges to exercise their utmost vigilance and circumspection in judging these birds. A bald face is artificially coloured, sometimes very dexterously; a small cap is enlarged and enriched in colour by the use of a Judson's dye or a strong solution of saffron; white flight or tail feathers are extracted, and corresponding but dark feathers, drawn from other birds, are cleverly substituted for them; the tweezers are frequently brought into requisition to remove some tiny dark feathers from the cap, and when the pinion covers are intermixed with white, the white feathers are skilfully clipped close off, and the legs and bills are often stained black; in fact, every Lizard sent to compete at an exhibition should be handled and minutely examined all over by the judge. If a wing or tail feather projects beyond the natural line, or falls short of it, examine it most particularly, for it is a suspicious circumstance; and be sure to see that none of the feathers have been cut or trimmed. When a judge discovers a bird that has been fraudulently tampered with, he should make the fact public, despite any entreaties that may be urged against his doing so. Those fanciers who are mean enough to perpetrate such barefaced deception cannot be too severely censured and condemned.

SHOW PLUMAGE.—Young Lizards in their nest feathers are devoid of spangles; but when they moult these are produced, and, when fully moulted, they are in full show plumage, and not afterwards. Every time a Lizard moults it becomes paler in colour, in the wings especially, and the colour sometimes runs. Particularly is this the case if a bird is out of health at the time of moulting. Lizards are known among Scotchmen as " macaronies."

BREEDING.—In order to breed high-class birds of this variety, the greatest care and discrimination are necessary in the selection of your stock birds. Quality is the first thing to be considered. See that the birds you select are of the correct ground colour, for this is an essential point to begin with; that of a Golden Spangled Lizard should be of a deep, rich, velvety, greenish-golden, bronze colour, and the surface of the feathers should be entirely pervaded with a silvery, greyish luminosity, that adds richness to the colour, and is a sure sign of quality. Avoid all shades of hard greens, and smudginess or dinginess of hue, as this denotes bad blood. In the Silver Spangled birds the ground colour should be a deep, greyish, silver green, with a slight tinge of golden yellow, and the bright silvery luminous shading of the upper surface should be more marked and conspicuous in this variety than in the Golden birds. Your next consideration is spangle, as no Lizard is of any value that fails in this respect, and moreover the spangling should be decided, clear, and distinct, and not broken

or variegated in form. I admire a bird with a profusion of
close, fine spangling about the neck, giving it the appearance
of having a superbly and delicately worked lace collar, or a
collar of superfine network, and as the spangling descends
it should become more open and enlarged, and form a series
of distinctive half-moons round the edges of ' the larger
feathers. It should appear in long uniform stripes down
the back of the bird, and perfectly regular in order.
Always select large birds when obtainable, birds with wide
skulls, broad backs, and full prominent breasts, but on no
account must size supersede quality. The advantage gained by
a good big bird is, that it shows the spangling and cap to
much greater advantage than a smaller specimen. Never breed
from bald-faced birds, that is, birds that show clear-coloured
feathers below the eye and at the root of the beak, nor from
birds that have white feathers on the wings or tail, as these
faults would be propagated in the offspring. A good broad
well-formed cap is an essential point in a Lizard, but it
frequently happens that the best capped birds are deficient in
spangling, and *vice versâ ;* therefore, I recommend a bird with
a well-formed full cap, and not too profuse in spangles, to be
mated with a bird of the opposite sex that is rich and full of
"work," as spangling is termed, and whose cap may be small
and even "broken;" but I do not advocate breeding from
"broken" capped birds, unless they are highly meritorious in
all other respects. It is equally objectionable to mate two
over-capped birds, but to put an over-capped bird—that is,
when the cap runs partly down the neck—with a bird that is
slightly under-capped, short, and barely reaching to the base
of the skull, is frequently attended with excellent results.
Never put two birds to breed that are both " under-capped,"
as it has a tendency to circumscribe this valuable appendage.
I once bred a magnificently spangled Lizard in this way, but
it was entirely destitute of a cap. I put it with an over-
capped bird the following year, and from this pair I reared
some wonderful youngsters. It is customary to mate a Gold
and Silver bird together, but to increase the size and stamina

and to improve the spangling it is advisable occasionally to put two Silvers together, but this must not be overdone, or the spangling will run together and give a hazy appearance, and the ground colour will become too grey and pale. Put a good, sound Golden cock, deep, rich, and mellow in colour, to a superior light grey hen, or *vice versâ*, and when you obtain young birds pretty nearly perfect in cap, spangles, &c., mate the most perfect of them together, brother and sister, or uncle and niece, or even father and daughter, or son and mother, as this will greatly aid you in establishing the proper type, and preserving the most salient features. Then you must have recourse to fresh blood, selecting birds similar in type, &c., to those you have bred. Of course, where you breed a lot for the purpose of exhibiting, you will have several pairs in no way related to each other, so that you will have no difficulty in following out the rule laid down, for no man can expect to compete with success that only breeds from two or three pairs. Continue to 'breed on the same plan with regard to selection, and every third year full cousins may be mated together to keep the blood pure. If this method is followed up, discarding all faulty specimens, in a few years you will be in possession of a strain of Lizards that will breed prize birds with regularity and certainty.

Do not put two birds together that are both dark in the ground colours or you will lose in spangling, as it would become short and indistinct. A Gold cóck put to a hen bred from Double Silvers, if both are carefully selected, will often produce the best show birds. Splendid Silver birds are often bred from a hen the produce of two Gold birds and a good Silver cock. I do not care for Lizards being too black in the legs and claws, as it is generally a sign that there is too much green colour in the blood; it is also considered a fault to have birds too pale or flesh coloured in .the legs or claws, although I have seen some grand Lizards with flesh-coloured legs. I prefer a medium between the two.

Where there is too much green in a strain, the colour and feathers are harsh and unpleasant to the sight. Birds with red legs are usually very rich and pure in the ground colour, and clear and well defined in spangling, but they are apt occasionally to throw youngsters with a white feather in the tail or wings, which is very undesirable. Lizards as a rule are quarrelsome and mischievous, especially the males, and cocks of this description should be removed from beside the hens during the period of incubation, or they will probably destroy the eggs or harass the hens until the eggs are addled. I have known one very successful exhibitor, who introduced a cross of the London Fancy among his Lizards, crossing and re-crossing the produce with Lizards again and again for several years, until his birds attained a very high position as prize winners, and at one time he was almost invincible on the show bench. This cross is said to improve the cap and spangles. A London Fancy should be selected with a good skull and cap, and if possible a bird with some vigour of body; it should be paired with a large strong Lizard, and one deficient to some extent in spangles. In three years, if the produce of the first cross is bred-in with good Lizards, selected with judgment, a marked improvement in the chief characteristics of the birds will be observable, but the result will depend greatly on the birds selected for this purpose.

The greatest care is needed to prevent the parent birds from plucking their young, as those which have the misfortune to get plucked never make such satisfactory show birds as those which are fortunate enough to escape the misfortune, and if a tail or a flight feather is withdrawn it is reproduced with a spangle, which counts· against the exhibit, If the parents are observed to indulge in this vicious practice it will be best to remove the young birds to a small cage. which can be fixed to the front of the breeding cage, and so arranged that the parents can feed their progeny through the wires. If the breeding cage is wired at the ends as well as the front, it will be found best to fix the cage containing the young birds to one end instead of the front.

Lizard canaries are very difficult to breed sufficiently good in all points for exhibition purposes, and they occasionally breed young birds with foul feathers—white feathers—among their pinion coverlets, or in their wings or tails. When these appear at the shoulder blades or pinions, the bird is called " shelly shouldered," meaning that it resembles a chaffinch. which is often called by bird-catchers the " shell apple "; and this is considered, as it unquestionably is, a great blemish ; but clear flight or tail feathers are the most detrimental of . all, and those fanciers who pride themselves · upon breeding good Lizards invariably give all such ill-favoured progeny their quietus ere they number many days in the calendar of life. Were it not that this practice savours strongly of wanton cruelty I would have endorsed it, as I verily believe that it is the only method of effectually stamping out all remnants of impure blood.

CLASSES.—There are two varieties of these birds, viz., yellows and buffs (jonques and mealies), or, as they are more frequently designated, golden-spangled and silver-spangled Lizards. These are divided into four classes as follows: Golden-spangled Lizards, silver-spangled Lizards, golden-spangled Lizards with broken caps, and silver-spangled Lizards with broken caps.

Thirty years ago and upwards there was a breed of Lizards known among fanciers by the name of " Blue Lizards." I have never seen but three of those magnificent birds, which I bought. It is twenty-seven or twenty-eight years since the last of these died, and I have never been able to procure another specimen of them, although I have used every effort to do so. I have been told by several very old fanciers that they were plentiful · enough fifty or sixty years ago; now they appear to be quite extinct. What a. pity ! They were totally different from the silver Lizards of the present day. The ground colour of these birds was a beautiful, soft bluish grey, but decidedly blue in tint, and the spangles were particularly well defined and clear, and as white as newly-molten silver. I consider they were by far the handsomest of all the Lizard varieties.

POINTS.—The golden-spangled Lizard should be in its ground or body colour a deep rich golden bronze green or fine old moss green, quite neutral in tint, and soft and somewhat velvety in appearance, with the green so subdued and blended with yellow, &c., as to lose that hard, harsh vividness, so peculiar to bad specimens of this variety. In fact, the ground colour of a good Lizard is somewhat difficult to describe accurately, and to imitate it correctly would require a combination of various colours in different proportions, such as green, yellow, sienna, umber, and black, with a slight tinge of red and blue, and it would probably prove a task of no mean difficulty to a practical and accomplished artist to represent it faithfully.

The silver Lizards are much lighter or greyer in colour than the golden birds; in other respects they should resemble each other very closely. The latter, however, are considered the greatest favourites with fanciers, and when good specimens and in fine condition they are most exquisitely beautiful, although it very frequently happens that the best capped birds are most deficient in spangles, and *vice versâ.*

The cap of a prize bird ought to be elliptic in form, and should commence at the top of the base of the upper mandible, and extend in a parallel line immediately over the top of each eye, leaving a slight mark above the eye like a pencil line, or slight eyebrow, and should terminate at the base of the skull. It is a most difficult matter to breed a Lizard with a perfect cap, or even an approximation to one. Some birds are over-capped, whilst others are considerably under-capped. Both are faults; but an over-capped bird, provided the cap does not extend too far below the line, is preferable to an under-capped bird. Some caps run in a line with the lower instead of the upper part of the upper mandible, and descend below the eye. This is a grave fault: and all birds possessing caps of this description are only fit for stock purposes. When the cap is formed from the lower portion of the bill, it makes the bird appear to have a white face; and a bird thus disfigured is termed " bald-faced." With the exception of white feathers in the wings and tail, this is probably one of the greatest defects a bird of this variety can possess. The cap is one of the essential qualifications in a good Lizard.

z

The flight and tail feathers of a Lizard, whether golden or silver spangled, should be black, as also the wing and tail coverts; and the more intense and brilliant they are the more valuable is the bird. But these feathers are all more or less fringed at the extreme outer edges with a golden or silvery hue, according to the variety of the bird; but neither the tail nor the flight feathers in the wings should be spangled in a show specimen. A bird may by accident shed a wing or tail feather, which they frequently do; and when they are reproduced they show the "half moon;" but this can in no wise be regarded as a disqualification, although it may to some extent be looked upon as a detraction, and might be considered as such in the event of two birds proving of equal merit in all other points. The throat, breast, sides of neck, belly, and vent of the bird should be as uniform in colour throughout as possible. Some birds are much lighter in colour at the sides of the belly near the thighs than they are on the breast, &c. This is a defect. The breast of a good bird is regularly spangled, although the spangles are so delicate that it requires a strong side light to see them distinctly. Some birds—and good birds, too—are striped with a darker shade of colour down the breast, but the less these stripes are observable the better. From the termination of the cap at the back of the head to the end of the saddle feathers the ground colour should be uniform, but darker than the breast and belly, as these feathers are shaded with black, and each of them should be clearly "mooned" or spangled round the end or bottom with yellow or buff (gold or silver), and the more distinct and well-defined these spangles are the more is the value of the bird enhanced. As the feathers upon the neck of a bird are much smaller in proportion to those which cover the back, the spangles, as a natural sequence, are much closer, and consequently they appear more numerous than they do upon the back of the bird, where the feathers are larger and the spangles more distinct. This gives the bird an appearance of being lighter in colour round the neck or collar, more especially in a silver-spangled bird, and. instead of being, as might be

The Lizard. 339

supposed, a drawback, it adds greatly to its beauty, and is indicative of very high breeding and superior quality. The spangling should not be broken up or laced, but ought to appear perfectly distinct throughout, both in form and finish, and this is one of the greatest points of beauty and attraction in the Lizard canary. Over the body feathers there appears, in the golden-spangled Lizards, a sort of subdued golden shade or light, called by some fanciers the "crine," and in the silver-spangled birds it is of a fine silvery-grey hue, and adds much to their beauty; some birds are quite destitute of this luminosity—a sure indication of coarse breeding or bad blood.

The legs, feet, and bills are considered by most fanciers to look best when dark, but, for my part, I attach very little importance to this feature, and I regard it only as a secondary consideration, as I have almost invariably noticed that such birds as possess it naturally (for in too many cases it is artificially produced) are too green in their ground colour—and the ground colour is a speciality which ought to be regarded as a *sine quâ non* in an exhibition bird. The two most beautiful and perfect specimens of this variety of bird I ever saw had red or flesh-coloured legs and feet; in all other respects they were the nearest approximation to perfection that could be imagined.

The Lizard canaries are from 4¾in. to 5¼in. in length upon an average. The head should be rather large than otherwise, with an abundance of width between the eyes, and flattish on the crown; the beak rather stout and short; the neck thick, and inclined to be short rather than long; the breast broad, round, and full; the shoulders broad; the back wide, slightly curved outwardly; the tail should hang obtusely from the body; the ends of the wings should rest upon the base of the tail; the legs should be somewhat short; and the carriage of the bird easy, graceful, and semi-erect. The cap, colour, "crine" and spangling are the chief characteristics in birds of this variety.

STANDARD OF EXCELLENCE.—The following is the standard, 100 points representing perfection:

z 2

STANDARD FOR JUDGING LIZARD CANARIES.

	Points.
Head and cap	20
Spangles	20
Ground colour	15
"Crine," or luminosity and quality	8
Size	7
Condition	7
Contour and carriage	6
Feathers, for quality and closeness	6
Wings and tail, for blackness in hue	6
Legs and feet	5
Total	100

The head must be full, broad, and flattish on the crown; the cap oval, clear, rich in colour, and well formed, and must not come below the eye; it ought to terminate in front at the top of the bill, and at the back at the base of the skull. The spangles must be clear, regular, and well defined. The colour must be rich, soft, and mellow, level throughout, and quite free from any decidedly green tinge.

TYPE.—The bird from which our illustration was taken was the property of Mr. T. W. Fairbrass, of Canterbury. It stood first in a class of fifteen at the Crystal Palace Show at Sydenham (1875), the majority of which had been successful competitors at other shows. He won with the most consummate ease, being vastly superior in all respects to any of his antagonists, and a thorough champion all over, his colour, cap, contour, and spangling being exquisitely grand, and almost perfect; the greatest fault observable was that he was rather too much striped down the sides of the abdomen. Mr. Fairbrass is probably one of the oldest and most extensive breeders of this greatly admired variety of canaries living, and a pretty successful exhibitor as well. Several prize winners in previous years have been bred from birds procured from his aviary by other fanciers. One of the most successful breeders and exhibitors of these birds is Mr. Robert Ritchie, of Darlington.

LONDON FANCY CANARY.

(First Prize Crystal Palace Show, 1899. Owner, Mr. T. Stokes.)

CHAPTER XXI.

THE LONDON FANCY.*

BREEDERS.—These birds are rare, handsome, and costly, and somewhat tender and delicate in their constitutions. They are great favourites with many of the London Fanciers, but owing to their want of stamina and vigour, combined with the exhorbitant prices that are demanded for good specimens, they are not very popular with the "fancy" at large. Indeed, this breed at the present time may be considered as being in the hands of a select few. Mr. W. Brodrick, of Chudleigh; Mr. James Waller, of London; and Mr. Thomas Clark, of Sutton, in Surrey, are probably the chief and most successful breeders extant.

ORIGIN.—Although many of the admirers of this variety of canary regard them as a distinct breed, I am decidedly of opinion that they have originated from the Lizard canaries, and I know that a great number of thoroughly practical and experienced fanciers entertain the same idea as myself. Having propounded a theory, it is only right that I should give some reason for so doing. The title "London Fancy" implies that the breed is peculiar to, or originated in London, in the same manner as the "Norwich Fancy" doubtless had its origin in the town of Norwich, the "Scotch Fancy" in Scotland,

---

* It is said that the London Fancy canary was first cultivated by the French Protestant refugee silk weavers, who came to London about two centuries ago, and that they were bred by them exclusively in Spitalfields for many years. I made every possible inquiry in my power on this point as to their origin, from Jas. Waller and others, some thirty-two or thirty-three years ago, but I was unable at that time to glean anything worthy of note respecting it.

and the "Yorkshire Fancy" in Yorkshire; and the bird not being indigenous, must necessarily have been manufactured. Indeed, it is a well-known fact that the latter varieties are produced by cross breeding, that is to say, by matching two or more distinct varieties together, and thereby producing a new variety. Some people do not like the idea that any of their pets should be considered mongrels; but I contend that when once a variety is established whose individuality is so marked and distinguishable by certain peculiarities, and which can be reproduced at pleasure, that it is no longer deserving of the term mongrel; and I further contend that to produce a new variety of any kind, whether it be in dogs, pigeons, poultry, or canaries, is to bring about a result indicative of the highest art or science of breeding, and, therefore, is more worthy of commendation than condemnation. If my first proposition is conceded, I do not think that anyone will doubt that the Lizard canary is the most prominent cross to be found in these birds, as it is well known that a young London Fancy in its nest feather, if a good specimen, so closely resembles the young of the Lizards that none other than really experienced fanciers can distinguish the one variety from the other; in fact, I have had young Lizards in one cage and young London Fancies in another adjoining, and I have known many men who have bred canaries for several years, who were totally unable to say which were which. Another reason in support of my supposition that the London Fancy canaries have in the first instance been artificially produced is that the young birds vary very much in plumage in their nest feather, some being all dark except the cap, whilst others are often pied like a common variegated canary; these specimens are produced in the same nest, and you require to breed a goodly number ere you succeed in getting two or three birds sufficiently perfect to show, and that exclusive of all accidents. In further support of my theory, I will quote a few facts within my own knowledge, and which have tended greatly to confirm me in my opinion.

I once put a Lizard canary and a London Fancy together; the produce of this cross resembled bad Lizards. The next

season I matched one of these birds with a clear Norwich canary;
the result of this cross was, to all intents and purposes, well-
bred Norwich canaries, but all were more or less marked—two
slightly, whilst the third, a hen, was a beautiful buff, with evenly-
marked wings and clear tail, no eye markings. I showed her in
an evenly-marked Norwich class twice, and she was very highly
commended at one show and third prize at the other. When she
moulted the next season her wing-markings disappeared, leaving
nothing beyond a grizzly trace of their former loveliness. I
coupled this hen with a ticked Norwich cock, and several of
their produce were marked about the head and neck, but on
moulting the marks vanished almost entirely. The colour of
the young birds from the last cross was remarkable for its
depth and richness of hue. I mention this circumstance to
show that the markings in these birds disappeared in the same
manner as the dark feathers do in the London Fancy variety,
and were changed for a clear, or almost clear plumage.

An acquaintance of mine, several years ago, bred a nest of
young birds between a London Fancy and a Lizard canary;
the offspring of this cross he mated, one with a London Fancy
and the other two with Lizards. He continued his experiments
for four or five years, putting those bred from the Lizard cross
with Lizards again, and those from the London Fancy cross
with that breed again, so that in the end no trace of the cross
breeding was discernible on either side; in fact, he always
contended that it greatly improved both breeds. I am not so
sure about the Lizards, although I know that some of the birds
so bred distinguished themselves at some of our best shows; to
my thinking, they were too light in body colour, and the
spangling not so regular and fine in finish as a good Lizard
ought to be. Another fact in confirmation of my theory, and I
have done. I once purchased a good yellow Lizard cock from
a noted breeder of these birds; he was about eighteen months
old when I got him, and in fine feather. I bred from him
several years in succession, and had him until he was eight
years old, when he died; every time this bird moulted he
became lighter and clearer in colour, until, at the age of seven

years, he could hardly have been distinguished from a London
Fancy bird at the age of six years; his ground colour was
almost clear, and he looked as if he had been slightly dredged
over with black pepper. These facts, I submit, speak volumes
in support of the idea I entertain in regard to the origin of
this wonderful and elegant variety of canary—the true London
Fancy. No doubt it required years of study and judicious
crossing to bring them to perfection.

Were I a regular breeder of this variety of birds, I would not
hesitate to cross them with a Lizard canary occasionally, say,
once in five or seven years; if this is not done, I am afraid that
the days of these lovely gems are numbered, and that they
will soon become extinct, for already the in-and-in breeding is
telling with painful effect upon their constitutions; in fact, to
quote the exact words of an old fancier, addressed to me, in
reference to that variety. not long ago, "I would not bother
with them; they are all as rotten as blown pears" (from in-
and-in breeding).

On July 19th, 1889, an illustration of a bird of this variety was
given in a London journal, *Poultry*, and a very good and even
elegant specimen it was; and singular to relate, the bird figured
had been bred from a pair of well-bred Lizard canaries, by
Mr. J. Green, of Leigh, in Lancashire. The father was a Golden
spangled bird, the winner of a first prize in a large class at
Manchester, and from a thoroughly reliable strain of well-bred
Lizards. The mother was a Silver, bred from a celebrated
pure strain. This incident goes far to corroborate my theory—
for I think I was the first to propound it in the first edition
of this work—that the London Fancy is an off-shoot from the
Lizard canary. I said that I thought the London Fancy canary
was bred between the Lizard and Norwich Fancy canary,
or between a Lizard and a Cinnamon variegated bird. I
am morally certain that it was originally produced by one
or other of these crosses, and this, no doubt, will account in
a great measure for the difficulty that has always been experienced—since I can remember them, for a period of thirty-
six years at least—in obtaining specimens free from patches of

body colour and frizzly markings after moulting; whereas in a good specimen, only the flight feathers of the wings and tail should have remained black or dark in colour. In consequence of the rarity and high price of these birds, and the difficulties experienced in breeding specimens fit for show, and the trouble required to keep them in show feather, I have never felt much interest personally in them, consequently I have not experimented with them as I usually do to prove my theories.

More than thirty years ago, I used to pay visits, at intervals, to Mr. J. Waller, a fancier and breeder of these birds, who, at that time, resided at Tabernacle Walk, Finsbury Square, London; but it was very rare even for him to breed anything approaching to a high-class specimen, although he put up from ten to fifteen pairs annually. Another reason why I felt no partiality for the London Fancy canary was, that they were so small and puny, so sickly and delicate looking, owing to their being so sib-bred—as the breed then was limited to a few fanciers—all the birds being as nearly related as possible, and no new blood obtainable. They were loose in feather, asthmatical, and short lived, a breed with many faults and few redeeming features. I regret now that I did not try some experiments to resuscitate this breed, for I feel sure it could have been done in a few years, and probably some of the prevailing faults might have been overcome, and the variety much improved in most respects.

NEST FEATHER BIRDS.—London Fancy canaries in their first or nest feathers should resemble very closely the young of the Lizard canaries; they should appear dark all over, except their caps, which should be clear, but very few of them reach this criterion of excellence, many of them appearing irregularly marked or pied, but in any case the tail and the larger or flying feathers of the wings ought to be all black. When these birds moult the first time they shed all their feathers except those of the wings and tail, the process of moulting being observed first on each side of the breast. The new coat comes clear as the dark feathers disappear, and when thoroughly moulted the bodies of the birds appear in a rich bright, almost clear plumage, with dark wings and tails. They are then in their most perfect state as show birds, and never afterwards, as when they moult the following season they shed their tail and wing feathers, and these are reproduced almost clear, being merely grizzled in place of being black. The young of these birds, however, although bred from parents which have moulted clear, appear in the dark plumage in their nest feather, and undergo the same process as their parents did before them; this is the great and attractive feature or peculiarity of this particular variety of canaries.

BREEDING.—In breeding London Fancy canaries, it is customary to match a jonque and mealy bird together, but it will be found advantageous to breed from two mealies occasionally, for by this plan you increase the size and substance of your birds, and it tends greatly to improve the feather, more particularly in firmness and fringe. It will detract slightly from the colour if too frequently resorted to, but this must be avoided.

These birds are not only difficult to breed in anything like perfection, but the greatest possible care is required in moulting, and when moulted in preserving them intact; for if a tail or wing feather (flight feather) is prematurely shed or beaten out, it is certain to be reproduced clear or grizzled, and this circumstance alone would debar a bird from competing successfully at any show. It is, therefore, of the greatest importance to moult these birds in separate cages, and in some quiet corner of a room. The principal London breeders have cages made expressly for moulting these birds. They are a sort of box cage, being made of wood on all sides, with a wire front, but immediately behind this is placed a glass slide, which is seldom wholly withdrawn; a portion of the top of the cage, too, is made to fold back with hinges, like a door, and inside of this is fixed a small wired frame This is used for supplying the occupant of the cage with fresh air. I do not advocate moulting birds in these boxed-in cages. I prefer an

open wire cage, with a very thin calico cover made to fit over
it and tie down with strings at the bottom, as it answers all
the requirements of the first-named cage, with the additional
advantage of furnishing the occupant with more ventilation
and fresh air.

CLASSES.—There are only two classes of this variety of
canary, viz., jonques and mealies (yellows and buffs).

POINTS.—The chief features in the London Fancy canaries
are their deep, bright, luxuriant plumage, their beautiful
black wing-markings and black tails, and the fine, soft, silky
appearance of their feathers. The jonque birds should be
almost orange in tint throughout the body feathers, with a
silvery luminous appearance pervading the outer surface; but
this appearance, which is commonly called the "meal," is
more conspicuous upon the buff birds, or "mealies," as they
are usually termed.

In size these birds vary from $4\frac{3}{4}$in. to $5\frac{1}{2}$in. in length. The
head should be large, and the cap broad and expansive, and
very rich in colour and free from any admixture of grey, or spots
of a dark colour; the neck rather short and thick; the chest
broad and full; the back broad, and slightly curved outwardly;
the legs short, and the position semi-erect. A great many of the
London fanciers regard the body colour as of the first importance, and this is looked for more particularly on the crown of
the head, or, as it is usually styled, the "cap;" also upon the
breast and throat, which must be very fully developed, likewise upon the scapulars or shoulder blades, and the rump; the
colour must be pure and brilliant, and as free from tinge or
mottle as possible, and even and regular, more especially on
the "cap" and breast; the wings and tails, too, are of great
importance, and to produce them free from that dingy, dusky,
grizzly-looking hue, is probably the most difficult task a breeder
has to encounter, and hence I think that too little weight is
frequently attached to this very important feature in a good
bird. The large feathers in the wings, and also the tail
feathers, should be as nearly jet black as they can be got, with
a nice gloss upon them; they should be entirely free from

348 *The Canary Book.*

grizzle; a good saddle, too, is a very decided advantage, and improves the appearance of a bird immensely.

STANDARD OF EXCELLENCE.—The following standard gives the relative value of each point, one hundred being the maximum:

STANDARD FOR JUDGING LONDON FANCY CANARIES.

Points.

Colour, for intensity, brilliancy and regularity, more particularly on head, breast, scapulars, and rump.. 35
Wings and tail, for depth of tone and brightness of colour throughout, and also for formation.......... 25
Saddle, for fulness, shape, and colour............... 10
Size of bird, length, and stoutness 7
Contour and carriage 7
Quality and firmness of feather 7
Legs and underflue, for blackness.................. 5
Throat, for expansiveness 4
                                                   ———
                    Total...................,......... 100

JUDGING.—In judging London Fancy canaries much care is needed, for they are a class of birds that can be wonderfully improved in the hands of skilful and unprincipled exhibitors.

The bird represented in our engraving is a fair specimen of the breed.

CHAPTER XXII.

THE BORDER FANCY.

THIS bird is also known by the name of the "Cumberland Fancy," and in some parts as the "Common Canary." It is an old variety regenerated and given a new name, but by careful cultivation and the admixture of foreign blood—such as Norwich and Yorkshire—it has been greatly improved, and is deserving of a better title than that of the "Common Canary."

The Border Fancy Canary is a small but rather neat-looking bird, light in build, short in length of body, and very tight in feather, which gives it a smart, bright, active, and compact appearance. It should be well-proportioned, and in fact look something like a diminutive specimen of a good Yorkshire canary. The head is small and round, with neat well-formed cheeks, as if chiselled; the beak should be small and slender, the neck thin, the back well filled and level in appearance, the chest neat and round, but not heavy looking; legs proportionate to the body, and to show very little thigh when standing in show position; the wings must be tight and close-fitting to the body, level, and must meet at the tips; the tail must be neat, close, and compact, and somewhat round, resembling the shank of a pipe—not fish-tailed; length of bird, 5¼in. to 5½in.; position inclined to be more erect than otherwise, the head being elevated, and the line from back of head to tail should form a rather acute angle. The colour must be soft and delicate; artificial colour, produced by feeding during the process of the moult is altogether ignored by the admirers of these birds. Good and robust health and fine condition are essential points in this variety.

There are clear and marked birds among the Border Fancy, but type and quality overrule markings, however perfect the latter may be; and, according to the rules of judging this variety, a bird possessing superior shape, feather, and style, would in a class for "any variety" of this breed, be placed before a perfect evenly-marked specimen which lacked in a marked degree the qualities named, and even in a class of marked birds, an unevenly-marked bird would not vie with an evenly-marked one on the same grounds—which to me is rather enigmatical—as even-marking is more difficult to obtain by far than the features which the fanciers of these birds so much esteem. For instance, a bird with even wings and one eye-mark, or with two uneven eye-markings and one wing-mark, would be placed before a bird with evenly well-balanced eye- and wing-markings, providing the contour and *tout ensemble* of the former somewhat exceeded the latter. This I consider rather hypercritical. Evenly- and unevenly-marked birds are, as a rule, shown in separate classes, and when exhibited together all the points should be separately considered, and full allowance made for markings as well as form and other properties.

This breed has evidently been originated by crossing the common German canary with the Norwich and Yorkshire fancy, selecting stock birds possessing the points sought after, and by careful and judicious breeding for a number of years the variety has been perfected.

The standard for judging may be summarised as follows:

	Points.
Shape, style, and general contour	35
Colour, for purity, softness, and delicacy; and feather; for soundness and silkiness in texture	15
Head and beak	10
Tail	10
Wings	10
Legs and feet	5
Condition and health	15
Total	100

The Border Fancy.

This breed is greatly esteemed on the borders of Scotland and Cumberland, and in the north and north-west of England generally; at Galashiels and Hawick, and in Carlisle, Whitehaven, and other border towns the best specimens are to be found. They are hardy and prolific birds, and well adapted to beginners in the bird fancy.

CHAPTER XXIII.

ANY OTHER VARIETY OF CANARY.

DUTCH CANARIES.—This variety, once so popular among English fanciers, is now almost obsolete. It is probably in size the largest of all the canary tribes—indeed, they may be fairly considered as the giants of their race.

A good specimen of a Dutch Fancy canary, or, as they are sometimes inaptly termed, "Dutch Belgians," is a large handsome bird, with a large full handsomely formed head, a long straight, full neck, a well-shaped body of considerable length, good substantial shoulders, broad and massive, but not elevated like a Belgian Fancy bird, a fine deep prominent chest, a good stout waist, long, well-formed legs, and a long, compact, sweeping tail, with a bold, erect, and noble carriage. They are mostly very rough in feather on their bodies, and are often heavily frilled both on the breast and back, some of them to such an extent as to give them a sort of woolly appearance. They are a hardy, robust race of birds, and it seems to be a great pity that they have become so unpopular and neglected—indeed, so much so, that they have completely fallen into disregard, having been entirely superseded by the Belgian Fancy canaries and Lancashire Coppies, the latter having originated from this breed.

GREEN CANARIES.—There are now very many fanciers to be found who are partial to a Green canary, and in Liverpool this variety is in great vogue, and special classes are provided for them at the principal shows. Size, colour, and form are the most essential points recognised in this variety.

The colour should be of a decided green throughout, clear and bright, and free from dinginess. Sometimes the colour is described as "grass green;" but at any rate it should be a pleasant yellowish green, free from stripiness and black marks, and as level and evenly distributed over the entire surface of the body as possible; light throats, rumps, vents, thighs and bellies are decidedly objectionable, and birds with these faults should be discarded, as also those of a dull blackish green shade.

BREEDING.—To produce good specimens fit for the show bench, I would recommend the crossing of pure Norwich Greens with birds bred between a good Cinnamon and a Green plain-head, bred from large modern Crested-Norwich birds. Select a bird with a large, broad skull, and a stout, massive body, not too long in feather, but of a good colour and shape— a good green Yorkshire bred from a Cinnamon strain may also be used with advantage—but for my own part I prefer a bird that is inclined to be bulky in body, and massive in head and neck, provided the colour is right, as I admire substance as well as length in these birds. Do not pair two dark Greens together, but a dark Green mated with a pale Green frequently produce progeny of the right stamp. It is not material whether the male or female is light or dark, but I prefer the hen to be light and the cock to be dark. The faults or negative properties of a Green bird are: Dark stripes on the back or breast, light coloured throats, sides, breasts, vents, rumps, and thighs. Like the present day Cinnamons, these birds are found in various sizes and styles; but a large, well-formed bird of the approved colour and free from the faults mentioned is pretty sure to win. Green, like Cinnamon, is a colour that is easily preserved, but I certainly would advise the breeders of this variety to select self-coloured birds to breed from as much as possible; but if large size is deemed essential, it will be necessary occasionally to use a flecked or variegated bird, and I know of no bird so

2 A

suitable as a good crested-bred Plain-head Norwich of the right stamp, or a large bird bred between a bird of that variety and a large Cinnamon bird.

STANDARD FOR JUDGING.

	Points.
Colour, for richness, clearness, brightness, and even distribution throughout	40
Skull, for size, and beak for neatness	8
Back and breast, for width and substance	10
Tail, for compactness and neatness	7
Style, for type, closeness and fineness of feather	20
Size, contour, and condition	15
Total	100

GERMAN CANARIES.—These are the common type of canaries, and they are prized solely on account of their song. They are taught by the Germans (artisans chiefly) to imitate the songs of other birds and the notes of musical instruments, and are valued according to their capabilities as musicians. But the most valued of all are the variety known by the name of the Hartz Mountain Rollers, which are reared in Hanover and Saxony, in the neighbourhood of the Hartz Mountains. Their song is varied by a series of notes or sounds which they warble or roll forth with great fervour, and those which have the longest and sweetest trills, and which run or roll their notes to the greatest length, or frequently repeat the most admired portion of them, are the most highly prized, and bring the highest prices. We have known as much as 35s. to have been given for an exceptional bird of this kind. They are imported annually by most of the respectable dealers in London and other large towns, and vary in price from 5s. to 15s. each; rare specimens bring larger prices. Those birds that are intended to be instructed in the art of song are removed from their parents at an early age and reared by hand. Almost as soon as they begin to twitter they are placed under their instructors in an apartment far removed from the sound of any canary still in possession of its " natural wood notes wild."

When they are able to feed themselves they are placed in a room with some five or six others that are intended to be taught

the same song or set of notes. It is customary to keep them in
total darkness during the early hours of tuition, and sometimes
it is found advisable to have recourse to hunger to make them
attentive and subservient. Great patience and perseverance
are needed to make them anything like proficient scholars in this
branch of education, and so powerful are their natural instincts
that instances are on record where some of the best taught and
most masterly songsters have been completely spoilt by being
hung in close proximity for a few months to a bird that was an
ardent exponent of his own natural lays. It must not be forgotten by those who delight in keeping canaries that have learnt
the song of other birds, or to imitate the notes of any musical
instrument, that they cease singing during the season for moulting, and at that time they are very apt to reject their artificial
notes for the natural melody of their race; therefore it will be
most prudent to remove them during this period beyond the
sound and hearing of any other bird of their kind.

The most notable breeders of these birds are the Messrs.
Trute Bros., of St. Andreasberg, in the neighbourhood of the
Hartz Mountains, and birds bred and reared by these men
bring higher prices than those of other breeders. In order to
procure the best songsters, the most reliable strain must be
used, for the voice and powers of vocalization, even in canaries,
appear to be hereditary. These birds are not at all difficult to
breed, being of the very commonest type of the canary
family. They may be bred in pairs in cages, or one male
may be mated with two females if thought desirable. If,
however, aviary breeding is preferred, one male may be
placed with four females, only they will need to be carefully
looked after, as sometimes hens prove mischievous, and interfere
with each other's nests, &c. In all such cases the delinquents
should be removed, and placed in cages.

The method adopted by the St. Andreasberg fanciers
in feeding and treating their birds will be found useful to
those fanciers who have a predilection for the trained
German songsters, or Hartz Mountain Rollers, as they are
usually styled. It is as follows: During the breeding season,

2 A 2

first meal at 5 a.m., second 9 a.m., third 1 p.m., and fourth at 5.30 p.m.; at all other times at 8 a.m. and 5 p.m. daily.

The food consists of zwiebacken (rusks) and hard-boiled eggs (both whites and yokes are used). The rusks are ground to a fine powder in a mortar, and the eggs passed through a fine wire sieve. The ingredients are used in equal proportions, thoroughly incorporated, and given dry. The seed consists of the very best German rape; avoid old seed. No canary seed is given by Germans to their birds; but occasionally as a treat, a mixture of lettuce seed and maw seed (the whole kind preferred) is given in equal proportions. It is usually given with the egg food; two or three teaspoonfuls of seed is placed in the egg pan, and a sprinkling of egg food is placed over it. The feeding troughs are cleaned out every day, or the food would become sour. The Germans run their best birds into a clean cage every alternate morning. The empty cages are placed in a tub of boiling water, in which a small quantity of soap and soda has been dissolved, and after being thoroughly washed they are rinsed in hot water and left to dry in the open air, or by the side of a fire. The cages used by the Germans for their song birds are very small, and are made entirely of wood, thin round sticks being used in place of wires. None but the best rusks are to be used for feeding, and if these are not obtainable Oswego biscuits are substituted, but the rusks are greatly preferred. On no account must those be used which have become musty. The St. Andreasberg fanciers' remedy for a cold is peppermint, dried—*i.e.*, the common mint of our gardens. This remedy is resorted to on the slightest appearance of a cold, or if the evacuations from the bowels are of a greenish colour; it is also used in cases of hoarseness or wheezing; and it is likewise given if a bird is observed to be dull and listless, or mopish, with its feathers ruffled up, a form known among fanciers as "sitting thick;" or if the excrement has a fetid or sour smell, generally the result of over-feeding with egg food, which disorders the liver. When a bird is observed to have a cold, they cease to give it egg food until it has recovered, and in its place they feed on milk

sop, made with stale bread soaked in milk, squeezed dry, and
sweetened with manna. If the patient refuses this food, a
little moist sugar or honey is substituted for the manna, but
the latter is considered preferable. The peppermint is prepared by pouring hot water over the dried leaves and allowing
them to infuse in a warm place for a couple of hours, when
they are strained through a piece of muslin. It is prepared
fresh every day, or every alternate day at the farthest, and
given in place of the drinking water. The Germans never
give their birds cold water to drink, they give it lukewarm,
and if a bird is in health they get a little egg food every
day or every alternate day, as they believe that it induces a
bird to eat its seed more freely. The Germans consider that
a newly-imported bird should not have a supply of sand given
him, and only very sparingly after he becomes acclimatised
until he gets accustomed to it, as otherwise it will kill it. I
cannot see the danger, nor understand the logic of this advice,
as birds cannot be kept in health without a supply of sand
or grit, but I reluctantly tell what the Germans say. Another
thing about which they are very particular is the temperature
in which their birds are kept. It varies from 60deg. to
65deg. Bird dealers in this country keep them in a much
higher temperature, say, from 70deg. upwards; the warmer
they are kept the more freely they sing, but the greater
the heat the sooner they will be brought into moult, when
they cease to sing, so that a moderate use of heat is preferable.

If a bird becomes too vivacious and begins to "scream"
he is gradually put into outer darkness, the cage being covered
by degrees with thick cloth until the light is entirely excluded.
After a few days he is allowed to have a little light, and if
he still "screams" he is again covered. After a few weeks
of this treatment he will understand the reason and refrain.
The great cause of failure among many fanciers of these lovely
songsters in our country is attributed to the manner in which
they are fed and treated, and more particularly is this the
case with imported specimens. The Germans have made a

life study of the subject, and their methods of feeding and treatment ought not to be ignored.

CROSS BREEDS.—Birds bred between the Lizard and Norwich Fancy canaries, or between the London Fancy and Belgian Fancy, or any other cross between separate and distinct varieties, are named cross breeds, but in some towns some of these crosses have distinguishing names given to them, as, for instance, some people call three-parts bred Lizard canaries "Spangle Backs." Then again, the birds frequently denominated "French Canaries" come within this category, as they are merely three-quarter bred Belgian Fancy canaries. None of these crosses, excepting the Cinnamon and variegated Cinnamon, are of any real intrinsic value, as they are used principally for experimental purposes only.

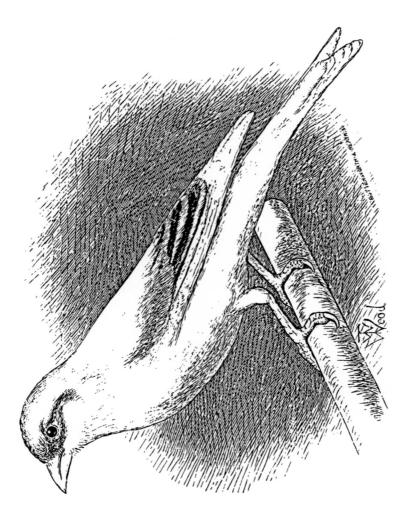

Buff Evenly-marked Goldfinch Mule.

Canary and Goldfinch Mules exist in a variety of colours and markings, but one with a

CHAPTER XXIV.

CANARY MULES.

GOLDFINCH AND CANARY MULES.—Formerly these elegant and highly-prized hybrids were all shown in one class, under the general name of "Goldfinch and Canary mules," and the rule for judging them in those days was, to use the vernacular of that period, "nearest the canary," which is meant to signify a bird with the fewest dark feathers on its body. At the present day, however, there are several classes for these birds at most of our "All England" shows, and they are capable of the following divisions and sub-divisions: Clear or ticked yellow, clear or ticked buff, evenly-marked yellow, evenly-marked buff, unevenly-marked yellow, unevenly-marked buff, dark jonque, dark buff.

A goldfinch and canary mule with a perfectly clear body and a rich, deep broad flourish round the beak, is the rarest and most valuable of all the canary hybrids, more particularly if the under flue or small body feathers next the skin are clear as well, Next in estimation to a bird of this description is one very lightly ticked; in fact, the one most nearly resembling a clear bird—hence the term "nearest the canary." Size, colour, contour, feather, and condition are all points of merit in birds of this kind; but the aforenamed qualities far outweigh every other consideration in judging them. The evenly-marked variety is to my thinking, by far the handsomest, and it is without doubt, the most popular. The even markings, the rich orange band that surrounds the bill, commonly called the "flourish," the colour, which should be clear, pure, and delicate in tint, and free from any slaty-coloured tinge, are among the chief points of merit in this class of mules.

The following Standard of Excellence for evenly-marked mules has been carefully made, each feature having been duly weighed and fully considered, and a percentage accorded to it separately, showing its relative value; 100 points is fixed as representing the highest excellence attainable:

STANDARD FOR JUDGING EVENLY-MARKED GOLDFINCH MULES.

	Points.
Head, beak, and flourish	10
Eye markings	15
Wing marking, saddle, and contour	20
Colour (to include the yellow bars on wings)	15
Size	5
Freedom from any dark tinge on cheeks, vent, rump and thighs	10
Clear underflue	10
Quality of feather and condition	10
Clear legs and feet	5
Total	100

A bird with even eye and wing markings, and a dark feather on each side of the tail, is considered a legitimate show bird in this class, and, in point of perfection, stands next to the " four pointed " birds.

The Standard of Excellence for Unevenly-marked Birds, the conditions being the same as those referred to in the last-named class, are as follows:

STANDARD FOR JUDGING UNEVENLY-MARKED GOLDFINCH MULES.

	Points.
Head, beak, and flourish	15
Colour	20
Size and contour	10
Markings	15
Saddle	5
Freedom from dark tinge on body feathers	10
Clear underflue	10
Quality and condition	10
Clear legs and feet	5
Total	100

In this class the markings are not nearly of so much importance as they are in the first named class—colour, size, and shape are weighty matters in judging these birds, and are allowed for accordingly. The markings to be preferred to all others are even wings and eyes, with a solitary dark feather on one side of the tail, or even wings and one eye marking only; next in point of merit to these we prefer a bird with evenly-marked wings and a small cap or spot on the head. A bird with eye-marks and a clear body should be shown as a ticked bird. When the ticked and unevenly marked birds are shown together in one class, the ticked birds are pretty sure to take precedence, unless the marked birds are extraordinarily good, and the ticked birds wanting in size, colour, and quality.

When hybrids between the goldfinch and canary can be procured resembling the one shown in our illustration, they may be considered both valuable and rare, and are very beautiful to look upon. The bird from which the cut was taken belonged to Mr. J. Doel, of Stonehouse, Devon. The eye-markings are not quite perfect in form, but in all other respects it was the bird *par excellence*, and very difficult to put aside, as it possessed good size, colour, form, and feather, and was in reality a gem.

Dark goldfinch mules are judged for size, colour, and contour principally, but rich dazzling colour, and more particularly a large fiery blaze round the beak and down the breast of the bird, are of the first importance.

The Standard of Excellence for Dark Goldfinch Mules is as under :

STANDARD FOR JUDGING DARK GOLDFINCH MULES.

	Points
Head, beak, and flourish	25
Body, colour, and breast	25
Size and contour	15
Quality of feathers	5
Condition	10
Saddle	5
Bloom or meal	10
Golden bars on wings, for extension and brilliancy in colour	5
Total	100

BROWN LINNET AND CANARY MULES.—There is seldom more than one class for these birds at any show. When this is the case they are judged for the resemblance to a clear canary. Next to a bird of this sort comes an evenly-marked bird; the dark varieties are of very little value. These hybrids are more frequently shown in the classes for "any other variety of canary mules" than otherwise. Personally, I prefer an evenly-marked specimen, but have never seen more than one. In the dark birds, size, colour, form, and condition are the chief characteristics.

SISKIN AND CANARY MULES.—Siskin mules are, generally speaking, not very attractive birds to look at, and ninety-five out of every hundred of them resemble the siskin so much, particularly if bred from a small green canary hen, that it requires a thoroughly practised eye to discern wherein the difference lies. The one forming the subject of the engraving is quite an exceptional bird; and I never remember having seen one in which the canary colours predominated so strongly. This bird was the property of Mr. R. Hawman, of Middlesbrough, a well-known and esteemed fancier and successful exhibitor.

It is said that siskin and canary mules are the only hybrids which propagate their species, but I have never tried the experiment, and cannot say, therefore, whether this is so or not.

OTHER VARIETIES OF MULES.—There are, in addition to the varieties of canary mules already specified, those bred between the greenfinch and canary; but they are regarded as of little value, as they invariably favour the greenfinch very much, both in colour and marking, as well as form, they have a poor song, and are only shown in an "any other variety of mule" class; but whenever a good specimen of a brown linnet mule or a mule bred between a bullfinch and goldfinch, is shown against them, it invariably happens that one or other of the last-named varieties bears away the palm. Bechstein, in his book entitled "Cage and Chamber Birds," at page 286 mentions an instance where a friend of his (Dr. Jassay, of Frankfort-on-the-Maine) succeeded in producing mules between a bullfinch and canary, but I have never seen a well-authenticated specimen of this cross. I know the birds pair readily enough, but their eggs, so far as my experience goes, never prove fruitful I have seen two birds, said to be hybrids

Siskin and Canary Mule.

The plumage of Siskin mules is generally unattractive, but in the bird here portrayed the Canary colour strongly predominates.

of this sort, but I am convinced that the one was a flecked canary with a malformed bill, and the other a mule between a canary and a greenfinch.

For further information on the subject of hybrids, see the chapter devoted to " Mule Breeding."

The bullfinch and brown or grey linnet will breed together, but their produce are rather *raræ aves* than specimens of elegance. I have likewise seen a bird exhibited as a hybrid between a yellow-hammer and a canary. I examined it very carefully and could trace no characteristics of the last-mentioned species. It appeared to me to be a yellow-hammer pure and simple. I have never observed any amatory tendency to exist between the yellow-hammer and canary, but the reverse.

CHAPTER XXV.

WASHING CANARIES.

To the uninitiated, washing birds is not only a tedious but a difficult operation, and one not unfrequently attended with fatal results in the hands of inexperienced manipulators, but to those who have been regularly accustomed to prepare birds for exhibition, for any lengthened period, it becomes a matter of small concern, and a bird is toiletted and put through its ablutions without the least compunction or misgiving; but for all that it requires great care and skill to do it well and satisfactorily. If a bird is improperly washed it looks worse than it would do if it were moderately dirty.

Fanciers who live in suburban residences or in the country do not require to wash their birds so frequently for exhibition as those people who live in large over-grown towns where smoke and dust appear as though they were component parts of the atmosphere, so that clean, sprightly, gay-coloured birds get so begrimed and so besmeared with dirt, that they are barely recognisable a week after they have been washed. In all such cases as these, birds shown for colour chiefly, or even where colour forms an important consideration, must of necessity be washed for each show at which they are intended to be exhibited, otherwise the labour and expense incurred in sending them will be entirely thrown away, for unless a bird is as clean "as paint" it has a meagre chance of success.

A number of amateur fanciers nowadays rush headlong into the too prevalent practice of claiming prize birds, thinking, as they no doubt do, that it is only necessary to secure a few birds of this stamp, and send them to a certain number of shows, when, according to their theory and calculations, they will be reimbursed for their outlay by obtaining prizes. But they appear to forget, or entirely ignore the fact that these birds require to be properly prepared for each essay; and if they are neglected the chances are that they will be inevitably overthrown, for it is astonishing what a change in position a slight difference in appearance will effect at times. But this is not to be so much wondered at after all, if people would only consider the great difficulties judges have to encounter, now and again, in discriminating between the relative qualities of two birds (especially in clears), so closely is the race for honours contested in some classes. To give an instance in point, I may relate that I have known a bird take prizes at every show it was sent to by one man, yet when it fell into the hands of another, and was sent to compete among the same birds that it had hitherto defeated, with the same judges officiating, it got nothing beyond a mere commendation, and in one instance was passed by without notice. I refer to these facts in order to show plainly the necessity for the closest attention and care in washing birds properly and thoroughly, and in preparing them in a systematic and artistic manner, without which it is a waste of time and money to attempt to show birds.

Before you begin to practise upon a bird it would be advisable, if an opportunity presented itself, to watch some experienced person perform the operation, as you would doubtless learn more readily in this way than in any other; but where it is not possible to do so, then it will be best to proceed in the following manner: First of all, supply yourself with a piece of good soap—I prefer old brown Windsor to all other kinds—two pieces of soft flannel, scrupulously clean; two or three nice soft cotton cloths, or old silk handkerchiefs, without spot, stain, or tinge upon them; two large-sized basins—washbasins are most suitable—two quart jugs, a large kettle full of boiling water, and a plentiful supply of pure cold water as well; a chair or two, and a stool made for a low seat. Some exhibitors use curd, Pears', white Windsor, or other soap. Pears' soap I have found to answer well, as also white curd, but if a bird is very dirty, thoroughly begrimed, then I advise the use of soft soap and powdered borax, 1dr. of the latter to 1oz. of the former. Mix these ingredients well together and use in moderate quantities, as this mixture makes a powerful lather and requires a good deal of rinsing off to get the soap out of the feathers, but if well done it makes the birds washed with it thoroughly clean. Another formula, which is used for both cleaning and beautifying the feathers, is as follows: Curd soap, dried and powdered, 1oz., good yellow soap (also dried and powdered) 1oz., three Jordan almonds, skinned and blanched, orange-flower water and rose water 1dr. each; put the powdered soaps into a jar with sufficient water to moisten them, but no more, and place the jar in a saucepan of hot water until dissolved. When the almonds have been skinned and dried with a clean towel, pound them well in a mortar, and when fine add the rose- and orange-flower water gradually, stirring them with the pestle all the time; then strain, and add the soap as soon as it is dissolved, and thoroughly incorporate the whole of the ingredients. When they begin to stiffen, pour into a small tin ready for use.

Catch the birds you intend to wash and put them in a cage altogether. If they quarrel, throw a cover over them; for, if they are show birds, which is generally presumed, they must not be permitted to pluck each other. Place them upon a table or some convenient spot near you; but, ere you begin to operate, you must provide yourself with another cage, which should be thoroughly cleaned out and washed, or well rubbed with a cloth, and the bottom of it sprinkled with silver sand; this is to put the birds in to get aired off. In addition to this, you will require a drying cage. Formerly I used a Belgian canary show cage, which I laid upon its side, with perches fixed crosswise inside of it, and I had it entirely covered externally with flannel, except the doorway, and firmly sewn all over it, with a long piece stitched at the hinge side of the door to fold over the opening cut out to allow the door to work when needed; this is a most essential and indispensable requisite, as the birds dry more rapidly in this way than in any other. Latterly, however, I have used a box which I contrived purposely for drying birds in, and it answers admirably; it is sixteen inches long, eight inches wide, and ten inches in depth; it is made with a solid wood bottom; the portion forming the body is framed with inch square laths, and then covered with flannel; one of the ends is done over with perforated zinc to admit the air, whilst the other has a framed glass door hung on hinges to let in light (the glass could be made to slide in a groove if need be), which enables the operator to see at a glance if all is right within, and likewise how the occupants progress. Two perches are fixed inside by letting two upright miniature posts into the bottom; these are three inches in height, and cross pieces are fastened to them with small screws from the top. When the drying box is not being used it should be folded in two paper covers and kept in another box or calico bag to keep the dust from it.

I will now proceed to describe minutely the process of washing: First of all place the stool a short distance from the fire; stir the fire if necessary and make it a good one, and rake out all the dust from the bars. Having done this, place the drying-box or cage upon the stool to get it thoroughly warmed through; spread the cotton cloths, or old silk handkerchief, over it so that they may get well warmed by the time they are required; pour out some hot water into one of the jugs and some cold into the other. Next wash your hands perfectly clean, and having poured some hot and cold water into one of the basins in such proportions as to leave it at about 75deg. to 85deg. temperature, commence to make it into a soap lather; and having folded the two pieces of flannel ready for use, rub some soap on to one of these also. Some fanciers prefer to use a shaving brush instead of a piece of flannel to rub in the soap lather. I do not approve of this plan, for the reason that the hairs of the brush often get into the eyes of the birds and cause irritation, and, in some cases, inflammation, whereas a piece of clean flannel or cotton waste is never productive of injury in any form. In the next place, you must pour some clean water into the other basin, hot and cold, to about the same temperature. I presume that you have already doffed your coat and folded back your shirt sleeves over your elbows ; you are now ready to begin. First, put a piece of soap or some of the compound into a basin and dissolve it in hot water, then add cold water until the proper temperature is obtained, afterwards take the bird you value least first, and place it in your left hand with its head from you; you must grasp it securely but not tightly; let it be as passive as possible, at the same time it must be held in such a way that it cannot by any possibility make its escape; let it lay somewhat loosely in your hand, and place your thumb or your forefinger over its neck, with sufficient pressure to hold it but no more.

You must be careful to avoid any undue pressure upon any part of its body, and more particularly over the region of the heart or bowels. If a bird makes a sudden dash, and you feel conscious that it will elude your grasp, let it go; for if you attempt to prevent it you will in all likelihood either hurt it or pull out some of its wing or tail feathers. It is an easy matter to catch it again. There is a great art in handling a bird properly, and, although it is very simple when discovered, it requires a large amount of practice to enable any person to do it efficiently. You must not be timid or fumble when handling a bird, for birds, like horses, appear to know instinctively when they have a novice to deal with. Always remember that to have confidence in your own prowess is half the battle won; without it, how many men have failed to achieve feats which otherwise they might have accomplished easily enough!

Commence to wash the back of the bird first from the junction of the neck downwards; the wings next. Let your middle and lower fingers recede a little, and spread the wing of the bird over them and wash it thoroughly; after doing one wing turn the bird round and do the other in like manner, and

---

the tail as well. Some fanciers place the thighs of the bird they are operating upon between their fingers whilst thus engaged, but it is not advisable for a novice to attempt this. Next wash the head and neck, and do not be sparing with the soap lather; get well into the hollows and about the cheeks and sides of the neck; then turn the bird over and place your little finger over the lower part of its body, and begin to wash the throat, breast, body, &c. Do not be afraid of giving it a complete lathering; never heed it if it gets the soap in its eyes or a few mouthfuls of the lather; it will not be harmed thereby.

After you have finished this part of the programme, you must take the other flannel and go over the bird in the same way as before, with clean water. Never be afraid of giving it a good sousing with the pure liquid, for one of the principal secrets in washing birds is to get the soap completely out of the feathers. Having accomplished this part of the operation to your satisfaction, you must proceed to dry the bird. Take the long wing feathers, and pressing them gently together, draw them between your lips to bring out the wet; having done the wings, draw the tail through your mouth in the same way; then proceed to pat the bird as gently as you can with one of the warm dry cotton cloths or handkerchiefs, spread out the wings and tail as before, and dry them as well as you can. Having got out all the moisture you are able, roll the bird in one of the other dry cloths, leaving its head partly out, and hold it to the fire pretty closely for about three minutes, with your finger over the region of the heart very lightly. As soon as you feel the pulsation return naturally you may release the little prisoner, and place it in the drying cage. The whole of this operation must be performed as close to the fire as you can bear to be, for if a bird gets chilled it may die.

Birds become very much exhausted by this process, and lie panting for several minutes after they are admitted into the drying compartment; but you must not be alarmed thereby, for I may tell you that I have washed hundreds of birds for shows during the past thirty years, and never lost one myself.

2 B

It takes about five minutes to wash a bird, and twenty minutes to get it quite dry. You must not let them get too dry in the box or cage used for that purpose. I have found it a good plan to place the drying box on the top of a basin containing hot water, as the moisture arising therefrom prevents the birds from drying too rapidly, which causes the feathers to become hard and loose fitting, and detracts so greatly from a bird's appearance as to risk its chance of winning a prize. As soon as you observe a bird to be about two-thirds dry, remove it to the airing-off cage. This cage should be placed upon a chair, not too far from the fire, with a light covering over it, and must be removed gradually as the birds get quite dry, to cool them. Lastly uncover the cage, and remove it to the far side of the room. An hour aftewards the birds may be returned to their domiciles. If the tail or wing feather should get twisted awry or curled up, give the bird some water to wash itself. If this does not remedy the fault, catch it, and put the feather or feathers so crumpled or ruffled in a little warm water, then draw them a few times gently between your finger and thumb, and they will soon resume their wonted appearance. If the soap is not thoroughly removed from the feathers, they will curl and twist and spoil the look of the birds.

After you have washed one bird you will require to put more hot water into each basin to bring up the temperature to about 80deg., and this will need to be done after each operation. Spread the damp cloths over the drying cage each time after they have been used. Carefully examine the wing and tail feathers of your bird, and if any are found broken they should be withdrawn at once, but until they grow again, the bird will not be in a fit condition to show. There should be eighteen flying feathers in each wing and twelve in the tail. It takes six weeks for a feather to grow to its full length, but if one feather is drawn from the tail or the wing the bird may be shown as soon as the new feather becomes distinctly visible to the naked eye. I think it is best to wash all birds intended for exhibition two or three days before they are required to be sent off.

CHAPTER XXVI.

Preparing Birds for Exhibition.

Before canaries can be exhibited, they require to be specially fed, washed (as described in the previous chapter), and otherwise prepared for the contest. This is the case with horses, dogs, poultry, pigeons, and other animals and birds, and canaries are no exception to the rule.

Norwich Plain-heads and Cinnamons are shown for colour chiefly; and at the age of from six to eight weeks, those intended for exhibition should be placed in separate cages, or, at any rate, apart from the ordinary stock birds, and fed with one or other of the compounds recommended for colour feeding, depending on whether you wish to produce yellow or red-fed birds. For colour feeding you must be careful to select birds of a recognised type, of good quality of feather, and large and robust, or your labours will be thrown away.

If the birds you select for this purpose are young, *i.e.*, of the first season, in order to give them a fair chance of success, they will require to be tailed and flighted, that is to say, the tails of the birds, as well as the majority of the wing feathers, will have to be drawn out, as it is only during the process of the moult that the colour feeding affects the plumage. It is a cruel and unnatural practice, and one I am greatly averse to myself, but what is to be done? Most exhibitors do it, as they know it is their only chance of success, as the best birds not so treated would probably fail to

2 B 2

get beyond the V.H.C. division in a good All England show. You must not draw a single feather until you are satisfied that the moulting process has begun, which is first noticeable at the sides of the breast; when this is observed, draw out the tail. It should be done by a single pull. Place the feathers together tightly, and grasp them firmly between the thumb and forefingers of the right hand, about the centre of the tail, give a sudden jerk to your hand, and the thing is accomplished. To pluck them out one by one is not only more cruel, but it would cause the new growth to spread and expand, which would be a very grave fault in any show bird.

A week after this operation, commence with the wings; leave the first two or three of the largest flight feathers, as the others cover them to such an extent that they are scarcely noticeable, and these are not only the worse to draw, but are the most likely to cause damage to the wings, and most pain to the birds. Begin by pulling two feathers out of each wing at one operation, commencing with the largest feathers, say the third or fourth, or fourth and fifth, according to your decision to leave two or three unplucked; let a day intervene before drawing the next four feathers, and so on, until the task is completed. Take the bird in your left hand, open the wing, then hold it firmly by placing your forefinger on one side of the shoulder and your thumb on the other side, and grip firmly during the operation of drawing the feathers. Some fanciers leave the wings until the bird is half over the moult, as the feathers come out more readily then, or are supposed to do so, but the objection to this practice is that it keeps the birds too long under the moulting process, which is weakening to the constitution. If the wings are not held firmly during the operation of drawing the feathers they will probably get broken, in which case the bird, however good in other respects, would be rendered useless as a show bird. It will be found advantageous to hold the wings of the bird over a cup containing hot water, as the steam causes the feathers to come out easier, and with less pain to the bird. A little magnesia or Epsom salts placed in the drinking-water a few days before the birds are operated upon is also of much service. If by accident the wing is caused to bleed it should be bathed with warm water and dressed with a few drops of the compound tincture of myrrh, applied by a feather or a camel-hair brush. It is advisable in the case of an inexperienced fancier or amateur to get an "old hand" to perform the operation, if one is procurable.

When the colour feeding is first begun, let the birds have a supply of canary seed in addition to the prepared food, and partly cover the cages with some thin material that will not altogether exclude the light. When the colour feed is freely consumed, remove the canary seed and substitute mustard seed, and gradually lower the cover until it reaches within two inches of the bottom of the wiring in front of the cage, but do not exclude any light except the direct rays of the sun, as light is necessary to health, but the direct rays of the sun affect the colour and make it much paler. (*See* Chapter on Moulting.)

When the birds have completed the process of the moult, the covers may be partly or entirely removed, provided there is not a strong or direct light upon them, and the ordinary seed diet may be substituted for the food used to produce colour. A varied diet will also be found of great benefit at this period.

A few groats, a little linseed, hemp, inga, or rape seed should be given sparingly once or twice a week. Great care must be taken to keep birds intended for exhibition scrupulously clean; they should be supplied with fresh sand and good grit at least once a week, and should have a bath twice a week, if the weather will permit and the temperature is above freezing-point. Before a bird is sent off to a show it should be washed, if dirty, at least three days before it is despatched on its journey, and if the tail is not tight and firm, the bird should be caught and its tail immersed in pure water (warm is best), and dried with a clean cloth, taking care to compress the feathers firmly during the operation. If the feathers show a little rough (the result of too quick drying), endeavour to induce the bird to take a bath; this can often be done by sprinkling a few drops of water over it from the tips of your fingers. Five or six days before a show feed your birds with stimulating food, such as egg and bread, with a little hemp seed, maw seed, and groats ; and if you add a few drops of whisky or brandy to the drinking water on the day the birds are sent off it will prevent them taking cold, and will keep them in good spirits during the journey.

Crested birds require to be groomed every day for a week before being sent off. Brush the crest carefully, and as gently as possible, with a perfectly soft tooth-brush, and if there are any troublesome or wayward feathers that do not lie so smoothly as they might, put a dram of spirits of wine into a small bottle, add to it twenty drops of almond oil and one ounce of rose-water, and moisten the brush with this before using it. Other things are used by some fanciers, such as a weak solution of gum arabic, &c.; but when birds require this they are not legitimate candidates for the show bench, as they require "faking," which is a dishonest practice.

In the case of Belgian canaries they must be trained to get into "position" (*see* Chapter on the Belgian canary). If "Scotch fancy," they must be taught to "travel" (*vide* Chapter on this variety). Lizards and London Fancy canaries require much care in handling, so that no feathers be knocked out. They should be trained to run from one cage to another by using a piece of stick, or placing the cages together with the doors open, until they get accustomed to go from one cage to the other of their own accord. In the case of Lizard canaries too much cayenne must not be given or the colours will run, and so disfigure them that they will not be eligible for the show bench.

Whenever birds are received from a show they should be placed in a warm room for a day or two, and fed liberally on the same diet that is recommended in preparing them for the show bench, and the addition of a few drops of spirit to their drinking-water, or half a teaspoonful of sherry wine, will be found very beneficial, often preventing them going into the moult. If they appear to have caught cold on the journey add a little cayenne to the egg food, and instead of the spirit of wine add twenty to thirty drops of the spirit of nitre to the drinking-water.

CHAPTER XXVII.

CANARY SOCIETIES, AND CLOSE AND OPEN SHOWS.

CANARY societies have existed is this country for a great number of years, and there are few towns, I should imagine, throughout the length and breadth of England at least, if not of Ireland, Scotland, and Wales, that cannot boast of an institution of this sort. Formerly the whole of these societies were of a purely conservative character, being restricted not only to the towns in which they were held, but, so far as the exhibitions held in connection with them were concerned, they were conserved to the sole use and benefit of the members forming the society. The main objects in promoting these institutions were undoubtedly to bring together in close and friendly intercourse the principal breeders and fanciers of canaries, and to diffuse among tnem a spirit of brotherhood and friendly feeling, as well as to infuse a spirit of emulation for the advancement of the canary cause.

These societies hold their meetings usually at an inn or tavern, and have an arrangement with the proprietor or landlord to have a room appropriated for their especial use; this is invariably conceded without demur.

The legitimate meetings, viz., those set apart for the transaction of the society's business, are held monthly, in the case of a "close show society," but the members thereof, which consist chiefly of the working classes, are generally drawn every Saturday evening to the inn where these meetings are held. and there discuss freely all topics pertaining to their favourite pastime; and this is, in my opinion, the only drawback to these and other kindred societies, as they are calculated to lead men into habits of intemperance; but where an "open" or "all England" show society exists this evil can be obviated almost entirely. As it is my intention to give all the details connected with the different systems of managing each, it is not necessary for me to offer any further remarks here on this part of the subject. One thing may be said in favour of the "close show societies," and that is, they are both instructive and entertaining, for the members, after the business of the meeting has been duly transacted, enter into a general conversation, the chief topic, as a matter of course, being canaries and their kindred species, and some member is almost invariably ready to relate something which he conceives to be new, or appeals to some older and more experienced member of the society for his opinion on some particular method of breeding, feeding, or what not, and new theories are often propounded in this way, and freely discussed for the edification of all present; and juveniles in the "fancy" can often gather a great deal of information which they need by this means. But for the fact of their being held at taverns, these meetings are highly favourable to the progress and well-being of this delightful and innocent recreation. At the end of the year a show is held in connection with each "close show" society, restricted to subscribing members only, and at its termination a supper is mostly held, and this is got up in the "landlord's best style" of course, and a convivial evening is spent.

To begin a society of this kind it is necessary, in the first place, for one or two of the most intelligent or prominent members of the "Fancy" to wait upon all the known lovers and admirers of the canary, and to inform them of the project, and to request their attendance at such a place or inn as may be considered most suitable and likely to meet the approval of the majority at least of those people who, it is anticipated, will become members and office bearers. Be sure that the inn is one of good repute, and in a respectable neighbourhood. If the landlord is a fancier of birds, so much the better, as

he will be able to understand the requirements of the association fully. In any case, you must state the circumstances
in detail, and make some preliminary arrangements with him.
After your first meeting you will be able to ascertain whether
there is a reasonable prospect of establishing a society, and,
if there is, then a private room, no doubt, will be readily
granted to hold all special meetings in.

It will be found in nine cases out of ten that the first meeting
will be badly attended, several fanciers prognosticating that
it will be a failure; but as soon as ever it goes forth that
it has been decided to form an institution of this sort they
will all flock to the rendezvous to join it. A sufficient
number of members having collected, some one must propose
a chairman. The person chosen to fill this office should be
fully acquainted with the duties required of him, and be able
to explain the objects of the society, its aim, and how it is
proposed to manage it, in a clear and intelligible way. After
this has been done, propositions can be made, and the feasibility
of the scheme fully discussed.

If it is decided to establish a society of this sort, then a
secretary must be appointed, either permanently or *pro tem.*,
and likewise a president, a treasurer, and a committee; but,
having fixed upon a secretary, the other office bearers can be
elected at a subsequent meeting. The president, secretary, and
treasurer must act in conjunction with the committee, which
should consist of not less than six members, exclusive of president, secretary, and treasurer; but this is not imperative.

The secretary must keep a diary in which he will record
all the propositions that are brought forward by the different
members, and will see that those which have been carried
by a majority are acted upon. He will likewise form a code
of rules, which he must hand to the president of the society,
who will submit them at the first meeting after the association
is fairly established, for the approval of its members. Each
rule must be put to the meeting separately, and if an amendment is moved by any member, he will proceed to put such
amendment to the meeting, and the secretary will record
the ayes and noes for or against it. He will then put the

original rule, and, if the majority is in favour of it, it will remain unaltered, but if, on the contrary, the majority is in favour of the amendment, then the rule must be altered accordingly. After the rules have been fully discussed and approved, they should be printed, and each member supplied with a copy on payment of sixpence, to assist in defraying the expense of printing them.

The following will be found to embrace all that is required in a code of regulations for the purpose of conducting a society of this description in a satisfactory manner :

RULES AND REGULATIONS.

Rule 1. That this society shall be called the ———— Ornithological Society.

2. That it shall consist of a president, vice-president, secretary, treasurer, and a committee, to be chosen by a majority of the members composing the meetings, provided always that they form at least a quorum. The officers so elected to serve twelve calendar months, to be computed from the termination of the society's annual show in each year.

3. Five members are to constitute a quorum, and the meetings of the society are to take place on the first Thursday in each month at the place appointed, at eight o'clock in the evening, for the transaction of business.

4. The duties of the president or vice-president shall be to keep order, and to submit any proposition made by any member to the meeting for approval or rejection. No member to be allowed to address the meeting except through the president or vice-president, who shall rule him in or out of order, or whether his question is relevant or not. Any member infringing this rule to be fined sixpence, to go to the funds of the society. The vice-president to act only in the absence of the president.

5. The secretary must keep a diary or minute book, in which he will be required to record the business transactions of each meeting, and likewise to keep a debtor and creditor account of all receipts and disbursements made on behalf of the society.

6. The treasurer is to receive all moneys and pay all bills on behalf of the society, and to keep an account of the same, and in conjunction with the secretary to make out an annual balance sheet, to be submitted for the inspection and approval of the committee.

7. That the committee be empowered to transact the business of the society, and to hold meetings at other times than those specified, when they deem it expedient to do so, and in such cases it will be the duty of the secretary to acquaint each member of the committee, individually, of the day and hour at which such meeting will be held. Any member, being an office bearer, failing to attend either the regular or special meeting without giving a full and satisfactory reason for so doing, to be fined fourpence, the amount to go to the benefit of the society's general fund.

8. Any person desirous of becoming a member of this society must be proposed by one of its members, and the proposition duly seconded by another ; he will

then be balloted for at the following meeting, and, if elected, he will have to pay the sum of two shillings and sixpence as an admission fee, to assist in defraying the expenses of the society.

9. Any person wishing to become an honorary member only, can do so on payment of the sum of five shillings annually; and in this capacity he will be permitted to attend the meetings of the society, and will be eligible to hold office, should he be elected; but he will not be allowed to exhibit birds at the shows of the society as a competitor.

10. All members of this society are to be resident in the town of or its environs.

11. Each member shall pay a subscription of sixpence monthly, which shall go towards a prize fund and for assisting to defray the expenses of the society.

12. The secretary shall, from time to time, receive such remuneration for his services as the committee think fit, but no other officer shall be paid for services rendered to the society, without the authority or sanction of three-fourths of the subscribing members.

13. All propositions made at any of the society's meetings to be disposed of on a show of hands, the result to be taken by the president or vice-president; and where a dispute arises a recount shall be taken by the secretary, which shall be final, unless there be an unexplained discrepancy between the counts, when a count out can be demanded by the proposer or seconder of a motion: in this case the members must divide.

14. That a show be held annually in connection with this society, to take place on the ofin each year, and that any member, not being in arrears with his payments, such as fees, subscriptions, or fines, and who has conformed with the rules of this society in every particular, shall be entitled to exhibit birds.

15. No member will be allowed to exhibit any bird at any of the society's shows except such birds as have been bred by himself, and are his own *bonâ fide* property at the time of exhibition. Any member infringing this rule shall be expelled from the society, and shall forfeit all benefits accruing therefrom, whether in prize money or otherwise.

16. Any members desirous of competing for prizes at any of the society's shows must give due notice of their intention to do so to the secretary, at the first monthly meeting after the bird or birds intended to be entered attain the age of three weeks; and they will be required to furnish such information relative to such bird or birds as the secretary may deem necessary. All such notices shall be handed to the president, who will announce the same at the first meeting after their receipt. If the committee consider it expedient to appoint two or any other number of their body, as a deputation to visit the homes of any member or members intending to exhibit, for the purpose of noting more fully the particulars of the specimens announced for competition, it shall be competent for them to do so. The last night for receiving any entry to be fixed at the meeting held in the month of July. All birds entered must be under twelve months old.

17. Every member of this society who has entered a bird or birds for exhibition shall be required to sign a declaration, certifying that such bird or birds as entered by him are his property, and were bred by himself, such certificate to be made and handed to the secretary of the show not later than 10 a.m. on the morning of exhibition, and must be in the following form:

I,   , do hereby solemnly and sincerely declare that the bird (or birds) entered by me for competition at the   Ornithological Society's Show, of which society I am a duly appointed member, was (or were) bred by myself, and is (or are) at this present time my *bonâ fide* property; and, furthermore, that the said bird (or birds) is (or are) under twelve months old.

Witness,   Signed,

Any member making a false declaration, or exhibiting a bird or birds contrary to the spirit or intention of these rules, shall, on proof thereof, be expelled from this society, and shall forfeit all prize money and claims of every description against the society.

18. If any member is more than three months in arrear of payments of any kind he will be fined the sum of sixpence; and if this sum, together with all other arrears then due, be not paid to the secretary or treasurer on or before the following meeting night, then it shall be competent for the committee (unless a satisfactory reason can be assigned) to expel the said member without further consideration from the society.

19. Any person who has been expelled from this society for an infringement of any of its regulations shall not be eligible for re-election before the end of the current year in which the expulsion takes place.

20. The place of exhibition to be decided upon by the committee of management at least one month before a show takes place, and all members will be required to deliver their birds at or before 8.30 a.m. on the morning of the show to the person appointed to receive them. Every member who has entered a bird or birds for competition will be furnished with a card or label for each separate entry by the secretary, naming the class, variety of bird, and number of such entry; and he will be expected to affix these labels to the cages containing the birds answering such particulars prior to his delivering the specimens on the morning of the show. All birds must be shown in separate cages, and any birds entered in a wrong class will be excluded from competing. A card or list, containing the names and numbers of the different classes for which prizes will be awarded, must be hung up in the "club room" on the nights of each meeting after the schedule has been arranged and approved for the information of the members, and the secretary shall furnish to any member any further particulars he may reasonably require. No member will be permitted to enter the show room except those who are engaged in the arrangements until after the birds have been judged and the show is declared open. All members are to be admitted free of charge.

21. The judges are to be elected by a majority of the members of the society, at a meeting called specially for that purpose. No judge to be allowed to enter the show room until the arrangements are fully completed, and no member of the society will be permitted to be present during the time the judge or judges are performing their duties. If a judge desires to ask a question, the secretary, accompanied by a member of the society, will attend together to answer his query.

22. The judges will be empowered to withhold a prize where they have reason for suspecting that a bird has been fraudulently tampered with; but it will be their duty to bring such a case before the committee, who will decide thereon. If the bird belongs to a member of that body, he (the member) must retire during the inquiry.

23. All birds with clipped, drawn, or artificially coloured plumage, if detected, will be disqualified, and the owner of such bird shall forfeit all prize moneys, and

be expelled the society without further consideration, and any member who has been so expelled shall not be eligible for re-election.

24. The decisions of the judges shall be final, except in cases where a bird is found deficient in plumage or has been tampered with. All such cases shall be decided by the committee.

25. No joint partners will be allowed to become members as such; but where two persons have joined together to breed and exhibit birds, they must divide their stock equally, and enter as if they were separate fanciers.

26. The secretary will be authorised to order a sufficient number of prize cards, which will be affixed to the cages of the winning birds; but no commendation cards will be printed at the expense of the society.

27. The amount of prize money and number of prizes shall be arranged by the committee of management, due regard being had to the expenses incurred by the society, such expenses to be paid before the distribution of the prize money; and should any deficiency appear, it will be deducted from each successful competitor in a proportionate degree, according to the amount of prize money he has won.

28. It shall be competent for the committee, with not less than a quorum of its members present, to frame any bye-law to meet a case of emergency; and, further, the president shall, at any meeting of the society where an equal division of members has taken place in regard to any motion, be allowed to give a casting vote in addition to his own vote as a member of the society.

29. It shall be competent for any member, being an office bearer, to resign his office at any time by giving his written resignation to the secretary, and the members of the society, at the following meeting, shall proceed to appoint a substitute in his stead.

30. Any member who shall conduct himself in an unbecoming manner during any of the society's meetings, or who shall use intemperate and improper language to a brother member, or to any office bearer, judge, or other person, during the exhibition, or who shall smoke or annoy any member or other person visiting the exhibition, shall be fined a sum not exceeding two shillings and sixpence, and may be suspended from membership or expelled the society at the discretion of the committee.

31. That the exhibition shall be held for one or two days, as may be decided by a majority of the members of the society, and that the public be admitted on payment of a charge for admission to be fixed by the committee of management, the proceeds to be applied towards the liquidation of the society's expenses.

32. That it shall be competent for any member of this society to report to the secretary any case of supposed fraud, in bird transactions or otherwise, perpetrated by any of its members; and the secretary, on receipt of such complaint, shall call a meeting of the committee of management, who shall, if they deem fit, depute one or more members to investigate the charges and report the result. If there appear any just ground for the complaint, then the person so accused shall be called upon for an explanation, and if it prove unsatisfactory the committee shall have power to suspend or expel him, as they shall think proper; but if, on the contrary, the complaint should prove frivolous, then the member making such complaint shall be fined the sum of two and sixpence, and receive a public censure at the next meeting of the society.

33. This society shall not be dissolved so long as six members can be found who

are able and willing to undertake the duties and responsibilities required for the transaction and management of the business of the society.

34. At the termination of each exhibition in connection with this society a supper shall be held, and each member shall be admitted on payment of two shillings and sixpence, and non-members on payment of five shillings each. Prior to such meeting the secretary shall prepare a statement of the society's prospects, showing its progress or retrogression, as the case may be, such meeting and supper to take place within two weeks from the closing of the show. The minutes of all the meetings held throughout the year to be produced on this occasion, and such as may be considered necessary shall be read over to the members.

35. No alteration shall be made in any of the society's rules unless due notice thereof shall have been given previously to each member, and unless it takes place at a general meeting and be approved by a majority of the members then present; in all such cases a full quorum must be in attendance.

36. That these rules be printed, and each member supplied with a copy on payment of sixpence.

"Close" shows are being superseded rapidly by the "open" or "all England" shows. Nevertheless, they answer admirably for fostering among the members composing them a spirit of enterprise and zeal, as well as schools of instruction, and they are well adapted as a groundwork for promoting the establishment of "all England" show societies, and for preparing fanciers for more extended and enlightened views. Beside these advantages, they will be found an excellent means for teaching those connected with them how to conduct a show in a methodical and systematic manner, for without this knowledge confusion and disorder are certain to prevail; furthermore, they are likely to cherish a feeling of confidence among their members, which is very necessary in order to manage an "open" show with satisfaction and success.

OPEN SHOWS.—Many years ago, I used to look upon all "close" show societies as narrow and selfish in principle and upon these grounds I condemned them. About thirty-five years ago, in conjunction with one or two others, who were favourable to my views, I got up a show "open to all England." The prizes were of a liberal character, and the show was held in a public hall, in a large and prosperous town in the North of England. Music was introduced as a further attraction in order to gain public patronage, but the Fates were against us, and the speculation was a "losing game." So far as the number of birds entered for competition was concerned, the show was successful enough, but the weather was wretched, for the rain came pelting down in torrents, at short intervals, during the whole time the exhibition was open, and consequently the attendance of the public was of the most meagre description possible. I acted as secretary, and the lesson which I learnt was not readily forgotten by me, nor by other individuals, I should imagine, who were likewise interested in the undertaking. However, after the lapse of a few more years, and with the infusion of "new blood" among us, we ventured to get up another upon a more extended scale, and this was attended with better success, and it continued to prosper for a little while; but through a too reckless expenditure and too liberal a programme, it ultimately proved a failure and its members had to "pay the piper." Since that time I have had a good deal of experience in getting up shows, and having been permitted to exercise my own discretion almost entirely in managing a new society, formed by myself, in a different town to the one previously referred to, and which has on every occasion been attended with brilliant success—a good balance having been left in hand after the conclusion of each show, after every expense was satisfactorily liquidated, and this, too, in the face of a liberal programme and no niggardly "cheeseparing" policy in the management—I will proceed, for the benefit of those fanciers who have repeatedly been called upon to put their hands in their pockets and pay large sums to make up the deficiencies caused by losses incurred by exhibitions of this sort, to detail fully the plan which I adopted, and which has been so far attended with beneficial and satisfactory results; and if the advice given be strictly followed, any show conducted with energy and determination will, I am convinced, be a success.

One of the principal requirements in commencing an "open" show is to get a good secretary, for much depends upon this functionary for the success or otherwise of the undertaking. What is required is a sober, steady, industrious, intelligent man, active in mind and body, of good address, bland and conciliatory manners, and capable of expressing himself in a gentlemanly and becoming style, for it will be part of his duty to enter into correspondence with the *élite* of the town and neighbourhood where the show is about to take place, asking them for their patronage and support; and if they were to receive a rude or badly-constructed missive, badly written, it would be calculated to hinder rather than facilitate the object sought to be accomplished.

OFFICERS.—There is no necessity for a code of rules for a society of this description. In the first place, a few fanciers meet together and decide to have a show, to be "open to all England." They then confer together, and select some person whom they consider most suitable to fill the office of secretary. One or two such individuals are usually to be found in most towns of any importance; but they are not always willing to act in that capacity, for it is both a laborious and an unthankful office. However, if they are of an enthusiastic temperament and are in good health, they rarely refuse when pressed, and more particularly if they are flattered a little, for all men are more or less vain enough to show a little weakness in this direction; and, if a man is not naturally an enthusiast, then he is unsuited for such an occupation. A secretary having been duly appointed and a day and place fixed to hold a meeting, it will be his duty to send a written notice, or call upon those fanciers personally whom he considers most capable of assisting him in carrying out the project. Halfpenny post-cards will be found exceedingly useful for giving notice to the office bearers whenever the secretary thinks it desirable to consult them upon any subject on which their advice appears to him necessary.

It is important that a respectable hotel should be selected for the purpose of holding meetings, &c., and not a low public-house, as is sometimes the case.

The next consideration of moment is to fix upon a president, and afterwards a vice-president. The office of president is simply honorary, but it is most desirable to have a gentleman of affluence and position, well known and highly esteemed to fill it, for obvious reasons. Having decided upon some

2 c

one with the requisite qualifications resident in the town, or closely adjacent thereto, where the exhibition is about to take place, one or two influential members who are interested in its welfare should be deputed to wait upon this personage. and explain the matter to him, and endeavour to obtain his consent to undertake the appointment, or the secretary could write to him something after this fashion :

Sir (*that is, if he is an untitled gentleman, but if titled, then address according to his title*),—I am directed by the committee of the ——— Ornithological Association to inform you that, at a meeting of its members, held in the ——— Hotel on the —— inst., you were unanimously elected to the office of president of the aforenamed society. I may inform you that it is merely a post of honour, and does not entail any service of any description. If you will kindly inform me at your earliest convenience whether it is agreeable to you to accept the office, I shall feel greatly indebted for your kindness.—I have, &c., your obedient servant,

To C. London, Esq.   N. N., Hon. Sec.
      Botheram, Sept. ——, 187—.

Having met with a suitable president, it will behove you in the next place to appoint a vice-president, or chairman ; a man holding a good position in society, and one likely to be esteemed and respected, so that he will have no difficulty in maintaining order—an essential consideration at all times. He must be acquainted with the duties which will devolve upon him. Having secured the services of some one likely to fill this office satisfactorily, a treasurer must be chosen. I hardly need point out, I should imagine, that it is desirable to have a highly respectable and thoroughly trustworthy person to fill this important office. Beyond these officers all that is needed is a committee of management, consisting of six or eight fanciers, men of good repute and respectability. Do not have more, for there is an old saying, which is as true as it is ancient, that "Too many cooks spoil the broth." These preliminary arrangements completed, a list must be compiled, which should include all the ladies and gentlemen in your town and district who are likely to become patrons, which means, of course, subscribers.

PATRONS.—I have always found the aristocracy of this country willing to lend a helping hand to their fellow men to carry out an object of this kind ; at least, I have found but few exceptions to this rule, either in England or Scotland (I have never tried Ireland or Wales), among that class of people who are justly entitled to rank among the nobility of our land—the great "Upper Ten"—and these exceptions are mostly either eccentric or crotchety individuals, but more frequently parvenus.

The plan I adopt in asking for patronage and subscriptions is to send letters, and I think it by far the best, although it entails a good deal of labour upon the secretary. The following is a specimen of an application of this kind (presuming the person applied to to be a peer of the realm):

B——, Sept., 187—.

My Lord,—At a meeting of the committee of the ——— Ornithological Association, held in the K——A——Hotel on the—inst., it was resolved to hold an exhibition in or about the month of November next in connection with this society, and I am directed to communicate this fact to your lordship, and to ask for your lordship's patronage and support, which would be cordially received and highly esteemed by its members. The president of the association is C. L., Esq., and the treasurer O. P., Esq. An early reply from your lordship would be esteemed an especial favour.—I am, my lord, your lordship's most obedient servant, N. N., Hon. Sec.

To the Rt. Hon. Lord H——.

It is hardly necessary for me to point out that it is advantageous to get as many patrons as possible, for the success of the undertaking depends very much upon this extraneous aid, as few patrons will subscribe less than a guinea, and none less than half a guinea, whilst some will give two guineas; in one case I knew three to be given, but this is quite exceptional, the rule being one guinea. Besides the acknowledged aristocracy resident in a town and neighbourhood, if a corporate body exists, the patronage of the mayor, sheriff, and other official dignitaries should be secured if possible. This is best done by a select deputation waiting upon them personally. Two or more members should likewise be chosen to wait upon the principal tradesmen and shopkeepers resident in the town where the show is held to solicit subscriptions. All patrons and subscribers of half a guinea and upwards must be furnished with a family ticket—*i.e.*, a ticket to admit the entire household, and to remain in force during the whole time the show is open. These tickets must be printed specially for the occasion.

2 c 2

MEETINGS—GENERAL BUSINESS.—The first meeting should be held six or eight weeks prior to the time fixed upon to hold the show. Four or five, or six meetings at most, will suffice to complete the arrangements. Sixteen or eighteen days will probably elapse between the first and second meetings, unless the secretary has received replies from all the ladies and gentlemen he has written to on the subject. If he fails to receive an answer from anyone within fourteen days, he may safely conclude either that his communication has been over-looked, forgotten, or ignored, or that the person written to is absent from home. It will be advisable under these circumstances to write a polite note to the absentee, calling attention to his former letter; but this will seldom happen, for with one or two exceptions I have always received a prompt, and, I am happy to say, satisfactory reply to my applications in less than ten days, and, in most cases, in less than a week. Until you are in receipt of these replies, and can form some estimate of the probable amount of aid that you are likely to derive from this source, it will not be prudent to issue a programme, for the arrangement of the latter must be governed in a great measure by the result of your success in obtaining subscriptions. It must not be forgotten, when a reply is received announcing that the writer will be glad to become a patron of the society, or a letter inclosing a subscription, to send a suitable acknowledgment thanking the donor on behalf of the association.

Among other things, the secretary must supply himself with a diary, in which he will note the day and hour of each meeting, and record therein the names of all members present and absent on each occasion; he will likewise detail fully all the resolutions and other matters of business transacted at each meeting. The minutes of a former meeting must always be read over as a preliminary proceeding at the one immediately subsequent thereto.

Although it is quite unnecessary to frame a code of rules for conducting a society of this description, it should be tacitly understood by every person holding office that, in the event of a deficiency arising, each member is personally responsible to pay an equal share with his *confrères* to make up the loss. This responsibility gives an impetus to the whole machinery, as every member is interested in promoting the success of the institution.

TICKETS.—The plan to be adopted is to have a quantity of tickets of admission printed, in different colours, so as to represent at a glance the different prices. For subscribers of 10s. 6d. and upwards I use white enamelled cards, with an ornamental margin, and the words "Family Season Ticket" and the year printed upon them in ornamental type. For single admission tickets of 1s. value I use an orange ground with the words "Admission, 1s., 188—," and have a plain ruled line below, on which I can sign my name. For 6d. single admission tickets I generally have a green ground, but otherwise as those just described, except the amount, &c., and in addition to the words mentioned, I have the name of the society printed on them as well. To each member of the committee I give so many of those tickets, having previously subscribed my name or initials, and I debit him with the number and amount. I likewise furnish penny memorandum books, and ask them, severally, to obtain all the subscriptions they can, instructing them at the same time that they are at liberty to furnish any subscriber to the amount of his or her subscription with these tickets. To every patron of the show I send a family season ticket, whether they choose to subscribe or not; but those who omit to do so are not asked for their patronage on any subsequent occasion. I think the plan of issuing tickets a good one, as it affords those members who are timid a good opportunity of introducing the subject at any rate, and it makes them feel more independent—it gives them an opportunity of selling some tickets if they are too modest or bashful to crave a donation. From £6 to £10 should be realised in this way in a town with a population of from twelve to fourteen thousand inhabitants, and of course an increase in proportion to the greater population in larger towns, if this plan is vigorously prosecuted.

EXPENSES.—A schedule of prizes ought to be framed in accordance with the amount of subscriptions received and the prospects of the association.

To get up a show in a decent and praiseworthy manner will cost from £40 upwards. The following comprise the principal items of expenditure: Prize moneys (say, £20), use of hall for exhibition purposes (say, £4, this to include gas, fires, &c.), two men (two days at 5s. per day) to attend the birds, including feeding and giving them water to drink, &c., £1; two men (two days at 5s. each) to collect money taken at door, and to check tickets, &c., £1; judges' fees, £2 2s.; travelling expenses, paid to judges and hotel bill for same, £2; printing, £5; postage stamps, stationery, and sundries, £1 15s.; advertising, £1; conveyance for taking birds from railway station to show room and back to station, 8s.; professional packers to pack birds, 15s.; amounting in all to £40. And this is a moderate bill of costs for a respectable show. The printing is the heaviest item, but I like everything connected with this department well done, as it reflects credit upon the management, and is, I imagine, a sort of credential by which the respectability of a society of this sort is measured; bad paper, bad printing, and bad type, are all emblematic of vulgarity, parsimony, and bad taste—at least, I think so.

SCHEDULES.—It will be found a tolerably safe plan in arranging a schedule of prizes for a bird show to keep the amount of prize money a few pounds within the sum total received in the shape of subscriptions. To meet an expenditure of £40, which we will select merely as an example, £20 should be realised from the patrons alone and £5 more by donations from the public. The entrance fees may be estimated at £13, the charges for admissions at the doors £6, the sale of tickets by members £1, sale of catalogues and commission charged on the sale of birds £1, total £46—which would leave a balance in the hands of the treasurer for the following year of £6, and this may be considered as a very modest estimate indeed, as, in an ordinary way, the subscriptions, as well as the entrance fees, and takings at the doors. should exceed the amounts just mentioned, say, in any town with a population of 14,000 inhabitants, but I prefer to be under rather than over the mark in my calculations. We will presume that a schedule of prizes has been submitted to the committee for approval by the secretary and sanctioned, that a president and vice-president have been duly elected, and the place of exhibition fixed upon; that the manager of the hall or other building has been seen, and the days when it will be vacant ascertained, with the terms for three days, for it must be taken for the day prior to the days of exhibition to the public. The regulations must state that all birds are to be at the place of exhibition on that day, for it takes a long time to arrange all the classes properly, and this should be done and the birds carefully attended to the night before they are to judged. By this arrangement the judges can begin their duties as soon as it is light enough for them to see the birds properly, and it will enable them to do their work in a calm and deliberate way, whereas, if birds are to be received on the morning of a show, and the arrangements are only completed in time to allow the judges an hour or so before the public are admitted, they are very apt to lose their equanimity, and consequently they perform their work in a hurried and unsatisfactory manner. If care is taken to explain this circumstance fully to the manager or secretary of the building, in which the show is to be held, two days only should be charged for.

Before finally fixing upon the show days it must be ascertained beyond all doubt whether another bird show is likely to take place at or about the same time in any other town, as it is an object of great moment to avoid clashing with any other show of the kind, and would be likely to prove detrimental to both. This can be easily ascertained by referring to the list of shows published weekly in any of the papers which provide for fanciers, such as the *Journal of Horticulture, Live Stock Journal, The Stockkeeper,* &c., or *The Bazaar**; the last contains as full a list as any of its contemporaries. As soon as

---

* *The Bazaar* has a system by which a show can be advertised in its columns three times a week for the whole season, from the time of fixing the date until date of holding, for 10s.

the schedules have been satisfactorily arranged and the days of exhibition decided upon, the hall agreed for, and other preliminary matters settled, let the schedules be printed without delay. Four hundred copies should be ordered, and one sent to every known exhibitor in the kingdom. To obtain the addresses of these, the secretary should write for a catalogue of each show preceding his own, or refer to catalogues of the previous year. With regard to the best time of year to hold a canary show, much will depend upon circumstances, but it should certainly take place between the months of September and February, unless it be a "nest feather" show, and then the month of July will be found most suitable. Ten days at least should elapse between the last day for receiving entries and the first day of the exhibition, to allow the secretary ample time to arrange the catalogue, &c.

ANNOUNCING THE NAMES OF JUDGES.—Some societies deem it expedient to announce the name of the judge or judges upon the schedule; as to the advisability of this plan there is a variety of opinions. It is unquestionably open to discussion, hence I must refrain from offering an opinion thereon. Of one thing, however, I am fully convinced, and that is the desirability of a change of judges occasionally, as I find it gives more satisfaction to exhibitors. I have sometimes thought it would be well to submit the names of a number of well-known judges, and allow each exhibitor to vote for two, and finally to select the one or two, as may be deemed expedient, who received the greatest number of votes, but even this plan is open to objection. Always endeavour to procure a straightforward, conscientious man to act in this capacity. Some men are so anxious to become judges that they offer their services gratis, and in some cases agree to pay their own expenses as well. These men are generally fanciers with very limited experience, and are dear even on these terms, as their awards rarely give satisfaction to exhibitors, and they not unfrequently perpetrate gross blunders through ignorance. By all means avoid such men.

SERVANTS.—The men selected to attend upon birds during

an exhibition should invariably be fanciers—men who have a thorough knowledge of what they are required to do, and are sure to do it properly and well. It is probably the best plan to employ strangers—that is, people unconnected with the show—to collect the charges for admission and take the checks; at the same time, there is no serious objection to members of the committee being employed in these capacities if they are considered suitable and are willing to act.

It is undoubtedly best to employ a man who has a conveyance of his own adapted to the purpose of taking the birds to and from the railway station and the place of exhibition; but when such an arrangement is impracticable a horse and waggon can be employed; Messrs. Carver and Co. will ' be able to supply this desideratum in most towns north of the Humber, I believe, and how far south of the river I cannot say; be sure to arrange for a steady, reliable driver. Two members of the committee, at least, should accompany the conveyance, particularly on the return journey, to see the birds safely sent off. The Railway Companies will deliver the birds, but it is highly desirable that a member of the Show Committee should be in attendance on the arrival of all trains to see that the birds are carefully dealt with, and not delayed in delivery, or exposed to cold draughts unnecessarily, by being left on the platform or other exposed places. The Companies will likewise collect the birds for the return journeys, free of charge, if proper arrangements are made with the local station-master. I have always found these men most obliging in this respect, and they will attend even at a late hour at night without a murmur.

ADVERTISING. — Large posters, giving a full and clear announcement of when the exhibition is to take place, should be printed and freely distributed, and posted in all conspicuous and convenient places, at least a week before the show takes place. In addition to sending out schedules or programmes, it will be found advantageous to insert an advertisement, giving all particulars of the show, in at least two journals published in London, and those which promote the welfare of all persons interested in exhibitions of this sort by printing a weekly list of all coming shows should be favoured with these announcements. .The best papers to advertise in are: *The Bazaar*, 170, Strand, London (see p. 391); *Poultry*, 171, Fleet Street, London; and *Feathered World*, 273, Strand, London. There are a few others, but those mentioned are doubtless the most popular and best. The notices should be sent for publication as soon as the programmes are ready for distribution. It is customary, likewise, to advertise in each of the local papers published in the town where the exhibition is about to take place; one insertion in each paper is generally considered sufficient. It should appear in the week prior to that in which the show is to be held. There are several reasons why this custom should not be overlooked or neglected, and one is that a favourable report of the proceedings, &c., is likely to follow, and these notices are calculated to bring the society into favour and public estimation.

POINTS PRIZES. — Silver cups and other special prizes of considerable value are frequently offered as inducements to fanciers to swell their entries. At one time I was in favour of this scheme, but experience, that unerring monitor, has taught me to regard this plan as objectionable, as it is open to so much abuse, and is found to tempt some exhibitors to place themselves in a false position, which proves a means of deluding fanciers at a distance, who are totally ignorant of the real facts of the case. I have known exhibitors who have succeeded in obtaining these trophies not only borrow birds from their brother fanciers, but do even worse, for, in order to comply with the rule (common to all shows of this kind) stipulating that "all birds must be *bonâ fide* the property of the exhibitor," they have agreed to mock purchases, the owner of the bird agreeing to sell, for a mere nominal sum, to the exhibitor, upon condition that at the termination of a certain show the said bird shall be re-sold to him for the same amount as he received for it, and that the said vendor (real owner) shall be entitled to all prize moneys won by such bird in its own individual capacity, and, furthermore, that he shall be entitled to participate in a proportionate share of the said special prize or prizes obtained by the exhibitor, the latter further agreeing to pay all entrance fees and other costs incident thereto, and in some cases binding himself to pay a certain sum to the vendor in the event of the bird dying or being lost, killed, maimed, or disfigured whilst in his custody or care; and this transparent and palpable device is considered by some men as a sufficient salve for their consciences.

Common sense should teach us that no man would withhold a bird from a show if he felt reasonably satisfied that it had a fair chance of success in obtaining a prize, and if he thought otherwise it is scarcely probable that he would be foolish enough to throw away money by entering it, unless it happened to be at a show held in the town where he resides, he might then be generous enough to send a few extra entries to swell the funds of the institution. If committees are wishful to stimulate breeders and exhibitors to greater exertions by offering additional inducements, why not confine themselves to medals of moderate value intrinsically, and offer them for the best birds in such-and-such classes, or to the exhibitor who gains the greatest aggregate number of points in certain classes which must be specified? This would be an honorary distinction, hardly capable of being abused, and one which would be sure to be appreciated. There is another matter in connection with this subject deserving of attention. It is this. In counting points for extra prizes the recognised rule hitherto followed at nearly all shows has been to count three for a first prize, two for a second, and one for a third; but I think that commended birds should be included as well, and in the event of this suggestion being adopted, the rule should be to count first prize six points, second five, third four, very highly commended three, highly commended two, and commended one. I feel satisfied that where this plan is resorted to, when cups are given, it will tend greatly to increase the number of entries.

Prizes are now offered at a great many shows by the manufacturers of special foods for canaries and other birds that are fed solely upon the specific food of the vendors. But the question is, are all the birds that compete in these classes so fed? Ah! that is the question! but there is no means of proving the fact. Nothing could be more unsatisfactory to judges than classes of this kind, for birds of every known variety are eligible to compete together in one class, and the question naturally arises, are these birds to be entered on their merits as show specimens, or for the condition in which they are shown? Should they be taken out of their cages and examined to ascertain which are the plumpest, the best fed, and conditioned? Are they on the same lines as trussed fowls and fat pigs, or what? Judges, in the absence of instructions to the contrary, go for the best bird, according to the rules for class judging, regardless of the amount of flesh each body may contain. I should not be surprised to learn that many of the birds exhibited in these classes have not partaken of a whole penny packet of the food upon which they are presumed to have been reared; and so far as legitimate fanciers are concerned, the whole proceeding appears to be a farce, and a mere method of advertising. Would it not be commendable for the Committee of Shows to refuse these special gifts on the conditions named, as they cannot be considered advantageous to either honest exhibitors or themselves, and they certainly open a wide gate for wrong doers?

DISTRICT PRIZES.—A few prizes of small amounts should be offered for competition to fanciers living in the town and neighbourhood where the show is held. A radius of five miles might be allowed, and the classes confined to working men or cottagers only. I have tried the experiment, and was extremely pleased with the result, as I found it had a tendency to foster a spirit of enterprise and emulation among this class of fanciers.

PRIZES FOR PACKING CASES.—I am of opinion, too, that it would be good policy on the part of committees if they were to offer special prizes for the two most approved packing cases sent to the exhibition containing specimens to be shown.

THE COMMITTEE, THEIR DUTIES, &c.—The duties of committee men are neither so onerous nor laborious as those of the secretary and treasurer of a show, particularly the former, for upon him the weight of the work rests. They should render all the assistance they can to these functionaries to enable them to carry out the arrangements of the show in an efficient and praiseworthy manner, by endeavouring to raise funds, offering suggestions, and by deliberating carefully and thoughtfully upon all matters submitted for their approval or rejection, in the arrangement of a schedule of prizes, of a code of regulations for exhibition, in fixing upon the place of exhibition, in the appointment of judges, in directing the various items of expenditure, such as printing, advertising, &c., and in giving all the assistance they possibly can during the exhibition by unpacking the birds, and classifying them, and all other and similar duties, and by striving to do all in their power to get the birds packed and despatched to their destinations with as little delay as possible after the termination of the show. Each member should strive against his neighbour in endeavouring to set an example of cordiality, industry, and cheerfulness; for when men lose their temper at these times it is greatly to be regretted.

THE SECRETARY'S DUTIES.—The duties of a secretary to a show of any kind are laborious, and are not unfrequently a self-imposed task. I can assure those who have never undertaken, such an office that it is by no means a sinecure, the emoluments derived therefrom are *nil*, the work is most arduous, and the thanks of the public and exhibitors are of the most meagre description; but if the show is not skilfully managed, and there are any hitches in the way, showers of abuse will most likely pour in on all sides. It is, therefore, by no means an enviable or thankful office, but somebody must undertake it, or what would become of our favourite hobby?

It will be seen from the foregoing remarks that a person, to fill an appointment of this kind, will need to possess several qualifications and some virtues, and be endowed with a good "thick skin" beside. In addition to keeping a minute book, in which all the business transactions of the society at each meeting are to be duly recorded, the secretary will have to keep a book containing a debtor and creditor account; on the debit side he will have to enter all sums received on behalf of the society from every source, and on the credit side he must record every payment, however trivial. It will likewise be his duty to arrange about the printing and advertising, the taking of a proper building for the exhibition, and, in fact, he must look after and arrange everything in connection with the carrying out of the show, as the entire responsibility, in one sense, rests with him; but he must do nothing of his own accord—everything must be submitted to and sanctioned by the committee of management before it is acted upon.

PRINTING.—In selecting a printer be sure to employ one upon whose veracity and punctuality in all matters of business you can confidently rely, for if there is the least delay in having the catalogues and awards of prizes ready, and they are not sent off by first post after the judges have completed their task to those exhibitors who have sent the requisite amount to procure one or more copies, you may prepare yourself for the receipt of a few missives containing epithets the reverse of complimentary. The first year is always the most expensive in the item of printing. You will require to order three or four hundred programmes, which cost about 4s. 6d. a hundred; two hundred and fifty forms of entry, which are charged at about the same rate; fifty patrons' tickets, which cost about 3s. 6d.; three hundred admission tickets, in various colours, say, 6s. 6d.; one hundred and fifty prize cards— first, second and third prizes—different colours, 5s,; fifty tickets V.H.C., one hundred H.C., and one hundred C., the lot 5s. 6d.; three hundred class and prize tickets, 6s.; and a number of large class tickets on a white ground, say, six inches square, according to the number of classes for which prizes are offered, 2s. 6d. per dozen; two hundred posters—bills for distribution and posting up in conspicuous places, announcing the particulars of the show—demy folio, 10s. 6d.; one hundred and fifty catalogues, three-quarter sheet, with covers, £2 14s. The programmes I like printed on tinted paper, pink, white, pea-green, and yellow, or purple, or blue. The prices quoted may be regarded as moderate, considering that they are intended to represent charges for first-class workmanship, good clear type, and the best quality of paper. The cards should be rather large, and neatly executed, particularly the prize cards. The printing can be done for much less by getting the programmes and entry forms combined in one sheet, and by curtailing some of the regulations, &c., and by using sheets instead of catalogues; but I am opposed to exhibiting a parsimonious and niggardly spirit in this direction, as I consider it detrimental and pernicious in its consequences. The quantities given here are for a show presumed to be managed upon a tolerably liberal basis; but in arranging these matters every circumstance of the case must be fully weighed and considered. The class tickets will last for years, if they are carefully preserved from show to show.

It will be found a good plan to get a piece of board, about two and a half to three feet long and six inches wide, stained and varnished, or plain, with varnished edges. This is for a sort of advertising board; slips of paper of the same or similar dimensions should be ordered with the words "Bird Show" printed upon them; one of these should be pasted on each side of the board, which should be secured with screw nails to the side of the door frame at the entrance to the place of exhibition, allowing it to project to its fullest extent outwards to the street. After the show is over it must be taken down and preserved until again required.

PROGRAMMES.—In arranging a programme the secretary ought to have the names of all persons forming the committee printed on the title page, which will cause them to be legally responsible with the secretary and treasurer for any deficiency in the event of a show proving a failure; otherwise they are, I presume, only morally. bound, and if so disposed might back out of the concern at a moment's notice. The following specimens of a programme, and form and certificate of entry, will be found useful and instructive to those who are unacquainted with the mode of establishing a bird show. The regulations and conditions have been supplemented where it was considered expedient and necessary, and they will now be found sufficient to meet all requirements. The schedule of prizes is a good ordinary one, and can be augmented when considered desirable.

[Specimen.]

PROGRAMME.

THE NORTHERN COUNTIES ORNITHOLOGICAL ASSOCIATION.

The First Annual Exhibition of

CANARIES, CANARY MULES, AND BRITISH CAGE BIRDS.

Open to the United Kingdom,
Will be held in the Victoria Hall, B——,
On Wednesday and Thursday, Nov. 10 and 11, 188—.

PRESIDENT.	VICE-PRESIDENT.
O. LONDON, Esq., M.P.	S. BRIGHTON, Esq.

PATRONESSES.

Mrs. Mayoress.	Mrs. P.
Lady M.	The Misses H.
Mrs. H.	Mrs. J.

PATRONS.

TheWorshipful the Mayor of B. (J.P.).	The Hon. R. B. H.
The Sheriff of B. (S.W.).	Lord D.
The Earl P.	J. C., Esq , M.P.
The Earl of H.	The Rev. the Vicar of B. (N.M.).
Capt. W.	&c., &c., &c.

MANAGING COMMITTEE.

Mr. D. Durham.	Mr. D. Derby.
Mr. Y. York.	Mr. W. Warwick.
Mr. L. Lancaster	Mr. L. Leicester.

With power to add to their number.

TREASURER : Mr. C. CHESTER.

HON. SEC. : Mr. N. NORTHAMPTON, 15, Claremont-villas, B——.

N.B.—Exhibitors are particularly requested to examine the regulations most carefully, and also the schedule of prizes, in order to avoid errors in making their entries.

REGULATIONS AND CONDITIONS.

1. The decisions of the judges shall be final, unless it be proved that a bird has been fradulently tampered with, in which case the decision shall be void, the committee reserving to themselves the right of adjudicating thereon.

2. When the entries do not exceed five in any class, the first prize will be withheld. The judges will be empowered to withhold a prize in any class when the specimens are considered inferior in quality and below the regular standard.

3. All specimens are to be *bond fide* the property of the exhibitor. Any person infringing this rule by any device shall, on proof of illegal ownership, forfeit all entrance fees and prize money.

4. Specimens entered in a wrong class shall be excluded, and the entrance fee forfeited.

5. A price must be named with each specimen—price to include the cage as well. Anyone offering the price specified will become the purchaser. No alteration in the prices of specimens will be allowed during the exhibition. All sales must take place through the secretary or other authorised member of the committee. Ten

per cent. will be deducted from all sales. All birds claimed must be paid for at the time, or the claim will not be entertained. All birds claimed to be removed at the expense and risk of the purchaser. Where two people claim a bird simultaneously, the person offering the highest price shall have the preference. The surplus over and above the catalogue price to go to the society's funds.

6. No bird shall be removed before the show is finally closed without a written order signed by two members of the committee and approved by the secretary.

7. The amount of entrance fees must be sent with the certificates of entry, and post office orders are to be made payable to Mr. N. Northampton, at B—. Postage stamps will not be taken in payment unless one additional 1d. stamp be sent for the amount of each separate entrance fee. No alteration will be allowed in any certificate after it has been received by the secretary.

8. Exhibitors will be held responsible for the correct descriptions of the specimens sent, and in the event of a dispute arising after purchase, they must, on proof of wrong entry, receive back the bird or birds so entered, and refund to the purchaser the full amount paid by him, with all costs and charges incident thereto. In all such cases the commission charged by the society will be forfeited.

9. The whole of the specimens must be in the Victoria Hall, B——, on Tuesday, the 9th of November. All cages are to be addressed to the secretary, Victoria Hall, B——. The carriage in all cases must be prepaid by exhibitors.

10. The specimens will be returned as desired; but, in the absence of special instructions, they will be forwarded by such trains as the committee consider most desirable. The show room will be properly warmed and ventilated, and every care will be taken of the specimens sent for exhibition. They will be carefully packed for the return journey, but the committee will not be responsible for any loss or damage that may happen to them, either on the way to or from, or during the exhibition.

11. No person will be admitted to the exhibition previous to its being opened, except those who are engaged in the arrangements.

12. Exhibitors requiring an award of prizes must send 6½d. in addition to their entrance fees.

13. The entries will close on Saturday, October the 30th, 188—.

☞ All prize moneys will be paid within ten days after the closing of the exhibition.

SCHEDULE OF PRIZES.

Class. Description.	First.	Second.	Third
1. Clear, ticked, or marked yellow Belgian	12s.	6s.	3s.
2. Clear, ticked, or marked buff Belgian	12s.	6s.	3s.
3. Clear yellow Glasgow Don	12s.	6s.	3s.
4. Clear buff Glasgow Don	12s.	6s.	3s.
5. Flecked Glasgow Don	12s.	6s.	3s.
6. Clear yellow Norwich	12s.	6s.	3s.
7. Clear buff Norwich	12s.	6s.	3s.
8. Evenly-marked yellow Norwich	12s.	6s.	3s.
9. Evenly-marked buff Norwich	12s.	6s.	3s.
10. Ticked or unevenly-marked yellow Norwich	12s.	6s.	3s.
11. Ticked or unevenly-marked buff Norwich	12s.	6s.	3s.
12. Any variety of crested yellow Norwich	12s.	6s.	3s.
13. Any variety of crested buff Norwich	12s.	6s.	3s.

2 D

SCHEDULE OF PRIZES—*(continued).*

Class.	Description.	First.	Second.	Third
14.	Golden-spangled Lizard	12s.	6s.	3s.
15.	Silver-spangled Lizard	12s.	6s.	3s.
16.	Clear yellow Yorkshire	12s.	6s.	3s.
17.	Clear buff Yorkshire	12s.	6s.	3s.
18.	Marked or variegated yellow Yorkshire	12s.	6s.	3s.
19.	Marked or variegated buff Yorkshire	12s.	6s.	3s.
20.	Jonque Cinnamon	12s.	6s.	3s.
21.	Buff Cinnamon	12s.	6s.	3s.
22.	Evenly-marked Cinnamon	12s.	6s.	3s.
23.	Any other variety of canary (distinct breed)	12s.	6s.	3s.
24.	Goldfinch mule, evenly-marked	12s.	6s.	3s.
25.	Goldfinch mule, unevenly-marked	12s.	6s.	3s.
26.	Dark Goldfinch mule	12s.	6s.	3s.
27.	Any other variety of mule	12s.	6s.	3s.
28.	Selling class (any variety of canary, price, with cage, not to exceed 15s.)	10s.	5s.	2s. 6d.
29.	Goldfinch	8s.	4s.	2s.
30.	Linnet	8s.	4s.	2s.
31.	Any other variety of British bird	8s.	4s.	2s

DISTRICT PRIZES.

Class.	Description.	First.	Second.	Third
32.	Best clear or marked bird (any breed), to be shown solely for form, style, and condition..	4s.	2s.	1s.
33.	The most evenly-marked bird (any breed)	4s.	2s.	1s.

Entrance fees for classes from 1 to 27 inclusive will be 1s. 6d. each bird, from 28 to 31 inclusive 1s. each bird. The district classes, confined to working men and cottagers, 6d. each entry; exhibitors to be resident in or within five miles of the town of B——. Exhibitors must provide their own cages.

Admission: Wednesday, from 1 to 6 p.m., 1s. each; from 6 to 9.30 p.m., 6d. each; and on Thursday, from 9 to 12 a.m., 1s. each; and from 12 to 6 p.m., 6d. each.

The exhibition will close punctually at the times stated, and visitors are respectfully requested to leave at the hours specified.

Subscribers of 10s. 6d. and upwards will be entitled to a family season ticket. Children under 12 years of age and schools will be admitted at half price.

Catalogues, 6d. each; by post, 6½d.

[Specimen.]

THE NORTHERN COUNTIES ORNITHOLOGICAL ASSOCIATION.
FORM OF ENTRY.

Class.	Description.	Age of Specimen.	Price.	Name and Address of the Breeder.	Name and Address of the Person from whom Purchased.	Remarks.

I hereby enter the above birds for competition, subject to the Rules and Conditions of this Society; and I most solemnly and sincerely declare that I have given the fullest information in my power respecting the specimens entered, and in the event of my declaration being proved to be erroneous, I agree to forfeit all my entrance fees, and any prize money which I may have won; and, furthermore, I authorize the committee to adopt any plan they may deem fit or expedient for publishing the same. I also solemnly declare that all the birds exhibited by me are truly and *bona fide* my own property, and I enclose the sum of.........................to entitle me to become an exhibitor at this show.

Signature.......................................
Address (in full) ....

Date...............

£   s.   d. enclosed for Catalogue, &c.

CATALOGUES.—After the schedules are printed and a copy sent to every well-known exhibitor in the United Kingdom, it will be necessary to obtain and prepare a book, from which the catalogues will have to be printed. Great care must be taken in its arrangement. The book used should be about fourteen inches long, eight inches wide, and from half to three-fourths of an inch in thickness, and ruled with £ *s. d.* columns. On the title-page you must set forth the name of the society and other particulars, similar to the following specimen:

CATALOGUE.

THE NORTHERN COUNTIES ORNITHOLOGICAL ASSOCIATION.

First Annual Exhibition of

BRITISH CAGE AND SONG BIRDS,

Open to the United Kingdom,

Held in the Victoria Hall, B——,

On Wednesday and Thursday, November 10th and 11th, 188—.

Judges—M. Herniman Toke, Puddletown; Mr. Jeremiah Smasher, Bowlover.

President—C. London, Esq., M.P. | Hon. Sec.—Mr. N. Northampton.
Vice President—S. Brighton, Esq. | Treasurer—Mr. C. Chester.

And upon the first leaf of the book begin the heading thus:

CATALOGUE.

THE NORTHERN COUNTIES ORNITHOLOGICAL ASSOCIATION.

CANARIES, &c.

N.B.—The cage is, in every case, included in the price of all specimens sent for competition. No specimen or other bird will be allowed to be disposed of privately, or removed during the exhibition. For addresses of exhibitors see index. Abbreviations: First signifies First Prize; Second, Second Prize; Third, Third Prize; V.H.C., Very Highly Commended; H.C., Highly Commended; C., Commended.

Then arrange the classes thus:

[Specimen.]

Class 1.—Clear, Marked, or Ticked Yellow Belgian.

First Prize, 12s.; Second, 6s.; Third, 3s.

		£	s.	d.
C.	No. 1. Mr. J. Nash, cock, age 4 months..........................	3	3	0
V.H.C.	No. 2. Mr. S. Jones, hen, 6 months...	2	0	0
Second.	No. 3. Mr. G. Smith, cock, 1 year	4	10	0
H.C.	No. 4. Mr. W. Thompson, cock, 16 months	5	0	0
First	No. 5. Mr. P. Brunt .... ;...........................	10	0	0

2 D 2

Do not begin to number them until all the entries have been received on November 1.

Continue to arrange all the classes in this way, leaving a separate page for each class. After you have received all the entry forms, which should reach you on the day following that advertised as the last day for receiving them, you must fill up and despatch by post to each exhibitor a class ticket for every entry made. These tickets must denote the number of the class, the consecutive number of the entry, and the price of the specimen, in the order mentioned. Having completed this part of your duty, you must proceed to compile an index at the back of the book, according to the plan given below, which will be found so arranged as to prevent the possibility of a mistake being made when the re-packing commences, provided always that the rules herein laid down are strictly observed on all occasions.

[Specimen.]

Con. No.	No. of Entries.	INDEX.
1	3	Adam, Timothy, Brick-place, Battle Town—40, 51, 62.
2	2	Abraham, Simon, Smoke-hill, Fryington—9, 55.
3	6	Barebell, William, Possum-row, Bogglesbury—1, 2, 6, 7, 52, 53.
4	1	Brunt, Peter, Scisson-grove, Raynortowne—3.
5	4	Codrake, Thomas, Over-terrace, Furness—4, 5, 54, 68.
6	8	Cauliflower, Charles, Garden-place, Orchardton—6, 7, 8, 12, 42, 43, 56, 57.
7	3	Duff, Nicholas, Brownlow-terrace, Wheatley—14, 15, 16.
7½	2	Dent, Isaac, Drinkwater-place, Templer-town—17, 21.
8	1	Eagle, Edward, Dove-place, Lambourney—30.
9	5	Easysides, Philip, Slow-hill, Snailsby—10, 11, 13, 31, 45.
10	3	Farthing, Benjamin, Silver-street, Stirling—46, 18, 20.
10½	7	Feast, Jonathan, The Esplanade, Bunkrun—23, 24, 25, 32, 33, 47, 48.
11	1	Goodfellow, George, Christian Bank, Bushwell—50.
12	2	Green, Patrick, Shiney-row, Emeralda—35, 61.

The index should always be arranged alphabetically; in front of the names you must arrange two columns of numbers. The first column should contain the consecutive numbers of the entries, beginning with number one, and afterwards continuing to the end of the list of exhibitors. In column number two you must enter the number of birds shown by each exhibitor opposite his name, and at the end of the address add the numbers of the entries according to the class arrangement of the catalogues.

RECEIVING AND STAGING THE BIRDS.—On the day announced for the receipt of the birds you should be in attendance at the place of exhibition at such times as birds may arrive; this you will ascertain on reference to a railway time-table giving the arrivals of the trains. One of the committee, or some duly authorised person specially appointed, and armed with an authority in writing duly signed by the secretary and dated, should be in attendance at the railway station to receive the birds and have them forwarded to the place of exhibition with the least possible delay. As soon as they arrive they should be opened out, and the secretary or one of the committee-men should chalk upon each cage at the top the number that is opposite the name of the exhibitor in the consecutive column. The object in doing this is to save much time in packing for the return journey. Numbered labels would be better than chalked numbers, as the latter are liable to get rubbed off or defaced. By adopting this plan, all that is necessary for the working members of the committee to do is to go through the different classes and pick out all the cages having the same numbers, and place them together; they should then be checked off by the secretary, assistant-secretary, or some member of the committee who may have been specially selected for this duty, and finally given over to one of the persons who have been appointed as packers. On reference to the index, the number of exhibits and the class numbers are readily seen, and can with the least possible · labour be checked off. The saving of time gained by the adoption of this method, to say nothing of the prevention of errors, is almost incredible. During the many years that I took an active part in shows, as secretary or otherwise, I never remember a single occurrence of a bird being wrongly sent, or one being left behind, and I have known instances where from three to four hundred birds have been carefully packed and sent off within three hours after the closing of the show. If one is wanting to complete the entry, the secretary can easily ascertain which bird is missing by referring to the class numbers in the index at the end of the name and address of the exhibitor; he will then communicate the fact to the owner. It sometimes happens that a bird is taken ill at the last moment, and not forwarded to a show in consequence. In such a case the exhibitor ought to intimate the fact to the secretary, but this is rarely done. Those birds which are sent in wrappers or other covers must be carefully dealt with. Before the birds are unpacked someone should be appointed to take charge of and fold up the wrappers and tie the address labels for the return journey outside of them. The number of birds packed in each wrapper should be marked upon the label, for some fanciers who make large entries are often necessitated to send their birds in two or three separate packages. As soon as the wrappers are properly folded and labelled they should be stowed away in a secure place and neatly arranged. It is a bad plan to have too many assistants in unpacking. There should be one person to open the packages; another to place the chalk numbers on the cages. The secretary should tick off the entries himself. A fourth person ought to be deputed to arrange the birds in their proper classes; a fifth to feed and give them water. More helpers than these are superfluous, and likely to be productive of mischief.

The secretary must be firm in keeping order among those officials entrusted to perform the various duties mentioned, and should prevent undue interference by one assistant with another, or other kind of obstructiveness.

LATE ENTRIES.—There are sure to be some late entries. By this I mean birds entered for competition after the stipulated time, and after you have arranged your catalogue in manuscript. Such entries are very troublesome, but it is quite optional with the secretary, whether he accepts them or not; in fact, I am not sure if he is legally justified in doing so without a proviso in the regulations to enable him to do it. About four years ago I introduced a system of post entries, charging an additional fee of sixpence for each entry for so many days after that specified for the ordinary closing, and I should like to see this plan more generally adopted, as fanciers who neglect to send their entries at the proper time should pay for their negligence. When you receive entries of this sort you must deal with them in this fashion. Suppose, for example, you receive two entries for Class 5, and the last entry in that class is numbered 47, you must enter the two additional birds thus: 47A, 47B, and so on; and in the index in this manner: Presuming the name of the person who has sent the late entry is Dunn, and the last person entered under letter D is represented by the consecutive number 22, you must distinguish the specimens entered by Mr. Dunn by adding a ½ to the figures 22, so that this number will be 22½. By this simple arrangement the packing for the return journey, which is always looked forward to as a formidable undertaking by most people, is greatly facilitated, and rendered quite an easy task.

PACKING AND RETURNING BIRDS.—As soon as the show is concluded and the room cleared of visitors the doors should be all secured. In the next place, all the birds should be gathered together and placed in lots—all the number one's, two's, and so on. The packers must then be told off, two being apportioned for each lot of birds. Three lots of packers are ample in ordinary cases, and, if good hands, should be able to clear out the place in a few hours. Each couple of packers should have an attendant, whose duty it is to pick out the wrappers for each different lot, and call out the numbers for the secretary to tick off each bird according to its class number. One of the packers will then tie each two cages together with twine, having first emptied the water out of the drinking tins, and hand them to the other packer to arrange in the cover. Whilst the packers are engaged sewing up the package, the attendant can be preparing the next lot. They should be packed consecutively, excepting those birds which are to be sent a long distance, as these should in all cases be sent off by the first train.* The secretary should pre-arrange matters with the station-master, and should furnish a list of the number of packages sent by each conveyance, or at each separate journey of the one engaged, and get the lists signed by the railway company's servants.

---

* When practicable, the night mail will in all cases be found most suitable.

ASSISTANCE AND TREATMENT OF JUDGES.—But there are other important duties to be performed beside, both before the opening and during the exhibition. As soon as all the birds are arranged, and examined to see that they are all properly classed, fed, and supplied with water, the room should be swept; the floor should be strewn all over with damp sand or sawdust previous to this being done to prevent the birds getting soiled with dust. These preliminaries being completed, you are now ready to admit the judges. You should prepare for each judge a lead pencil and a small memorandum or judging book, in which you have previously written the number and heading of each class; request each of them (if more than one) to mark down the number and particulars of every bird to which they award a prize or commendation. With the judges you should send a person to act as amanuensis to them; he must not be an exhibitor, nor connected directly or indirectly with one. This person should be furnished with slips of paper, which must be obtained from the printer, being in reality leaves of a catalogue minus the awards; he should keep behind the judges, and ought not to hold any communication with them whatever, beyond marking down the awards when they are called over. A boy should likewise be in attendance to tie on the prize tickets, under the supervision of the person attendant upon the judges (unless the "Field Duplicate Judging Books" are used, in which case an attendant is not necessary. The whole of these officials should be regaled, say, once in two or three hours, with some light refreshment whilst performing their duties. It is usual to consult them as to what they prefer—tea, coffee, or a glass of sherry and a biscuit, or bread and cheese and beer. After every two or three classes have been judged, the boy or atten-dant should hand out the slips that are ready to the secretary, who should keep a copy of them for his own guidance, and send the originals to the printer; by adopting this method you are enabled to have your catalogues ready very shortly after the judges have finished their work. As soon as they have com-pleted their task have a good substantial dinner ready for them. After dinner the judges should check the catalogue with the books supplied them by the secretary, to see that no error has been made; they should then sign them, having first certified that they are correct. These books should be retained by the secretary for future reference in case of any dispute. He will then pay them their fees and travelling expenses, taking a receipt for the same, unless the treasurer is present to do so.

SELLING TICKETS.—With regard to the arrangement for selling tickets, he must give the person authorised to receive the admission charges so many tickets of each kind, debiting him with their value. Another person must be employed to collect these and to act as check. Instruct the latter to admit no one without a ticket. To distinguish between the tickets sold at the door and those sold by members or given to subscribers, put your name or initials to the latter and leave the former blank. Every hour or two the ticket collector or check should hand in to the secretary or treasurer the tickets collected by him, which should be sorted and entered on a sheet, and afterwards placed under lock and key. The secretary will likewise supply the ticket salesman with catalogues to sell to visitors; these must form a separate account.

CHECKING ACCOUNTS.—After the show is over the secretary must make out a list of prize money payable to each exhibitor, and hand it to the treasurer; he will likewise account to the treasurer for all cash he receives for subscriptions, &c., every meeting night, if the treasurer is present, taking his receipt for each payment in a memorandum book which should be used for this purpose. The secretary will likewise, on each show night, check over the amount of the takings at the door, in the presence of the treasurer and committee, and after counting and entering the same in his book, hand the money over to the treasurer, taking his acknowledgment as before. No false delicacy should be exercised on these occasions, but everything should be done in a straightforward business-like manner, and with exactness. The secretary will, furthermore, gather in the various accounts, and hand them to the treasurer for payment; when paid, the treasurer will hand them to the secretary, who will enter them on the credit side of his account before filing them.

REMOVAL OF PRICES FROM CAGES.—Before the judges enter the show room I have always made it a rule to cut off all the prices from the class tickets, so that they may not in any way be influenced in their opinion by a fancier's own estimation of his birds, for some judges if they observe two birds in the same class precisely alike, are apt to refer to the prices before giving their verdicts, and if not thoroughly self-reliant men and endowed with moral courage, they are wont to pander to the opinions of the owners. Another reason is, that it is often the means of causing a good sale for catalogues, as many people purchase them on purpose to get to know the price of the specimens; it is also a sort of key to fanciers, as it enables them to estimate the qualities of a judge; for there are few fanciers of experience who do not know as well, and sometimes better, than some of those people who act in that capacity, the real merits and qualifications of their specimens.

ORDERS FOR CATALOGUES.—Whenever an exhibitor sends an order and prepayment for one or more catalogues, I make an entry in front of his name in the index thus, " 1 c." or "2 c.," and so on, according to the number paid for; this I do with red ink, to appear more conspicuous. I afterwards make out a list of the names and addresses of those fanciers who have paid for them, and as soon after as convenient I direct a stamped newspaper wrapper to each of them ready to fold the catalogue in as soon as received from the printer. When more than one is paid for, I put the number required immediately below the address in plain figures, so that they can be got ready in a few minutes for the post. Exhibitors of six birds and upwards are generally admitted to the exhibition free of charge.

MISCELLANEOUS HINTS.—The secretary or treasurer and one or two of the committee, alternately, should be in constant attendance to give any explanation to patrons and others desiring it, and to keep proper order in the show room.

Sometimes flowers, stuffed birds, evergreens, or music are introduced as additional attractions, but these are merely accessories, and may be adopted or rejected at the discretion of the committee. It is sometimes considered desirable to have a show opened by some person in a high social position, and to charge an extra fee to witness the ceremony, but this plan has never been attended with success within my knowledge. Exhibitors are in some cases admitted to the show at any time, when open, on payment of sixpence. No birds can be sold or removed without the authority of the secretary and in conformity with the regulations. An account of all sales should be kept.

After the receipt of entries, if you find that the show is badly supported, write a letter to each of the principal exhibitors who have not already patronised your show, pressing them to do so; your appeal is sure to meet with some responses. The Editors of *Feathered World* and *Poultry* will, if the entries are deficient, willingly insert a paragraph free of charge, stating that entries will be received until a later date, if the secretary requests them to do so.

Every night that the specimens are in the show room a diligent search should be made to see that no cat, or person, is concealed on the premises, prior to the lights being extinguished, and the room secured for the night. Someone should take charge during the night, unless a hall-keeper resides in some part of the building, when it may be considered unnecessary. If you find it desirable during any period of the exhibition to have a policeman in attendance, you can get one by giving timely notice to the superintendent of the town or district where the show is held.

Be sure to see that the drinking tins are always returned with the cages to which they belong; this is often neglected, and causes annoyance and needless expense to exhibitors.

Refreshments should be supplied to those people who are engaged in any arduous duties, such as packing and unpacking birds, arranging the tables or stands for the cages, and similar duties. Members of the committee should each have a family season ticket given to them, unless they wear favours in their coats by which they can be easily recognised by the ticket collector and check-taker.

TREASURER'S DUTIES.—The duties of a treasurer to an ornithological association are more confidential than onerous. He will be required to take charge of all moneys collected on behalf of the society; he will furthermore be required to pay all accounts, or depute the secretary to do so, incurred on its behalf; he must likewise keep a debtor and creditor account as well as the secretary, so that they will act as a check to each other, and be a means of preventing errors or irregularities. After the conclusion of the show, and all the disbursements are completed, he will be required to prepare a balance sheet *in extenso*, setting forth the source from which the funds have been derived, showing at a glance the amount received by subscriptions, entrance fees, sale of tickets, admissions to the exhibition, &c., separately, and on the debit side every item of expenditure should be plainly and clearly specified, so that it is intelligible to the meanest capacity. After it is completed it should be submitted to the committee for their inspection, information, and approval, at a special meeting called for that purpose. If it is satisfactory to all, it is customary for a vote of thanks to be accorded to both the secretary and treasurer, and also to the vice-chairman; but this duty devolves upon the committee. If a balance remains in favour of the society, it should be placed in the Post-office or other savings bank in the names of three trustees, which should always include the secretary and treasurer and one of the committee or the vice-chairman. In the event of the society being in arrears, the secretary and treasurer are liable to be sued in the county court for any debt legally contracted on behalf of the society, and they in turn can sue every member of the committee for his rateable proportion should he refuse to pay it voluntarily. This is, I believe, the law on the subject.

ACCOUNTS.—The specimen of a balance sheet given on p. 413 will doubtless be found very serviceable, especially to those who are unacquainted with practical book keeping. The names used for the society, secretary, committee, and all and every

THE NORTHERN COUNTIES ORNITHOLOGICAL SOCIETY IN ACCOUNT WITH C. CHESTER, TREASURER.

	£ s. d.	£ s. d.
To subscriptions collected by—		
N. Northampton	8 10 0	
C. Chester	6 0 0	
D. Durham	2 15 0	
Y. York	0 12 6	
L. Lancaster	0 10 6	
D. Derby	0 9 6	
W. Warwick	0 6 6	
L. Leicester	0 4 0	
		19 7 0
To entrance fees—		
189 at 1s. 6d.	14 3 6	
23 at 1s.	1 3 0	
		15 6 6
To amount collected at door—		
November 10th	4 6 6	
,, 11th	3 7 6	
		7 14 0
To tickets sold by—		
D. Durham	0 6 0	
L. Lancaster	0 3 0	
W. Warwick	0 4 6	
D. Derby	0 2 6	
L. Leicester	0 2 0	
		0 18 0
To catalogues sold		0 16 0
To commission on birds sold		0 10 0
		£44 11 6

	£ s. d.	£ s. d.
By amount paid for prizes		19 13 0
By expenses of show—		
Victoria Hall (hire and gas)	3 17 6	
W. Smith (for attendance)	0 10 0	
T. Jones ,,	0 5 0	
G. Thompson ,,	0 10 0	
F. Popham ,,	0 5 0	
Mr. Y. Z. Primrose (judge)	1 1 0	
Mr. P. F. Daisy ,,	1 1 0	
,, ,, travelling expenses	0 17 6	
Dinners for judges	0 10 0	
P. Typo, account for printing	5 3 6	
Postage stamps, stationery, &c.	1 15 0	
Advertisements, *Bazaar*	0 10 0	
,, The *Gazette* (local)	0 4 0	
,, ,, *Journal* ,,	0 4 6	
,, ,, *News* ,,	0 5 0	
Commission on Post-office orders	0 3 6	
T. Small's Account (bird seed)		
P. Jerk (twine, &c.)		
Bones Brothers (account for refreshments)	0 10 6	
R. Spice (for conveying birds, &c.)	0 7 6	
T. Stone (for notice board)	0 1 0	
Packing needles and sundries	0 1 6	
		18 11 0
Total expenditure		38 4 0
Balance in hands of Treasurer		6 7 6
		£44 11 6

The Canary Book.

name which appears not only in the account, but likewise those in the specimens given for arranging a schedule and catalogue, are, as a matter of course, imaginary or fictitious. After the conclusion of the meeting, the treasurer should hand over to the secretary all the accounts he has paid, and the balance sheet, which should be carefully checked, and afterwards filed. Sometimes auditors are appointed to examine the accounts, and certify their correctness; but in a matter of this kind such a course appears to me to be unwarrantable and offensive, unless there is some just ground for adopting it, more especially when the appointments are purely honorary. A treasurer should render the secretary all the assistance in his power, as he is the individual on whom the brunt of the battle falls.

SENDING PRIZE MONEY.—When the prize money is sent to the exhibitors, an acknowledgement should be obtained. Keep the numbers, dates, and amounts of the Post-office Money Orders sent to each, so that payment can be proved if necessary. Never send postage stamps in payment of prize money, however small the amount, nor Postal Orders, which are not by any means secure.

ADVICE TO JUDGES.—Never accept an appointment to officiate as judge at any show unless you feel morally certain that there is no reason why you should not be able to fulfil your engagement, as it is a great disappointment to the managers when a judge, after accepting office, fails to attend. Should you happen to feel at all unwell a few days before a show is about to take place, where you are under an engagement to act in that capacity, it will be advisable to communicate the fact to the secretary without delay, so that he may be prepared, in the event of your not being able to officiate, with a substitute to fill your place. Be sure always to be in attendance in good time on the day fixed for your services. If the show is held at a town situated a great distance from the one in which you reside, it will be best for you to arrive there the previous night, unless you prefer to travel all night, or can reach it before 9 a.m. by proceeding by an early morning train on the day of the show. It is not a commendable practice to travel all night, as it is very likely to unfit a man for the proper performance of his duties. As soon as you accept an·appointment as judge at a show, you should request the secretary to furnish you with a schedule or programme of prizes and the regulations, which you should read over attentively, and if there is anything in it which you do not clearly comprehend, write at once for an explanation. Before you proceed on your journey to the town where the show is to take place, you should prepare yourself with a small memorandum book, which you must arrange in the same way as the schedule, that is, so far as the classification is concerned. You should likewise write the word "prize" on three separate and consecutive lines, and also immediately below these the letters V.H.C., leaving two lines on which to enter the numbers, then H.C. and C., acting in the same way. You then only require to fill in first, second, and third prizes, and the numbers of the other birds entitled to distinction, which saves much time. It is, however, generally understood that the secretary of a show will provide the judges with properly prepared judging books and a lead pencil. The *Field* judging books are well adapted for this purpose, and save much time and labour to the judges and secretary alike, and are not expensive. This book I always fill in from my own, and afterwards check it over with the printed catalogue. I then certify it as being correct, sign it, and then hand it to the secretary; but the catalogue I keep, and after I return home I compare it with my own book; if I discover a discrepancy I write to the secretary to rectify it without delay. You should likewise prepare yourself with a good eyeglass—a powerful magnifier—and three small phials, containing tests for stained birds, one of spirits of wine, another of liquor of potass, and the third should contain a good strong solution of common washing soda, or a little well diluted hydrochloric acid, but unless the latter is properly prepared it is dangerous to use; the fumes of this acid will remove most dyes, but this, too, is a dangerous process, and should not be practised by anyone who does not thoroughly understand how to use it. A pair of small

tweezers will be found useful for examining the pinion
and body feathers, &c., of the specimens. You must likewise be supplied with one or two spotless white handkerchiefs
and a piece of nice clean cotton wadding, in case you should
require to test the genuineness of the colour of any birds. If
the legs of a bird are stained with a colouring matter, or the
underflue, when blown, appears discoloured, or if the colour be
quite uniform throughout and void of bloom, it is pretty
evident that the bird has been tampered with. I have detected
several in this way. Whilst you are judging be sure to
partake of some light refreshment, but avoid alcoholic
beverages, unless it be a glass of sherry or good bitter beer.
After you enter the show room, and before you commence
your duties, take a walk round the hall or room, and satisfy
yourself that you thoroughly understand the class arrangements. If you observe any birds drooping, or any saturated
with water from bathing, remove them to the fire to get
warmed or dried, as the case may be, but be sure not to
overlook them when you come to judge the classes to which
they belong. If you find a bird in a wrong class, call the
attention of the secretary to the fact. Always use your own
judgment independently in giving awards; pander to no man
in this respect. Should there be two judges, and you fail
to agree after carefully going into all the points of the birds
in dispute, let the secretary appoint another person to act
as referee to decide between you; his opinion must be final.
Where there are three judges, the majority must prevail.
When you commence to judge a class of birds look them
through very carefully, and place all the best birds—that
first strike you—together; then commence to compare and
examine them minutely, and give your awards. Do nothing
hurriedly, and always act conscientiously, honestly, and
fearlessly, and with the greatest impartiality, regardless of
all consequences; any man who acts otherwise is unworthy
to fill the office. There is no specific rule for judges' charges,
but well-known and competent judges generally charge £2 2s.
and £3 3s. for judging a show, according to distance, say,
between 50 and 150 miles from home, which is inclusive

of travelling and hotel expenses, but where the distance is very great a proportionate charge to cover additional railway fare, &c., is made. Incompetent judges are dear at any price. If a show is likely to prove a failure, you might give your services gratuitously, charging bare expenses only.

If, on your way to a show, you happen to miss the train, or if a break-down or other accident should occur which is likely to delay your arrival at the expected time, telegraph to the secretary all necessary particulars, giving the time when you expect to reach your destination. If it should be a dull or wet day, and the light is bad, leave those classes judged principally for colour to the last. Proceed with Yorkshire Fancies or the marked classes, and always count the wing and tail feathers of all the prize birds shown in the evenly-marked classes; if any are wanting in a specimen it should be disqualified. Write on the class ticket the words "Disqualified," Deficient in plumage." The same rule is applicable to Lizards, Cinnamons, London Fancies, and Green birds, but in judging birds for shape, such as Belgians and Scotch Fancies, or even Lancashires and clear birds, this rule need not apply, as the loss of a tail or a wing feather would not imperil their chance of taking a prize; of course, if several feathers are missing from the tail or wings of a show specimen in any class, it would at once debar it from taking a prize, as the bird would not be in a fit condition to compete successfully. The great thing to guard against is dishonest practices, where birds have been systematically trimmed in such a way as to give them an unfair chance of obtaining a prize. A bird may have lost a feather by accident, and if it is in the cage you should mention the fact to the secretary, who will consult with the committee, and if they are satisfied that the feather has been shed whilst in their custody it should not be considered a disqualification, or counted as such. The bird should stand, but the committee should look well to this, as an unscrupulous exhibitor might extract a foul feather from the tail or wing of a show specimen and place a dark one (or *vice versâ*) in the bottom of the cage, taken from another bird. I have heard of such things being done.

2 E

In judging Lizard canaries, handle them, and blow them all over, and notice particularly that the bird has not a bald face which has been "blacked in," and that there are no white feathers in the pinion covers. Examine their legs minutely, as they are often found to be stained, and also the upper mandible. In judging crested birds, see that the crests are not gummed down. These and a variety of similar dishonest practices are often resorted to by unprincipled fanciers.

In judging an "any other variety" class of canaries, you should select the three best specimens of each distinct variety shown, and place them first, second, and third, according to their individual merits; never giving two prizes to the same variety, unless much superior in merit to birds of a different variety; but in awarding prizes in a selling class, you should give them to the best birds exhibited—to those of the greatest intrinsic value, apart from any other consideration.

In serving as judge several times during the past twenty-five years at the Crystal Palace, Alexandra Palace, and many other important shows, I have always acted in accordance with the plan herein set forth, and I never was found fault with. Of late, I have reluctantly been necessitated to refuse a great many invitations to be judge at different shows, owing to the nature of my employment (and through ill-health), as I have great difficulty in getting from home. I would add, in conclusion: a judge should always bear in mind that he is as much the servant of the exhibitors as he is of the managers of a show, and that if he is faithful in the discharge of his duties, he must act with the most studied impartiality.

INDEX

INDEX.

Feather-eating, 139.
Feathers, drawing, 371.
Feeding, hand, 77.
Feet, dirty, 80.
    Sore, 80, 151.
Felt lining for nests, 59.
Fertile eggs, to know, 195.
Fever, scarlet, 149.
    Typhus, 154.
Fire and gas in rooms with birds, 194
First brood, 77.
Fits, 139.
Flight-cages, 36.
Flighting stock birds, 51.
Food, 122.
    Cheap, for young birds, 207.
    During moult, 163.
    For Belgians, 228.
    For newly-paired birds, 56.
    Green, 63.
Food, hoppers for, 44.
    Influence of, on colour, 170.
    Prepared, 57.
Forcing a moult, 166.
Foster mothers, 78.
French canaries, 358.

G.

Gas and fire in rooms with birds, 194.
German canaries, 354:
    Breeding, 355.
    Price of, 354.
    Teaching, to sing, 355.
German paste, 199.
Glasgow Don, 235:
    Breeding, 233.
    Classes, 238.
    "Going Light," 133.
    Origin of, 237.
    Packing-case for, 47.
    Points of, 239.
    Standard of excellence, 241.
    Style of, 241.
    Travelling, 240.
Goldfinch and canary mules, 92, 107, 359.

Goldfinches, Cheverell and Pea-throat, 101, 109.
    For mule breeding, 109.
    Newly-caught, 112.
Grain, poisoned, for vermin, 186.
Green canaries, 352:
    Breeders of, 355.
    Breeding, 353.
    Points of, 354.
    St. Andreasberg fanciers' treatment of, 355.
    Standard of excellence, 354.
Green food, 63.

H.

Hand-feeding, 77.
Hartz Mountain Rollers, 355.
Hatching, 70, 90.
Health, hens with delicate, 77.
Heating bird room, 86.
Hens, barren, 81.
    Irregularly laying, 82.
    Leaving cocks beside, during incubation, 73.
    Mule, rearing canaries, 197.
    Refusing to feed their progeny, 76.
    Ruptured, 148.
    Singing, 81.
    Sweating young birds, 74.
    Young, breeding from, 72.
Hepatitis, 140.
Hints, miscellaneous, for shows, 309.
Holes in wire cages, 5.
Hoppers, seed, 44.
Hind claw, deformed, 133.
Hybrids or mules, marked canaries mistaken for, 196.

I.

Importing Belgians, 215.
Impregnating eggs, 195.
Incubation, 64, 89, 111.
    Leaving cocks beside hens during, 73.

Norwich. modern crested: prices of, 323.
  Size of, 317.
  Standards of excellence, 322, 330.
Norwich, modern plainhead, 308:
  Breeding, 310.
  Origin of, 308.
  Points of, 312.
  Preparing for exhibition, 371.
  Size of, 318.
Numbers, moulting in, 168.

O.

Officers of societies, 385.
Open and close shows, 376, 383.
Ophthalmia, 144.
Orders for catalogues of shows, 410.
Original canary, 209.
Origin of Belgian, 212.
  Border Fancy, 350.
  Glasgow Don, 237.
  Lancashire Coppy, 251.
  London Fancy, 341.
  Manchester Coppy, 251.
  Norwich Fancy, 284, 308, 314.
  Scotch Fancy, 237.
  Scotch Fancy, modern, 247.
Outdoor aviaries, 37.
Overgrown claws and beaks, 80, 130.
Overtrained Belgians, 232.

P.

Packing Belgians for show, 230.
  Birds and returning after shows, 47, 407.
Packing-cases, 47.
  Prizes for, 396.
Painting cages, 12.
Pairing, 54.
Pairs, managing single, 68.
Pampering, evil effects of, 123.
Pans, nesting, 62.
Parasites, 52, 143, 145.
Parentage of young birds 67

Parents, influence of, on progeny, 92.
Paring claws and beaks, 80.
Paste, German, 199.
Patrons of shows, 386.
Pea-throat goldfinches, 101, 109.
Phthisis, 130.
Pip, 147.
Plainhead Norwich, modern, 308.
  See Norwich modern plainhead.
Plucking of young, 75.
Pneumonia, 147.
Points of Belgian, 225.
  Border Fancy, 349.
  Cinnamon, 272.
  Glasgow Don, 239.
  Green canary, 354.
  Lancashire Coppy, 252.
  Lizard, 336.
  London Fancy, 347.
  Manchester Coppy, 252.
  Modern Cinnamon, 275.
  Modern crested Norwich, 316.
  Modern plainhead Norwich, 312.
  Modern Scotch Fancy, 250.
  Norwich Fancy, 295, 312, 316.
  Scotch Fancy, 239.
  Yorkshire Fancy, 263.
Points, prizes for, 394.
Poisoned grain for vermin, 186.
Polishing cages, 14.
Powdering food, 57.
Prepared food, 57.
Preparing birds for exhibition, 371.
Preserving colour, 179.
Prices of canaries, 211.
  From cages, removals of, 410.
  Of prize Belgians, 217.
Printing for shows, 398.
Prize money, sending, 414.
Prizes, best variety for breeding for, 191.
  District, 396.
  For packing-cases, 396.
  Points, 394.
Progeny, hens refusing to feed their, 76.
  Influence of parents on, 92.

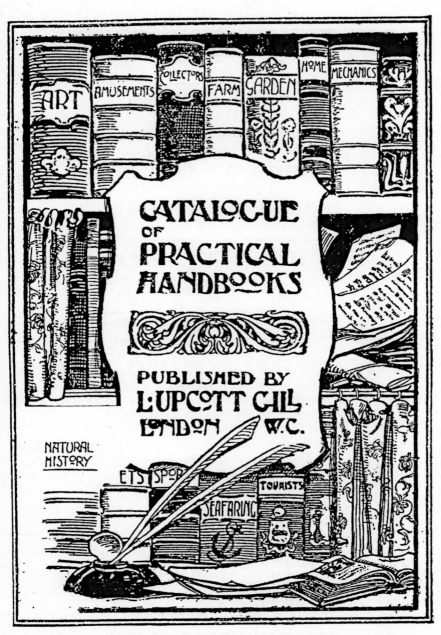

CATALOGUE
OF
PRACTICAL
HANDBOOKS

PUBLISHED BY
L. UPCOTT GILL
LONDON W.C.

NOTE.—*All Books are at* <u>Nett Prices.</u>

INDEX
To the Practical Handbooks
Published by L. Upcott Gill, London, and
Chas. Scribner's Sons, New York,

ART.

	PAGE
Churches, Old English	9
Designing, Harmonic	10
Lace, Hand-Made	13
Old Violins	18
Paper Work, Ornamental	14
Painting, Decorative	14
Poker Work	15

AMUSEMENTS.

	PAGE
Card Games	8, 9, 10, 11, 15, 17, 18
Conjuring	10, 17
Entertainments	1, 8, 11, 17, 18
Fortune Telling	11
Lawn Tennis	13
Magic Lanterns	14
Palmistry	14
Paper Work	14
Photography	15
Pianoforte	15
Poker Work	15
Pool	15
Vamping	18

COLLECTING.

	PAGE
Autographs	7
Books	14, 17
Butterflies	8, 9
Coins	9, 10
Dragonflies	11
Engravings	11
Handwriting	13
Hawk Moths	13
Moths	9
Painting	14
Postage Stamps	16
Postmarks	16
Pottery & Porcelain	16
Violins	18
War Medals	18

FARMING.

	PAGE
Bees	7, 8
Goats	12
Horses	13
Pigs	15
Poultry	11, 13, 16
Sheep	17
Stock Records	8, 15, 17, 18

GARDENING.

	PAGE
Alpine	7
Begonias	8
Book of Gardening	12
Bulbs	8
Cactus	9
Carnations	9
Chrysanthemums	9
Cucumbers	10
Dictionary of Gardening	12
Ferns	11
Fruit	12, 18
Gardening in Egypt	12
Grapes	12
Greenhouse Construction and Heating	12
Greenhouse Management	12, 13
Home Gardening	12
Mushrooms	14
Open-Air Gardening	12
Orchids	14
Perennials	13
Roses	16
Tomatoes	18
Vegetables	18

HOME.

	PAGE
Cookery	7, 10, 11
Decorative Painting	14
Gardening	12
Lace, Hand-Made	13
Medicine	14
Needlework	13, 14

MECHANICS.

	PAGE
Bookbinding	8
Cane Basket Work	9
Chip Carving	9
Firework Making	11
Fretwork	12
Marqueterie	14
Metal Working	8, 16, 17, 19
Model Yachts	14
Poker Work	15
Repoussé Work	16
Ticket Writing	19

	PAGE
Wood Working	9, 12, 14, 15, 19

NATURAL HISTORY.

	PAGE
Aquaria	7
Insects	8, 9, 11, 13
Naturalists' Directory	14
Taxidermy	18
Vivarium	18
Wild Birds	19

PET-KEEPING.

	PAGE
Birds	8, 9, 11, 15, 19
Cats	9
Dogs	10, 11, 12, 13, 17, 18
Guinea Pigs	13
Mice	14
Pigeons	15
Rabbits	16

SPORTING.

	PAGE
Angling	7, 17
Cycling	10
Ferreting	11
Game Preserving	12
Lawn Tennis	13
Sailing	8, 13, 14, 16, 17
Skating	17
Trapping	18
Wildfowling	19
Wild Sports	19
Wrestling	19

SEAFARING.

	PAGE
Boat Building	8
Boat Sailing	8
Sailing Tours	16, 17
Sea Life	17
Sea Terms	17
Solent Guide	16
Yachting Yarns	13

TOURING.

	PAGE
Friesland Meres	12
Route Map	10
Seaside Watering Places	17
Welsh Mountaineering	14

212 C 10/03.

All you have
to do

If you want to Buy, Sell, or Exchange ANY article of <u>Private</u> Property quickly and to the best advantage, is to send a short notice of it to "The Bazaar, Exchange and Mart," with stamps or P.O. at 1d. for 3 words. You will get plenty of replies. If you like you can have a private number at the Office. For further particulars get a copy of the paper—of all Newsagents, price 2d.

OFFICES:

BAZAAR BUILDINGS, DRURY LANE, LONDON, W.C.

Catalogue of
Practical Handbooks

Published by
L. Upcott Gill, London, and
Chas. Scribner's Sons, New York.

Alpine Plants. A Practical Method for Growing the rarer and more difficult Alpine Flowers. By W. A. CLARK, F.R.H.S. With Illustrations from photographs by Clarence Elliott. *In cloth, price 3/6, by post 3/9.*

American Dainties, and How to Prepare Them. By an AMERICAN LADY. *In paper, price 1/-, by post 1/2.*

Angler, Book of the All-Round. A Comprehensive Treatise on Angling in both Fresh and Salt Water. By JOHN BICKERDYKE. With over 220 Engravings. *In cloth gilt, price 5/6, by post 5/10.* Also in Four Divisions as follow :—

Angling for Coarse Fish. Bottom Fishing, according to the Methods in use on the Thames, Trent, Norfolk Broads, and elsewhere. New Edition, Revised and Enlarged. Illustrated. *In paper, price 1/-, by post 1/2.*

Angling for Pike. The most approved methods of Fishing for Pike or Jack. New Edition, Revised and Enlarged. Profusely illustrated. *In paper, price 1/-, by post 1/2.*

Angling for Game Fish. The Various Methods of Fishing for Salmon, Moorland, Chalk-stream, and Thames Trout; Grayling and Char. New Edition. Well illustrated. *In paper, price 1/6, by post 1/9.*

Angling in Salt Water. Sea Fishing with Rod and Line, from the Shore, Piers, Jetties, Rocks, and from Boats; together with Some Account of Hand-Lining. Over 50 Engravings. *In paper, price 1/-, by post 1/2.*

Angler, The Modern. A Practical Handbook on all Kinds of Angling, both Fresh Water and Sea. By "OTTER." Well illustrated. New Edition. *In cloth gilt, price 2/6, by post 2/9.*

Aquaria, Book of. A Practical Guide to the Construction, Arrangement, and Management of Freshwater and Marine Aquaria; containing Full Information as to the Plants, Weeds, Fish, Molluscs, Insects, &c., How and Where to Obtain Them, and How to Keep Them in Health. By REV. GREGORY C. BATEMAN, A.K.C., and REGINALD A. R. BENNETT, B.A. Illustrated. *In cloth gilt, price 5/6, by post 5/10.*

Aquaria, Freshwater: Their Construction, Arrangement, Stocking, and Management. Second Edition, revised and enlarged. By REV. G. C. BATEMAN, A.K.C. Fully Illustrated. *In cloth gilt, price 3/6, by post 3/10.*

Aquaria, Marine: Their Construction, Arrangement, and Management. By R. A. R. BENNETT, B.A. Fully Illustrated. *In cloth gilt, price 2/6, by post 2/9.*

Autograph Collecting: A Practical Manual for Amateurs and Historical Students, containing ample information on the Selection and Arrangement of Autographs, the Detection of Forged Specimens, &c., &c., to which are added numerous Facsimiles for Study and Reference, and an extensive Valuation Table of Autographs worth Collecting. By HENRY T. SCOTT, M.D., L.R.C.P., &c. *In cloth gilt, price 7/6, by post 7/10.*

Bazaars and Fancy Fairs: Their Organization and Management. A Secretary's *Vade Mecum.* By JOHN MUIR. *In paper, price 1/-, by post, 1/2.*

Bee-Keeping, Book of. A very practical and Complete Manual on the Proper Management of Bees, especially written for Beginners and Amateurs who have but a few Hives. By W. B. WEBSTER, First-class Expert, B.B.K.A. Fully illustrated. *In paper, price 1/-, by post 1/2; In cloth price 1/6, by post 1/8.*

All Books are Nett.

Bees and Bee-Keeping: Scientific and Practical. By F. R. CHESHIRE, F.L.S., F.R.M.S., Lecturer on Apiculture at South Kensington. *In two vols., cloth gilt, price* 16s., *by post* 16s. 6d.
  Vol. I., Scientific. A complete Treatise on the Anatomy and Physiology of the Hive Bee. *In cloth gilt, price* 7s. 6d., *by post* 7s. 10d.
  Vol. II., Practical Management of Bees. An Exhaustive Treatise on Advanced Bee-Culture. *In cloth-gilt, price* 8s. 6d.; *by post,* 8s. 11d.

Begonia Culture, for Amateurs and Professionals. Containing Full Directions for the Successful Cultivation of the Begonia, under Glass and in the Open Air. By B. C. RAVENSCROFT. New Edition, Revised and Enlarged. Illustrated. *In paper, price* 1/-, *by post* 1/2.

Bent Iron Work: A Practical Manual of Instruction for Amateurs in the Art and Craft of Making and Ornamenting Light Articles in imitation of the beautiful Mediæval and Italian Wrought Iron Work. By F. J. ERSKINE. Illustrated. *In paper, price* 1/-, *by post* 1/2.

Birds, British, for the Cages and Aviaries. A Handbook relating to all British Birds which may be kept in Confinement. Illustrated. By DR. W. T. GREENE. *In cloth gilt, price 3/6, by post* 3/9.

Birds, Favourite Foreign, for Cages and Aviaries. How to Keep them in Health. By W. T. GREENE, M.A., M.D., F.Z.S., &c. Fully Illustrated. *In cloth gilt, price* 2/6, *by post* 2/9.

Birds, Wild, Cries and Call Notes of, described at Length, and in many instances Illustrated by Musical Notation. By C. A. WITCHELL. *In paper, price* 1/-, *by post* 1/2.

Boat Building and Sailing, Practical. Containing Full Instructions for Designing and Building Punts, Skiffs, Canoes, Sailing Boats, &c. Particulars of the most suitable Sailing Boats and Yachts for Amateurs, and Instructions for their Proper Handling. Fully Illustrated with Designs and Working Diagrams. By ADRIAN NEISON, C.E., DIXON KEMP, A.I.N.A., and G. CHRISTOPHER DAVIES. *In one vol., cloth gilt, price* 7/6, *by post* 7/10. Also in separate Vols. as follows:—

Boat Building for Amateurs, Practical. Containing Full Instructions for Designing and Building Punts, Skiffs, Canoes, Sailing Boats, &c. Fully Illustrated with Working Diagrams. By ADRIAN NEISON, C.E. Second Edition, Revised and Enlarged by DIXON KEMP, Author of "A Manual of Yacht and Boat Sailing," &c. *In cloth gilt, price* 2/6, *by post* 2/9.

Boat Sailing for Amateurs, Practical. Containing Particulars of the most Suitable Sailing Boats and Yachts for Amateurs, and Instructions for their Proper Handling, &c. Illustrated with numerous Diagrams. By G. CHRISTOPHER DAVIES. Second Edition, Revised and Enlarged, and with several New Plans of Yachts. *In cloth gilt, price* 5/-, *by post* 5/4.

Bookbinding for Amateurs: Being descriptions of the various Tools and Appliances Required, and Minute Instructions for their Effective Use. By W. J. E. CRANE. Illustrated with 156 Engravings. *In cloth-gilt, price* 2/6, *by post* 2/9.

Breeders' and Exhibitors' Record, for the Registration of Particulars concerning Pedigree Stock of every Description. By W. K. TAUNTON. In 3 Parts. Part I., The Pedigree Record. Part II., The Stud Record. Part III., The Show Record *In cloth gilt, price each Part* 2/6, *or the set* 6/-, *by post* 6/6.

Bridge Whist: Its Whys and Wherefores. The Game taught by *Reason* instead of, by Rule, on the same popular lines as "Scientific Whist" and "Solo Whist," and by the same Author, C. J. MELROSE. With Illustrative Hands in Colours. New and Revised Edition. *In cloth gilt, price* 3/6, *by post* 3/10; *in half leather, gilt top, price* 5/6, *by post* 5/10.

Bulb Culture, Popular. A Practical and Handy Guide to the Successful Cultivation of Bulbous Plants, both in the Open and Under Glass. By W. D. DRURY. New Edition. Fully illustrated. *In paper, price* 1/-, *by post* 1/2.

Bunkum Entertainments: A Collection of Original Laughable Skits on Conjuring, Physiognomy, Juggling, Performing Fleas, Waxworks, Panorama, Phrenology, Phonograph, Second Sight, Lightning Calculators, Ventriloquism, Spiritualism, &c., to which are added Humorous Sketches, Whimsical Recitals, and Drawing-room Comedies. By ROBERT GANTHONY. Illustrated. *In cloth, price* 2/6, *by post* 2/9.

Butterflies, The Book of British: A Practical Manual for Collectors and Naturalists. Splendidly illustrated throughout with very accurate Engravings of the Caterpillars, Chrysalids, and Butterflies, both upper and under sides, from drawings by the Author or direct from Nature. By W. J. LUCAS, B.A. *In cloth gilt, price* 3/6, *by post* 3/9.

All Books are Nett.

Butterfly and Moth Collecting : Being Practical Hints as to Outfit, most profitable Hunting Grounds, and Best Methods of Capture and Setting, with brief descriptions of many species. Second Edition, revised, re-arranged, and enlarged. Illustrated. *In paper, price 1/-, by post 1/2.*

Cabinet Making for Amateurs. Being clear Directions How to Construct many Useful Articles, such as Brackets, Sideboard, Tables, Cupboards, and other Furniture. Illustrated. *In cloth gilt, price 2/6, by post 2/9.*

Cactus Culture for Amateurs: Being Descriptions of the various Cactuses grown in this country ; with Full and Practical Instructions for their Successful Cultivation. By W. WATSON, Assistant Curator of th) Royal Botanic Gardens, Kew. New Edition. Profusely illustrated. *In cloth gilt, price 5/-, by post 5/4.*

Cage Birds, Diseases of: Their Causes, Symptoms, and Treatment. A Handbook for everyone who keeps a Bird. By DR. W. T. GREENE, F.Z.S. *In paper, price 1/-, by post 1/2.*

Cage Birds, Notes on. Second Series. Being Practical Hints on the Management of British and Foreign Cage Birds, Hybrids, and Canaries. By various Fanciers. Edited by DR. W. T. GREENE. *In cloth gilt, price 6/-, by post 6/6.*

Canary Book. The Breeding, Rearing, and Management of all Varieties of Canaries and Canary Mules, and all other matters connected with this Fancy. By ROBERT L. WALLACE. Third Edition. *In cloth gilt, price 5/-, by post 5/4 ; with COLOURED PLATES, price 6/6, by post 6/10.* Also in separate Vols. as follow :

Canaries, General Management of. Cages and Cage-making, Breeding, Managing, Mule Breeding, Diseases and their Treatment, Moulting, Pests, &c. Illustrated. *In cloth gilt, price 2/6, by post 2/9.*

Canaries, Exhibition. Full Particulars of all the different Varieties, their Points of Excellence, Preparing Birds for Exhibition, Formation and Management of Canary Societies and Exhibitions. Illustrated. *In cloth gilt, price 2/6, by post 2/9.*

Canary-Keeping for Amateurs. A Book for the Average Canary-Keeper, Plain and Practical Directions for the Successful Management and Breeding of Canaries as Pets rather than for Exhibition. By DR. W. T. GREENE, F.Z.S. *In paper, price 1/-, by post 1/2.*

Cane Basket Work: A Practical Manual on Weaving Useful and Fancy Baskets. By ANNIE FIRTH. Series I. and II. Illustrated. *In cloth gilt, price 1/6, by post 1/8 each.*

Card Tricks. By HOWARD THURSTON. A Manual on the Art of Conjuring with Cards, including many hitherto unpublished Novel and Unique Experiments, as presented by the Author in the Leading Theatres of the World. Illustrated. *In paper, price 2/6, by post 2/8 ; in cloth, price 3/6, by post 3/9.*

Card Tricks, Book of, for Drawing-room and Stage Entertainments by Amateurs ; with an exposure of Tricks as practised by Card Sharpers and Swindlers. Numerous Illustrations. By PROF. R. KUNARD. *In illustrated wrapper, price 2/6, by post 2/9.*

Carnation Culture, for Amateurs. The Culture of Carnations and Picotees of all Classes in the Open Ground and in Pots. By B. C. RAVENSCROFT. Illustrated. *In paper, price 1/-, by post 1/2.*

Cats, Domestic and Fancy. A Practical Treatise on their Varieties, Breeding, Management, and Diseases. By JOHN JENNINGS. Illustrated. *In paper, price 1/-, by post 1/2.*

Chip-Carving as a Recreation. A Practical Manual for Amateurs, containing a Full and Clear Description of the Manipulation and Use of the Tools, with a Chapter on the Principles and Construction of Designs. By W. JACKSON SMITH. Profusely Illustrated with Specially Prepared Illustrations, showing how the Tools should be Held and Used, and the way to Prepare Designs. *In paper, price 1/-, by post 1/2.*

Chrysanthemum Culture, for Amateurs and Professionals. Containing Full Directions for the Successful Cultivation of the Chrysanthemum for Exhibition and the Market. By B. C. RAVENSCROFT. Third Edition. Illustrated *In paper, price 1/-, by post 1/2.*

Chrysanthemum, The Show, and Its Cultivation. By C. SCOTT, of the Sheffield Chrysanthemum Society. *In paper, price 6d., by post 7d.*

Churches, Old English: Their Architecture, Furniture, Decorations, Monuments, Vestments, and Plate, &c. Second and Enlarged Edition. By GEO. CLINCH, F.G.S. Magnificently illustrated. *In cloth gilt, price 6/6, by post 6/9.*

Coffee Stall Management. Practical Hints for the Use of those Interested in Temperance or Philanthropic work. *In paper, price 1/-, by post, 1/1.*

Coins, a Guide to English Pattern, in Gold, Silver, Copper, and Pewter, from Edward I. to Victoria, with their Value. By the REV. G. F. CROWTHER, M.A. Illustrated. *In silver cloth, with gilt facsimiles of Coins, price 5/-, by post 5/3.*

All Books are Nett.

Coins of Great Britain and Ireland, a Guide to the, in Gold, Silver and Copper, from the Earliest Period to the Present Time, with their Value. By the late COLONEL W. STEWART THORBURN. Third Edition. Revised and Enlarged by H. A. GRUEBER, F.S.A. Illustrated. *In cloth gilt, price 10/6, by post 10/10.*

Cold Meat Cookery. A Handy Guide to making really tasty and much appreciated Dishes from Cold Meat. By MRS. J. E. DAVIDSON. *In paper, price 1/-, by post 1/2.*

Collie Stud Book. Edited by HUGH DALZIEL. *In cloth gilt, price 3/6 each, by post 3/9 each.*

> *Vol. I.*, containing Pedigrees of 1308 of the best-known Dogs, traced to their most remote known ancestors; Show Record to Feb., 1890, &c.

> *Vol. II.* Pedigrees of 795 Dogs, Show Record, &c.

> *Vol. III.* Pedigrees of 786 Dogs, Show Record, &c.

Conjuring, Book of Modern. A Practical Guide to Drawing-room and Stage Magic for Amateurs. By PROFESSOR R. KUNARD. Illustrated. *In paper, price 2/6, by post 2/9.*

Conjuring and Card Tricks, Book of. By PROF. R. KUNARD. Being "The Book of Modern Conjuring" and "The Book of Card Tricks" bound in one vol. *Cloth gilt, price 5/-, by post 5/4.*

Conjuring for Amateurs. A Practical Handbook on How to Perform a Number of Amusing Tricks, with diagrams, where necessary, to explain exactly how the trick is carried out. By PROF. ELLIS STANYON. *In paper, price 1/-, by post 1/2.*

Conjuring with Cards: Being Tricks with Cards, and How to Perform Them. By PROF. ELLIS STANYON. Illustrated. *In paper, price 1/-, by post 1/2.*

Cookery, The Encyclopædia of Practical. A complete Dictionary of all pertaining to the Art of Cookery and Table Service. Edited by THEO. FRANCIS GARRETT, assisted by eminent Chefs de Cuisine and Confectioners. Profusely Illustrated with Coloured Plates and Engravings by HAROLD FURNESS, GEO. CRUIKSHANK, W. MUNN ANDREW, and others. *In demy 4to half morocco, cushion edges, 2 vols., price £3 3/-; 4 vols., £3/3/6.*

Cucumber Culture for Amateurs. Including also clear Directions for the Successful Culture of Melons, Vegetable Marrows and Gourds. Illustrated. By W. J. MAY. *In paper, price 1/-, by post 1/2.*

Cyclist's Route Map of England and Wales. Shows clearly all the Main, and most of the Cross, Roads, Railroads, and the Distances between the Chief Towns, as well as the Mileage from London. In addition to this, Routes of *Thirty of the Most Interesting Tours* are printed in red. Fourth Edition, thoroughly revised. The map is printed on specially prepared vellum paper, and is the fullest, handiest, and best up-to-date tourist's map in the market. *In cloth, price 1/-, by post 1/2.*

Dainties, English and Foreign, and How to Prepare Them. By MRS. DAVIDSON. *In paper, price 1/-, by post 1/2.*

Designing, Harmonic and Keyboard. Explaining a System whereby an endless Variety of Most Beautiful Designs suited to numberless Manufactures may be obtained by Unskilled Persons from any Printed Music. Illustrated by Numerous Explanatory Diagrams and Illustrative Examples. By C. H. WILKINSON. *Demy 4to, cloth gilt, price £3 3/-, by post £3/3/8.*

Dogs, Breaking and Training: Being Concise Directions for the proper education of Dogs, both for the Field and for Companions. Second Edition. By "PATHFINDER." With Chapters by HUGH DALZIEL. Many new Illustrations. *In cloth gilt, price 6/6, by post 6/10.*

Dogs, British. A Modern History of the Domesticated Canine Race: Their Points, Selection, and Show Preparation. Third Edition. By W. D. DRURY, Kennel Editor of "The Bazaar," assisted by eminent specialists. Beautifully Illustrated with full-page engravings of typical dogs of the present time, mostly produced from photographs of living dogs, and numerous smaller illustrations in the text. This is the fullest work on the various breeds of dogs kept in England. In one volume, *demy 8vo, cloth gilt, price 12/6, by post 13/-.*

All Books are Nett.

Dogs, Diseases of: Their Causes, Symptoms, and Treatment; Modes of Administering Medicines; Treatment in cases of Poisoning, &c. For the use of Amateurs. By HUGH DALZIEL. Fourth Edition. Entirely Re-written and brought up to date. *In paper, price 1/-, by post 1/2; in cloth gilt, price 2/-, by post 2/3.*

Dog-Keeping, Popular: Being a Handy Guide to the General Management and Training of all Kinds of Dogs for Companions and Pets. By J. MAXTEE. Illustrated. *In paper, price 1/-, by post 1/2.*

Dragonflies, British. Being an Exhaustive Treatise on our Native Odonata; Their Collection, Classification, and Preservation. By W. J. LUCAS, B.A. Very fully Illustrated with 27 Plates, Illustrating 39 Species, exquisitely printed in Colour, and numerous Black-and-White Engravings. *In cloth gilt, price 31/6, by post 32/-.*

Egg Dainties. How to Cook Eggs, One Hundred and Fifty Different Ways, English and Foreign. *In paper price 1/-, by post 1/2.*

Egg and Poultry Raising at Home. A Practical Work, showing how Eggs and Poultry may be produced for Home Consumption with little expenditure of time or money. By W. M. ELKINGTON. Illustrated. *In paper, price 1/-, by post 1/2.*

Eggs Certificate, Fertility of. These are Forms of Guarantee given by the Sellers to the Buyers of Eggs for Hatching, undertaking to refund value of any unfertile eggs, or to replace them with good ones. Very valuable to sellers of eggs, as they induce purchases. *In books, with counterfoils, price 6d., by post 7d.*

Engravings and their Value. Containing a Dictionary of all the Greatest Engravers and their Works. By J. H. SLATER. Third Edition. Revised with an appendix and illustrations, and with latest Prices at Auction, &c. *In cloth gilt, price 15/-, by post 15/5.*

Entertainments, Amateur, for Charitable and other Objects; How to Organise and Work them with Profit and Success. By ROBERT GANTHONY. *In paper, price 1/., by post 1/2.*

Feathered Friends, Old and New. Being the Experience of many years' Observations of the Habits of British and Foreign Cage Birds. By DR. W. T. GREENE. Illustrated. *In cloth gilt, price 5/-, by post 5/4.*

Ferns, The Book of Choice: for the Garden, Conservatory, and Stove. Describing the best and most striking Ferns and Selaginellas, and giving explicit directions for their Cultivation, the formation of Rockeries, the arrangement of Ferneries, &c. By GEORGE SCHNEIDER. With numerous Coloured Plates and other Illustrations. *In 3 vols., large post 4to. Cloth gilt, price £3 3/-, by post £3 5/-.*

Ferns, Choice British. Descriptive of the most beautiful Variations from the common forms, and their Culture. By C. T. DRUERY, F.L.S. Very accurate Plates, and other Illustrations. *In cloth, gilt, price 2/6, by post 2/9.*

Ferrets and Ferreting. Containing Instructions for the Breeding, Management and Working of Ferrets. Second Edition. Re-written and greatly Enlarged. Illustrated. New Edition. *In paper, price 1/-, by post 1/2.*

Firework Making for Amateurs. A complete, accurate, and easily understood work on making Simple and High-class Fireworks. By DR. W. H. BROWNE, M.A. *In coloured wrapper, price 2/6, by post 2/9.*

Fish, Flesh, and Fowl. When in Season, How to Select, Cook, and Serve. By MARY BARRETT BROWN. *In paper, price 1/-, by post 1/3.*

Fortune Telling by Cards. Describing and Illustrating the Methods by which the would-be occult Tells Fortunes by Cards. By J. B. PRANGLEY. Illustrated. *In paper, price 1/-, by post 1/2.*

Fox Terrier, The. Its History, Points, Breeding, Rearing, Preparing for Exhibition, and Coursing. By HUGH DALZIEL. Second Edition, Revised and brought up to date by J. MAXTEE (Author of "Popular Dog-Keeping"). Fully illustrated. *In paper, price 1/-, by post 1/2; in cloth, with Coloured Frontispiece and several extra plates, price 2/6, by post 2/9.*

All Books are Nett.

Fox Terrier Stud Book. Edited by HUGH DALZIEL. *In cloth gilt, price* 3/6 each, *by post* 3/9 each.

> *Vol. I.*, containing Pedigrees of over 1400 of the best-known Dogs, traced to their most remote known ancestors.
>
> *Vol. II.*   Pedigrees of 1544 Dogs, Show Record, &c.
>
> *Vol. III.*   Pedigrees of 1214 Dogs, Show Record, &c.
>
> *Vol. IV.*   Pedigrees of 1168 Dogs, Show Record, &c.
>
> *Vol. V.*   Pedigrees of 1562 Dogs, Show Record, &c.

Fretwork and Marquetry. A Practical Manual of Instructions in the Art of Fret-cutting and Marquetry Work. By D. DENNING. Profusely Illustrated. *In cloth gilt, price* 2/6, *by post* 2/9.

Friesland Meres, A Cruise on the. By ERNEST R. SUFFLING. Illustrated. *In paper, price* 1/-, *by post* 1/2.

Fruit Culture for Amateurs. An illustrated practical hand-book on the Growing of Fruits in the Open and under Glass. By S. T. WRIGHT. With Chapters on Insect and other Fruit Pests by W. D. DRURY. Second Edition. Illustrated. *In cloth gilt, price* 3/6, *by post* 3/9.

Game Preserving, Practical. Containing the fullest Directions for Rearing and Preserving both Winged and Ground Game; and Destroying Vermin; with other information of Value to the Game Preserver. By W. CARNEGIE. Illustrated. *In cloth gilt, demy 8vo, price* 10/6, *by post* 11/-.

Gardening, Dictionary of. A Practical Encyclopædia of Horticulture, for Amateurs and Professionals. Illustrated with 3150 Engravings. Edited by G. NICHOLSON, Curator of the Royal Botanic Gardens, Kew; assisted by Prof. Trail, M.D., Rev. P. W. Myles, B.A., F.L.S., W. Watson, J. Garrett, and other Specialists. *In* 5 *vols., large post* 4to. *Cloth gilt, price* £4, *by post* £4 2/-.

Gardening, Home. A Manual for the Amateur, Containing Instructions for the Laying Out, Stocking, Cultivation, and Management of Small Gardens—Flower, Fruit, and Vegetable. By W. D. DRURY, F.R.H.S. Illustrated. *In paper, price* 1/-, *by post* 1/2.

Gardening in Egypt. A Handbook of Gardening for Lower Egypt. With a Calendar of Work for the different Months of the Year. BY WALTER DRAPER. *In cloth gilt, price* 3/6, *by post* 3/9.

Gardening, Open-Air: The Culture of Hardy Flowers, Fruit, and Vegetables. Edited by W. D. DRURY, F.E.S. Beautifully Illustrated. *In cloth gilt, demy 8vo, price* 6/-, *by post* 6/5.

Gardening, the Book of. A Handbook of Horticulture. By well-known Specialists, including J. M. Abbott, W. G. Baker, Charles Bennett, H. J. Chapman, James Douglas, Charles Friedrich, A. Griessen, F. M. Mark, Trevor Monmouth, G. Schneider, Mortimer Thorn, J. J. Willis, and Alan Wynne. Edited by W. D. DRURY (Author of "Home Gardening," "Insects Injurious to Fruit," "Popular Bulb Culture," &c.). Very fully Illustrated. 1 *vol., demy 8vo, about* 1200*pp, price* 16/-, *by post* 16/9.

Goat, Book of the. Containing Full Particulars of the Various Breeds of Goats, and their Profitable Management. With many Plates. By H. STEPHEN HOLMES PEGLER. Third Edition, with Engravings and Coloured Frontispiece. *In cloth gilt, price* 4/6, *by post* 4/10.

Goat-Keeping for Amateurs: Being the Practical Management of Goats for Milking Purposes. Abridged from "The Book of the Goat." Illustrated. *In paper, price* 1/-, *by post* 1/2.

Grape Growing for Amateurs. A Thoroughly Practical Book on Successful Vine Culture. By E. MOLYNEUX. Illustrated. *In paper, price* 1/-, *by post* 1/2.

Greenhouse Construction and Heating. Containing Full Descriptions of the Various Kinds of Greenhouses, Stove Houses, Forcing Houses, Pits and Frames, with Directions for their Construction; and also Descriptions of the Different types of Boilers, Pipes, and Heating Apparatus generally, with Instructions for Fixing the Same. By B. C. RAVENSCROFT. Illustrated. *In cloth gilt, price* 3/6, *by post* 3/9.

All Books are Nett.

Greenhouse Management for Amateurs.'. The Best Greenhouses and Frames, and How to Build and Heat them, Illustrated Descriptions of the most suitable Plants, with general and Special Cultural Directions, and all necessary information for the Guidance of the Amateur. By W. J. MAY. Second Edition, Revised and Enlarged. Magnificently illustrated. *In cloth gilt, price* 5/-, *by post* 5/4.

Guinea Pig, The, for Food, Fur, and Fancy. Its Varieties. and its Management. By C. CUMBERLAND, F.Z.S. Illustrated. *In paper, price.* 1/-, *by post* 1/2. *In cloth gilt, with coloured frontispiece, price* 2/6, *by post* 2/9.

Handwriting, Character Indicated by: With Illustrations in Support of the Theories advanced, taken from Autograph Letters, of Statesmen, Lawyers, Soldiers, Ecclesiastics, Authors, Poets, Musicians, Actors, and other persons. Second Edition By R. BAUGHAN. *In cloth gilt, price.* 2/6, *by post* 2/9.

Hardy Perennials and Old-fashioned Garden Flowers. Descriptions, alphabetically arranged, of the most desirable Plants for Borders, Rockeries, and Shrubberies, including Foliage, as well as Flowering Plants. By J. WOOD. Profusely Illustrated. *In cloth gilt, price* 3/6, *by post* 3/9.

Hawk Moths, Book of British. A Popular and Practical Manual for all Lepidopterists.. Copiously illustrated in black and white from the Author's own exquisite Drawings from Nature. By W. J. LUCAS, B.A. *In cloth gilt, price* 3/6, *by post* 3/9.

Horse Buying and Management.' A Practical Handbook for the Guidance of Amateurs in Buying a Horse, with Instructions as to its after-management. By HENRY E. FAWCUS. Illustrated. *In paper, price* 1/-, *by post* 1/2.

Horse-Keeper, The Practical. By GEORGE FLEMING, C.B., LL.D., F.R.C.V.S., late Principal Veterinary Surgeon to the British Army, and Ex-President of the Royal College of Veterinary Surgeons. *In cloth gilt, price* 3/6, *by post* 3/10.

Horse-Keeping for Amateurs.. A Practical Manual on the Management of Horses, for the guidance of those who keep one or two for their personal use. By FOX RUSSELL. *In paper, price* 1/-, *by post* 1/2; *cloth gilt, price* 2/-, *by post* 2/3.

Horses, Diseases of: Their Causes, Symptoms, and Treatment. For the use of Amateurs. By HUGH DALZIEL. *In paper, price* 1/-, *by post* 1/2; *cloth gilt, price* 2/-, *by post* 2/3.

Incubators and their Management. By J. H. SUTCLIFFE. New Edition, Revised and Enlarged. Illustrated. *In paper, price* 1/-, *by post* 1/2.

Jack All Alone. Being a Collection of Descriptive Yachting Reminiscences. By FRANK COWPER, B.A., Author of "Sailing Tours.". Illustrated. *In cloth gilt, price* 3/6, *by post* 3/10.

Kennel Management, Practical. A Complete Treatise on the Proper Management of Dogs for the Show Bench, the Field, er as Companions, with a chapter on Diseases—their Causes and Treatment. By W. D. DRURY, assisted by well-known Specialists. Illustrated. *In cloth, price* 10/6, *by post* 11/-.

Lace, A History of Hand-Made. By MRS. E. NEVILL JACKSON. With Supplementary Remarks by SIGNOR ERNESTO JESURUM. Exquisitely Illustrated with numerous high-class Engravings of Old and Valuable Laces and their application to Dress as shown in Portraits and Monochrome and Sepia Plates of great beauty. *In crown* 4to, *cloth gilt, price* 18/-, *by post* 18/6. *Edition de Luxe, on large paper, containing* 12 *specimens of Real Lace, handsomely bound in full leather, gilt, price* £4 4/-, *by post* £4/5/6. (A few copies only left at this price, after which there are 60 at £5 5/-, when the entire stock will be exhausted.)

Lawn Tennis, Lessons in. A New Method of Study and Practise for Acquiring a Good and Sound Style of Play. With Exercises. Second and Revised Edition. By E. H. MILES. Illustrated. *In paper, price* 1/-, *by post* 1/2.

Laying Hens, How to Keep, and to Rear Chickens in Large or small Numbers, in Absolute Confinement, with perfect Success. By MAJOR G. F. MORANT. *In paper, price* 6d., *by post* 7d.

All Books are Nett.

Library Manual, The. A Guide to the Formation of a Library, and the Values of Rare and Standard Books. By J. H. SLATER, Barrister-at-Law. Third Edition. Revised and Greatly Enlarged. *In cloth gilt, price 7/6, by post 7/10.*

Lip-Reading, Practical; for the use of the Deaf. By E. F. BOULTBEE. *In cloth gilt, price 2/-, by post 2/3.*

Magic Lanterns, Modern. A Guide to the Management of the Optical Lantern, for the Use of Entertainers, Lecturers, Photographers, Teachers, and others. By R. CHILD BAYLEY. *In paper, price 1/-, by post 1/2.*

Marqueterie Wood-Staining for Amateurs. A Practical Handbook to Marqueterie Wood-staining, and Kindred Arts. By ELIZA TURCK. Profusely Illustrated. *In paper, price 1/-, by post 1/2.*

Medicine and Surgery, Home. A Dictionary of Diseases and Accidents, and their Proper Home Treatment. For Family Use. By W. J. MACKENZIE, M.D. Illustrated. *In paper, price 1/-, by post 1/2.*

Mice, Fancy: Their Varieties, Management, and Breeding. Third Edition, with additional matter and Illustrations. *In coloured wrapper representing different varieties, price 1/-, by post 1/2.*

Model Yachts and Boats: Their Designing, Making, and Sailing. Illustrated with 118 Designs and Working Diagrams. By J. DU V. GROSVENOR. *In leatherette, price 5/-, by post 5/3.*

Mountaineering, Welsh. A Complete and Handy Guide to all the Best Roads and Bye-Paths by which the Tourist should Ascend the Welsh Mountains. By A. W. PERRY. With Numerous Maps. *In cloth gilt, price 2/6, by post 2/9.*

Mushroom Culture for Amateurs. With Full Directions for Successful Growth in Houses, Sheds, Cellars, and Pots, on Shelves, and Out of Doors. By W. J. MAY. Illustrated. *In paper, price 1/-, by post 1/2.*

Naturalists' Directory, The. Invaluable to all Students and Collectors. *In paper, price 1/6, by post 1/8.*

Needlework, Dictionary of. An Encyclopædia of Artistic, Plain, and Fancy Needlework. By S. F. A. CAULFEILD and B. C. SAWARD. Magnificently Illustrated with 41 Embossed and Coloured Plates of Lace, Raised, and other Needlework, besides a large number of Wood Engravings. 528pp. A cheap re-issue. *In demy 4to, cloth, 18/6; Special Edition with satin brocade, price 21/-, postage 6d. extra.*

Orchids: Their Culture and Management. By W. WATSON (Curator, Royal Botanic Gardens, Kew). New Edition, thoroughly Revised and Enlarged. Contains Full Descriptions of all Species and Varieties that are in General Cultivation, a List of Hybrids and their Recorded Parentage, and Detailed Cultural Directions. By HENRY J. CHAPMAN, one of the finest growers and judges in the kingdom (member of the Orchid and Scientific Committees of the Royal Horticultural Society). Beautifully Illustrated with 180 Engravings and 20 Coloured Plates. *In cloth gilt, price 25/-, by post 25/6.*

Painting, Decorative. A practical Handbook on Painting and Etching upon Textiles, Pottery, Porcelain, Paper, Vellum, Leather, Glass, Wood, Stone, Metals, and Plaster, for the Decoration of our Homes. By B. C. SAWARD. *In cloth gilt, price 3/6, by post 3/9.*

Palmistry, Life Studies in. The hands of Notable Persons read according to the practice of Modern Palmistry. By I. OXENFORD. Illustrated with 41 Full-Page Plates. *In 4to, cloth gilt, price 5/-, by post 5/4.*

Palmistry, Modern. By I. OXENFORD, Author of Life Studies in Palmistry. Numerous Original Illustrations by L. WILKINS. *In cloth gilt, price 2/6, by post 2/9.*

Paper Work, Instructive and Ornamental. A practical book on the making of flowers and many other articles for artistic decoration, including a graduated course of Paper Folding and Cutting for children five to twelve years of age. Especially useful as preparatory exercises to the making of artificial flowers in silk and velvet, increasing that dexterity of hand and niceness of finish so necessary to that work. By Mrs. L. WALKER. Fully Illustrated. *In crown 4to, cloth gilt, price 3/6, by post 3/10.*

All Books are Nett.

Parcel Post Dispatch Book (registered). An invaluable book for all who send parcels by post. Provides Address Labels, Certificate of Posting, and Records of Parcels Dispatched. By the use of this book parcels are insured against loss or damage to the extent of £2. Authorised by the Post Office. *Price 1/-, by post 1/2, for 100 parcels ; larger sizes if required.*

Parrakeets, Popular. How to Keep and Breed Them. By W. T. GREENE, M.D., M.A., F.Z.S., &c. *In paper, price 1/-, by post 1/2.*

Parrot, The Grey, and How to Treat it. By W. T. GREENE, M.D., M.A., F.Z.S., &c. *In paper, price 1/-, by post 1/2.*

Patience, Games of, for one or more Players. How to Play 173 different Games of Patience. By M. WHITMORE JONES. Illustrated. Series I., 39 games ; Series II., 34 games ; Series III., 33 games ; Series IV., 37 games ; Series V., 30 games. *Each, in paper, 1/-, by post 1/2. The five bound together, in cloth gilt, price 6/-; by post 6/4. In full leather, solid gilt edges, price 10/6; by post 10/11.*

Pedigree Record, The. Being Part I. of "The Breeders' and Exhibitors' Record," for the Registration of Particulars concerning Pedigrees of Stock of every Description. By W. K. TAUNTON. *In cloth gilt, price 2/6, by post 2/9.*

Photographic Printing Processes, Popular. A Practical Guide to Printing with Gelatino-Chloride, Artigue, Platinotype, Carbon, Bromide, Collodio-Chloride, Bichromated Gum, and other Sensitised Papers. By H. MACLEAN, F.R.P.S. Illustrated. *In cloth gilt, price 2/6, by post 2/10.*

Photography (Modern) for Amateurs. Fourth Edition. Revised and Enlarged. By J. EATON FEARN. *In paper, price 1/-, by post 1/2.*

Pianofortes, Tuning and Repairing. The Amateur's Guide, without the intervention of a professional. New Edition. *In paper, price 1/-; by post 1/2.*

Picture-Frame Making for Amateurs. Being Practical Instructions in the Making of various kinds of Frames for Paintings, Drawings, Photographs, and Engravings. By the REV. J. LUKIN. Illustrated. *In paper, price 1/-, by post 1/2.*

Pig, Book of the. The Selection, Breeding, Feeding, and Management of the Pig; the Treatment of its Diseases ; The Curing and Preserving of Hams, Bacon, and other Pork Foods ; and other information appertaining to Pork Farming. By PROFESSOR JAMES LONG. Fully Illustrated with Portraits of Prize Pigs, Plans of Model Piggeries, &c. *In cloth gilt, price 10/6, by post 10/11.*

Pig-Keeping, Practical: A Manual for Amateurs, based on personal Experience in Breeding, Feeding, and Fattening; also in Buying and Selling Pigs at Market Prices. By R. D. GARRATT. *In paper, price 1/-, by post 1/2.*

Pigeon-Keeping for Amateurs. A Complete Guide to the Amateur Breeder of Domestic and Fancy Pigeons. By J. C. LYELL. Illustrated. *In cloth gilt, price 2/6, by post 2/9 ; in paper, price 1/-, by post 1/2.*

Poker Work, A Guide to, including Coloured Poker Work and Relief Turning. A Practical Manual for Amateurs, containing a full Description of the necessary Tools, and Instructions for their use. By W. D. THOMPSON. Illustrated. *In paper, price 1/-, by post 1/2.*

Polishes and Stains for Woods : A Complete Guide to Polishing Woodwork, with Directions for Staining, and Full Information for Making the Stains, Polishes, &c., in the simplest and most satisfactory manner. By DAVID DENNING. *In paper, price 1/-, by post 1/2.*

Pool, Games of. Describing Various English and American Pool Games, and giving the Rules in full. Illustrated. *In paper, price 1/-, by post 1/2.*

Portraiture, Home, for Amateur Photographers. Being the result of many years' incessant work in the production of Portraits "at home." By P. R. SALMON (RICHARD PENLAKE), Editor of *The Photographic News.* Fully Illustrated. *In cloth gilt, price 2/6, by post 2/9.*

All Books are Nett.

Postage Stamps, and their Collection. A Practical Handbook for Collector of Postal Stamps, Envelopes, Wrappers, and Cards. By OLIVER FIRTH Member of the Philatelic Societies of London, Leeds, and Bradford. Pro fusely Illustrated. *In cloth gilt, price 2/6, by post 2/10.*

Postage Stamps of Europe, The Adhesive: A Practical Guide to thei Collection, Identification, and Classification. Especially designed for the us of those commencing the Study. By W. A. S. WESTOBY. Beautifull Illustrated. Cheap and Revised Edition. ' *In 2 vols., price 7/6, by post 8/.*

In connection with these Publications on Postage Stamps we have arrange to supply Gauges for Measuring Perforations. These Stamp Gauges are mad in brass, and can be carried in the waistcoat pocket. *Price 1/-, by post 1/1.*

Postmarks, History of British. With 350 Illustrations and a List o Numbers used in Obliterations. By J. H. DANIELS. *In cloth gilt, price 2/6 by post 2/9.*

Pottery and Porcelain, English. A Guide for Collectors. Handsomel Illustrated with Engravings of Specimen Pieces and the Marks and Mono grams used by the different Makers. New Edition, Revised and Enlarged By the REV. E. A. DOWNMAN. *In cloth gilt, price 3/6, by post 3/9.*

Poultry-Farming, Profitable. Describing in Detail the Methods that Giv the Best Results, and pointing out the Mistakes to be Avoided. By J. H SUTCLIFFE. Illustrated. *In paper, price 1/-, by post 1/2.*

Poultry-Keeping, Popular. A Practical and Complete Guide to Breedin and Keeping Poultry for Eggs or for the Table. By F. A. MACKENZIE. Secon Edition, with Additional Matter and Illustrations. *In paper, price 1/-, b post 1/2.*

Rabbit, Book of the. A Complete Work on Breeding and Rearing all Varietie of Fancy Rabbits, giving their History, Variations, Uses, Points, Selection Mating, Management, &c., &c. SECOND EDITION. Edited by KEMPSTEI W. KNIGHT. Illustrated with Coloured and other Plates. *In cloth gilt, pric 10/6, by post 10/11.*

Rabbits, Diseases of: Their Causes, Symptoms, and Cure. With a Chapte on THE DISEASES OF CAVIES. Reprinted from "The Book of the Rabbit". an "The Guinea Pig for Food, Fur, and Fancy." *In paper, price 1/-, by post 1/2.*

Rabbits for Prizes and Profit. The Proper Management of Fancy Rabbit in Health and Disease, for Pets or the Market, and Descriptions of ever known Variety, with Instructions for Breeding Good Specimens. By CHARLE RAYSON. Illustrated. *In cloth gilt, price 2/6, by post 2/9.* Also in Sections, a follow:

Rabbits, General Management of. Including Hutches, Breeding, Feeding Diseases and their Treatment, Rabbit Courts, &c. Fully Illustrated. *In paper price 1/-, by post 1/2.*

Rabbits, Exhibition. Being descriptions of all Varieties of Fancy Rabbits their Points of Excellence, and how to obtain them. Illustrated. *In paper price 1/-, by post 1/2.*

Repoussé Work for Amateurs. Being the Art of Ornamenting Thi Metal with Raised Figures. By L. L. HASLOPE. Illustrated. *In paper price 1/-, by post 1/2.*

Roses for Amateurs. A Practical Guide to the Selection and Cultivation o the best Roses. Second Edition, with Many Plates. By the REV. J. HONY WOOD D'OMBRAIN, Hon. Sec. Nat. Rose Soc. *In paper, price 1/-, by post 1/2.*

Sailing Guide to the Solent and Poole Harbour, with Practical Hint as to Living and Cooking on, and Working a Small Yacht. By LIEUT.-CO T. G. CUTHELL. Illustrated with Coloured Charts. *In cloth gilt, price 2/6 by post 2/9.*

Sailing Tours. The Yachtman's Guide to the Cruising Waters of the Englis and Adjacent Coasts. With Descriptions of every Creek, Harbour, and Road stead on the Course. With numerous Charts printed in Colours, showing Dee water, Shoals, and Sands exposed at low water, with sounding. By FRAN COWPER, B.A. *In crown 8vo, cloth gilt.*

Vol. I. The Coasts of Essex and Suffolk, from the Thames to Aldborough Six Charts. *Price 5/-, by post 5/3.*

All Books are Nett.

Vol. II. The South Coast, from the Thames to the Scilly Islands. Twenty-five Charts. New and Revised Edition. *Price 7/6, by post 7/10.*

Vol. III. The Coast of Brittany, from L'Abervrach to St. Nazaire, and an account of the Loire. Twelve Charts. *Price 7/6, by post 7/10.*

Vol. IV. The West Coast, from Land's End to Mull of Galloway, including the East Coast of Ireland. Thirty Charts. *Price 10/6, by post 10/10.*

Vol. V. The Coasts of Scotland and the N.E. of England down to Aldborough. Forty Charts. *Price 10/6, by post 10/10.*

St. Bernard Stud Book. Edited by HUGH DALZIEL. 2 Vols., containing Pedigrees of over 1800 Dogs. *In cloth gilt, price 3/6 each, by post 3/9 each.*

Sea-Fishing for Amateurs. A Practical Book on Fishing from Shore, Rocks, or Piers, with a Directory of Fishing Stations on the English and Welsh Coasts. Illustrated by numerous Charts, shewing the best spots for the various kinds of fish, position of rocks, &c. Second Edition, revised, enlarged, and copiously illustrated. By FRANK HUDSON. *In paper, price 1/-, by post 1/2.*

Sea-Life, Realities of. Describing the Duties, Prospects, and Pleasures of a Young Sailor in the Mercantile Marine. By H. E. ACRAMAN COATE. With a Preface by J. R. DIGGLE, M.A., M.L.S.B. *In cloth gilt, price 3/6, by post 3/10.*

Seaside Watering Places. A description of the Holiday Resorts on the Coasts of England and Wales, the Channel Islands, and the Isle of Man, giving full particulars of them and their attractions, and all information likely to assist persons in selecting places in which to spend their Holidays, according to their individual tastes. Illustrated. Twenty-fourth Year of Issue. *In cloth gilt, price 2/6, by post 2/10.*

Sea Terms, a Dictionary of. For the use of Yachtsmen, Voyagers, and all who go down to the sea in big or little ships. By A. ANSTED. Fully Illustrated. *In cloth gilt, price 5/-, by post 5/4.*

Shadow Entertainments, and How to Work them: being Something about Shadows, and the way to make them, Profitable and Funny. By A. PATTERSON. Illustrated. *In paper, price 1/-, by post 1/2.*

Sheep Raising and Shepherding. A Handbook of Sheep Farming. By W. J. MALDEN, late Principal of the Colonial College, Hollesley Bay, Suffolk, and of the Agricultural College, Uckfield. Illustrated. *Cloth gilt, price 3/6, by post 3/9.*

Sheet Metal, Working in: Being Practical Instructions for Making and Mending Small Articles in Tin, Copper, Iron, Zinc, and Brass. By the Rev. J. LUKIN, B.A. Illustrated. Third Edition. *In paper, price 1/-, by post 1/1.*

Show Record, The. Being Part III. of "The Breeders' and Exhibitors' Record," for the Registration of Particulars concerning the Exhibition of Pedigree stock of every Description. By W. K. TAUNTON. *In cloth gilt, price 2/6, by post 2/9.*

Skating Cards: An Easy Method of Learning Figure Skating, as the Cards *can be used on the Ice. In cloth case, price 2/6, by post 2/9.* A cheap form is issued printed on paper and made up as a small book, *price 1/-, by post 1/1.*

Sleight of Hand. A Practical Manual of Legerdemain for Amateurs and Others. New Edition, Revised and Enlarged. Illustrated. By E. SACHS. *In cloth gilt, price 6/6, by post 6/10.*

Solo Whist. Its Whys and Wherefores. A Progressive and Clear Method of Explanation and Illustration of the Game, and how to Play it Successfully. With Illustrative Hands printed in Colours. By C. J. MELROSE. *In cloth gilt, price 3/6, by post 3/10; in half leather, gilt top, 5/6, by post 6/-.*

Sporting Books, Illustrated. A Descriptive Survey of a Collection of English Illustrated Works of a Sporting and Racy Character, with an Appendix of Prints relating to Sports of the Field. The whole valued by reference to Average Auction Prices. By J. H. SLATER, Author of "Library Manual," "Engravings and Their Value," &c. *In cloth gilt, price 7/6 by post 7/10.*

All Books are Nett.

Stud Record, The. Being Part II. of "The Breeders' and Exhibitors' Record," for the Registration of Particulars concerning Pedigree Stock of every Description. By W. K. TAUNTON. *In cloth gilt, price 2/6, by post 2/9.*

Taxidermy, Practical. A Manual of Instruction to the Amateur in Collecting, Preserving, and Setting-up Natural History Specimens of all kinds. With Examples and Working Diagrams. By MONTAGU BROWNE, F.Z.S., Curator of Leicester Museum. Second Edition. *In cloth gilt, price 7/6, by post 7/10.*

Tomato Culture for Amateurs. A Practical and very Complete Manual on the subject. By B. C. RAVENSCROFT. Illustrated. *In paper, price 1/-, by post 1/1.*

Trapping, Practical : Being some Papers on Traps and Trapping for Vermin, with a Chapter on General Bird Trapping and Snaring. By W. CARNEGIE. *In paper, price 1/-, by post 1/2.*

Vamp, How to. A Practical Guide to the Accompaniment of Songs by the Unskilled Musician. With Examples. *In paper, price 9d., by post 10d.*

Vegetable Culture for Amateurs. Containing Concise Directions for the Cultivation of Vegetables in small Gardens so as to insure Good Crops. With Lists of the Best Varieties of each Sort. By W. J. MAY. Illustrated. *In paper, price 1/-, by post 1/2.*

Ventriloquism, Practical. A thoroughly reliable Guide to the Art of Voice Throwing and Vocal Mimicry, Vocal Instrumentation, Ventriloquial Figures, Entertaining, &c. By ROBERT GANTHONY. Numerous Illustrations. *In cloth gilt, price 2/6, by post 2/9.*

Violins (Old) and their Makers. Including some References to those of Modern Times. By JAMES M. FLEMING. Illustrated with Facsimiles of Tickets, Sound-Holes, &c. *In cloth gilt, price 6/6, by post 6/10.*

Violin School, Practical, for Home Students. Instructions and Exercises in Violin Playing, for the use of Amateurs, Self-Learners, Teachers, and others. With a Supplement on "Easy Legato Studies for the Violin." By J. M. FLEMING. *Demy 4to, cloth gilt, price 9/6, by post 10/2.* Without Supplement, *price 7/6, by post 8/-.*

Vivarium, The. Being a Full Description of the most Interesting Snakes, Lizards, and other Reptiles, and How to Keep Them Satisfactorily in Confinement. By REV. G. C. BATEMAN. Beautifully Illustrated. *In cloth gilt, price 7/6, by post 8/-.*

War Medals and Decorations. A Manual for Collectors, with some account of Civil Rewards for Valour. By D. HASTINGS IRWIN. Revised and Enlarged Edition. Beautifully Illustrated. *In cloth gilt, price 12/6, by post 12/10.*

Whippet and Race-Dog, The : How to Breed, Rear, Train, Race, and Exhibit the Whippet, the Management of Race Meetings, and Original Plans of Courses. By FREEMAN LLOYD. *In cloth gilt, price 2/6, by post 2/10.*

Whist, Bridge : Its Whys and Wherefores. The Game taught by *Reason* instead of by Rule, on the same popular lines as "Scientific Whist" and "Solo Whist," and by the same author, C. J. MELROSE. With Illustrative Hands printed in Colours. New and Revised Edition. *In cloth gilt, price 3/6, by post 3/10; in half leather, gilt top, 5/6, by post 5/10.*

Whist, Solo: Its Whys and Wherefores. A Progressive and Clear Method of Explanation and Illustration of the Game, and how to Play it Successfully. With Illustrative Hands printed in Colours. By C. J. MELROSE. *In cloth gilt, price 3/6, by post 3/10; in half leather, gilt top, 5/6, by post 5/10.*

Whist, Scientific: Its Whys and Wherefores. The Reader being taught by *Reason* rather than by arbitrary Rules. With Illustrative Hands printed in Colours. By C. J. MELROSE. *In cloth gilt, price 3/6, by post 3/10; in half leather, gilt top, 5/6, by post 5/10.*

All Books are Nett.

Wildfowling, Practical: A Book on Wildfowl and Wildfowl Shooting. By HY. SHARP. The result of 25 years' experience of Wildfowl Shooting under all sort of conditions of locality as well as circumstances. Profusely Illustrated. *Demy 8vo, cloth gilt, price 6/-, by post 6/4.*

Wild Sports in Ireland. Being Picturesque and Entertaining Descriptions of several visits paid to Ireland, with Practical Hints likely to be of service to the Angler, Wildfowler, and Yachtsman. By JOHN BICKERDYKE, Author of "The Book of the All-Round Angler," &c. Beautifully illustrated from Photographs taken by the Author. *In cloth gilt, price 6/-, by post 6/4.*

Window Ticket Writing. Containing full instructions on the Method of Mixing and using the Various Inks, &c., required, Hints on Stencilling as applied to Ticket Writing, together with Lessons on Glass Writing, Japanning on Tin, &c. Especially written for the use of Learners and Shop Assistants. By WM. C. SCOTT. *In paper, price 1/-, by post 1/2.*

Wire and Sheet Gauges of the World. Compared and Compiled by C. A. B. PFEILSCHMIDT, of Sheffield. *In paper, price 1/-, by post 1/1.*

Wood Carving for Amateurs. Full instructions for producing all the different varieties of Carvings. SECOND EDITION. Edited by D. DENNING. *In paper, price 1/-, by post 1/2.*

Workshop Makeshifts. Being a Collection of Practical Hints and Suggestions for the use of Amateur Workers in Wood and Metal. By H. J. S. CASSALL. Fully Illustrated. *In cloth gilt, price 2/6, by post 2/9.*

Wrestling. A Practical Handbook upon the Catch-hold and Græco-Roman Styles of Wrestling; a splendid system of Athletic Training. By PERCY LONGHURST, winner in the Light-weight Competition, G.G.S., 1899. Profusely Illustrated. *In paper, price 1/-, by post 1/2.*

All Books are Nett.

British Dogs.

A modern History of the Domesticated Canine Race: their points, selection, and show preparation. Third Edition, by W. D. DRURY, Kennel Editor of the "Bazaar," assisted by eminent specialists. Beautifully illustrated with full-page engravings of typical dogs of the present time, mostly produced from photographs of living dogs, and numerous smaller illustrations in the text.

This is the fullest work on the various breeds of dogs kept in England. In one Volume, demy 8vo. cloth gilt. Price 12s. 6d., by post 13s.

L. UPCOTT GILL,
BAZAAR BUILDINGS, DRURY LANE, W.C.

Lightning Source UK Ltd.
Milton Keynes UK
UKOW04f1935060214

226046UK00001B/51/A